Embodying Black Religions in Africa and Its Diasporas

D1602762

RELIGIOUS CULTURES OF AFRICAN AND AFRICAN DIASPORA PEOPLE
Series editors: Jacob K. Olupona, Harvard University, Dianne M. Stewart, Emory University, and Terrence L. Johnson, Georgetown University

This book series examines the religious, cultural, and political expressions of African, African American, and African Caribbean traditions. Through transnational, cross-cultural, and multidisciplinary approaches to the study of religion, the series investigates the epistemic boundaries of continental and diasporic religious practices and thought and explores the diverse and distinct ways African-derived religions inform culture and politics. The series aims to establish a forum for imagining the centrality of Black religions in the formation of the "New World."

Embodying Black Religions in Africa and Its Diasporas

Yolanda Covington-Ward and Jeanette S. Jouili, editors

Duke University Press   *Durham and London*   2021

Project editor: Lisa Lawley
Designed by Courtney Leigh Richardson
Typeset in Whitman and Helvetica Neue by Westchester
Publishing Services.

Library of Congress Cataloging-in-Publication Data
Names: Covington-Ward, Yolanda, [date] editor. | Jouili,
Jeanette Selma, editor.
Title: Embodying Black religions in Africa and its diasporas /
Yolanda Covington-Ward and Jeanette S. Jouili, editors.
Other titles: Religious cultures of African and African
diaspora people.
Description: Durham : Duke University Press, 2021. | Series:
Religious cultures of African and African diaspora people |
Includes bibliographical references and index.
Identifiers: LCCN 2020053565 (print)
LCCN 2020053566 (ebook)
ISBN 9781478010647 (hardcover)
ISBN 9781478011750 (paperback)
ISBN 9781478013112 (ebook)
Subjects: LCSH: Religion and culture—Africa. | Religions—
African influences. | African diaspora. | Religion—Social
aspects—Africa. | Africa—Religion. | Africa—Religious life
and customs.
Classification: LCC BL2400 .E49 2021 (print) | LCC BL2400
(ebook) | DDC 200.896—dc23
LC record available at https://lccn.loc.gov/2020053565
LC ebook record available at https://lccn.loc.gov/2020053566

Cover art: Frank Wimberley, *Siempre (Always)*, 1998. Collage of cut painted paper with pastel, 22¼ × 27⅛ inches. © Frank Wimberley. Courtesy of the artist and the Saint Louis Art Museum, The Thelma and Bert Ollie Memorial Collection, Gift of Ronald and Monique Ollie.

Contents

Foreword

JACOB K. OLUPONA

The chapters in this volume collectively observe that the body, as expressed in embodied practices, ways of knowing, and spiritualities, rightly warrants increasing amounts of scholarly attention. As Yolanda Covington-Ward and Jeanette S. Jouili remind us in their introduction, in African and African diaspora religions there is a new way of understanding that calls into question the mind-body dualisms inherited from Western models of interpretation, which have long influenced the way scholars construct religious realities.

Most impressively, the contributors to this work bring recent scholarship on embodiment to bear on a host of disciplines under current scholarly investigation in the humanities and the study of religion. I name only a few of the broader themes here. *Embodying Black Religion in Africa and Its Diasporas* addresses the ways in which conceptions of self and personhood are intricately caught up in ritual and bodily practices. A much-needed focus is given to embodied selves as relational beings and to the processes and factors that influence, give shape to, and constitute intersubjectivity. At several points in the volume, critical appraisals of the body and modes of bodily representation are set forth, including the radicalization of bodies and their presence in different religious, political, and cultural contexts.

The work also offers insightful reflections on the subjects of embodiment and the arts, communal formation, ethnicity, funerary rites, health, immigration, gender, sexuality, spiritual beliefs, and spirit possession. Consequently, it succeeds, as the title hints, in furthering a welcome discussion between African studies and African diaspora scholarship. The reader will pick up readily and easily enough on these generous gleanings in the introduction and in the essays that make up this volume.

What I offer here is a reflection on the concerns of the various authors in this work, who agree with a central thesis: only by taking the body paradigm seriously will we be able to bring embodied practices into the understanding of the totality of religion, particularly practices that are often marginalized in Western traditions because they do not neatly fit into the models and modes of Western religious interpretation. By presenting African and African diaspora religious practices in a new way, this volume enables us to truly see ourselves! Consequently, the understanding of African indigenous religions as embodied traditions might turn out to be not an alternative but a central method of understanding African spirituality, cultures, and societies.

Throughout my career, my mindset and scholarly approach have led me to the understanding that there are multiple ways of being religious. While texts and myths are incredibly valuable, a significant entry into the understanding of African religion is through praxis—the lived traditions that are embodied in sacred festivals, ceremonies, and rituals, and the material culture that animates African spiritual traditions. Indeed, in the past decades, even scholars of the so-called world religions have turned to these ways of interpretation and genres to provide a more in-depth understanding of their respective traditions, demonstrating their recognition of the importance of embodied practices and relationships in religions.

The phenomenological interpretation of religious traditions with which I began my academic journey in the late 1970s—particularly the works of Edmund Husserl and Maurice Merleau-Ponty—recognized the pivotal importance of religious experience and practices, particularly as they relate to the body, intentionality, and relationality. Forms of African indigenous religions are deeply embedded in the imagery of the body, especially as revealed through many cultural expressions. The body provides the most cardinal metaphors and symbols for understanding how one encounters and relates to the multiple deities, devotees, and sacred persons and officiants of the religious community we encounter.

One way to observe and analyze this centrality of the body is through the study of oral traditions and histories, particularly proverbs, the wisdom texts of African elders and the *open sesame* to African worldviews and cultures. For example, when an elderly person has a faraway look and sighs deeply in the presence of a group, the Yoruba will quickly say as a response: "Oro gbe inu agba se hun!" Literally translated, this means "The word (or thought) is embedded in the deep stomach." That is, the painful and joyful silences of the elders as expressed in deep sighs are presumed to be kept in the stomach, which is conceived as the womb and the home of wisdom. In other words, it is the stomach, not only the brain as in the Western context, that houses our intellectual capacities. The Amharic word for "lover" is *hode*, which means the stomach—thus, in Ethiopia, interrelational experience is connected again to the stomach, not to the heart!

A major expression of embodied practice is the ritual of spirit possession. I agree with Paul Stoller's (1995) critique of the Western fascination with and fixation on spirit possession, particularly on spirit possession as text. While this is an important dimension of embodiment, it is only one aspect of religious phenomena that not everyone necessarily has access to. Zones of contact between Islam and indigenous religion, for example, include subversive elements of possession with regard to gender and identity. For example, women in some African Muslim cultures are able to gain access to different sectors of society through possession. As such, there are elements of embodiment and relationality in the phenomenon of spirit possession that could be highlighted here, including in modern-day Pentecostal and evangelical traditions and Sufism. Similarly, we are reminded of the fascinating study conducted by Aisha Beliso-De Jesús (2015) on the centrality and pivotal role of possession in Orisha traditions.

Embodiment, as an object of study, cannot be divorced from the discussion of an individual's relational connection with the human, animal, nonhuman, and natural world around them. In general, Africans frown upon a life of loneliness devoid of relational connection to others. There is a tree that grows in the western region of Africa that by nature stands alone in the forest without the benefit of sharing space with other trees. This loner tree, the opposite of other trees growing together in the forest, is referred to by the Yoruba as *oko*—that is, "the oko tree that grows alone." Not having any connection with others, it is often employed to describe the relationship of avoidable loneliness that causes an individual to detach from his or her community and turn into an antisocial human being.

So how should we understand African traditional and diasporic practices that Western epistemological theories have not been able to decipher and that do not fit within Western Protestant-centric conceptions of religion? These include empirical observation of such traditions and practices as in twin cultures (*Ibeji*), so-called magical practices (*Oogun*), born-to-die children, children of repeated birth (*abiku*), the display of medicinal power, and actively spoken words that alter our understanding that words not only have meaning but enforce a practical action and effect (the ritual specialist on his way to the farm uses his extrasensory gift to perceive danger in the forest; he faces a tree, and like a prophet says, "This tree is harboring something negative" and then curses the tree, and by the evening, when he returns from the farm, the leaves of the tree have withered). Why is a tradition (such as African Christianity) willing and able to attest to such a miraculous event when cited in the biblical scriptures and yet either denies its authenticity in African religion or condemns it as purely diabolical? These are occurrences and activities that I grew up witnessing and experienced as a teenager living in African villages and towns. Western scholarship has come up with vocabularies to suggest that these are "magical" things, excluding them from the domain of proper religion. The epistemological violence done to the understanding of African ways of being religious by the Western mindset is immeasurable and reflects why today appointed texts, often termed *classic readings*, are chosen for the education of graduate students of color that do not have relevance to their lived experiences or to the realities of their lives.

When African studies was beginning to emerge as a credible field of knowledge, philosophy and religion focused on systems of thought and beliefs. Scholars paid very little or no attention to the significance of the practice of religion, and when they did, in the context of anthropological studies, they left out the centrality and importance of the body in ritual discourse. In fact, many books describing African belief systems were shaped by conversations in Europe, where religious worldview scholarship was tailored toward the understanding of God and belief in the Western philosophy of religion. The critical discipline of the philosophy of religion arose from this context and mindset. These trends resulted in the absence of embodiment-oriented analysis in the study of African indigenous religion and a disciplinary focus on myths and orature, which in turn reflected the text-oriented methodology employed for the study of Abrahamic traditions.

In the remaining section, I explore how Africans, particularly the Yoruba in West Africa, deploy messages of the body to explain religious sentiments, philosophies, and practices. I argue that the embodied practices of African religious traditions provide not only alternate modes of interpreting experiences of being religious but also central modes of being religious. The authors in this volume argue that only by taking them seriously will we be able to bring these practices into the picture, practices that are often marginalized in Western traditions because they do not neatly fit into the models and modes of Western religious interpretation.

In Yoruba cosmology, *ori*, often termed the source of wisdom in Western philosophy and primarily seen as an embodied spiritual part of humans, has the most important and influential presence. There are two forms of ori, the physical ori, which is the outer head, and the spiritual ori, which is the inner head. In Yoruba oral tradition, both are regarded as relational, and, as such, both are spiritual. However, it is believed that the inner head acts as a conduit for the physical head. References like *ori mogunje* ("It is one's ori that guarantees the potency of the ritual specialist's/healer's medicine") and *ori l'onise* ("It's one's ori that assures one's fortune in life") illustrate that ori is central to determining one's success in life.

In one of the Yoruba myths of creation, after Obatala, the Yoruba deity, molds human beings, they travel to the home of Ajala on their way to the earth, where they pick their ori. It is assumed that one's choice of ori will determine one's fortune in the world. Similarly, in a situation of stiff competition among the group, the one with the strongest ori will win. This, of course, touches on the question of predestination and choice. Consequently, diviners pay a lot of attention to how one's ori dictates one's fortune in the world. Even in naming ceremonies, ori forms prefixes in names such as Orimolade ("ori is the one that knows who will be the king"), Orire ("good ori"), and Orimolusi ("ori knows the future").

In fact, it could be argued that ori, also a deity in the Yoruba pantheon, is regarded as more sacred than the rest of the deities (*Orisha*), and that is because the ori is a true physical manifestation, more visible and tangible than the other orisa. While the orisa may reveal themselves via images and material objects and sometimes in human representations of kings and twins, they are not humans but rather superhumans who are above human temporalities. The significance of the ori suggests that the Yoruba cosmology posits that humans are potential gods, which in turn reflects divinization of the human body.

That Matter matters is a truism in African religious traditions—in fact, matter is central to religious experience. Material practices are not a manipulation of the sacred, but the sacred itself. The so-called taboos are a worthy illustration of this point. Food taboos are very common in the African context; different individuals, as well as communities and settlements, have to follow certain food restrictions. As Lawrence E. Sullivan rightly puts it, "Because the mouth controls contact with the cosmic powers that order one's shape and meaning, the symbolism of diet distinguishes groups and qualities of relations within a given society" (1988, 295). Beliefs surrounding food and dietary restrictions clearly demonstrate the materiality of religion, where food is understood not simply as a source of sustenance in a physical sense but rather also in a spiritual sense. Moreover, food taboos are linked to totemic concepts and ideas and therefore are not to be overlooked in religious practice. As Émile Durkheim explains in his *Elementary Forms of the Religious Life* (1961), totems are the symbols of god and the symbols of the clan; hence, obeying totemic restrictions is an expression of utter respect.

For example, as a twin in Yoruba traditions, I am forbidden from eating the flesh of a monkey, partially because of the religious affinity between twins and the colobus monkey. Twins and monkeys are both held sacred by certain Yoruba, and twin lineages represent multiple births, which are revered in Yoruba traditions. Among the BaKongo, twins could not eat the double-spotted leopard, which was considered to mediate between the visible realm of humans and the invisible realm of spirits. To speak more broadly about communities, in the city of Ile Oluji, Nigeria, the inhabitants are forbidden from eating buffalo meat because of the belief that the buffalo led the inhabitants of the city to safety in the past.

Beliefs regarding food function both in a direct sense (i.e., food taboos) and in an allegorical sense. As James Aho argues in *The Orifice as Sacrificial Site*, "The experience of our personal bodies reflects the workings of our social arrangements." Private entry and exit zones, that is, our orifices, are "doorways out of and penetration routes into the social bodies of which we are members" (2002, 10). In the Yoruba context, the proverb "ona ofun, ona orun" (the way to the belly is also the way to heaven/death) teaches that gluttony can lead to physical and social death. The idea here is that one should fend for what one eats, since gluttony can lead the consumer to betray their community. When a pot of porridge is accepted by an individual in exchange for the group interest, it is interpreted as not only a betrayal of the whole but also a form of social death. In short, as Aho explains, "the personal body . . . is a metaphor of the social body; orifices in particular stand for a group's weak spots. The more defensive and exclusionary a group is, the more pressure is placed on its members to police what goes into and what comes out of the bodies" (11).

The Body and Ritual Process

The ritual process can be entirely reimagined as an embodied practice. African rites of passage, the ideology and rituals of sacred kingship, festivals and the ceremonial calendar, and worship of the deities are all tied to the signification of the body. The body becomes a special agent through which those performances and ritual actions take place. Given what we now know through empirical research, we can boldly construct a new paradigm that we could label as the "spirituality of the body."

Embodied deities run through the entire African cosmology. In the cosmogonic myths of many African societies, we come across assemblies of deities who not only are represented as human-like—they eat, dance, and fornicate—but also manifest deep meanings and metaphors through their embodied imagery. If we take the example of Obatala, the most senior deity in the Yoruba pantheon of 201 gods, we can see that the deity is represented as the epitome of purity, as revealed in the use of white clothes among members of his household. More significantly, Obatala honors those with disabilities and physical differences—who are collectively regarded as *eni orisa*, that is, "people of the deity," meaning that they are beloved and protected by Obatala. As a Yoruba proverb says, "Owo orisa lafi nwo afin" (It is the honor given to Obatala that we extend to the albino). Albinos, for instance, are regarded in many African societies as spiritual agents of the deities. Among the Yoruba in Nigeria, these individuals are given so much freedom that if they show up in traditional marketplaces, they will be showered with gifts because it is believed that they are a good omen for a successful business. Obatala is praised as a perfect fashioner of human beings—"eni soju, eni semu, orisa ni ma sin" (he who fashions eyes and the nose, it is the orisa that I will worship)—and thus the Yoruba are careful not to make fun of individuals with disabilities or peculiar physical traits such as protruding teeth, because those individuals are fashioned by the orisa. If we take this point further, we could even argue that a significant relational role of Obatala and the disabled in the Yoruba divine economy is providing the theological rationale for protecting these individuals.

But in the ideology and rituals of sacred kingship, we see the strongest evidence of embodied beliefs and practices. Among the Baganda of Uganda and the Akan people of Ghana, the king is regarded as sacred, and his sacred body is held in reverence. From his hair to his toes, all segments of his body are sacred and therefore tabooed against profanity. In a number of cultures such as the Benin, Fon, and Yoruba, one must keep an informed distance from the king—one relates to the king not like a human being but like a deity. Greetings and interactions must reflect these relationships. As such, the Yoruba say, "Mo sun m'oba egbeje, mo jina s'oba, egbee fa, enit o ba ri oba fin, ni oba npa." (I move close to the king, two hundred times six times, I keep a distance from the king, two hundred and seven times. He who disrespects the king, the king kills.) In other words, it is crucial to keep an informed distance from the Yoruba sacred kings if one wants to live long. As the example illustrates, in this context, relationality is an ontological process—the need and ability to maintain ritual distance, while at the same time having secular interactions, emphasizes the importance of the body in ritual and relationship. The king covers his head at all times (also, in Ghana, the kings cannot touch the ground with their feet); in ritual, the king dips his left toe in the blood of the sacrifice, which represents the continuity and maintenance of the ancestral relationships from which he derives his authority and power once he has ascended the throne of his father.

REFERENCES

Aho, James. 2002. *The Orifice as Sacrificial Site: Culture, Organization, and the Body.* New York: Aldine de Gruyter.

Beliso-De Jesús, Aisha M. 2015. *Electric Santería: Racial and Sexual Assemblages of Transnational Religion.* New York: Columbia University Press.

Durkheim, Émile. 1961. *The Elementary Forms of Religious Life.* New York: Collier Books.

Stoller, Paul. 1995. *Embodying Colonial Memories: Spirit Possession, Power, and the Hauka in West Africa.* New York: Routledge.

Sullivan, Lawrence Eugene. 1988. *Icanchu's Drum: An Orientation to Meaning in South American Religions.* New York: Macmillan.

Editors' Acknowledgments

As always with collaborative projects, we are indebted to a large number of people and organizations without whom this book would not have been possible. This edited volume emerged from a symposium organized at the University of Pittsburgh in April 2017: Diverse Spiritualities: Embodiment and Relationality in Religions of Africa. We thank all the participants in the symposium, who all agreed to contribute their chapters to this book. In addition, we thank the three distinguished keynote speakers, Stephanie Mitchem, Rudolph Ware, and Jacob K. Olupona, whose lectures all helped to push our collective thinking in new directions.

We are incredibly grateful to the respondents to the individual presentations who offered stimulating thoughts, questions, and provocations that allowed us all to develop our contributions further: Brock Bahler, Mari Webel, and Oronde Sharif.

Particular thanks go out to our departments and previous department chairs, the late Linda Penkower and Christel Temple, for their encouragement and support throughout the years, from the symposium to the book project. A special word of gratitude goes to Joanna Reed, the former program assistant at the Humanities Center at the University of Pittsburgh, who provided essential logistical and organizational help during the symposium.

We appreciate the University of Pittsburgh sponsors who funded the symposium and made this project possible, including the Year of Diversity; the Humanities Center (Faculty Collaborative Grant); the Faculty Research Scholarship Program (Dietrich School of Arts and Sciences); the Department of Africana Studies; the Department of Religious Studies; the African Studies Program; the Global Studies Center (through the Kabak Endowment); the Center for Latin American Studies; the World History Center; the Department of History; the

Gender, Sexuality, and Women's Studies Program; the Cultural Studies Program; and the Department of Theatre Arts.

We also thank our editor at Duke University Press, Miriam Angress, who has provided valuable support from the beginning of this project throughout the production stages. We also want to express our gratitude to the editors of the Duke series Religious Cultures of African and African Diaspora People, Jacob Olupona, Dianne Stewart, and Terrence Johnson, who encouraged us so enthusiastically to move forward with this book project.

We also want to thank the three anonymous peer reviewers who provided excellent feedback that has significantly improved the quality of each of the contributions.

Finally, we want to thank our families for their steadfast support in our busy academic and personal lives. Yolanda wants to thank Lincoln, Leyeti, and Lincoln Ward II. Jeanette wants to especially thank Idrissou, Mounir, and Aqeel Mora-Kpai.

Introduction: Embodiment and Relationality in
Religions of Africa and Its Diasporas
YOLANDA COVINGTON-WARD AND JEANETTE S. JOUILI

Melodically rocking Sufi bodies remember God on a former plantation in South
Carolina, reconnecting with ancestors and an imagined homeland. Dancers in
Martinique use the sound of the *bèlè* drum to achieve emotional transcendence
and resist alienation caused by centuries of French assimilation. Devotees of
Mama Tchamba in Togo use shuffling steps, dress, and ritual to placate the
spirits of formerly enslaved people from the North whom their own ancestors
bought and sold. All of these examples foreground one thing: the role of the
body specifically in the shaping, transmitting, and remaking of African and
African diasporic religions and religious communities.

Embodying Black Religions in Africa and Its Diasporas is an edited volume that
critically examines the role of the body as a source of religiously motivated
social action for people of African descent across the geographic regions of the
African continent, the Caribbean and Latin America, the American South, and
Europe. From a variety of religious contexts—from Pentecostalism in Ghana
and Brazil to Ifá divination in Trinidad to Islam in South Carolina, Nigeria,
and London—the contributors investigate the complex intersections between
the body, religious expression, and the construction and negotiation of particular social relationships and collective identities. A series of case studies explore
how embodied practices—such as possession and spirit-induced trembling,
wrestling in pursuit of deliverance, ritual dance, and gestures and postures of
piety—can inform notions of sexual citizenship, challenge secular definitions
of the nation, or promote transatlantic connections as well as local and ethnic

identities beyond the nation-state. Together these chapters offer a substantial contribution to understandings of relationality, embodiment, and spirituality within the context of various global Black experiences.

The turn to the body and embodiment over the past thirty years within religious studies and related disciplines in the humanities and the social sciences has led to a reappraisal of the body's role in social and cultural practices. While embodied religious practices have been studied in scholarship on religion and in anthropology from early on, they have been disregarded (following the Cartesian body-mind paradigm) as inconsequential or symbolic or, especially when encountering the non-Western other, used as markers of difference and primitivism (Asad 1997; Baker 1998). Thus, articulations of the body-mind were from their inception used to organize and order the world in hierarchies, not only between Europeans and non-Europeans, between colonizer and colonized, and between white, Black, and brown but also between men and women. Here reason not only defined the West (at least its white male inhabitants) but also became the basis for defining humanity (the "cogito") in highly *racialized* terms. An excess of embodied practices signified a lack of interiority, rationality, discipline, and morality—and was thus a sign of not having a "real" religion and lacking in humanity (Maldonado-Torres 2014; Wynter 2003).[1] Hence, the new attention to the body has engendered a veritable epistemological shift that discloses the ontological relevance of corporeality.

Critical race, postcolonial, and feminist scholarship's engagement with poststructuralism, phenomenology, and/or praxis theory but also non-Western philosophical and religious approaches has provided scholars with analytic tools to revalorize embodied practices, allowing them to more completely grasp bodies' potential for shaping selves and society, religious life and religious communities. Over the past three decades, scholars of religion have deconstructed the body-mind dichotomy and its underlying assumptions (Asad 1993; Masuzawa 2005; Smith 1998). Having turned from body-mind dualism to recognition of our "mindful body" (Schepers-Hughes and Lock 1987), scholars have at long last begun to fully do justice to Marcel Mauss's understanding of the "biological means of entering into 'communion with God'" (1973, 2; see also Asad 1997, 48). A flourishing literature on religion and the body now takes seriously the "somatic quality of . . . piety" (Bynum 1991, 16), the "intense ambiguity of the individual body as locus both of potential sanctification and of defilement" (Coakley 1997, 9), examining "how religions speak to . . . body-oriented human concerns" (McGuire 1990, 284).

Yet the empirical world is still struggling with powerful modern narratives that have been globalized since the advent of European hegemony. Without being overdetermined, let alone fully oppressed, by these narratives, non-Western religious practitioners are still grappling with these legacies, which have downgraded their religious traditions and questioned their humanity. However embodied practices were reevaluated—whether suppressed, altered, reaccentuated, or reinvented—the body has always mattered in various forms of religious expression and practice. Indeed, the body continues to creatively transform people's shared spiritual lifeworlds in multiple ways. This situation is particularly true for people of African descent, the concern of this volume.

While scholars of African and African diasporic religions have focused for many years on the role of the body, they have only rarely been in conversation with each other. Furthermore, their conversations about religious embodiment were limited by a focus on particular religions (i.e., Santeria, Islam) or by geography (African religions, Caribbean religions, African American religions). This debate has additionally been divided by contested understandings of what counts as African diasporic or "traditionally African" religions, where often traditions like Islam or Christianity have not been considered to be authentically African (see Carter, this volume; see also Matory 2005; Routon 2006). Bringing these different areas of research together in one volume is not merely a response to a geographic disconnect; the objective of this volume is to transcend often-ideological divisions in academic debates in order to enable different analytic perspectives. Structural conditions are also relevant to this discussion, as Africans on the continent and throughout its many diasporas are dealing with related historical and current social and economic challenges. These are the consequences of colonialism, enslavement, global racial hierarchies, and racial oppression, as well as social exclusion and marginalization, both within nation-states and within global systems of power. As a result of neoliberal reforms—such as structural adjustment programs, the reduction of social services, and the outsourcing of industrial jobs—people of African descent on the continent and elsewhere endure massive deteriorations in the social fabric of often-vulnerable communities. Religion has come to play a major role, both historically and in the contemporary moment, in coping with these changes and also causing larger social transformations. In this volume we examine how these related structural conditions have impacted spiritual embodied practices and religiously defined forms of sociability and solidarity in African and African diasporic religions. We also question to what extent the investigated practices of embodiment and relationality partake in the constitution of a Black Atlantic (Gilroy 1993) or larger global Black social imaginary.

Theorizing the Black Body in Religions of
Africa and Its Diasporas

There are several trends in scholarly studies of embodiment and the body in the religions of Africa and its diasporas. By placing these trends into dialogue with each another, we aim in this volume to illuminate connections, divergences, and myriad understandings and practices that help us to expand studies of religion and embodiment in new and exciting directions. We home in on thematic connections across Africa and its diasporas in certain key texts that illustrate broader trends in the field concerning embodiment in relation to the politics of representation, healing, spirit possession, affect, and memory. Our volume extends discussions around these existing themes, while also refocusing attention on (1) materiality, (2) mobility, and (3) relationality, belonging, and community formation in studies of embodiment in the religions of Africa and its diasporas.

Existing research on embodiment in the religions of Africa and its diasporas contributes to understanding the politics of representation and the ways it informs religious and spiritual beliefs and practices. The long history of enslavement, colonialism, segregation, apartheid, and other forms of racialized oppression over the past five centuries has created a context in which European misconceptions and representations of the bodies of people of African descent have shaped and continue to influence Black people and their religions in myriad ways. Across time and geographic space, the Black body became the site of interrogation for larger judgments about morality and even questioning whether people of African descent were fully human. Fanciful European travel narratives about deviant, monstrous, and idle African bodies were used to justify the slave trade and European colonialism in Africa (Morgan 1997). On the other side of the Atlantic, discourses about Black people as irrational, immoral, and sexually deviant, having bodies with superhuman strength and higher thresholds for physical pain, proliferated throughout the era of enslavement (W. Johnson 1999; Pernick 1985; Roberts 1997). M. Shawn Copeland (2010) has highlighted the relationship between Christianity and perceptions of Black women's bodies as objects of property, production, reproduction, and sexual violence in slavery, such that Black women were seen as incapable of rational thought and the interiority that defined Protestantism at the time. Discourses about Black religious practices that described them as "'heathenish observances,' 'insane yellings' and violent contortions of the body" were used to categorize Black people as an Other in juxtaposition to whiteness and support their ill treatment and exclusion from citizenship (Evans 2008, 69). Indeed, theologians Anthony Pinn (2010) and Stephanie Mitchem (2014) explore these troubling histories as the reason for a lack of attention to the body in African American theology (see also CERCL Writing Collective 2017).

In the African context, religion as an aspect of culture became a critical marker of difference in European-African relationships (Pierre 2013). Cases such as the Tswana ethnic group in South Africa encountering European Nonconformist missions highlight how negative perceptions of African belief systems and practices shaped Western missionary attitudes toward African spirituality and religions while also helping to bolster Western claims of superiority, modernity, civilization, and the supposed benefits of the colonial empire (Chidester 2014; Comaroff and Comaroff 1991). In Latin America and the Caribbean, nation-states and proponents of certain forms of Catholicism and Protestantism used discourses about "paganism" and "evil" to actively suppress African-inspired religions such as Santeria, Candomblé, and Vodou and Abrahamic faiths such as Islam, both during and after enslavement (Diouf 2013; Matory 2005; Palmié 2002; Ramsey 2011). The control of both bodies and embodiment played a central role in all of these efforts.

Religious communities and individuals of African descent have reacted to these stereotypes about Black bodies and embodiment and these proscriptions against certain embodied practices in various ways, whether in Chicago, Colombia, or Côte d'Ivoire. In the United States during the nineteenth century, for instance, "black religious capacity became the lens through which blacks were judged as fit or unfit for participation and inclusion in the nation" (Evans 2008, 5). Thus, Black people often used their own self-presentation and worship practices to disrupt prevailing narratives of degeneracy and difference. For instance, Evelyn Brooks Higginbotham (1993, 190–191) explores how Black Baptist women in the late nineteenth- and early twentieth-century United States resisted being categorized as "the embodiment of deviance" by emphasizing "respectable behavior," using their dress, conduct, manners, and morals to present "alternate images of black women." Marla Frederick's (2003) more recent ethnography of Southern Black Baptist women even shows how religious body politics impacts sexual intimacy as another form of respectability for single and married women alike. Embracing respectability is one among many manners of addressing Western stereotypes about Blackness and Black bodies in worship, both in Africa (Ross 1999) and in its diasporas (White 2012), and both historically and contemporaneously. However, it is not the only option, as other Black religious communities have opted to create more oppositional cultures where white conceptions of Blackness are intentionally decentered, rejected, and marginalized. Rastafarian religion in Jamaica is one example where adherents profess an unabashed love for Blackness and self-elevation and wear their hair in unruly dreadlocks as an intentional break with notions of proper appearance and respectability (Price 2009). Historical studies of African religions (especially relating to the colonial era) tend to pay more attention to the politics of representation than do contemporary studies; however, these concerns continue to influence religious practices across the continent in different ways. All of these responses clearly illustrate the impact of external gazes and perceptions on Black religious expression. Accordingly, *Embodying Black Religions in Africa and Its Diasporas* pays attention to the many ways that religion directly responds to, subtly engages, and even ignores processes of racialization and stigmatization on both sides of the Atlantic. The chapters explore how the social context shapes understandings of and reactions to the politics of representation in Black religions across the globe. Moreover, this volume highlights how misconceptions and stigmas related to certain forms of religious embodiment are internalized or even explicitly rejected.

Scholarly studies of spirit possession and religious and spiritual healing in the religions of Africa and its diasporas are another fruitful area for examining the relationship among religion, relationality, and embodiment. This is especially the case in disciplines such as anthropology, where spirit possession has "long been an explicit topic of inquiry" (Boddy 1994, 408). While much valuable research has emerged from studies of spirit possession, we recognize that outsized scholarly attention to such practices over others is not without its own problems, as it leads to questions about the privileging of perceived "exotic" religions or an emphasis on difference in the religious communities that scholars choose to study (Ware 2014), adding another layer to our previous discussion of the politics of representation. Nevertheless, this caveat does not diminish the value of classic texts such as *Mama Lola: A Vodou Priestess in Brooklyn* (Brown 1991), *Wombs and Alien Spirits: Women, Men, and the Zar Cult in Northern Sudan* (Boddy 1989), and *Body of Power, Spirit of Resistance: The Culture and History of a South African People* (Comaroff 1985), all of which illustrate the effectiveness of privileging the body in studies of everyday religion. More recent volumes, such as *Spirited Things: The Work of "Possession" in Afro-Atlantic Religions* (P. Johnson 2014), investigate the politics and power dynamics of spirit possession in everyday life. Other research has emphasized spirituality and religion as a source of healing for both the individual physical body and the larger social body (Douglas 1970).

In the existing literature, one significant difference seems to be that research on spirit possession and healing in Africa often focuses on more social aspects of healing, examining processes for healing larger communities and individuals, especially through examining their relationships with others. In contrast, research in the diaspora tends to focus more on individuals, with less emphasis on healing families or communities. Studies of mind-body healing and biological mechanisms in Brazilian Candomblé (Seligman 2014) and African American folk healing practices (Mitchem 2007) illustrate how religion and spirit possession can be utilized to heal individual selves. Similarly, studies of the interrelational politics of affliction in the Democratic Republic of the Congo (Janzen 1992), traditional healing practices in Tanzania (Langwick 2011), and spiritual healing in charismatic Apostolic churches in Botswana (Werbner 2011) highlight how spirituality-based healing is enmeshed in social and spiritual relationships and plays a key role in repairing social discord and healing the body politic. However, these trends are not absolute, as more recent work on the global spread of Pentecostal and charismatic religions across Africa stresses how the breaking of social relationships is emphasized in discourses of success and prosperity (Meyer 1999). These questions concerning individuality/dividuality (Coleman 2011; Klaits 2011), relationships with human and spiritual beings, and illness and health continue to be explored in this volume as our contributors consider collective aspects of healing and spirit possession across the Atlantic divide.

The recent turn to emotion, the senses, and affect has also influenced studies of spirit possession and healing. In her work on Santeria in Cuba and in the United States, Aisha Beliso-De Jesús notes that practitioners say Orishas are "sensed and felt on the body" through what she calls copresence between the person and the deity. These shared experiences of copresence then help to foster a religious community as "an embodied epistemology of copresence enables unification through sensing diaspora" (2014, 519; see also Beliso-De Jesús 2015). Overall, healing and spirit possession are used to create new relationships and larger communities within diverse contexts across the religions of Africa and its diasporas. These religious practices and communities can also be better understood in relation to one another, as one goal of this volume is to bring studies of Africa and those of the diaspora into dialogue. For example, studies of African diasporic religions often focus on Africa as a past place of origin for beliefs and practices rather than seeing Africa as coeval (Herskovits [1941] 1990; Pierre 2013), while studies of African religions often fail to make reference to African diasporic religions. Several chapters in this volume disrupt these tendencies by highlighting trends and connections across geographic space in understanding embodiment and relationality, an approach that has been championed in a few recent studies (Matory 2005).

Other typical approaches in studies of embodiment and relationality in African and African diasporic religions include attention to memory. Genealogy and perceived connections to familial or spiritual ancestors inform the character of embodied practices that come to define membership in religious congregations. Examples include Ethiopian Jews and African Hebrew Israelites in the United States (Jackson 2013; Weisenfeld 2017) and Kongo prophetic movements and churches in the Democratic Republic of the Congo (Covington-Ward 2016). A common use of kinship (whether real or imagined) connects these different works, which create new social identities and stake political claims on larger sociopolitical contexts of racial oppression and social exclusion.

Other approaches to memory in African and African diasporic religions highlight embodied practices and belief systems as ways to actively reestablish connections to ancestors and specific geographic and linguistic spaces (Daniel 2005; Olupona 2011). Like in studies of spirit possession in African diasporic religions, attention to memory in religions in the diaspora often privileges looking back to a distant, unchanging African homeland in the past. In the case of Africa, the memories that are invoked often emphasize time (e.g., the precolonial era or early twentieth century) rather than both time and space, while also revealing dynamic transformations in beliefs and practices. This volume places these perspectives and regions into conversation with one another by highlighting mobility as a concept that helps us to move beyond the limitations of either approach.

The contributors also build on and extend these existing trends (politics of representation, spirit possession, healing and affect, and memory) in scholarship on embodiment in the religions of Africa and its diasporas by emphasizing relationality and social processes of religious community formation. Moreover, by exploring materiality, mobility, and local political and social contexts, they highlight a vast continuum of articulations and strategies around embodiment and relationality for people of African descent. They consider a range of expressions from the explicit and intentional employment of embodiment pursuing particular aims to approaches shaped by existing social structures and power dynamics to reactions that lie beyond the realm of consciousness and draw on habitual memory.

Embodiment: Self-Formation, Epistemology, and Intersubjectivity

The theoretical musings among scholars of religion enabled through a body-centered perspective are vast. For the purpose of our volume, we want to foreground in particular three distinct but related insights that are fundamental for the shared theoretical perspectives elaborated throughout the different chapters. These insights refer to (a) the significance of the body for self-formation, (b) the acknowledgment that the body generates knowledge, and (c) the role of the body in producing relationality and intersubjectivity.

The first fundamental insight developed by the literature in regard to the ontological status of the body underscores the centrality of bodies for understanding the self, personhood, or subjectivity (Bynum 1991; McGuire 1990), which has even caused some scholars to argue for a "conflation of subjectivity and embodiment" (Furey 2012, 13). These claims point to the capacity of the body in shaping interiority, rather than merely being material that gives expression to the already realized interior self. Whether inspired by a poststructural emphasis on discipline, learning, and habituation (see, for instance, Asad 1993, 2003; Mahmood 2005) or a phenomenological focus on experience and consciousness (see Csordas 1993, 2008; Stoller 1995, 1997), scholars have demonstrated that the body is a key site for fashioning and refashioning interiority and selfhood.

Scholars of religion have studied how religious practitioners, through a vast array of embodied practices ranging from dietary practices, dress styles, spirit procession, dance, and trembling to prayer chant or pilgrimage, employ their bodies to self-cultivate, transform, remold, perfect, and heal their selves and realize various kinds of religious selves (Covington-Ward 2016; Jackson 2013; Jouili 2015; Seligman 2014). In turn, these cultivated bodies represent and re-signify the religious self (Jouili 2015; Abdul Khabeer 2016). By making these claims, scholars furthermore have questioned understandings of agency as located within consciousness. In place of being read in terms of "oppressed subjectivity" (Keller 2005, 5), the religious body has emerged as a locus of agency.

A second crucial aspect developed in this literature is the challenge to epistemologies underlying the duality between body and mind, which locate reason, understanding, and knowledge within the mind, while cognition is produced only linguistically. In contrast to this view, scholars have paid extensive attention to how our human "bodies are involved in our various ways of knowing" (McGuire 1996, 111–112; see also Csordas 1993; Sullivan 1990). This insight has proved especially fruitful for researchers of religion who investigate how the body (as well as its culturally elaborated senses) is engaged in generating religious knowledge, spiritual ideas, alternative states of reality, mystic experiences, and in "knowing" the divine. A number of studies have furthermore shown how bodies produce knowledge of the past and thus become a locus of collective memory (Connerton 1989; Covington-Ward 2016; McCall 2000).

Scholars have provided ample evidence in a variety of religious and spiritual contexts of the human body's significant capacity to produce different kinds of knowledge, leading scholars to speak of "embodied" or "sensory" epistemologies—or of "knowing bodies." At the same time, this should not be taken as an understanding of *primordially* knowing bodies. As Talal Asad (1997, 48) has astutely observed, knowing bodies have to be trained to know and have to learn to generate knowledge. In other words, the question of bodily knowledge also always brings up the question of "bodily ignorance" (Dilley 2010). In addition to drawing on culturally shaped body habits or techniques, religious practitioners quite often set out to consciously train and retrain their bodies. The recent study by Rudolph Ware on embodied learning in Senegambian Qur'anic education has powerfully demonstrated the intense training that enables bodies to "archive, transmit, decode, and actualize religious knowledge" (2014, 67). He further challenges still-existing binaries between textual and embodied learning by arguing that rather than texts being learned and acquired through the mind, in West African Qur'anic schooling the body can be equated with the text, and the text can be taught "via the body" (67).

Central to the present volume's underlying theoretical framework, the third and most significant contribution of the literature is the shift in studies on embodiment from a focus on individual bodies, subjectivity, and individual personhood to a better recognition of the relational character of subjectivity—namely, *intersubjectivity* (Beliso-De Jesús 2015; Covington-Ward 2016; Jouili 2015; Ware 2014). In other words, the initial critique of the body-mind split and the foregrounding of the embodied self does not automatically lead to a thinking that transcends the isolated, bounded, independent ego. Even studies that recognized the social or societal impact of embodied practices still often analyzed embodied (individual) selves as only secondarily and contingently entering into communication and interaction with others, as Thomas Csordas (2008) critiqued. The ongoing difficulty of thoroughly grasping the relational nature of the self is, as Constance Furey puts it, connected to a general misconception of the self, standing in contrast to the social: "The split and fragmented subject is still more often studied in relation to society, the material world, social norms, and physical constraints and conditioning than as part of a relational dynamic, in the context of intimate and influential relationships" (2012, 21). Such an understanding also has consequences for how agency is frequently theorized as oppositional to the social (see Mahmood 2001). At the same time, Furey cautions against conceptualizing these relationships naively or romantically. Relationships do not eschew power because "power is relationally internalized, enacted, and transformed" (Furey 2012, 21; see also Asad 2003).

The recognition that the self is embodied and relational has furthermore prompted discussion about intersubjectivity being related to "intercorporeality" (Csordas 2008). As Gail Weiss has noted, "To describe *embodiment as intercorporeality* is to emphasize that the experience of being embodied is never a private affair, but is always already mediated by our continual interactions with other human and nonhuman bodies" (1999, 5). This insight has allowed for a more capacious understanding of how human bodies, nonhuman material bodies, and nonmaterial entities (e.g., spirits, divinities, and deities) interact with each other, which is crucial for the study of religion. While scholars writing on non-Western societies have furthered the critique of the modern Western ideology of the self as singular, exposing different ideas and practices of selfhood, some scholars have also rightfully cautioned against postulating a simple binary between the individualist or individuated Western self versus the non-Western (for example, African collectivist or relational) self (Coleman 2011).

Together these studies have enabled a deeper sense of subjectivity as embodied, an understanding of the relational dimension of the embodied subject, and an appreciation of the knowing capacities of human bodies. These three arguments are by far not the only important insights these studies on religion and embodiment have contributed. Nonetheless, these three strands are to varying degrees the focus of the individual contributions to this volume.

Chapter Routes and Circuits

The twelve chapters in this volume are organized thematically into four parts that investigate different aspects of the relationship between embodiment and religion in African and African diasporic religions. In the first part, "Spiritual Memories and Ancestors," contributors interrogate how material bodies have become the locus for remembrance of the past, including collective histories and ancestors. They also consider related processes that build new connections, identities, and communities. In chapter 1, "Spirited Choreographies: Embodied Memories and Domestic Enslavement in Togolese Mama Tchamba Rituals," Elyan Hill examines Ewe dance rituals in Togo, in which the descendants of slave traders commemorate the domestic slave trade through celebrating Mama Tchamba, a pantheon of enslaved spirits. Hill demonstrates not only how these dancers mobilize their bodies to (re)produce narratives of the past through associative, metonymic strategies but also how, through this remembrance, they are able to diagnose obstructions to collective unity and self-examine historical and social disjuncture within their communities. Through these rituals, Hill argues, established power relations are inversed by destabilizing boundaries between master and mastered, enabling new ethical relationships.

Youssef Carter discusses in chapter 2, "Alchemy of the *Fuqara*: Spiritual Care, Memory, and the Black Muslim Body," how African American Muslims pursue spiritual healing of the past through the cultivation of a particular embodied West African Sufi discipline. The mosque he investigates is situated on land that was formerly a slave plantation in South Carolina; today it belongs to a transatlantic Sufi Order that originated in Senegal and operates as an important site for remembrance among African American Sufi Muslims. Carter examines how remembrance of the past is imprinted on their bodies through the enactment of specific embodied Sufi disciplines that retrain bodies and spirits via specific bicoastal collaborations, whether through remembrance of the enslaved Muslim ancestors that populated the Carolinas, of the dead and living Sufi saints, or of God and his Prophet. These forms of remembrance reconnect African American Muslims to a tradition of inward spiritual mastery that functions to cleanse them of their race-based trauma. For the practitioners, these practices therefore constitute techniques of self-care and are also embedded in concrete discourses of healing.

In chapter 3, "Spiritual Ethnicity: Our Collective Ancestors in Ifá Devotion across the Americas," N. Fadeke Castor examines a Yorùbá religious conference in Trinidad in order to reflect on the tensions that can emerge when a particular *spiritual ethnicity* is produced across ostensibly disparate racial assemblages through participation in embodied spiritual performances. Her analysis shows that, on the one hand, embodied movements enacted by practitioners from across Latin America, the Caribbean, and North America serve to reinforce a ritual collectivity established on the grounds of a shared imagined religious heritage. Through embodied rituals for the ancestors, historical memory is created that locates the practitioners within the African diaspora. On the other hand, she also shows how racial formations and the lived experience of heritage cannot always be fully transcended.

The three chapters in part II, "Community, Religious Habitus, and the Senses," consider how a variety of different embodied and material practices contribute to producing a religious habitus or shaping a particular kind of pious sensorium. Chapter 4, entitled "Faith Full: Sensuous Habitus, Everyday Affect, and Divergent Diaspora in the UCKG," by Rachel Cantave, deals with the expansion of Pentecostalism in traditionally Catholic Brazil. Here the adaptation of ecstatic practices used in traditional Afro-Brazilian religions, which are re-dressed as evangelical, has proved to be highly attractive to Pentecostal church members. She examines how Pentecostal practitioners in Salvador de Bahia work through a variety of intersubjective affective registers (including touch and sight) to develop a particular pious sensory experience that affiliates them to their faith—

and, paradoxically, ultimately reaffirms an individualist discourse. Through a discourse among practitioners about the role of feeling, Cantave shows how ideological and embodied knowledges are internalized by Afro-Brazilian adherents and rearticulated as a form of divergent Blackness, connected to a quest for social uplift.

In chapter 5, "Covered Bodies, Moral Education, and the Embodiment of Islamic Reform in Northern Nigeria," Elisha P. Renne explores the religious politics of Islamic dress by examining the significance of cloth coverings in the embodiment of Islamic religious practice. In Zaria, Kaduna, and Kano in northern Nigeria, which are home to numerous Islamic institutions and schools, the injunction for men and women to cover their bodies has been widely observed, although distinctive forms of dress and head covering are associated with different Islamic reform groups. Paying specific attention to the Islamic reform movement Jama'atu Izalat al-Bid'a wa Iqamat al-Sunna—known as Izala—Renne examines the gendered implications of Izala's emphasis on dress within its broader educational approaches. Moreover, Renne underscores the interconnectedness of spiritual, bodily, and material religious practice in the moral education promoted by the Izala movement.

In chapter 6, "Embodied Worship in a Haitian Protestant Church in the Bahamas: Religious Habitus among Bahamians of Haitian Descent," Bertin M. Louis Jr. is concerned with a context of massive conversion, in this case a traditionally Catholic migrant population converting to Protestantism in their host country. Louis uses the case of Haitian migrants in the Bahamas to show that conversion entails not only a reworking of a religious habitus but also the reworking of a cultural Haitian habitus. In the context of Bahamian xenophobia and anti-Haitian sentiments, Haitian religious expressions—hybrid Catholic Vodou—are deemed backward, primitive, and too African; becoming Protestant in the Bahamas also means to become, through bodily work, less markedly Haitian. He describes particular forms of individual and collective self-remaking through embodied practices, which allows Haitian Bahamians to negotiate their different contested identities. On the one hand, they resist the constant marginalization of their community and integrate certain altered forms of Haitian cultural practices. On the other hand, they seek, through their newly adopted Protestant identity as it manifests in a reformed embodied habitus, to increase their chances for citizenship and cultural belonging in the Bahamas.

Part III, "Interrogating Sacredness in Performance," investigates how dance and spoken-word performances deploy, work through, or recover a variety of different spiritual and religious identities. Chapter 7, "The Quest for Spiritual

Purpose in a Secular Dance Community: *Bèlè's* Rebirth in Contemporary Martinique," by Camee Maddox-Wingfield, describes the ancestral dance practice *bèlè*, brought to Martinique by enslaved Africans. Bèlè was repressed by the Catholic Church and discouraged by France's national model of assimilation, but it has witnessed a cultural revival in recent decades, instigated by cultural activists and artist intellectuals. Maddox-Wingfield challenges popular accounts claiming that all elements of African religiosity have dissolved from Martinique's cultural landscape by showing the spiritual and religious significance bèlè can carry for practitioners who are searching for healing from feelings of alienation, dispossession, and vulnerability associated with Martinique's so-called identity crisis. Ultimately, she reads the bèlè revival as embodied resistance to the French colonial, secular assimilation project.

In chapter 8, "Embodying Black Islam: The Ethics and Aesthetics of Afro-Diasporic Muslim Hip-Hop in Britain," Jeanette S. Jouili turns her attention to the quickly growing Islamic hip-hop scene in urban Britain, a phenomenon that has been spearheaded mainly by British Muslims of African descent. She particularly examines how Black British Muslim hip-hop artists, by employing their bodies in particular ways, strive to outline a Black Muslim authenticity. Forms of corporeal conduct on stage, such as dress, gestures, and movement, become consequential for a performed embodied ethics that builds on Islamic *and* Black liberationist traditions of social justice and criticizes global structures of racial oppression. Jouili further shows how such an understanding of the body as ethical material transpires particularly in hip-hop lyrics by Black Muslim female artists. These lyrics challenge racialized discourses by recentering the (Black female) body, which in turn becomes a key conduit to formulate a socially engaged and racially aware Islamic ethics.

In chapter 9, "Secular Affective Politics in a National Dance about AIDS in Mozambique," Aaron Montoya investigates a form of secular body politics that proliferates within state productions that promote certain types of secular religiosity in Mozambique's capital, Maputo. Produced in the late 1990s, *Amatodos*, a state-sponsored dance performance piece, promotes proper religiosity conducive to neoliberal rule by performing contrasts between proper AIDS-free subjects as restrained, disembodied, and interiorized and complicit, downright criminal subjects who are unrestrained, ecstatic, promiscuous, and African. Montoya argues for further attention to this state-sponsored secular religiosity while also acknowledging how Mozambicans continue to engage in embodied spiritual practices in secular performances that promote a notion of intercorporeality as well as commenting on precarity, violence, and dashed expectations brought by the neoliberal regime.

The final part of the volume, "Religious Discipline and the Gendered and Sexual Body," examines similar questions with respect to gender and sexuality. In chapter 10, "Wrestling with Homosexuality: Kinesthesia as Resistance in Ghanaian Pentecostalism," Nathanael Homewood takes up the question of homosexuality within Ghanaian Pentecostalism. Going beyond studies that analyze the role of religious institutions in opposing homosexuality discursively, Homewood examines how embodied rituals within Pentecostalism are at least as relevant as discourses for understanding what he calls an increasing "antiqueer animus" in Ghana. He opens with a particular deliverance session performed by a Pentecostal prophet aimed at freeing two young women from the "spirit of lesbianism." He then reflects how, through physical exchanges in deliverance, sexuality is not only publicized but also constructed materially and metaphysically. But he also shows how bodies are able to resist the scripts that are written onto them and encrypted in deliverance. From this observation, he argues how embodied affect produced for a specific purpose can always take on a life of its own, exceeding and even reversing the intended outcome, enabling bodies to become sites of resistance.

In chapter 11, "Exceptional Healing: Gender, Materiality, Embodiment, and Prophetism in the Lower Congo," Yolanda Covington-Ward explores how the routinization of nonmainstream religious embodied practices such as trembling impacts the role of women in the Dibundu dia Mpeve Nlongo mu Afelika, a small Protestant African independent church in Luozi, a town in the Democratic Republic of the Congo. Trembling indicates the embodiment of the Holy Spirit in the bodies of members and can be used to heal and bless others. In this church everyone may receive the Holy Spirit, yet only men may channel the Holy Spirit to heal and bless others. Covington-Ward shows how ideas about purity in regard to material culture restrict women's roles but also how the potential for embodied trembling allows women with spiritual gifts to continue to practice healing, especially as they are embedded in a larger prophetic tradition in the region. Her chapter highlights the sometimes-ambivalent relationship between material culture and embodiment for studies of African and African diasporic religions.

Casey Golomski concludes the fourth part of the volume in chapter 12, "Dark Matter: Formations of Death Pollution in Southeastern African Funerals," discussing funerary rites in southeastern Africa. He compares rites in the neotraditionalist Kingdom of Eswatini (formerly known as Swaziland) and neighboring cosmopolitan, urban South Africa by focusing on the local perceptions of *sinyama*, a dark penumbral emission akin to symbolic pollution. By tracing multiple reformulations of practices related to sinyama, Golomski shows how histories of racialization have transformed the value of darkness as a negative quality of materiality in religious ritual, affecting human bodies and places, with particular consequences for women. He argues that, as a gendered and racialized religious formation, this inauspicious spiritual penumbra is a manifestation of ongoing ethical and embodied engagements with a changing world, materially shaped by modernity and life in the postcolony.

NOTE

1. When we use conceptual terms like *Western* (and, alternatively, *non-Western*), we refer to the geopolitical North Atlantic region, which—through a range of epistemological, cultural, economic, and military-expansionist practices—has legitimated its supremacy and globalizing power over the past several hundreds of years and continues to shape the contemporary present of people and societies across the globe.

REFERENCES

Abdul Khabeer, Su'ad. 2016. *Muslim Cool: Race, Religion, and Hip Hop in the United States.* New York: New York University Press.

Asad, Talal. 1997. "Remarks on the Anthropology of the Body." In *Religion and the Body*, edited by Sarah Coakley, 42–52. Cambridge: Cambridge University Press.

Asad, Talal. 1993. *Genealogies of Religion: Discipline and Reasons of Power in Christianity and Islam.* Baltimore: Johns Hopkins University Press.

Asad, Talal. 2003. *Formations of the Secular: Christianity, Islam, Modernity.* Stanford, CA: Stanford University Press.

Baker, Lee D. 1998. *From Savage to Negro: Anthropology and the Construction of Race, 1896–1954.* Berkeley: University of California Press.

Beliso-De Jesús, Aisha M. 2014. "Santería Copresence and the Making of African Diaspora Bodies." *Cultural Anthropology* 29 (3): 503–526.

Beliso-De Jesús, Aisha M. 2015. *Electric Santería: Racial and Sexual Assemblages of Transnational Religion.* New York: Columbia University Press.

Boddy, Janice. 1989. *Wombs and Alien Spirits: Women, Men, and the Zar Cult in Northern Sudan.* Madison: University of Wisconsin Press.

Boddy, Janice. 1994. "Spirit Possession Revisited: Beyond Instrumentality." *Annual Review of Anthropology* 23:407–434.

Brown, Karen McCarthy. 1991. *Mama Lola: A Vodou Priestess in Brooklyn.* Berkeley: University of California Press.

Bynum, Caroline Walker. 1991. *Fragmentation and Redemption: Essays on Gender and the Human Body in Medieval Religion.* New York: Zone Books.

CERCL Writing Collective. 2017. *Embodiment and Black Religion: Rethinking the Body in African American Religious Experience.* Sheffield, UK: Equinox.

Chidester, David. 2014. *Empire of Religion: Imperialism and Comparative Religion.* Chicago: University of Chicago Press.

Coakley, Sarah, ed. 1997. *Religion and the Body*. Cambridge: Cambridge University Press.

Coleman, Simon. 2011. "Introduction: Negotiating Personhood in African Christianities." *Journal of Religion in Africa* 41 (3): 243–255.

Comaroff, Jean. 1985. *Body of Power, Spirit of Resistance: The Culture and History of a South African People*. Chicago: University of Chicago Press.

Comaroff, Jean, and John Comaroff. 1991. *Of Revelation and Revolution: Christianity, Colonialism, and Consciousness in South Africa*. Chicago: University of Chicago Press.

Connerton, Paul. 1989. *How Societies Remember*. Cambridge: Cambridge University Press.

Copeland, M. Shawn. 2010. *Enfleshing Freedom: Body, Race, and Being*. Minneapolis: Fortress.

Covington-Ward, Yolanda. 2016. *Gesture and Power: Religion, Nationalism, and Everyday Performance in Congo*. Durham, NC: Duke University Press.

Csordas, Thomas J. 1993. "Somatic Modes of Attention." *Cultural Anthropology* 8 (2): 135–156.

Csordas, Thomas J. 2008. "Intersubjectivity and Intercorporeality." *Subjectivity* 22 (1): 110–121.

Daniel, Yvonne. 2005. *Dancing Wisdom: Embodied Knowledge in Haitian Vodou, Cuban Yoruba, and Bahian Candomblé*. Urbana: University of Illinois Press.

Dilley, Roy. 2010. "Reflections on Knowledge Practices and the Problem of Ignorance." *Journal of the Royal Anthropological Institute* 16 (1): 176–192.

Diouf, Sylviane. 2013. *Servants of Allah: African Muslims Enslaved in the Americas*. New York: New York University Press.

Douglas, Mary. 1970. *Natural Symbols: Explorations in Cosmology*. New York: Pantheon Books.

Evans, Curtis. 2008. *The Burden of Black Religion*. New York: Oxford University Press.

Frederick, Marla. 2003. *Between Sundays: Black Women and Everyday Struggles of Faith*. Berkeley, CA: University of California Press.

Furey, Constance M. 2012. "Body, Society, and Subjectivity in Religious Studies." *Journal of the American Academy of Religion* 80 (1): 7–33.

Gilroy, Paul. 1993. *The Black Atlantic: Modernity and Double Consciousness*. Cambridge, MA: Harvard University Press.

Herskovits, Melville. (1941) 1990. *The Myth of the Negro Past*. Boston: Beacon.

Higginbotham, Evelyn Brooks. 1993. *Righteous Discontent: The Women's Movement in the Black Baptist Church, 1880–1920*. Cambridge, MA: Harvard University Press.

Jackson, John L., Jr. 2013. *Thin Description: Ethnography and the African Hebrew Israelites of Jerusalem*. Cambridge, MA: Harvard University Press.

Janzen, John. 1992. *Ngoma: Discourses of Healing in Central and Southern Africa*. Berkeley: University of California Press.

Johnson, Paul C., ed. 2014. *Spirited Things: The Work of "Possession" in Afro-Atlantic Religions*. Chicago: University of Chicago Press.

Johnson, Walter. 1999. *Soul by Soul: Life inside the Antebellum Slave Market*. Cambridge, MA: Harvard University Press.

Jouili, Jeanette S. 2015. *Pious Practice and Secular Constraints: Women in the Islamic Revival in Europe*. Stanford, CA: Stanford University Press.

Keller, Mary. 2005. *The Hammer and the Flute: Women, Power, and Spirit Possession*. Baltimore: Johns Hopkins University Press.

Klaits, Frederick. 2011. "Introduction: Self, Other and God in African Christianities." *Journal of Religion in Africa* 41 (2): 143–153.

Langwick, Stacey Ann. 2011. *Bodies, Politics, and African Healing: The Matter of Maladies in Tanzania*. Bloomington: Indiana University Press.

Mahmood, Saba. 2001. "Feminist Theory, Embodiment, and the Docile Agent: Some Reflections on the Egyptian Islamic Revival." *Cultural Anthropology* 16 (2): 202–236.

Mahmood, Saba. 2005. *Politics of Piety: The Islamic Revival and the Feminist Subject*. Princeton, NJ: Princeton University Press.

Maldonado-Torres, Nelson. 2014. "AAR Centennial Roundtable: Religion, Conquest, and Race in the Foundations of the Modern/Colonial World." *Journal of the American Academy of Religion* 82 (3): 636–665.

Masuzawa, Tomoko. 2005. *The Invention of World Religions, or, How European Universalism Was Preserved in the Language of Pluralism*. Chicago: University of Chicago Press.

Matory, J. Lorand. 2005. *Black Atlantic Religion: Tradition, Transnationalism, and Matriarchy in the Afro-Brazilian Candomblé*. Princeton, NJ: Princeton University Press.

Mauss, Marcel. 1973. "Techniques of the Body." *Economy and Society* 2 (1): 70–88.

McCall, John Christensen. 2000. *Dancing Histories: Heuristic Ethnography with the Ohafia Igbo*. Ann Arbor: University of Michigan Press.

McGuire, Meredith B. 1990. "Religion and the Body: Rematerializing the Human Body in the Social Sciences of Religion." *Journal for the Scientific Study of Religion* 29 (3): 283–296.

McGuire, Meredith B. 1996. "Religion and Healing the Mind/Body/Self." *Social Compass* 43 (1): 101–116.

Meyer, Birgit. 1999. *Translating the Devil: Religion and Modernity among the Ewe in Ghana*. Trenton, NJ: Africa World Press.

Mitchem, Stephanie. 2007. *African American Folk Healing*. New York: New York University Press.

Mitchem, Stephanie. 2014. "Embodiment in African American Theology." In *The Oxford Handbook of African American Theology*, edited by Anthony Pinn and Katie G. Cannon, 308–317. New York: Oxford University Press.

Morgan, Jennifer L. 1997. "'Some Could Suckle over Their Shoulder': Male Travelers, Female Bodies, and the Gendering of Racial Ideology, 1500–1770." *William and Mary Quarterly* 54 (1): 167–192.

Olupona, Jacob. 2011. *City of 201 Gods: Ilé-Ifè in Time, Space, and the Imagination*. Berkeley: University of California Press.

Palmié, Stephan. 2002. *Wizards and Scientists: Explorations in Afro-Cuban Modernity and Tradition*. Durham, NC: Duke University Press.

Pernick, Martin. 1985. *A Calculus of Suffering: Pain, Professionalism, and Anesthesia in Nineteenth-Century America*. New York: Columbia University Press.

Pierre, Jemima. 2013. *The Predicament of Blackness: Postcolonial Ghana and the Politics of Race*. Chicago: University of Chicago Press.

Pinn, Anthony. 2010. *Embodiment and the New Shape of Black Theological Thought*. New York: New York University Press.

Price, Charles. 2009. *Becoming Rasta: Origins of Rastafari Identity in Jamaica*. New York: New York University Press.

Ramsey, Kate. 2011. *The Spirits and the Law: Vodou and Power in Haiti*. Chicago: University of Chicago Press.

Roberts, Dorothy. 1997. *Killing the Black Body: Race, Reproduction, and the Meaning of Liberty*. New York: Pantheon Books.

Ross, Robert. 1999. *Status and Respectability in the Cape Colony, 1750–1870: A Tragedy of Manners*. Cambridge: Cambridge University Press.

Routon, Kenneth. 2006. "Trance-Nationalism: Religious Imaginaries of Belonging in the Black Atlantic." *Identities: Global Studies in Culture and Power* 13 (3): 483–502.

Schepers-Hughes, Nancy, and M. Margaret Lock. 1987. "The Mindful Body: A Prolegemenon to Future Work in Medical Anthropology." *Medical Anthropology Quarterly* 1 (1): 6–44.

Seligman, Rebecca. 2014. *Possessing Spirits and Healing Selves: Embodiment and Transformation in an Afro-Brazilian Religion*. New York: Palgrave Macmillan.

Smith, Jonathan Z. 1998. "Religion, Religions, Religious." In *Critical Terms for Religious Studies*, edited by Mark C. Taylor, 269–284. Chicago: University of Chicago Press.

Stoller, Paul. 1995. *Embodying Colonial Memories: Spirit Possession, Power, and the Hauka in West Africa*. London: Routledge.

Stoller, Paul. 1997. *Sensuous Scholarship*. Philadelphia: University of Pennsylvania Press.

Sullivan, Lawrence E. 1990. "Body Works: Knowledge of the Body in the Study of Religion." *History of Religions* 30 (1): 86–99.

Ware, Rudolph T., III. 2014. *The Walking Qur'an: Islamic Education, Embodied Knowledge, and History in West Africa*. Chapel Hill: University of North Carolina Press.

Weisenfeld, Judith. 2017. *New World A-Coming: Black Religion and Racial Identity during the Great Migration*. New York: New York University Press.

Weiss, Gail. 1999. *Body Images: Embodiment as Intercorporeality*. New York: Routledge.

Werbner, Richard. 2011. *Holy Hustlers, Schism, and Prophecy: Apostolic Reformation in Botswana*. Berkeley: University of California Press.

White, Calvin, Jr. 2012. *The Rise of Respectability: Race, Religion, and the Church of God in Christ*. Fayetteville: University of Arkansas Press.

Wynter, Sylvia. 2003. "Unsettling the Coloniality of Being/Power/Truth/Freedom: Towards the Human, after Man, Its Overrepresentation—An Argument." CR: *The New Centennial Review* 3 (3): 257–337.

PART I

Spiritual Memories and Ancestors

1. Spirited Choreographies: Embodied Memories and Domestic Enslavement in Togolese Mama Tchamba Rituals

ELYAN JEANINE HILL

Coastal Ewe Vodun communities located along the Bight of Benin elaborate on memories of enslavement through mnemonic gestures complete with sacred offerings, embodied spirits, and evocative accoutrements.[1] In many Ewe communities, men, women, and children participate in Vodun practices to present and transmit collective memories of the domestic trade in enslaved persons. This chapter demonstrates how ritual movements, like stylized walking, complement oral histories while also diagnosing social disjuncture within local communities. Through events for specific pantheons of spirits, called Vodunwo (plural of Vodun), practitioners perform intersubjective choreographies. By identifying ritual performances as a type of intersubjectivity—the intersection of individual and collective experience—this chapter extends scholarship on collective memory and religious practice in West Africa (Baum 1999; Rosenthal 1998; Shaw 2002; Stoller 1994; Wendl 1999).

Theorizing ritual performances as dynamic, ongoing catalysts for understanding memories of domestic enslavement in West Africa, I examine practices honoring a dangerous pantheon of slave spirits called Mama Tchamba. This group of northern spirits of "bought [enslaved] people" (*amefleflewo*) commandeers ritual performances through spirit possession (Rosenthal 1998, 130). The spirits of bought persons advise and critique practitioners, who are typically the descendants of enslaved and enslaving ancestors. Since many of the enslaved were practicing Muslims captured in northern Togo, devotees exaggerate Muslim aesthetics as they dance adorned with fez hats and sparkling head ties understood to come from "the North."[2] Specialists reinvent choreographies framed as traditional as forms of ritual exchange with northern spirits.

By attending to the creation of choreographic cooperation through which devotees assert their religious, cultural, and historical group identities, I conjoin theories of embodied cultural transmission (Connerton 1989; Taylor 2003) with an investigation of the significance of spatialized memories. By *spatialized memories*, I indicate ways performers connect historical narratives to contemporary ritual gestures to bring memory into the spatiotemporal present and provide opportunities for collective historicizing through the use of the space to enact intergenerational transmission and embodied tellings. Few studies have explored ritual dance choreographies as tactics for interrogating histories of enslavement. My research on Mama Tchamba devotions traces ways ritual choreographies often structure and activate embodied memories and the transmission of historical knowledge to intergenerational communities.

Among practitioners, Ewe Vodun persists as a site of social commentary and historical discourse as well as an ecstatic collective experience. The words Vodun and *spirit* interchangeably indicate nonhuman persons with their own histories, personalities, whims, and desires. Vodun practitioners communicate and collaborate with intermediary pantheons of spirits to elicit healing and positive changes in their communities (Cosentino 1995, 29). The multivalent term *Vodun* also denotes ancestors, nature spirits, and the malicious spirits of the previously enslaved. For Ewe practitioners, Vodun is a way of seeing the world and weaving the presence of histories viewed as neither dead nor past into the seasonal rhythms, movements, and practices of the body and of community life.

During field research conducted in 2015, I apprenticed with a traditional association in Tsévié, Togo, to learn Ewe indigenous dances and observe rituals.[3] Tsévié is a semirural town located about forty-two minutes north of Togo's capital, Lomé, in the maritime region on the nation's southern coast. I trained with Mamissi Sofivi Dansso, a seasoned Vodun practitioner.[4] Mamissi Sofivi, like other Ewe practitioners, endows traditional practices with particular significance and selects them to represent collectively constructed views of the past interpreted for use in the present. Using choreographic analysis, personal interviews, and my own experiences learning and observing Ewe dances, I demonstrate how specific West African communities use ritual dance practices to inhabit and remap histories of enslavement.

Ewe rituals include formal parameters for the behavior of both performers and spectators. Those whose dancing was most commonly lauded by onlookers and participants were priests and priestesses, called *hounoun* and *mamissi* respectively, who are highly susceptible to spirit possession, skilled in the artistic practices preferred by the spirits they host, and trained to perform annual sacraments and rites to appease the spirits and reinforce relationships with them. By lifting their pointer and middle fingers in a V pointing toward the most proficient performers, Ewe spectators display approval of the arrangement or presentation of movements. Skilled performers maintain calm and coordinated body positions, bending forward at the hips with their elbows neatly bent and lifted just above waist level as their relaxed hands complement delicate arms swinging from side to side across their bodies, just in front of their flexing thighs. These dancers choose in the moment when to deepen the energy of the movements by slowing the motion of their hands or speeding up and thrusting their feet forward in ways that reveal the determination or playfulness of the dancer. In such cases, the doleful tip of the head—as if inclining one ear to the ground—may also indicate narratives of weariness or grief as accomplished dancers push rapidly syncopating and alternating feet across outdoor spaces. Individuals, especially initiated practitioners, train for their roles in such performances through codified processes, and each participant performs specific tasks within ritual proceedings and, furthermore, within their communities.

Though the performers do not claim the role of choreographer for themselves—since the term *choreography* includes all decisions made about performance, training, and the presentation of a dance (O'Shea 2007, 11)—their performances demonstrate the types of intellectual labor inherent to choreographic practice. Community members assess the choreographic labor of producing and adapting movement vocabularies based on religious efficacy. Since choreographers structure and select dance movements, I claim this terminology from dance studies to acknowledge the labor of Ewe ritual specialists, especially the women, who often access leadership positions in their communities through the frameworks of ritual events and masterful selection and placement of ritual gestures. A row of nine hounoun and mamissi—well-known priests and priestesses, including Mamissi Sofivi—who took the floor to dance for Tchamba exemplified this type of respected mastery. *Drummers, singers, and other dancers buzzed with anticipation. A flurry of motion ensued around the gathering row of initiated priests and priestesses, who serenely shifted their weight from foot to foot, as onlookers reacted to the preparatory movements of the dancers, embodying the crackling anticipation of the building performance by throwing colorful sparkling scarves across their heads and necks. When these dance masters bent into the triplicate steps of Tchamba, the movements of others toward them, peripheral to their performance, briefly intensified as others gleefully enshrouded them in additional scarves and literally fanned their rapidly intensifying steps with large colorful cloths as the performers continued their collective progress across the dance space. Some practitioners began to fall behind the line as they emphasized the steps of the left or right foot, repeating rather than alternating. One dancer raised her knees high in a more strident and regal tread than her companions.* Such Vodun ritual choreographers engage in presentations of histories that they perpetually reenvision, generating movements in response to drumming rhythms and overarching frameworks of acceptable innovations.

In privately funded, small-scale community events hosted in home court-yards, like the ritual performance just described, Ewe Vodun adepts perform memories of their enslaved ancestors.[5] By the mid-eighteenth century, coastal ethnic groups looked to the northern regions of present-day Ghana and Togo for the majority of "bought persons." Possibly as many as a million captives came from northern polities between 1700 and 1850 at the height of the Atlantic slave trade (Akyeampong 2001 3; Piot 1999, 30; 2001, 160). During the transatlantic slave trade, some Ewe communities profited by participating in the expanding ivory trade and by buying and selling enslaved captives. Ewe society included both free persons (*ablodeto*) and enslaved persons (*amefleflewo*) (Wendl 1999, 111–112). Contemporary Vodun practitioners in Ghana, Togo, and Benin continue to integrate histories of involvement in the trade in enslaved persons through religious practices that connect these histories to contemporary social relations (Akyeampong 2001; Brivio 2016; Montgomery and Vannier 2017 Rosenthal 1998; Rush 2013; Venkatachalam 2015). Ewe ritual practices model experiencing and representing memories of enslavement in ways that question the boundaries between master and mastered, since Mama Tchamba devotees embrace the spirits of enslaved persons portrayed as "strangers" in order to reason through past and present shifts in power and authority.

This project advocates for expanding ethnographic tools to include choreographic and dance analysis as a means of understanding the submerged forms of communication through which women contribute to polyvocal histories of exploitation, wealth, and debt and the ways women use such histories-in-process to negotiate and comment on current political circumstances and hierarchies. To address silences and taboos around memories of enslaved ancestry, I explore memories of the domestic trade in bought persons through embodied forms, including ritual choreographies. Drawing on Black feminist frameworks that emphasize the "self-defined standpoint" (Collins 1989, 747) and interpretive strategies of Black women, I examine ways that West African women theorize and contextualize their own performances as a means of presenting themselves to outsiders and incorporating local youth into performances of partially forgotten family histories of enslaved women.

Ewe communities see themselves as intricately entangled within rather than as either perpetrators or victims of domestic slave trading while pointing to ways women narrate and evaluate memories of domestic enslavement as intimate family histories. In Tsévié skilled practitioners choreograph dances in cooperation with one another and with nonhuman spirits called Vodunwo to remember the part played by their ancestors in histories of domestic enslavement. By focusing on how ritual choreographers present these histories through the linked steps of Tchamba dances, I underscore the local frameworks through which women remember domestic enslavement. To stage my own experience as witness to and participant in ritual choreographies while also designating ways that Vodunwo interrupt and inform ongoing narratives during spirit possession as they transform the movements of spirits' hosts, I use interruptive italicized segments in this essay. I argue that by calling on spirits of the dead to reorder current circumstances of wealth, debt, and illness, devotees use ritual performances to map the legacies of the capture and purchase of bought persons onto contemporary social relations and create a corpus of embodied women's histories that emphasize the influence of enslaved women ancestors on Ewe communities.

Embodied Memories of Enslaved Others

As a Vodun priestess descended from both purchasers of bought persons and their enslaved wives of northern origin, Mamissi Sofivi references local theoretical frameworks of the meanings of the body to signify such intimate family histories. In November 2015, toward the end of my yearlong research in Togo, I sat on the porch of Mamissi Sofivi's home compound in Tsévié. With her back to the door of her shrine for Mama Tchamba, she relaxed in a plastic chair. When I asked her why she dances for Tchamba, her voice pitched lower as she explained that worshipping Tchamba identifies her adepts, or "spirit wives," as people coming from historically very wealthy person-purchasing families. She recounted:

> In historical times there were very rich people among them. They were rich in cowries, and these rich people sold other Africans to the colonizers. In order to find the people that they would sell, they went up North to a town called Tchamba. From there they would take slaves to sell on the coast. They would take iron bars and use them to make shackles to bind their prisoners around their wrists and ankles. The bracelets and chains, these objects made of iron, we now call Tchamba, and they have

become a symbol or sign of slavery. Tchamba has also become a Vodun that we worship. (Dansso, 2015)

Sofivi confirmed that Ewe families remember northerners captured and purchased during wars and interethnic raids through iron bars and shackles (represented by bracelets called *Tchambagan*, or Tchamba rings) and through rituals for the Vodunwo associated with such objects and histories (Rush 2013). Ewe raiders often sold captives from neighboring groups to European merchants or local intermediaries so that they could be resold into the transatlantic slave trade. Wealthy Ewe families like Sofivi's retained many of the northern captives within the domestic trade since they were far enough from home that the chances of escape or rescue were very low (Montgomery and Vannier 2017, 252–253; Wendl 1999, 113).[6] Sofivi and other Ewe Vodun practitioners typically broached discourses of domestic and transatlantic enslavement as discussions of wealth rather than confrontations of guilt, shame, and grievance. For many Ewe people, the abolition of the transatlantic slave trade by the British in 1807 started the global processes that resulted in the decline of the slave trade after the 1870s and corresponded with the end of a golden age of wealth and prosperity when Ewe chiefdoms had prospered from revenues obtained through the trade in human captives (Hochschild 2005, 307; Venkatachalam 2015, 4; Wendl 1999, 112). The descendants of enslaving families view such histories through the lens of their obligations to the spirits of the enslaved persons through which their families gained wealth, prosperity, and security.

Though Mamissi Sofivi identifies with her wealthy ancestors, through spirit possession the desires of enslaved people purchased by her family manifest in her body. Sofivi mentioned that she has experienced "manifestations" of Tchamba spirits in her body since she was "very, very small," when she started to fall into trances after the death of her aunt, who had been a devotee of Tchamba. Through familial narratives, Sofivi views her allegiance to Tchamba as an inheritance from her aunt. Such deductions and interpretations of the manifestations of spirits in the bodies of those who are both their descendants and the descendants of their captors illustrate how Ewe people continue to attach distant histories to lived realities.

During our discussion my Togolese research assistant Richard and Sofivi described embodied dimensions through which local Ewe communities interpret histories of enslavement. I turned to Richard and asked, "Why does Sofivi have Tchamba?" He then relayed her answer: "Her ancestors were rich, so they bought slaves. From among these slaves that were bought by her family, one manifested in Sofivi." Wondering how this knowledge was passed on, I persisted, "But how will they know if their family owned slaves? Will they ask the Vodunwo? Or do they know from their families?" Richard turned to me, still listening as Sofivi continued to speak, then responded, "It is an oral history that people know through word of mouth to this day. In her family, for example, you will see that there are people who are very, very dark . . . because the people from the North were very, very dark." Though Richard mentions oral histories, both he and Sofivi assess the presence of histories of enslavement in their lives through embodied factors. Local people familiar with Tchamba worship interpret Sofivi's body as a visible indication of her northern heritage.

Ewe people view the bodies of the descendants of enslaved persons based on complex local concepts of skin tone, race, and ethnic difference. Though northern areas were ethnically heterogeneous, Ewe people referred to the entire region as *adonko*, or "the slave country," since they viewed people from those regions as potential captives.[7] Sofivi's and Richard's recognition of northern people based on their "very, very dark" skin exists within global frameworks of racial and cultural hierarchy that were historically formalized within global frameworks of European domination (Trouillot 1994, 148).[8] That Ewe communities evaluate and assess the bodies of the descendants of the enslaved based on skin tone further contributes to the unspoken narratives of identity at play within danced rituals for Mama Tchamba. These interpretations indicate the inversion of historical hierarchies since the incorporation of dark-skinned others, rather than those with light or fair skin, indicates proximity to power in Tchamba dances.

In Mama Tchamba performances, domestic enslavement is remembered by embracing otherness as an essential aspect of Ewe identity and many Ewe family structures. Since the vast majority of enslaved Africans sold through the domestic trade in Togo were brought from northern Togo, many from a place called Tchamba, Tchamba spirits often manifest as foreigners clothed in northern or Muslim clothing carrying objects imported from the imagined and resymbolized North (see figure 1.1). To attract these Vodunwo, performers dance wearing kufi hats and sparkling head ties and place bits of white chalk and bowls of kola nuts imported from the north in teetering piles on altars (Rosenthal 1998, 113). During events honoring Tchamba, devotees carnivalize and exaggerate imagined Muslim aesthetics by modeling their adornment after the dress and practices of Muslim Hausa traders and other groups understood to come from "the North."[9] These performances also indicate and embrace the ways that Ewe identity intertwines with the imported religious and cultural practices brought from the North by enslaved women, whom Ewe devotees frame as practicing Muslims.[10]

FIGURE 1.1. The adornments of enslaved northerners, including kufi hats, sequined scarves, imported textiles, and Islamic prayer beads, called *misbaha*, in the left hand of the priestess on the far left (2015). Photograph by author.

Carnivalesque elaborations on histories of enslavement by Tchamba performers exhibit the tensions among what Michel-Rolph Trouillot (1995, 3) distinguishes as historical processes ("what happened") and the mechanisms of sharing knowledge, stories, and performances about "what happened" with others ("what is said to have happened"). These performances of scenarios from the past capture "what is said to have happened" and what Ewe communities judge as most important for understanding contemporary circumstances, rather than any positivist portrayal of "what happened."[11] The mechanisms through which Tchamba devotees remember and share histories present northern regions and peoples as historical sources of power and wealth that play a significant role in local concepts of ethnic identity and power dynamics in the present.

Sofivi provides one example of how devotees of Mama Tchamba incorporate narratives of domestic enslavement into family histories of prosperity. Tchamba devotees claim the historical legacies of the domestic trade as embodied memories passed down within families. In such ways, Ewe people incorporate and interpret the otherness of northerners—based on religion, dress, and embodied markers, like skin color—into narratives of personal identity and family history. After exploring how practitioners represent northern others, let us now turn to ways Tchamba performances depict power reversals, disputes, and complications among Ewe community members and northern spirits.

Dancing Mama Tchamba

Though choreographic practice functions differently within possession dance than in concert dances, Mama Tchamba devotees structure and prepare culturally legible and comprehensible movements.[12] As culturally decipherable patterns, symbols, and shapes (Browning 1995, 35), spirit possession dances are clearly choreographic, relating to the etymological root of the term *choreography*, which—when deconstructed in Greek into *choreo-*, meaning "dance" or "dancing," and *-graphy*, denoting "drawing" or "writing"—means "dance writing." Though performers improvise within culturally and collectively determined frameworks based on the movement patterns that best represent ancestors and nature Vodunwo, such "dance writings" (Browning 1995, 50) constitute forms of cultural literacy and unspoken communication.

In October 2015 Mamissi Sofivi held a ritual in Tsévié, Togo, to consult with Mama Tchamba. The ceremony was meant to address her loss and the implications of wrongdoing within the household since in a single year she had suffered the deaths of four close family members. Sofivi assumed that her family members had fallen sick and died owing to failures within the family to properly remember and honor the spirits, including those of their enslaved ancestors. She hosted a ritual that included performances for Tchamba as a means of navigating her own loss and communicating with her community, including her enslaved ancestors. Such performances are neither spontaneous nor unconscious. Practitioners performing in relationship with invisible spirits and power objects, like shackle bracelets and cowrie shells, use choreographic practices to reach into the past to preempt future difficulties.

Though the town of Tsévié is only an hour from the port city of Lomé by motorbike, the trip sometimes took me the better part of two hours. Riding in a shared van, crammed behind women holding babies and baskets of dried plantains and the "mate" sitting on the foldaway jump seat, I arrived at the gas station bus stop in Tsévié.[13] After choosing a motorcycle taxi, I sped toward Mamissi Sofivi's home compound, where ritual preparations had been underway since the dark of the morning.

The drummers were assembling when I arrived. The other devotees were reposed, the children circling from one area of the courtyard to another. The children arrived eager to learn, training both mind and memory by imitating their elders and disciplining their bodies to perform within the frameworks of the dances. When the drumming began in earnest, the trickles of laughter, experimentally struck drums, and the shifting of performers on the edge of Mamissi Sofivi's home courtyard coalesced into the multilayered crescendos of *brekete* drumming.[14] A group of women holding percussion sticks, seated across the courtyard from the drummers, joined the polyrhythms of the initial songs of the event.

The structure of dances for Tchamba necessitates three main stages: preparation, engagement, and conclusion. Performers prepare themselves to traverse the dance space with slower, calmer movements that hint at the short journey to come as they wait for the call of the lead drummer, marking the music by smoothly shifting their weight onto their right and then left feet while remaining in place. Following the signal of the drummers, dancers launch into the faster, energetic marching steps of Tchamba (see figure 1.2). Finally, each performer closes the dance with their own version of a short concluding motion, in which they stop marching as the body pitches forward and their arms slacken wearily as if dropping something at their feet.

Mamissi Sofivi's courtyard bustled with the efforts of dancers, singers, instrumentalists, and onlookers. As the music and the prompting of friends moved them, performers rose and lined themselves up shoulder to shoulder. The dances for Tchamba are all variations of walking. With downcast eyes, participants crouch low until their elbows seem able to brush their knees. Their feet shuffle forward as slightly bent arms slide across the frame of the body to bring balance to the swaying of the hips and the pumping motion of the lower legs that shoot out and come back together in alternation, moving the performers across the dirt-packed surface of the courtyard to face the drummers. After concluding their first pass of the dance, performers then return to their original spots with the same movements. A number of dancers traced a path from the onlookers on one side of the courtyard to the drummers on the other. One dancer shifted her weight in preparation, her movements easy and almost distracted as she waited for the music. She launched into the dance, her arms waving with languid grace as her simultaneously fluid and frenetic feet pumped purposeful steps away from the drummers. When she reached another pair of dancers, she released both arms forward as a type of punctuation and casually returned to her seat.

With soft hands and rigid feet, speedy steps and brushing arms, performers position themselves within ritually framed spaces in order to dramatize their relationships with enslaved spirits. In these cases, specialists perform to materialize the foot travels implied in oral histories of slave raiding. By moving repeatedly across the dance space, performers literally retrace their own steps

FIGURE 1.2. Performers launch into exaggerated Tchamba walking steps, setting imported scarves in motion with their hands. Their feet part only slightly as they advance (2015). Photograph by author.

and those of their fellow dancers while figuratively reinscribing the histories of their ancestors and revisiting the historical paths that led to current situations of need or illness. Through the "act of stylization" (DeFrantz 2004, 73), a process of personal invention, performers manipulate set movement patterns, like simple walking, to invite Vodun spirits through physical changes in gesture, pace, and demeanor. As in Sofivi's ritual to inquire about the deaths in her family, individuals employ embodied techniques to trace the sources of contemporary circumstances of illness, poverty, and death to distant pasts by acknowledging obscured relationships among persons living and dead.

Reversals of Power in Tchamba Performance

Tchamba rituals reverse the power relationships between dominant and exploited parties so that practitioners must serve, appease, and please the spirits of the bought persons who inhabit their bodies and take control of their sacred spaces. By welcoming Tchamba spirits to command and orchestrate the lives of practitioners, rituals honoring bought persons also destabilize binary notions of the location of power and mastery by blurring the lines between masters and those mastered. Ewe categories of enslaved persons trouble and redefine easy distinctions between "us" and "them" and between foreigners and family.[15]

Ewe danced enactments of journeys between the north and the south of Togo portray many narratives of the movements of enslaved northerners, who often became children and wives to the Ewe families they served (Rosenthal 1998, 131). For Tchamba devotees, reanimating the perspective of enslaved persons cannot be decoupled from the perspectives and subjectivities of the families who purchased them.[16] These stories of the descendants of enslaved and enslaving persons hosting the spirits of the enslaved in their bodies complicate the dichotomies through which many define the roles played by West Africans in the domestic and transatlantic slave trade. When the other is a part of the self, the process of dancing narratives of enslavement becomes a process of contending with the hegemony in the fibers of the self (Rushdy 1999, 227).

During Sofivi's ritual, initiated practitioners became possessed by the wild spirits of previously enslaved persons. They moved in distinctive ways that interrupted and recomposed their previous movements honoring Tchamba. At such times, practitioners abandoned the shuffling, stylized tread of the second phase of Mama Tchamba's walking dance step in favor of more variation, demonstrating the fusion of the worshipper with the spirit. The escalation of the dances and the transformations from the baseline of stylized steps to more grandiose gestures—through which the possessed make demands on all those present—demonstrate social, political, and historical transformations in status and authority.

In the midst of performing her own version of Tchamba's stylized step, a possessed priestess began to trail behind the others, dancing backward as her movements transitioned into the drunken quality of a danced spirit host. As the others continued to march forward, she relished a small area, returning to a limited patch of dirt and gliding backward on bobbing knees and backpedaling feet. Her feet began to cross, her arms to raise, the movements taking on a separate personality and intention. An attendant rose from the onlookers, running to her aid as if surprised by the sudden change in the movements of the dancer. She began to adjust the sequined scarves adorning the possessed priestess even as other initiated performers gathered to care for the priestess and the spirit of the bought person dancing her limbs. By the time four other women had gathered around her, the Tchamba spirit had modified the motion of the spirit host's arms and legs into commanding marching steps. Her movements sped into a rapid stomping triple step. As two women placed firm hands on her back, she stiffened in a half crouch with her knees bent. A priest dancing beside her seemed to challenge the drummer to play faster, beating out quick stomping rhythms on the ground and delaying the alternation of his legs. He tapped his feet frolicsomely, as if insisting on his way. He arrived at a point where libation had been poured and moved no further. An attendant came to his side. He initially resisted, causing a disruption in the dancing as two women tried to lead him to his seat. He lifted his foot high off the ground as if preparing to step onto a high platform. He stretched his body erect, pivoting on one foot as if off balance. Then, suddenly complying with the attendants surrounding him, with a vague smile on his face, he was led to his seat to receive offerings of libation and cooling perfume. Others, surrounding the first dancer in a tight huddle, poured libations of water from a plastic kettle before the woman's feet to appease the spirit visitor animating her body.

In the choreographic moment presented here, attending initiates called *senterua* cared for those dancers who became possessed by Tchamba spirits.[17] Before the moment when the spirit arrived, the two ritual choreographers, a hounoun and a mamissi, had interpreted the music based on their own stylistic requirements as a form of invitation and offering to the spirits. The man and woman had moved in line with a long row of other priests and priestesses, performing the same basic advancing, foot-thrusting steps. The surprise and sudden speed of the helper who came to the aid of the priestess indicated a recognizable change in the ways she was moving. The Vodunwo appropriated and transformed the movements of both dancers, slowing down those of the hounoun and prompting more insistent gestures by the mamissi, who stomped out a buoyant, crossing triple step as she raised her arms with a loose-limbed, "drunken" ease of movement. Entranced performers emphasize the weightiness of their bodies by taking up larger swaths of space or by cutting the lines of the dance when they cross their feet. These dances emphasize shifts in control and the need for the enslaved to reorder and challenge dangerous consumption. By illustrating the need for collective voices and including even stigmatized ancestors within the social fabric of Ewe communities, practitioners navigate complex shifts in social hierarchies.

Through embodied shifts of tempo, Tchamba spirits take control of the pace of the ritual and force Tchamba devotees to modify their behavior and movements. The hounoun and mamissi who fell into trance abandoned the small, concatenated steps necessitated by movements inviting Mama Tchamba. As Tchamba arrived, the priestess crossed her feet and intensified her tempo; the priest, by contrast, took gaping steps and slowed his movements until he was slowly pivoting on one foot, as if suspended mid-movement, rather than stepping forward into the rhythms of Tchamba (see figure 1.3). Ewe people interpret movements like the abrupt disruption of prevailing choreographic patterns seen in the ritual I described as the work of Tchamba spirits who take control of the pace of the ritual, often by intensifying or interrupting the dancing to demand that those present perform in new ways or offer additional gifts, like the libation poured for the priestess. Especially at moments when the enslaved arrive and wish to demonstrate their presence and dominance, performers

FIGURE 1.3. Entranced Tchamba devotees break the rhythm and defy the patterns of the Tchamba steps and drumming rhythms by changing the pace. The priest's feet stretch wide apart in opposition to the usual parameters of movements for Tchamba (2015). Photograph by author.

intentionally defy and displace the rhythmic structure of Tchamba dances by accelerating and retarding movements to indicate their control of the space and the ways that debts to the enslaved take precedence over previous power structures. The descendants of enslaving families view such rituals in terms of their obligations to the spirits of enslaved persons, through whom their families gained wealth and security.

The role reversal of Islamic others controlling the lives and bodies of Ewe performers, rather than wealthy Ewe people exploiting and controlling the labor of northerners, represents understandings of the tenuousness of power and affluence. Mamissi Sofivi later identified these shifts in movements as demonstrations of power, claiming that "once Tchamba arrives, the [spirits] unveil everything and impose rituals [on us] to arrest misfortune. The Tchamba spirits will show us these rituals through the movements of their entranced adepts" (Dansso 2017). These unfolding encounters with the spirits of previously enslaved people demonstrate that Tchamba practitioners question nineteenth-century (European) notions of memory as a fixed record of past experience (Gyatso 1992). The ongoing negotiation of these ritual gestures suggests that memories constitute a "system of categorization in which the past is recreated in ways appropriate for the present" (Lopez 1992, 36). Through performances of hierarchical tensions, Ewe people present their bodies, including skin tones, as indicators of kinship with enslaved strangers from the North whose spirits return to take control of sacred places.

Ewe people interpret histories of enslavement in relation to current political tensions between north and south that Togolese are also loath to speak of aloud. President Faure Gnassingbé and his father, Eyadéma, belong to another minority group from northern Togo, called Kabre people (not to be confused with people from Tchamba), who have held power in the neocolonial nation of Togo since 1967 (Piot 1999, 3).[18] Even as tensions mount between northern groups and Ewe people in response to Gnassingbé's stranglehold on the presidency, Vodun practitioners continue to perform dances through which they embody northerners and stage opportunities for metaphysical exchanges with northern "others."[19] Relations between the north and south were amicable before the bloody conflicts between Ewe people and northerners over control of the government in the 1990s (Piot 1999, 159). Since performers intentionally avoid making rigid historical connections that would exclude further interpretation and accumulations of meanings and complexities, these performances remain flexible enough to evoke current political tensions and danger as well as past exploitative relationships.

Ewe Vodun practitioners simultaneously communicate about slavery and contemporary politics through tactile, acoustic, and visual means. They do so by compounding signifiers through adornments affiliated with northerners, movements hinting at bondage and migration, and performances of dramatized tensions and danced ritual communication occurring between Ewe people and the embodied spirits of ethnic others. Even the fear of economic decline and resulting poverty and illness as repercussions of unpaid debts of remembrance to Tchamba pantheons may house memories not only of the financial downturn experienced soon after the decline of the transatlantic slave trade in the 1880s but also of the ways that the economy suffered during the political turmoil from 1991 to 1994 that was inflamed, in part, by violent Ewe opposition to Eyadéma's regime (Piot 1999, 47; Venkatachalam 2015, 4). During this historical moment, "development money fled, expatriates returned to Europe, [and] shops were closed for months" (Piot 1999, 47–48). Using a processual approach to indexing histories, Ewe devotees claim past hegemony over northern spirits (see Brivio 2016, 63) while also performing their experience of the current political power of Kabre politicians and the spiritual power of enslaved persons—all originating from northern regions—over their economic and physical well-being.

These interpretations represent the "potentiality" (Rush 1999, 61) through which practitioners use Tchamba performances to remember and reinterpret countless circumstances, themes, and histories, as they express views displaced from political discourses. In other words, owing to the multivalence of Tchamba dances, performers can interpret multiple time periods and contemporary circumstances through ritualized narratives of shifts in control and the tensions among dominance, service, and cooperation. Tchamba performers weave histories together in order to apply them to circumstances of illness, death, and debt faced by the descendants of enslaved people. They supplement and reinforce oral histories of enslavement through personal experiences of ongoing arbitration and shifts in "movement dialectic[s]" (A. Roberts 2013, 60, 84). Performers also make space for interpretations of political changes, while refusing to assert rigid applications and meanings for each movement. They also demonstrate the instability of power and the plasticity of identity through carnivalesque excess and exaggeration (Bakhtin [1965] 1984, 18–19). By offering gifts of libation, dance, music, and delicacies imported from the northern regions, practitioners seek to please Tchamba spirits and to allay fears of harmful repercussions for neglecting to honor them. Entranced adepts of Mama Tchamba demonstrate shifts in power and dramatize unvoiced fears of the generational consequences of the sale and purchase of bought persons while also reversing sociopolitical hierarchies in the space of the dance.

Unspeakable Fears

During our interview Mamissi Sofivi grew increasingly nervous. The small group of visitors who had gathered to listen and comment gradually left as I continued to ask about Tchamba. Sofivi expressed a sense of impending danger. When I asked Sofivi about the importance of Tchamba, she began to answer, paused, and then picked up a plastic water kettle. She poured libation for Tchamba as she said a soft prayer, then admitted:

> Tchamba is . . . very, very powerful. So powerful that it is making everyone afraid. . . . I am afraid for myself when I speak of these things. . . . That is why everyone else has returned to their homes, because they were becoming afraid when we started to speak of these things. It is because of this that I poured the libation. . . . I will explain it to you since I know that you are doing your research, but usually we would not explain. They are things that we do not commonly speak of.[20] This is a very dangerous Vodun. To make sacrifices for them, you must just put your hand on the animal, and it will suddenly die. If Tchamba becomes angry with you, you will just begin to bleed out and die. (Dansso 2015)

Though Ewe people carefully retain histories of domestic enslavement, they often convey them through unwritten, embodied forms of communication rather than discussing them openly. They do so in part because Ewe people historically buried bought persons as "bad dead" outside of the village in "the wilderness" (Wendl 1999, 114). Since these northern spirits could not return as proper ancestors, they became malicious, vengeful spirits.[21] Even the fact that Mama Tchamba spirits do not allow the use of knives for animal sacrifices to them (Dansso 2015) may reference ways enslaved persons were forced to give lifetimes of service, bloodless deaths for which the spirits now require person-purchasing families to show gratitude through memory performances (Rush 2013, 116).

Tchamba spirits attack the bodies and economic prosperity of their own descendants as well as the descendants of the families who purchased them. They punish those who neglect the necessary rituals. Performing rituals incorrectly may also result in Tchamba's wrath, expressed through illness or sudden death. Mamissi Sofivi once reasoned that many people in Tsévié who were "born to the Vodunwo" could not stop practicing Vodun because "if you neglect them, they will harm you" (Dansso 2015). Devotees conceive of memories of Tchamba as realities that can animate their limbs in new ways and as insidious forces that threaten their lives and livelihoods.

By demonstrating shifts of power and the interconnectivity between bought persons and their devotees, Tchamba dances mold silences as foundations for new narratives. Despite Tobias Wendl's (1999, 114) suggestion that the chaining of enslaved people to prevent escape became one of the major symbolic attributes of enslaved status, I saw no chains represented in any of the dances for Tchamba. The shackle bracelets that Vodun practitioners call *Tchambagan*, the "metal of Tchamba" (Rush 2013, 116), and the cowries that Sofivi mentioned as the currency of her wealthy ancestors were often evident on Tchamba altars. Such elements of ritual remembrance of enslavement were also included in ritual choreographies for Tchamba as adornments and jewelry. Through the inclusion of objects assembled on the body rather than on a stationary altar, Tchamba dances offer different and complementary perspectives on enslavement compared with Tchamba altars. Where Tchamba altars present objects in an arrangement intended to represent the body of the enslaved prepared for burial, spirit possession presents the living, dissenting, and commanding bodies of the enslaved as part of the social fabric of Ewe communities. By unfolding interactions between spirits and spirit hosts in ways that redefine sacred spaces choreographically, practitioners acknowledge their participation in and contributions to such systems as a means of repositioning themselves within interpreted and localized elements of foreign cultures through the walking of the body. By performing memories in multivalent ways that link certain types of recollection to specific, though imagined, landscapes, practitioners conjoin place and memory through lived experience. Since Ewe community members often choose not to give voice to fraught histories of the slave trade, choosing instead to perform and convey them through unspoken forms of communication, choreographies, and gestures that display the internal conflicts of slave-holding West Africans serves as a pathway through which community members communicate about these histories to outsiders and young people.

Intersubjectivity and Intergenerational Transmission

Tchamba performances enact a version of intersubjectivity, the consolidation of personal and collective concern, as a tool for communication across difference. I follow literary scholar Ashraf Rushdy in defining *intersubjectivity* as the intersection between individual and collective experience, essentially, the ability of individuals to see others as parts of the self (Rushdy 1994, 129, 132). Tchamba choreographies fusing northern spirits with southern worshippers demonstrate that "memory always lies on the border between self and other. The body constitutes the frontier of difference and sameness, a sieve through which historical facts are negotiated through remembrance, oblivescence, and signifying games of representation" (M. Roberts and A. Roberts 1996, 41). At moments when Tchamba spirits break prevailing patterns, their movements open paths for multiple interpretations of the behavior of the spirit. Such intersubjective choreographies involve the ability to recognize other persons as extensions of one's own body and consciousness and to acknowledge individuals as contiguous with larger communities, including both human and nonhuman persons.

Through structured improvisational movements, including dramatic breaks or pauses in brisk, stylized walking steps meant to portray the experiences and communicate the perspectives of enslaved ancestors, Ewe Vodun practitioners question the importance of the self and the notion of individuality. Communities use structured improvisation, ritual choreographies developed within culturally determined frameworks, to foster collectivity and extend its limits. Practitioners employ processes of embodied utterance to collapse the barriers between the self and others, between northern spirits and Ewe bodies, and between various time periods and locations. They posit ways the actions of an ancestor are not separate from the actions of their children and how inherited debts transform the lives of entire families and communities, rather than merely the individual. In this way, Vodun practice treats the full life text of the individual, including mental, physical, economic, and spiritual ailments, without "teasing apart . . . the body from the mind or from the numerous souls that make up an individual in all his or her overlapping with totemic plants, animals, deities and ancestors" (Rosenthal 1998, 42). Ewe Vodun practitioners examine the bonds of violence and exchange between themselves and those they identify as northerners by using the past as a lens for the present. Tchamba performers present techniques through which intersubjectivity serves as a means of constructing territories of memories and mapping internalized mnemonic geographies of enslavement. Practitioners place their own situations in dialogue with the plights, triumphs, travels, and exchanges of their forebears. Through such efforts Tchamba performers participate in the maintenance of spiritual legacies that reframe understandings of distant places. Communities foster social cohesion and intergenerational transmission of cultural knowledge through ongoing intersubjective performances.

Performers also use their bodies to activate sites and convey difficult histories to young initiates and the uninitiated alike through various realms of experience. In Vodun rituals, past and present narratives are layered to construct new interpretations of the past that build on and reframe past narratives. Many competing versions of historical events accumulate, displace one another, overlap, and merge depending on the social usefulness of various versions of histories. These debates—often taking place in Ewe contexts in the form of ritual performances—are the fertile ground on which groups adapt historical imaginaries. Yet Tchamba dances, as evidenced by the multiplicity of danced and spoken interpretations of music and movement by Ewe community members, constitute evocative mnemonic processes, rather than direct representations of events. These movements reveal the bare bones of historical narratives in the moment of creation, reinterpretation, and debate. During Sofivi's ritual for Tchamba, the young uninitiated girls joined the dancing from the slightly removed refuge of the porch as the adult dancers occupied the courtyard, dancing toward and away from the drummers.

Two girls stood side by side across the porch from me as I watched avidly, hoping to internalize the steps before my turn to dance. Eva, a girl of nine who danced with sophisticated grace, and Sophie, a jokester of seven often in trouble for not taking the dances seriously enough for the sensibilities of her instructors and elders, stood side by side across the porch from me. The drummer stood, while the other participants sat on wooden benches on either side of the porch. Many sang or played small percussion sticks as they watched the two young girls traverse the space. Their bodies bent far over as they inched their feet slowly forward. Eva's hands hung below her knees, her head cocked as if in grief, pain, or exhaustion. Her feet shot forward as her legs straightened at intervals. When her feet left the ground, she carefully flexed them, showing the whole sole of her foot. The girls' feet never moved far from each other as they sustained a syncopated gallop forward, alternating their feet as if they were enchained by invisible threads. Their arms continued to wave across their bodies as the movements of both arms and legs wove between the rhythm as if evading the downbeats. At times they appeared to dance to music that I could not hear, or perhaps as if their bodies—feet, hands, knees, elbows, and arms—made their own whispering music as they wound their way across, a melody hidden beneath the rhythms of Tchamba. Their heels slapped down in dialogue with the sounds of the percussion sticks and the hollow, jarring clang of a rusty metal barrel.

Through whispering gestures and familiar rhythms, uninitiated girls learn the movements through which practitioners invite Tchamba spirits to join the celebrations of the living (see figure 1.4). Through the symbolism of stylized walking and implied ties to northern regions through adornment, ritual choreographies provide a path into histories of enslavement and entice observers and performers to learn more. Yet, by participating in such performances, these young performers also add the motion of their bodies—their foibles, missteps, personalities, and individual heritage—to the histories being woven within dances honoring the spirits of ancestors purchased as bought persons and transported from homes and villages in northern Togo to foreign southern coastlands. Even as apprentices, the youngest members of the association—the uninitiated young girls—actually coproduce histories about their communities and encounters with outsiders and participate in lived and vibrantly enfleshed history lessons.

While I was attending Mamissi Sofivi's Tchamba ritual, Sofivi invited me to join the dances along with some of the young girls: *My feet pounded out an insistent shuffling triple step next to five young girls. Though we all danced with elbows akimbo and forearms crossing in front of our bodies, each of us danced in our own style. Some moved their arms as if gently waving a skirt in front of their legs, others as if rhythmically brushing something from their thighs. I labored to keep time, my heels hitching on shallow depressions, as my feet moved over the uneven surface of the porch.* The danced theories promoting the necessity of acknowledging inheritance from masters and mastered alike in Tchamba movements apply to my own personal identity as a Liberian American. As a descendant of both the native Liberian Gola people, who inhabited Liberia's capital, Monrovia, and the African American freedpersons who drove them from the area when they established Liberia as an independent African republic in 1847, my identity and heritage hinge on a series of transatlantic passages and hierarchical inversions.[22] As I perform Tchamba, I dance and stumble toward my own understandings of the paths through which Ewe religious practices forge connections between histo-

FIGURE 1.4. The author and other uninitiated apprentices demonstrate the small, enchained steps of Tchamba (2015). Photograph by Dodou Njie. Used by permission.

ries of enslavement and present realities. I add my own embodied harmony to the chorus of enacted assertions of kinship, hegemony, and passage inherent to Tchamba ritual choreographies.

Conclusion

Ewe Vodun communities use spirited choreographies to assuage debts to the spirits of enslaved persons. Within dance spaces and through the interplay between performing and interpreting those performances, devotees overturn and question political and economic hierarchies. Tchamba practitioners also navigate fears that reprisals by the uneasy spirits of the previously enslaved might manifest as an economic downturn owing to political conflicts in their small, neocolonial nation. Ewe women dance their narratives from positions as ritual specialists, dance masters, skilled choreographers, and local historians. Emphasizing these roles, this study illustrates how attention to embodied communication can broaden ethnographic practice. The combined testimonies and ritual performances of the women ritual specialists reveal the bare bones of grassroots historical narratives in the moment of creation and reinterpretation. The danced crossing and marking of the space constitute culturally specific gestures that imply and unearth often-unspoken narratives of enslaved women. By performing these movements, dancers train their bodies to remember the narratives that their gestures invoke and participate in processes of interpretation through which they continue to fashion personalized narratives of enslavement. In short, Ewe Vodun communities engage with obscured legacies of slavery and with incompletely forgotten women's histories by creating sites for healing through performances of memory.

NOTES

1. Ewe people primarily reside between the Volta region of Ghana on the east and the Mono River on the western side of the Republic of Benin. On an orthographic note, the terms *Vodun* and *Vodou* indicate separate but related bodies of knowledge and religious practice. Vodou commonly refers to Haitian Vodou, while Vodun is associated with the Bight of Benin, especially coastal indigenous religious practices in present-day Ghana, Togo, Benin, and Nigeria.

2. *North* with a capital *N* indicates the imagined place of authority that Tchamba devotees create within rituals.

3. Though scholars have problematized the term *tradition* as relating African practices to a static past (Barber 1997, 1; Comaroff and Comaroff 1993, xii; Drewal 1992, xiv), I use the term because the "traditionalization" (Gilman 2004; Hymes 1975, 353–354) of religious dance practices continues among Ewe people. Communities rhetorically affix the term *traditional* to certain practices as a means of lending them credence and authority (Gilman 2004, 33). Yet boundaries between "traditional," "modern," and "popular" practices are "fluid, permeable, and historically contingent" (Reed 2003, 10).

4. "Mamissi" is a Vodun title meaning "Mami priestess" or "wife of Mami." Communities also use the word *Tchambasi* (wife of Tchamba spirits) to specifically designate devotees of Mama Tchamba (Montgomery 2019, 60).

5. Though there are no clear records to indicate when practices honoring Mama Tchamba spirits emerged in their present form, ritual practices associated with spirits understood to originate from the north of Togo continue to grow in popularity.

6. Anthropologist Charles Piot (2001, 159) notes that Kabre people in northern Togo still have cultural memories of slave raids by many groups, including the ancestors of present-day Ewe people, and that some villages even paid human tributes to keep raiders at bay.

7. Though the majority of Africans enslaved by Ewe families were of Kabre and Tchamba (or Tamberma) origin, enslaved people purchased from northern Togo included Tem, Bassar, Mossi, Hausa, and Moba as well (Rosenthal 1998, 44, 110; Wendl 1999, 113–114).

8. Anthropologists Michel-Rolph Trouillot (1994, 170) and Jemima Pierre (2008) both frame colorism in predominantly Black nations as an important aspect of local ways of classifying social strata based on race.

9. I use the word *carnivalize* to encompass the imaginative excesses theorized by Mikhail Bakhtin in which "all that is bodily becomes grandiose, exaggerated, immeasurable" ([1965] 1984, 5, 18–19).

10. Alessandra Brivio (2016, 169–170) notes that although not all northern enslaved persons were practicing Muslims, Ewe people affiliate all of them with Muslim practices and dress as signs of enslavement and northern origin.

11. Performance studies scholar Diana Taylor defines such scenarios as "meaning-making paradigms that structure social environments, behavior, and potential outcomes" (2003, 28).

12. Dance studies scholar Anthea Kraut argues that Western audiences and scholars of staged concert dances often create a distinction between cultural traditions that they present as the product of anonymous performers and Western artists with "intellect" and "intellectual property." Drawing from anthropologist Joann Kealiinohomoku (2001, 35), Kraut (2009, 77) observes that traditionalized dance contexts still boast dance patrons, masters, choreographers, and performers.

13. The mate is an employee who collects the cash paid for journeys and returns change to passengers to avoid distractions for the driver.

14. Brekete drumming ensembles require rusty metal barrels and the *gon gon* drum borrowed from Dagbamba people in northern Ghana to produce the distinctive sound of the musical style, which entered Ewe music styles in the 1930s (Friedson 2009, 26). Drummers secure gon gon with a shoulder band and often move among the dancers to interact with the performers and contribute to the efficacy of ritual petitions for healing from northern spirits.

15. In Ewe there is no clear or direct word for "enslave," and even bought persons referred to those who purchased them as *afeto* and *afeno*, father and mother of the house, the Ewe equivalent of "sir" and "ma'am" (Rosenthal 1998, 130).

16. These complex paradigms are also at play in Octavia Butler's 1979 novel *Kindred*, in which an African American woman's body becomes a historical anchor through which she is forced back in time to rescue the slave master who is also her distant ancestor. Yet, in Tchamba performances, these dynamics between master and mastered play out based on markers of ethnicity and religious differences rather than through clear racial distinctions. Both the novel and Tchamba spirit possession rituals resist and confound neat binaries in favor of processes of coping with and assuaging debt.

17. The senterua support priests and priestesses and care for Vodun adepts once they fall into a trance. Such assistants may pour white powder, water, or liquor over the entranced performer; lead enraptured devotees into the shrine; or change them into appropriate clothing to please and represent whichever Vodun manifests (Rosenthal 1998, 265).

18. Although ethnically distinct from groups originating in the town of Tchamba, Kabre people were also enslaved by coastal families, and the term *kableto* ("person from Kabre") was sometimes used as a synonym for the term *adonko*, meaning "slave country" (Wendl 1999, 114).

19. On September 6, 2017, BBC News reported how, since the summer of 2017, Togolese protesters have called for an end to what they call the "Gnassingbé Dynasty." "Togo Protests against Faure Gnassingbé," *BBC News*, September 6, 2017, http://www.bbc.com /news/world-africa-41174005.

20. Owing to the social taboos around publicly acknowledging the heritage from enslaved persons, festival planning committees in Togo typically exclude dances for Mama Tchamba from government-funded festivities meant to portray regional diversity and celebrate local migration histories (Brivio 2016, 159).

21. Of the burial practices of enslaved Africans in Jamaica, historian Vincent Brown (2008, 65) notes that *duppies*, spirits of the dead, could harm or aid the living and that proper burial was necessary to send the spirits on their way and to ensure their benevolence toward the living. Since neither of these conditions was met in the case of domestically enslaved northerners in Togo, devotees continue to pacify and negotiate with these powerful spirits to avoid physical and financial ruin.

22. My Americo-Liberian ancestors first became Americans through Middle Passage journeys that brought them from various parts of the African continent. Many returned to West Africa between 1820 and 1867 through the American Colonization Society to reclaim national ties to Africa through conquest and colonial ambition (Ciment 2016). My parents left Liberia for the United States as teenagers in the 1970s to seek asylum from the Liberian Civil War.

REFERENCES

Akyeampong, Emmanuel. 2001. "History, Memory, Slave-Trade and Slavery in Anlo (Ghana)." *Slavery and Abolition* 22 (3): 1–24.

Bakhtin, Mikhail. (1965) 1984. *Rabelais and His World*. Translated by Helene Iswolsky. Bloomington: Indiana University Press.

Barber, Karin. 1997. Introduction to *Readings in African Popular Culture*, edited by Karin Barber, 1–12. Bloomington: Indiana University Press.

Baum, Robert M. 1999. *Shrines of the Slave Trade: Diola Religion and Society in Precolonial Senegambia*. New York: Oxford University Press.

Brivio, Alessandra. 2016. "Understanding Slavery Possession Rituals." In *African Voices on Slavery and the Slave Trade*, edited by Alice Bellgamba, Sandra E. Greene, and Martin A. Klein, 2, 154–173. Cambridge: Cambridge University Press.

Brown, Vincent. 2008. *The Reaper's Garden: Death and Power in the World of Atlantic Slavery*. Cambridge, MA: Harvard University Press.

Browning, Barbara. 1995. *Samba: Resistance in Motion*. Bloomington: Indiana University Press.

Butler, Octavia. 1979. *Kindred*. Boston: Beacon Press.

Ciment, James. 2016. "Americo-Liberia as a Settler Society." In *The Routledge Handbook of the History of Settler Colonialism*, edited by Edward Cavanagh and Lorenzo Veracini, 215–229. New York: Routledge.

Collins, Patricia Hill. 1989. "The Social Construction of Black Feminist Thought." *Signs* 14 (4): 745–773.

Comaroff, Jean, and John L. Comaroff. 1993. Introduction to *Modernity and Its Malcontents: Ritual and Power in Postcolonial Africa*, edited by Jean Comaroff and John Comaroff, xi–xxxvii. Chicago: University of Chicago Press.

Connerton, Paul. 1989. *How Societies Remember*. New York: Cambridge University Press.

Cosentino, Donald J. 1995. "Imagine Heaven." In *Sacred Arts of Haitian Voudou*, edited by Donald J. Cosentino, 28–29. Los Angeles: UCLA Fowler Museum of Cultural History.

Dansso, Mamissi Sofivi. 2015. Personal communication. November 22.

Dansso, Mamissi Sofivi. 2017. Personal communication. November 29.

DeFrantz, Thomas F. 2004. "The Black Beat Made Visible: Hip Hop Dance and Body Power." In *Of the Presence of the Body: Essays on Dance and Performance Theory*, edited by Andre Lepeki, 64–81. Middletown, CT: Wesleyan University Press.

Drewal, Margaret Thompson. 1988. "Ritual Performance in Africa Today." TDR *The Drama Review* 32 (2): 25–30.

Drewal, Margaret Thompson. 1992. *Yoruba Ritual: Performers, Play, Agency*. Bloomington: Indiana University Press.

Friedson, Steven M. 2009. *Remains of Ritual: Northern Gods in a Southern Land*. Chicago: University of Chicago Press.

Gilman, Lisa. 2004. "The Traditionalization of Women's Dancing, Hegemony, and Politics in Malawi." *Journal of Folklore Research* 41 (1): 33–60.

Gyatso, Janet. 1992. Introduction to *In the Mirror of Memory: Reflections on Mindfulness and Remembrance in Indian and Tibetan Buddhism*, edited by Janet Gyatso, 1–20. Albany: State University of New York Press.

Hochschild, Adam. 2005. *Bury the Chains: Prophets and Rebels in the Fight to Free an Empire's Slaves*. New York: Houghton Mifflin.

Hymes, Dell. 1975. "Folklore's Nature and the Sun's Myth." *Journal of American Folklore* 88 (359): 345–369.

Kealiinohomoku, Joann. 2001. "An Anthropologist Looks at Ballet as a Form of Ethnic Dance." In *Moving History/Dancing Cultures: A Dance History Reader*, edited by Ann Dils and Ann Cooper Albright, 33–43. Middletown, CT: Wesleyan University Press.

Kraut, Anthea. 2009. "Race-ing Choreographic Copyright." In *Worlding Dance*, edited by Susan Leigh Foster, 76–97. New York: Palgrave Macmillan.

Lopez, Donald. 1992. "Memories of the Buddha." In *In the Mirror of Memory: Reflections on Mindfulness and Remembrance in Indian and Tibetan Buddhism*, edited by Janet Gyatso, 22–46. Albany: State University of New York Press.

Montgomery, Eric J. 2019. "The Past Is Present: Slavery, Personhood, and Mimesis in Ewe Gorovodu and Mama Tchamba." In *Shackled Sentiments: Slaves, Spirits, and Memories in the African Diaspora*, edited by Eric J. Montgomery, 59–84. Lanham, MD: Lexington Books.

Montgomery, Eric J., and Christian N. Vannier. 2017. *An Ethnography of a Vodu Shrine in Southern Togo: Of Spirit, Slave and Sea*. Leiden: Brill.

O'Shea, Janet. 2007. *At Home in the World: Bharata Natyam on the Global Stage*. Middletown, CT: Wesleyan University Press.

Pierre, Jemima. 2008. "'I Like Your Color!': Skin Bleaching and Geographies of Race in Urban Ghana." *Feminist Review*, no. 90: 9–29.

Piot, Charles. 1999. *Remotely Global: Village Modernity in West Africa*. Chicago: University of Chicago Press.

Piot, Charles. 2001. "Atlantic Aporias: Africa and Paul Gilroy's Black Atlantic." *South Atlantic Quarterly* 100 (5): 155–170.

Reed, Daniel B. 2003. *Dan Ge Performance: Masks and Music in Contemporary Côte d'Ivoire*. Bloomington: Indiana University Press.

Roberts, Allen F. 2013. *A Dance of Assassins: Performing Early Colonial Hegemony in the Congo*. Bloomington: Indiana University Press.

Roberts, Mary Nooter, and Allen F. Roberts. 1996. *Memory: Luba Art and the Making of History*. New York: Prestel.

Rosenthal, Judy. 1998. *Possession, Ecstasy, and Law in Ewe Voodoo*. London: University of Virginia Press.

Rush, Dana. 1999. "Eternal Potential: Chromolithographs in Vodunland." *African Arts* 32 (4): 60–75, 94–96.

Rush, Dana. 2013. *Vodun in Coastal Benin: Unfinished, Open-Ended, Global*. Nashville, TN: Vanderbilt University Press.

Rushdy, Ashraf H. A. 1994. "Ishmael Reed's Neo-HooDoo Slave Narrative." *Narrative* 2 (2): 112–139.

Rushdy, Ashraf H. A. 1999. *Neo-slave Narratives: Studies in the Social Logic of a Literary Form*. Oxford: Oxford University Press.

Shaw, Rosalind. 2002. *Memories of the Slave Trade: Ritual and the Historical Imagination in Sierra Leone*. Chicago: University of Chicago Press.

Stoller, Paul. 1994. "Embodying Colonial Memories." *American Anthropologist* 96 (3): 634–648.

Taylor, Diana. 2003. *The Archive and the Repertoire: Performing Cultural Memory in the Americas*. Durham, NC: Duke University Press.

Trouillot, Michel-Rolph. 1994. "Culture, Color, and Politics in Haiti." In *Race*, edited by Steven Gregory and Roger Sanjek, 146–174. New Brunswick, NJ: Rutgers University Press.

Trouillot, Michel-Rolph. 1995. *Silencing the Past: Power and the Production of History*. Boston: Beacon.

Venkatachalam, Meera. 2015. *Slavery, Memory and Religion in Southeastern Ghana, c. 1850–Present*. New York: Cambridge University Press.

Wendl, Tobias. 1999. "Slavery, Spirit Possession and Ritual Consciousness: The Tchamba Cult among the Mina of Togo." In *Spirit Possession: Modernity and Power in Africa*, edited by Heike Behrend and Ute Luig, 111–123. Oxford, UK: James Currey.

2. Alchemy of the *Fuqara*: Spiritual Care,
Memory, and the Black Muslim Body

YOUSSEF CARTER

Dhikru-llāh or remembrance of Allah, is any practice that is intended to bring the
memory of Allah back to the recollection of the rememberer, or the *dhākir*. The
remembrance of Allah is therefore assumed to be about something that the *dhākir*
already knew, but has forgotten. It only stands to reason that you remember what
you already knew, not something you have never known. —Imam Fode Drame,
Illuminated Remembrance of God, 2017

Mikhail Abdullah, an African American Muslim from South Carolina, is an
integral member of the *zawiyah*-mosque (Masjidul Muhajjirun wal Ansar) of
Moncks Corner, South Carolina.[1] He is a devoted student of Shaykh Arona Faye,
who is a trusted and charismatic spiritual guide of the Mustafawi Sufi order in
the United States. Mikhail had performed music in a secular context before
becoming enveloped in the Mustafawi tradition and has since decided to engage himself in a West African Sufi training regimen that emphasizes bodily
discipline and inward mindfulness through *dhikr* (remembrance of Allah). To
achieve this manner of growth, he uses his body as a vehicle for mobilizing spiritual transformation to produce a consistent sense of attentiveness in remembering God. However, the performance of remembering for African-descended
Muslims in Moncks Corner includes a reconnection to lost ancestors and an
imagined homeland that is deployed through reciting the Mustafawi odes in a
space that has been purposefully devoted to spiritual care. Through the guidance

of their teacher, Shaykh Faye, African American *fuqara* like Mikhail transform their lives for the better by subjecting their bodies to daily Muslim devotions and arduous Sufi observances.[2] Moreover, the majority of the training that Mikhail and others have undergone has occurred at the zawiyah, which is situated in a location that contributes directly to reconnecting themselves to Muslim ancestors.

This chapter centers on a Sufi Muslim community composed primarily of African-descended Muslims who practice their religion in and around the mosque, which is situated on land that was formerly a slave plantation. Relying on Mikhail as emblematic, this chapter discusses how Black diasporic Muslim identities are shaped through bodily performances within the framework of a West African Islamic pedagogy, which, in turn, is impacted and enlivened by its African American initiates. This analysis aims to understand precisely the manner in which particular Muslim subjectivities are shaped within the bounds of a specific practice of spiritual cultivation. Spiritual cultivation is informed in this case, as I show, through the medium of *tarbiyah* (moral training/alchemy of the human being)—of which the religious poetry of Shaykh Mustafa Gueye Haydara is a part—and the call to actualize a return to the *fitra* (the original state of humanity, inclined toward God-consciousness and cleansed of negative or harmful experiences). Remembrance of Allah involves, and is contingent on, an intimate knowledge of one's inner self that is achieved through attending to cleansing the body and spirit. African American fuqara seek to reconnect themselves to a West African Sufi practice because the process of tarbiyah allows them to be cleansed of trauma and to reassert their full humanity in ways that, they believe, would otherwise be impossible. In so doing, they enact an entirely different route toward resisting racial oppression that emphasizes inward spiritual mastery and bodily discipline. This analysis of dhikr performance in the Moncks Corner zawiyah draws in many ways on work on Muslim ethical cultivation via embodiment in Muslim-majority contexts (Mahmood 2011) and in the diaspora (Eisenlohr 2018; Jouili 2015). However, my own analysis extends beyond these studies by examining how ethical cultivation operates as a work of self-healing in the context of racial violence and oppression.

The Mustafawi *tariqa* is a transatlantic Sufi order that originated in Senegal through the efforts of the late Shaykh Mustafa Gueye Haydara (d. 1989) and established a presence in South Carolina in 1994 through the efforts of Shaykh Arona Faye, leader of the fuqara in the United States, and Umm Aisha Faye, an African American Muslimah (Muslim woman) and the local matriarch of the Moncks Corner zawiyah. Dhikr within the Mustafawi Order serves as an avenue through which transatlantic solidarities are configured in this small blue-collar town and beyond. To discuss the cultivation of religious selves among Muslims of African descent in that space, I analyze remembrance in two major ways: I illustrate how African-descended Muslims use their bodies to perform and internalize specific knowledges that result in the emergence of those diasporic identities (Connerton 1989; Kugle 2011; Ware 2014), and I explore how those bodily performances play a part in forging and maintaining transatlantic religious relationships (Clarke 2004; Cohen 2008; Garbin 2013; Griffith and Savage 2006; Holsey 2004; Lovejoy 1997; Matory 2005). To interrogate how remembrance is activated through bodily dispositions and performances, this analysis highlights how and by what means a long-established West African Sufic tradition of moral-ethical training is deployed to address the needs of African American Muslims in the United States. What most interests me here is the multiple ways that remembrance operates. Dhikr is both a form of bodily practice (a corporeal form of memory) used as a device for religious instruction and a form of social memory among and between two distinct groups of diasporic Africans that possess variant relationships to the American South. I offer, therefore, that through dhikr African and African American Muslims access spiritual and historical reconnections that are grounded in affective diasporic relationships between the American South and coastal Senegal—a discursively imagined homeland as it emerges in the Moncks Corner mosque (Alpers 2000; Clarke 2004; Ho 2006; Kane 2011; Yamba 1995).

Ethnographic research conducted in the zawiyah of Moncks Corner from late 2014 to early 2016 has revealed to me the manner in which African American Mustafawi Muslims participate in dhikr as a means of remembering Allah while simultaneously engaging in a process of healing. The zawiyah is also the only mosque in Moncks Corner and is named Masjidul Muhajjirun wal Ansar—translated roughly as "place of worship for migrants and their (Indigenous) assistants."[3] The aptly named mosque is situated on Old U.S. 52 highway adjacent to Gippy Plantation—land where enslaved Africans were forced to labor before the American Civil War. In my talks with other members of the mosque, they reflected quite openly on the likelihood that enslaved Africans had been forced to labor and were abused in the vicinity. Furthermore, they noted the incongruity between how African American Muslims understand the sheer anguish of the enslaved in that space and how that history is presented in the Berkeley County Museum and Heritage Center, located nearby.[4] That Muslims who are descended from enslaved Africans, some of whom are believed to have been Muslim, are reciting the *qasidas* (odes) of a Senegalese spiritual master, which are incorporated into their dhikr sessions to activate healing and protection from harm, is significant.[5] By performing the poetic supplications of Shaykh Mustafa, the tariqa's founder, believers in the Moncks Corner mosque access a tradition through which Black transatlantic Muslim identities are fashioned and mobilized. Of course, these identities are also built from participating in other activities, such as studying the writings of Shaykh Mustafa, attending lectures provided by Shaykh Faye, and traveling to the Senegambian region of West Africa. However, I focus here on how those identities relate to the performance of Shaykh Mustafa's qasidas in that space.

Dhikr and Alchemy in Moncks Corner

In 1996 Mikhail Abdullah was attending an art institute in Atlanta, where he was pursuing a music career and owned an independent record label. Engaged in a life of public performance and entertainment, he had yet to become acquainted with the life of devotion that Sufism had to offer. He was already a practicing Muslim and had agreed to accompany his father-in-law from a prior marriage in visiting the Moncks Corner mosque for the Eid al-Adha that year.[6] The robust camaraderie and lively atmosphere evinced by the Moncks Corner community (at Masjid Muhajjirun wal Ansar) contrasted with the dullness of Mikhail's home mosque back in Charleston, South Carolina. In fact, it was while visiting the zawiyah of Moncks Corner that day that Mikhail first experienced dhikr. After the Eid festivities ended, Shaykh Faye sat down with some of his followers and led the group in singing the qasidas of Shaykh Mustafa:

> That evening they sat down in the zawiyah. . . . We actually had a place that was designed just for worshipping God outside of the obligatory worship that we do inside the mosque, where we do dhikr. . . . I didn't understand any of that. I had never even heard of dhikr before then. Well, that night, [Shaykh] pulled out a big red book, and he began to dhikr. And everyone at that time was just going over refrains. So we would go over refrains. He would read the qasida, and we would do the refrain. That was the icing on the cake for me because I was a musician and I was at a crossroads. And this sounded more and more like music, but it was music for God. At that point, I told him that I'm moving to Moncks Corner. (Mikhail Abdullah, interview, August 28, 2016)

While, in general, dhikr can be done rather randomly, the Mustafawi circles in which the qasidas of Shaykh Mustafa are performed tend to be well ordered. During the many instances during my fieldwork in which the fuqara sang the Mustafawi qasidas at the zawiyah of Moncks Corner, I always witnessed such collective performances enacted in a ritualized manner, and they were always led by Shaykh Faye. The proper way to formally initiate a dhikr session, according to Shaykh Faye, was to always recite the first chapter of the Qur'an (Suratul-Fatiha) and then recite "Laa ilaha illa Allah" ("There is no deity except God") one hundred times before uttering the words of Shaykh Mustafa. While one was in the circle, the intent was to use the body to activate mindfulness (and remembrance). Those in the circle needed to ensure that their bodies were ritually clean and that their clothing was tidy. In line with the social norm of Islamic religious space, men sat in circles separately from the women in attendance, who formed an adjacent circle. We were always expected to maintain a dignified posture while seated—we danced with our hearts rather than our bodies. It is not that voices were simply utilized to match rhythms and achieve a collective melody; the participants also tended to sway back and forth as if the upper body was relied on as a metronome to keep pace with the group. In my experience, this melodic rocking while seated seemed to occur naturally and was less a predetermined act than the result of witnessing other bodies in motion and following their method. In fact, rocking my upper body during my performance seemed to naturally force me to keep the established rhythm—even when I had not memorized enough of the qasida to avoid making noticeable mistakes. Regarding the embodiment of West African Islamic training and the programmatic disciplining of Muslim bodies in the American South, I find Rudolph Ware's notion of *incorporation* instructive in order to describe how performance and rituals work to apply or embed a specific manner of knowing (and, by extension, remembrance) onto and into the body.[7] Therefore, as Muslims of African descent in Moncks Corner use their voices to utter the words of Shaykh Mustafa and their bodies to perform his poetry in concert with other Mustafawi Muslims, they join in a process of incorporating into (and onto) themselves a West African Sufi technique of disciplining the self.

In the moment that Mikhail first experienced dhikr, he decided that he would actually relocate to Moncks Corner to be a part of the community and study with Shaykh Faye as his teacher. The performative nature of dhikr, introduced through a West African tradition, animated Mikhail's choice to pursue a life of such dedication to spiritual expansion. This moment marked the beginning of Mikhail's path to personal transformation, which occurred in the context of a broader collective effort on the part of his fellow fuqara to improve themselves. His initiation into a life of intensified Islamic devotion also marked the beginning of a profound connection to a tradition of corporeal pedagogy mediated through West African Sufism and a reconnection to the worship of and strategies of spiritual care for imagined ancestors.

In describing how West African religiosities are embodied by Muslims of African descent in the American South, I use the term *alchemy*—a popular term among Sufi groups—not only to refer to the programmatic, scientistic transformation of objects that carries with it connotations of spiritual growth and expansion but also to highlight the very nature of the relationship between African American students and the West African Sufi tradition of spiritual care.[8] Therefore, I deploy this term to suggest the transformative relationship that emerges as African American Muslims, in particular, learn to dissolve their egos (*tazkiyyat-ul-nafs*), seeking to move beyond the residues of racial trauma, and attain a higher sense of Islamic piety. Moreover, this process of transformation includes, according to the ethnographic data I have collected, the cultivation of African diasporic religious identities via the application of secret prayers, devotional performances in concert and in solitude, and journeys taken to pay homage to their *shuyukh* (Arabic plural of *shaykh*) in an imagined spiritual homeland. If alchemy is the transformation of matter, the goal here is to transform hearts. This transformation is achieved, however, through disciplining the body.

When I think back on witnessing various performances of dhikr throughout my time conducting ethnographic research in Moncks Corner, what I find most compelling is the combining of African American voice and West African tradition. The way in which American Muslims (predominantly African American) in the southern United States perform communal invocations, participate in religious instruction, and consume and circulate artifacts such as religious texts, recorded sermons, and poetry signals a relationship between communal religious practices and the construction of social identities. The repetitive nature of dhikr and qasidas works to embed the various spiritual formulae for praise and supplication into the memory and consciousness of the practitioner. It is not a requirement that the performer have achieved a heightened piety per se—it is believed that the performance of the composition itself at once is a pious act and paves the way for the development of piety (or at least a heightened sense of awareness of piety), whether through the training of the body and spirit to bend to the rhythm of righteousness or through the willingness to be supervised and corrected by Shaykh Faye directly. Such performances are done mostly in congregation as the fuqara collaboratively engage in spiritual care, and thus remembrance—in both senses—is largely intersubjective (Beliso-De Jesús 2015; Covington-Ward 2016; Jouili 2015; Ware 2014) insofar as the engagement in dhikr performance overwhelmingly relies on a deeply held bodily relation among the fuqara.[9]

Following others who have studied the religious practices of Muslims, I believe strategies of bodily care among Muslims in Moncks Corner and what Ware calls an "embodied knowledge" are best understood via analysis of participation in dhikr circles and other religious performances. In other words, approaches to knowledge gathering and religious study are dramatically shaped by a tradition of embodiment whereby certain corporeal practices (Qur'an memorization, mimesis, repetitive phrasings, ritual prayer, travel for scholarship, and even domestic chores) cultivate postures of piety. The entire community is commonly invited to gather weekly (generally on Fridays or Saturdays) after Maghrib prayer to sing the qasidas composed by Shaykh Mustafa so many years ago.

The path of inward transformation—of alchemy—occurs through training the physical body toward mindfulness, which is provided through the recitation of dhikr and through acts of attentive listening. Therefore, an emphasis on embodiment is the key to understanding processes of *knowing* in (and beyond) the West African Islamic context. "Human 'bodies of knowledge' are made, not born. Islamic learning is brought into the world through concrete practices of corporal discipline, corporeal knowledge transmission, and deeds of embodied agents. Knowledge of Islam does not abide in texts; it lives in people" (Ware 2014, 9). Such emphasis on the embodiment of knowledge—in other words, the *performance of knowing*—is similarly exemplified in the Mustafawi tradition. To be considered knowledgeable, one must embody piety and display righteous behavior. Attentiveness to Islamically ethical behavior and mindfulness toward etiquette (*adab*) with regard to interpersonal relationships and worship are assumed to be a primary step in the pathway to knowing. Just as in Ware's characterization of West African religiosity as a backdrop to Qur'anic memorization that emphasizes embodying through upright behavior the principles that one memorizes, Muslims in Moncks Corner are expected to embody, or perform, the knowledge that Shaykh Faye gives them. Following the mode of West African spiritual pedagogy, the Mustafawi tradition similarly necessitates an inseparability between knowledge and action. The mode of spiritual training analyzed in this chapter involves rectifying behavior and requires a corporeal modeling of piety learned from both the living and the dead.

Expanding the Ocean: Social Memory, Transatlantic Connections, and Ancestors

Whereas social scientific literatures and religious studies have both found the body to be central to understanding how religious subjects extract meaning from faith traditions and how it shapes their experiences, I have sought to take this approach further in order to bring to bear how Black Muslim practitioners engage in specific rituals and performances as they perform remembrance of the past and activate healing. Works that have used the Black Atlantic (Gilroy 1993) as a device for better understanding the flows and migrations of peoples and the traditions that circulate around this space have placed much emphasis on "traditional" African religiosity (e.g., Matory 2005; Routon 2006).[10] However, some argue that the focus on *trance-nationalism* (Routon 2006) has perhaps overstated the presence of traditions like Santeria and Candomblé in the exchange between Luso-America and continental Africa.[11] For my own purposes, however, I situate the religion of Islam, particularly in its West African configuration, as central to my own usage of the Black Atlantic in describing the circuits of exchange and transmission that take place between Muslims of African descent on either side of the ocean.[12] When built on other works (Curtis 2009; Diouf 2013; GhaneaBassiri 2010; Gomez 2005; McCloud 2014), such analyses help to concretize the analytic ground for understanding the long historical religious presence of West Africans in the Americas. Hence, the analysis here centers on the project of gathering ground for discussing how Sufism in a transatlantic context creates pathways for diasporic mobility regarding the migration of peoples and identities-in-motion. In fact, it is the *interrelatedness* between varying kinds of Black Muslimness that is of interest in the quest to apprehend the very nature of how and why Mustafawi members on either side of the Atlantic are drawn to each other so profoundly, beyond mere religious commonalities.

By analyzing exactly how African American fuqara mobilize a West African Sufi tradition for the purpose of addressing the past and present, I interrogate a conception of diaspora that has automatically included African Americans in a larger global African diasporic body.[13] As Edward Curtis (2014) asserts, a rigorous study of the religious dimensions of the African diaspora is vital to extend our collective understanding of the diasporic concept. Much as scholars have studied how African-descended people have incorporated themselves into diasporic networks via religion (Clarke 2004; Garbin 2013; Griffith and Savage 2006; Matory 2005), this discussion aims to ground this inclusion via analysis of religious observances that have animated Black religious identities. The motive here, then, is to analyze how and by what means Muslims of African descent living in Moncks Corner and beyond engage a West African Islamic pedagogical tradition that coheres the politics of Black Muslimness in an American context and among diasporic subjects.

Like the chapters by Elyan Hill and other contributors to this volume, this analysis of bodily performance relies on an approach that emphasizes memory not solely as a process of individual cognition but, more important, as a social process that contextualizes past events as devices for the expression and transmission of transatlantic identities. Therefore, such processes, in which the individual Muslim of African descent is situated, are collectively shaped and inform particular kinds of belonging while they also animate specific religious discourses seen in the Moncks Corner zawiyah in South Carolina and beyond.[14] Paul Connerton (1989) has argued that the past is constructed, or "remembered," via collective envisioning and that *performances* provide the glue through which shared knowledge of the past is attained. Therefore, ceremonial practices transmit collective vision by way of performance, which allows the individual to embody a shared envisioning of the past. Bodily practices, moreover, provide a pathway beyond two types of memory (personal and cognitive) into a third type: *habit-memory*. This third type has less to do with actively remembering how to perform an action by relying on cognitive recollection and more to do with a kind of interiorized memory—an embedded, more automatized process of embodying the past. I relate this notion to the manner in which Islamic conversion in Moncks Corner is collapsed with narratives of return to a lost religious tradition as a consequence of the transatlantic slave trade (i.e., reversion).[15] During interviews and informal conversations, all of my interlocutors displayed some vital connection between their own path to the religion of Islam and the likelihood that many of their own ancestors were Muslims when they were forcibly transported away from West Africa. Once again, this mobilization of identity does not involve tracing actual genealogies through time and space. Rather, it is a process that encourages the *faqir* (singular of fuqara) to locate himself in a tradition that spans continents and centuries by engaging the body in an appropriation of an already established spiritual network that affixes present students to past teachers through Shaykh Faye.

Protection Is in the Performance

The Moncks Corner fuqara, like most Muslims, utilize dhikr as a means of maintaining a heightened awareness and mindfulness of Allah. This can include the meditative repetition of phrases such as "Laa ilaha illa Allah," done in quiet solitude or in collaboration with others, and is performed to elicit a general piety. However, the weekly collective performance of Mustafawi odes (qasidas) is done to achieve more than this. The odes written by Shaykh Mustafa were composed to provide the student with a heightened spiritual vocabulary with which to praise Allah and His Prophet, beg for forgiveness, and ask for mercy, protection, and sustenance. Indeed, such performances are done with the intent of raising the station (*maqam*) of the performer also and stand as their own kind of formalized dhikr, insofar as one is in the act of remembering Allah.

Ritual action is a meaningful and transformational exercise whereby the training and disciplining of the body provide a means of achieving sainthood (Kugle 2003). However, beyond rote action, the repetitive nature of Sufi training aims to produce inward and outward transformation. That is, the task is to change the body into a pious entity through the consistent and intentional observance of a particular ritual act. While the performance of a Sufi ritual can lead one to conclude that intent and purpose are embedded within the ritual itself, repetitive or not, it does not automatically follow that we should find meaning solely within the act of performance. In fact, it is not merely the act itself that produces change. Without intention and an orientation toward being changed, words are but words, and gestures are only gestures. As the body becomes more apt and routinized in its performance of a pious behavior, the disposition becomes aligned with the bodily act. As the disposition becomes more inclined toward that particular mode of conduct, the body then is more exacting in its performance of pious conduct (see Mahmood 2001).

During weekly gatherings at the zawiyah, Shaykh Faye usually took the opportunity to "unfold knowledge" about the particular qasida we had just finished performing as we prepared to transition to the next one. He consistently provided those who surrounded him with an intimate awareness of the finer benefits of reciting specific lyrics, with the intention that they would practice the qasidas in order to master them. After all, mastery of the spiritual poetry lay not in committing it to memory but rather in gaining a deeper knowledge of its spiritual advantages by embodying a love of the Prophet and strengthening taqwa (consciousness/mindfulness of Allah). At the same time, however, I argue that the aspects of spiritual cultivation encouraged by the Mustafawi training regimen are combined with prescriptions for healing racial trauma through the performance of the Mustafawi odes.

Shaykh Mustafa's ode "Al-Bahrul Muhit" (The Vast Ocean) was conceived as resistance to religious repression and a source of spiritual power for his students. When the ode was composed in the late 1960s, Senegal had recently achieved its independence from colonization (in 1959) and was still grappling with the impact of French policies that favored secular modernization while imposing a Eurocentric approach to (disembodied) education on West African Muslims.[16] Shaykh Mustafa's religious poetry was meant to combat this trend by inscribing spiritual efficacy into the hearts and onto the bodies of those he led. Performance of "Al-Bahrul Muhit" was therefore, in that context, simultaneously an act of Islamic piety and an act of resistance to colonial shifts toward secularization—in spite of Senegal's fairly recent independence. In the present-day American South, where the legacy of political and economic repression of Black people is pronounced, African and African American Muslims collectively find solace and healing in Shaykh Mustafa's qasidas.

By reciting "Al-Bahrul Muhit," the Moncks Corner fuqara send praises and salutations to the Prophet Muhammad and use a formulaic approach to utter a comprehensive supplication for health, protection, wealth, and continued spiritual growth. Through elevating Muhammad, the supplicants hope to elevate themselves. The alternative title of the ode, which comprises 288 verses, is "Leave Me with My Love of the Prophet," and it begins by thoroughly praising his attributes. Its opening page includes the Qur'anic recommendation for Muslims to continually send blessings upon the Prophet Muhammad for their own sake: "Indeed, Allah sends His Blessings on the Prophet and also His Angels too ask Allah to bless him. Oh you who believe! Send your Salat on him and salute him with peace" (Qur'an 33:56—as it appears in "Al-Bahrul Muhit"). This Qur'anic verse shares the first page with the special prayer of the Mustafawi, the "Salaatul Samawiyyah," placed below it.[17] The poetic framing of the entire "Al-Bahrul Muhit," drenched in ecstatic applause, hinges on the following refrain, which was sung repeatedly in concert before each verse:

Ahmaduna Mahmaduna Nabiyyunaa Tabiibunaa Mughiithunaa
    shafii'unaa shamsul huda fil 'Aalami.
Our Ahmad, Our Mahmud, Our Prophet and Our Doctor, Our Helper and
    Our Intercessor. The Sun of Guidance in the realm of the Universe.[18]

The lyrics of the celebratory ode provide a specific language that allows the fuqara to pray for protection from external harms and internal shortcomings. In addition to praying for physical healing, the verses seem to request alleviation of oppressive forces described as "enemies." In addition to "Al-Bahrul Muhit," Shaykh Mustafa composed another qasida, entitled "The Cloak of Protection and the Soldiers of Divine Care."[19] It differs from the former insofar as it more directly provides the fuqara with a supplication for protection.[20] In this sense, protection from the lower self and the repelling of enemies are the central foci of this ode as Moncks Corner Muslims rely on it to ensure their bodily security as well:

12. And I will never fear my enemies as You are my protection from all
    of creation.
13. With the cutting sword of Your name on my breath, I am protected
    from every type of enemy.
14. Repel evil and treachery from me by Your great soldiers of divine care. . . .
23. Repel anyone who wants to harm my physical body by Your sword
    which is broad in its scope. . . .

50. O you who can work paper with your knowledge [transforming and transferring it], put it into action at the French mint.

We should consider that Mustafawi odes were written with the intent of also providing a regimen for future students not yet present and unknown in the time of the odes' composition. Thus, supplication for intimate knowledge ('irfan) and protection would apply to recently decolonized Senegal as well as the present-day United States. My own experience of participating in the dhikr circle and reciting the qasidas of Shaykh Mustafa while living at the zawiyah of Moncks Corner afforded me the opportunity to view these performances as part of a broader process of alchemy. In all of the instances in which I partici-pated in the circle, dhikr participants were always instructed or guided directly by Shaykh Faye in terms of how to engage in the recitation of dhikr, or the per-formance of the qasidas, with the aim of providing a systematic and practiced methodology for spiritual care.

West African Sufism and the Black Body

I do not highlight the role of African-descended Muslims in the process of shar-ing and transmitting knowledge simply because the fuqara I discuss here are Black and Muslim. I read these particular qualia of recipient bodies as signifi-cant. The linkages between present Black Muslim learners in the American South and supposed African Muslim ancestors are also meaningful. Black Mus-lims (whether American-born or not) can see their own selves as profoundly connected to the enslaved African Muslims who are believed to have been pres-ent in and around South Carolina before emancipation. It is not lost on them that before the American Civil War, those who now inhabit the Moncks Corner mosque would have been rendered chattel property, and therefore unapproved religious gatherings and at-will travel would have been impossible a century and a half ago. Such realities are quite apparent as we consider the significance of the Moncks Corner mosque's role as a space for worship, spiritual healing, and the dispensation of knowledge. Therefore, the act of reciting Islamic for-mulations of supplication and remembrance in that space is imbued with a specific politics of Black Muslimness, which is grounded in a broader transat-lantic region.

As observed in Moncks Corner, the performance of Islamic rituals is fused with the sociopolitical realities of Blackness insofar as the politics of Black Muslimness includes what one does with the body, what one puts on the body, and where one places one's body. The ideal body of the Black Muslim, although in the context of the Nation of Islam, became a symbol for racial uplift in the mid-twentieth century (Curtis 2006; Taylor 2017). Consequently, ritualization emerged as a vital demarcation of disciplined Black Muslims who would be protected from racial and economic dispossession. Throughout my research, national discourses surrounding racial violence and police brutality made their way into the homes of community members. During community dinners held at the houses of the Moncks Corner Muslims, discussions about the latest instances of violence seemed to repeatedly explode onto the tablecloth as Shaykh Faye, and those surrounding him, identified the United States as a place that would eventually worsen with regard to its social-political difficulties. Dhikr has therefore provided them with a strategy of self-care and healing that has the potential to undo both the pronounced and the subtle effects of race-based trauma.

Other zawiyah members have intimated to me how they have been affected by witnessing Ku Klux Klan parades in Moncks Corner in the past and instances of police brutality, and more recently they have had to deal with the psychological impact of events like the racially motivated massacre of Emanuel African Methodist Episcopal (AME) churchgoers in Charleston in 2015. Rather than immediately turning their attention outward to combat racist violence, which seems at times too large and too deeply embedded in the sociopolitical landscape, the fuqara first turn inward to heal themselves by relying on an otherworldly power and praying for change—and protection from their enemies. They do this because they understand quite thoroughly that any true and lasting change begins inside.

In recounting his own experience with the Mustafawi dhikr, Mikhail highlights how in spite of being intimately aware of racial oppression, being naturally drawn to the qasidas of Shaykh Mustafa provided him with a pathway toward shifting his outlook to find empowerment through spiritual cultivation. By choosing to address himself rather than the behaviors and attitudes of others, placing inward transformation over and above undoing racially motivated discrimination, Mikhail takes an alternative approach to uplift:

> As an African American, [dhikr] was something . . . that I could put in the place of music, because the people that I had been around and the lifestyle that I was living, scripture was not what guided their life—it was music. The music and the lyrics was the scripture of the African Americans that I was around. So . . . I guess that the [equivalent] to that would be the Qur'an, but outside of the Qur'an, something that I can walk around with and contemplate on was that dhikr . . . that "laa ilaha illa Allah" . . . and

knowing what it meant . . . and keep saying it over and over again, it affected me in a way where when the things that would make my parents upset or make the people that I was around upset, dealing with police brutality or the way the police was dealing with the African Americans inside the environments that I came from, it kind of softened my heart in a way where I started to understand that those were problems that they were dealing with within themselves . . . and the dhikr actually uplifted me in a way where I felt sorry for them even though they were attempting to oppress me. (interview, August 28, 2016)

As a result of his participation in the Moncks Corner zawiyah, performance of the Mustafawi qasidas seems to have alleviated the more acute impacts of racism for Mikhail. He uses his body to perform the protective and curative odes of Shaykh Mustafa, but through this act he acknowledges that power does not lie within or around oppressive forces. True power, in fact, lies with Allah. Through using the body to recite these odes, one acknowledges this truth that empowers the believer. This re-placement of power becomes evident as one sits to listen to the impromptu lectures of Shaykh Faye. Dhikr, the remembrance of Allah, is a lived practice that Mikhail takes seriously as part of his spiritual regimen. This includes both recitation of the Mustafawi qasidas, in which corporeal movement is a part, and connection to a perceived lost religious tradition; Islamic practice is thought of as reconnection with African Muslim ancestors as well as a present-day West African Muslim tradition of healing. Through collective recitation of the Mustafawi qasidas, African American Muslims in Moncks Corner, like Mikhail, access a tradition of spiritual cultivation and call on the curative power of prophetic salutation in order to overcome trauma.

During my observations of Mustafawi performances of the qasidas, I noted that Shaykh Faye imparted to his students that the compositions had the capacity to transform those who consistently recited them. Like Kathryn Linn Geurts's (2003) analysis of how listening practices configure the ethical grounds on which listeners use their bodies as receptacles for the consumption of moral guidance, this study proposes that Moncks Corner Muslims enact a bodily discourse in a twofold manner. On the one hand, they perform the religious poetry of Shaykh Mustafa in concert to enliven the knowledge he offers by using their voices. Animating a West African Sufi tradition through the medium of Black American Muslim voices in collaboration with West African ones marks a specific mode of ethical and moralizing performance that brings one closer to the other—or, rather, *incorporates* one in the other. On the other hand, inclusion of the witness (as in listening), impacted by the articulation of dhikr performance as an ethical behavior (discourses often initiated by Shaykh Faye), provides an opportunity for even the novice to participate in observances that lead to the embodying of historical religious memory on both sides of the Atlantic. Such listening practices, as described in Charles Hirschkind's (2006) work, deployed in conjunction with consistent practice, produce an affective power that leads to a cleansing, or vital transformation, of the heart in which the trauma of persistent racial hierarchy is addressed.[21] And this process of alchemizing bodies, through performative discourses, envelops Black American Muslims within an interconnected social world—a broader Atlantic intersubjectivity that operates across time and space.

Conclusion

As a result of Mikhail's dedication to transforming himself and abiding by the prescriptions of his teacher, Shaykh Faye has honored him with a mantle by which other fuqara may recognize him as particularly knowledgeable of Qur'an and hadith.[22] This also indicates that Shaykh Faye has entrusted Mikhail, now referred to as Shaykh Mikhail, with carrying on the tradition of the Mustafawi in Dakar, Senegal, on his behalf. According to Mikhail, consistent recitation of the Mustafawi qasidas and constant attentiveness to the guidance of Shaykh Faye contributed heavily to raising Mikhail's station. Through the story and words shared here, I bring attention to how the fuqara of Moncks Corner use their bodies as receptacles for knowledge transmission in such a way that piety is pronounced while the impacts of racism and historically embedded trauma are addressed. Not only are Muslim bodies alchemized in relation to other bodies, but they are also altered in relation to the space in which corporeally transformative religious practices take place. Masjidul Muhajjirun wal Ansar, the zawiyah-mosque of Moncks Corner, represents the reorientation of a physical space where Black people were historically disembodied (or rendered as *only* bodies) into a refuge for Black Muslim selves who desire healing and care. In this space dhikr simultaneously operates as a spiritual technology of remembering Allah and remembering the past. The fuqara use the qasidas of Shaykh Mustafa to engage their selves in a process of bodily cultivation and in a project of psychic healing and liberation. Accessing the past through a West African Islamic pedagogical tradition, moreover, provides the African American fuqara with a historical connection to the Islamic traditions of their imagined Muslim ancestors.

Sufi odes in the context of the Mustafawi regimen provide the African American participants a means to transform themselves into more disciplined and mindful Muslims who are empowered to envision themselves as having been cleansed of race-based trauma. In so doing, the Muslims living in Moncks Corner simultaneously envelop themselves in the vision for spiritual expansion that Shaykh Mustafa held as he composed his qasidas many decades earlier in Senegal. The performance of Shaykh Mustafa's qasidas by these particular American fuqara marks a desire for such growth; however, this willful, bodily engagement of Black Muslims in a West African Sufi program of spiritual disciplining is more than a mere religious observance. Certainly, the yearning for spiritual mastery and the rectification of the lower ego is a central motivation for the performance of remembering. Yet, against the backdrop of the political realities of navigating Black Muslimness in the American South, I read the structure and participation of Black adherents in this context as indicating the desire to protect the self from both spiritual decay and other kinds of cultural harm—corporeal and psychological. As well, collective ritual performance provides for an intersubjective experience of healing and mindfulness of the body in which performance is the result of a textual transmission from West Africa to the American South. Thus, such performances become infused with a politics of Black Muslimness whereby the diasporic collaborations—the animation of West African Sufi technologies via collective Black Muslim performance—present in such a way that they provide routes for inward transformation and bodily discipline. On a practical level, the knowledge of how to pray for protection, funds for travel, and spiritual expansion via specific religious formulae is embodied as a West African religious approach to alchemizing the self. Remembrance, as the words that open this chapter remind us, is an exercise that involves regaining what was lost or forgotten.

NOTES

1. While the word *zawiyah* in Arabic literally means "corner" or "nook," it refers more specifically to a place of retreat and reflection, particularly for those in a Sufi brotherhood. Moreover, there are strong connotations of community and mutual assistance.

2. Conceptually, the term *fuqara* ("the impoverished" is sourced from the Qur'an and is used by Shaykh Faye to express an utter and complete dependence on God. For example, the Qur'an states, "If they are poor, God will provide for them from His bounty: God's bounty is infinite and He is all knowing" (Qur'an 24:32). Shaykh Faye has taken this as a name to recognize his own dependency in relation to God and has named his students/followers in a similar fashion to signify their respective dependence.

At the same time, the name *fuqara* is extended to the entirety of a community which, in the context of Sufi tradition and in spite of the difficulty of finding regular employment in the blue-collar town of Moncks Corner, actively chooses to reside there with the aim of renouncing the world while realizing its members' utter dependence on Allah.

3. Shaykh Faye named the Moncks Corner mosque in honor of the relationship between the companions of the Prophet Muhammad, who fled to Medina from Mecca, and the original inhabitants of Medina, who welcomed them as refugees.

4. The museum, located in Moncks Corner, less than three miles away from the Masjidul Muhajjirun wal Ansar, is a modestly sized structure that houses a number of quaint exhibits that display various aspects of the area's early history. One of those displays includes a historical showcase that discusses the nearby plantations and their owners. Less focus, however, is placed on any intimate knowledge of the enslaved African Americans who labored on those plantations. Thus, the presence of white wealth is emphasized and framed as an aspect of Southern heritage—with little attention to Black dispossession.

5. There is a distinction between dhikr (remembrance) and qasidas (odes): while dhikr are public or private observances that involve the repetitive chanting of one or more of the ninety-nine names of Allah (*'asma al-husna*), for example, or religiously inflected phrasings, qasidas are religious poems or odes, usually composed by spiritual masters (*shuyukh* or *murshidun*) for the purpose of praising Allah and the Prophet Muhammad.

6. Eid al-Adha is a Muslim holiday that commemorates Abraham's sacrifice.

7. In the concluding chapter of his text on Islamic education and embodied knowledge in West Africa, Ware (2014, 239) discusses how "incorporation" provides a language that brings to bear two ways in which knowledge becomes inculcated into the body through techniques of discipline as well as how forms of knowledge become embodied through practices of sharing and collective study.

8. Literature on Sufism and works by notable Sufi masters are replete with references to alchemy. For example, see *The Sufi Message of Hazrat Inayat Khan: The Alchemy of Happiness* (Khan 1960) or M. Waley's (1993) *Sufism: Alchemy of the Heart*. In fact, Shaykha Maryam Kabeer Faye, a devoted companion of Shaykh Arona Faye, has penned a memoir of her own spiritual journey, entitled *Journey through Ten Thousand Veils: The Alchemy of Transformation on the Sufi Path* (2009).

9. Yolanda Covington-Ward and Jeanette S. Jouili provide a succinct review of intersubjectivity in the introductory chapter of this volume.

10. In spite of this focus, the aforementioned studies of diasporic religious communities are instructive in that they lead us to consider how both African American practices within a Senegalese Sufi tradition and the Senegalese institutions in which African Americans participate are reciprocally shifted by their combined presence.

11. Ramon Sarró and Ruy Llera Blanes (2009) depart from this trend by firmly placing African Christianity, particularly in its postcolonial formations (e.g., prophetism), as more central to the discussion of circuitous African traditions around the Atlantic.

12. At the same time, Jeffry Halverson (2016) urges us to rethink how the role of trance and lively formations of worship might also signal the historical presence of Islam in the coastal American South, the Caribbean, and beyond, as he argues that Gullah praise houses in colonial South Carolina served as spaces where West African Muslim forms of worship that were informed by a Sufi orientation were practiced.

13. I do not assert that studies that automatically include African Americans in a broader African diaspora need to be undone or invalidated. A valuable body of analysis

has pushed the field to recognize that diasporas have as much to do with identity and imagination as they do with actual dispersal—perhaps even more so. I argue, however, that there exists an opportunity to further illuminate how inclusion in religious networks has deepened and complicated the Black religious identities of African American Muslims in particular.

14. As David Berliner (2005) suggests, memory has been utilized in a multitude of ways in social scientific scholarship for the past few decades. Therefore, it has swiftly become a placeholder for referring to processes of continuity and transmission that have become transcultural through wide use and the word risks becoming emptied of meaning. I use memory as a lens through which to elaborate on the collective processes of memorialization that result in specific discourses of liberation and religious recollection ("reversion") embedded within distinct interpretations of sacred text and enacted via recitation of Sufi odes and other forms of learning.

15. Unlike *conversion*, which describes a fundamental transition from one religious tradition to another or the adoption of beliefs and attitudes that inform devotional practices, *reversion* connotes the regaining of a religious heritage that was previously forgotten or lost by the religious practitioner or by ancestors. Reversion therefore includes the rediscovery of a prior religious worldview or the reclaiming of a tradition imagined to be somehow lost by the adherent.

16. Ware (2014) juxtaposes the French system of education in colonial West Africa with the traditional Islamic approach to learning. While the French system emphasizes the mental faculties in what Ware characterizes as a "disembodied" approach, traditional Qur'anic schooling values the spiritual integrity of the body in which knowledge is placed.

17. Translated into English, the Prophetic salutation of the Mustafawi reads: "Oh Allah send blessings upon our Master Muhammad, the one who precedes all others, the one whose brilliant light radiates and fills the heavens. May Allah bless him and his Family and companions in the amount of every grain of sand and every star in the sky."

18. Shaykh Mustafa Gueye Haydara, excerpts from "Al-Bahrul Muhit (The Vast Ocean)," translated and printed by Shaykh Arona Faye al-Faqir, Zawiyyah of Moncks Corner.

19. Shaykh Mustafa Gueye Haydara, "The Cloak of Protection and the Soldiers of Divine Care," translated and printed by Shaykh Arona Faye al-Faqir, Zawiyyah of Moncks Corner, August 2014.

20. The introductory page of "The Cloak of Protection and the Soldiers of Divine Care" briefly discusses its author and intent: "This qasidah was written by Shaykh Muhammad Mustafa Gueye Haydar, who was the son of Shaykh Sahib Gueye, may Allah Ta'ala be pleased with both of them. With this qasidah he beseeches Allah to draw towards him all forms of goodness. He titled it 'The Cloak of Protection and the Soldiers of Divine Care.' He said that it would be exactly as the title suggests, in the open and in secret, for those who recite it morning and evening for the sake of Allah and with the intention of attracting all goodness and blessings repelling harm."

21. See Hirschkind's (2006) *The Ethical Soundscape: Cassette Sermons and Islamic Counterpublics*. Hirschkind's study of cassette-sermon listeners in Egypt is quite instructive

about the power of moralizing discourses that have the capacity to shape individual and collective ethical behavior.

22. Hadith are the documented sayings and actions of the Prophet Muhammad as directly narrated by and transmitted through his companions. In combination with Qur'an scriptures, Muslims around the world generally rely on direct accounts of the Prophet's decision-making to explicate appropriate behaviors and etiquette and to determine how specific kinds of worship should be enacted.

REFERENCES

Abdullah, Zain. 2009. "African 'Soul Brothers' in the 'Hood': Immigration, Islam, and the Black Encounter." *Anthropological Quarterly* 82 (1): 37–62.

Alpers, Edward A. 2000. "Recollecting Africa: Diasporic Memory in the Indian Ocean World." *African Studies Review* 43 (1): 83–99.

Beliso-De Jesús, Aisha M. 2015. *Electric Santería: Racial and Sexual Assemblages of Transnational Religion.* New York: Columbia University Press.

Berliner, David. 2005. "The Abuses of Memory: Reflections on the Memory Boom in Anthropology." *Anthropological Quarterly* 78 (1): 197–211.

Clarke, Kamari. 2004. *Mapping Yorùbá Networks: Power and Agency in the Making of Transnational Communities.* Durham, NC: Duke University Press.

Cohen, Robin. 2008. *Global Diasporas: An Introduction.* Abingdon, UK: Routledge.

Connerton, Paul. 1989. *How Societies Remember.* New York: Cambridge University Press.

Covington-Ward, Yolanda. 2016. *Gesture and Power: Religion, Nationalism, and Everyday Performance in Congo.* Durham, NC: Duke University Press.

Curtis, Edward E., IV. 2006. *Black Muslim Religion in the Nation of Islam, 1960–1975.* Chapel Hill: University of North Carolina Press.

Curtis, Edward E., IV. 2009. *Muslims in America: A Short History.* New York: Oxford University Press.

Curtis, Edward E., IV. 2014. *The Call of Bilal: Islam in the African Diaspora.* Chapel Hill: University of North Carolina Press.

Diouf, Sylviane A. 2013. *Servants of Allah: African Muslims Enslaved in the Americas.* New York: New York University Press.

Drame, Imam Fode. 2017. *Illuminated Remembrance of God.* Vancouver, BC: Tasleem.

Eisenlohr, Patrick. 2018. *Sounding Islam: Voice, Media, and Sonic Atmospheres in an Indian Ocean World.* Oakland: University of California Press.

Faye, Maryam Kabeer. 2009. *Journey through Ten Thousand Veils: The Alchemy of Transformation on the Sufi Path.* Clifton, NJ: Tughra Books.

Garbin, David. 2013. "The Visibility and Invisibility of Migrant Faith in the City: Diaspora Religion and the Politics of Emplacement of Afro-Christian Churches." *Journal of Ethnic and Migration Studies* 39 (5): 677–696.

Geurts, Kathryn Linn. 2003. *Culture and the Senses: Embodiment, Identity, and Well-Being in an African Community.* Berkeley: University of California Press.

Ghanea Bassiri, Khambiz. 2010. *A History of Islam in America: From the New World to the New World Order.* New York: Cambridge University Press.

Gilroy, Paul. 1993. *The Black Atlantic: Modernity and Double Consciousness*. Cambridge, MA: Harvard University Press.

Gomez, Michael. 2005. *Black Crescent: The Experience and Legacy of African Muslims in the Americas*. New York: Cambridge University Press.

Griffith, R. Marie, and Barbara Dianne Savage, eds. 2006. *Women and Religion in the African Diaspora: Knowledge, Power, and Performance*. Baltimore: Johns Hopkins University Press.

Gueye Haydara, Shaykh Mustafa. 2013. "Al-Bahrul Muhit (The Vast Ocean)." Translated by Shaykh Arona Faye al-Faqir. Moncks Corner, SC: Zawiyah of Moncks Corner.

Gueye Haydara, Shaykh Mustafa. 2014. "The Cloak of Protection and Soldiers of Divine Care." Translated by Shaykh Arona Faye al-Faqir. Moncks Corner, SC: Zawiyah of Moncks Corner.

Halverson, Jeffry R. 2016. "West African Islam in Colonial and Antebellum South Carolina." *Journal of Muslim Minority Affairs* 36 (3): 413–426.

Hirschkind, Charles. 2006. *The Ethical Soundscape: Cassette Sermons and Islamic Counterpublics*. New York: Columbia University Press.

Ho, Engseng. 2006. *The Graves of Tarim: Genealogy and Mobility across the Indian Ocean*. Berkeley: University of California Press.

Holsey, Bayo. 2004. "Transatlantic Dreaming: Slavery, Tourism, and Diasporic Encounters." In *Homecomings: Unsettling Paths of Return*, edited by Frank Markowitz and Alex Stefansson, 166–182. Lanham, MD: Lexington Books.

Jouili, Jeanette. 2015. *Pious Practice and Secular Constraints: Women in the Islamic Revival in Europe*. Stanford, CA: Stanford University Press.

Kane, Ousmane. 2011. *The Homeland Is the Arena: Religion, Transnationalism, and the Integration of Senegalese Immigrants in America*. New York: Oxford University Press.

Khan, Hazrat Inayat. 1960. *The Sufi Message of Hazrat Inayat Khan: The Alchemy of Happiness*. Vol. 1. Ashland, OH: Library of Alexandria.

Kugle, Scott A. 2003. "The Heart of Ritual Is the Body: Anatomy of an Islamic Devotional Manual of the Nineteenth Century." *Journal of Ritual Studies* 17 (1): 42–60.

Kugle, Scott A. 2011. *Sufis and Saints' Bodies: Mysticism, Corporeality, and Sacred Power in Islam*. Chapel Hill: University of North Carolina Press.

Lovejoy, Paul. 1997. *The African Diaspora: Revisionist Interpretations of Ethnicity, Culture and Religion under Slavery*. Boston: Northeastern University Press.

Mahmood, Saba. 2001. "Rehearsed Spontaneity and the Conventionality of Ritual: Disciplines of Ṣalat." *American Ethnologist* 28 (4): 827–853.

Mahmood, Saba. 2011. *Politics of Piety: The Islamic Revival and the Feminist Subject*. Princeton, NJ: Princeton University Press.

Matory, J. Lorand. 2005. *Black Atlantic Religion: Tradition, Transnationalism, and Matriarchy in the Afro-Brazilian Candomblé*. Princeton, NJ: Princeton University Press.

McCloud, Aminah Beverly. 2014. *African American Islam*. New York: Routledge.

Routon, Kenneth. 2006. "Trance-Nationalism: Religious Imaginaries of Belonging in the Black Atlantic." *Identities: Global Studies in Culture and Power* 13 (3): 483–502.

Sarró, Ramon, and Ruy Llera Blanes. 2009. "Prophetic Diasporas Moving Religion across the Lusophone Atlantic." *African Diaspora* 2 (1): 52–72.

Taylor, Ula. 2017. *The Promise of Patriarchy: Women and the Nation of Islam*. Chapel Hill: University of North Carolina Press.

Waley, M. 1993. *Sufism: The Alchemy of the Heart*. San Francisco: Chronicle Books.

Ware, Rudolph, III. 2014. *The Walking Qur'an: Islamic Education, Embodied Knowledge, and History in West Africa*. Chapel Hill: University of North Carolina Press.

Yamba, C. Bawa. 1995. *Permanent Pilgrims: The Role of Pilgrimage in the Lives of West African Muslims in Sudan*. Washington, DC: Smithsonian Institute Press.

3. Spiritual Ethnicity: Our Collective Ancestors in Ifá and Orisha Devotion across the Americas

N. FADEKE CASTOR

"Wole wa! Eriwo" rang out, asking for our attention and beckoning us forward. In response, we abandoned our seats to gather on the stage deep in Trinidad's Santa Cruz Valley. "Thwap, thwap, boom, boom, thwap, thwap" rang out as the drummers echoed the call, the skin of their hands hitting the skin of the drumhead. Soon the rhythms were supporting and energizing our own call-and-response as we sang, "Egun Alagba, Egun Alagba." The ancestors were calling, and we had gathered in response. Or was it that we were calling the ancestors and they were responding? Yes, indeed, the ancestors were coming! *Egun wa o!* As the energy built, the drums and song demanded a physical response. It became harder and harder for me to hold my hand steady (I was recording video for my research) as my hips went one way and my head moved another. I tried to direct all movement to my foot, tapping with the drums, though the visible sways and dips on the video attest to my ultimate failure.

Emerging from this interplay of movement and rhythms were the voices of the elders as they invoked the spiritual energies of the ancestors. This impromptu ritual found us deep in Trinidad's Santa Cruz Valley at the Orisha Shrine (Ile Eko Sango/Osun Mil'osa; IESOM) and their Ifá temple, Irentengbe.[1] A diverse group of devotees had gathered from across the Americas in 2012 for a multiday conference on Ifá called Alásùwadà.[2] As we paid homage to the Egungun (Yorùbá masquerade of the collective ancestors), what became visible was the construction of a shared affect between Spirit and participants.[3] The ancestral ritual created community through a combination of dialogic reflections on

African diasporic belonging and embodied ritual greetings. The boundaries and borders of nationality, language, race, and color bridged in this ritual moment created subjectivities I characterize under the term *spiritual ethnicity*.

Performatives of Spiritual Ethnicity

In a previous work I introduced the term *spiritual citizenship* to apply to how members of African diasporic religions in Trinidad access Yorùbá cosmology and spiritual practices to inform their belonging (including rights and responsibilities) in community, the nation, and, at the broader level, in transnational formations (Castor 2017).[4] In doing so, I postulated the idea of spiritual ethnicity as "the religious ethnic identities of 'Yoruba' priests and devotees throughout Latin America who situate themselves within the framework of the African diaspora, though ethnically and racially they are marked as Hispanic and largely not marked as 'black' or African descended socially, politically, or phenotypically" (2017, 68). I did not elaborate on this concept in the book, as my argument and narrative flowed in a different direction. Here I explore some of the possibilities of spiritual ethnicity in the context of the Ifá and Orisha religions in the African diaspora, which are closely associated with the Yorùbá people, culture, and religion of West Africa.[5]

The conference that brought people from Los Angeles, United States; Caracas, Venezuela; Toronto, Canada; and Medellín, Colombia, together in a valley of Trinidad's northern mountain range explored how Ifá could guide communities to face "global political, economic, and environmental challenges." The goal of the conference was to use Ifá "to suggest more harmonious ways to live in balance with each other and the earth." People crossed not only large geographic distances but separations of language, culture, race, and ethnicity to gather under the banner of Alásùwadà, "an obscure divinity . . . whose responsibilities include bringing balance into human societies."[6] I explore this journey across both place and space through the lens of diaspora while grounding my analysis on embodied ritual and the resultant shared affect (which I reference as spiritual affect). This chapter's focus on Egungun (our collective ancestors) calls attention to the entanglements of race, ethnicity, language, nation, and culture through a pivotal ritual moment of spiritual unity. I argue that during the multiday international Ifá conference, this ancestral ritual laid the groundwork for a shared identity or spiritual ethnicity that in the moment privileged a shared imagined Yorùbá identity over other markers of difference. I take into account how my own body was implicated in this bringing together of community and how this informs my ethnographic analysis of this 2012 ritual.[7]

My autoethnographic recollections, video recordings, photos, and notes (that is, my ethnographic archive) form my primary sources of data. Additionally, in my analysis I draw from a range of literature (by no means exhaustive) focusing on African and African diasporic religions (Beliso-De Jesús 2013, 2014; Clarke 2004, 2007; Hucks 2012; Matory 1994, 2005, 2009; Tweed 1997); embodiment, affect, and performance (Csordas 1990, Daniel 2005, 2011, 2018; E. P. Johnson 2006; Mazzarella 2009; Stewart 2017); and race and ethnicity (Hall 1996, 1999, 2003; Yelvington 2001), as well as some pieces on historical memory (Routon 2008; Scott 1991; Trouillot 1995). My critical ethnographic background in African diasporic religions, race and identity, and performance informs this analysis while pushing me in new directions on the body and the interpolation of affect, ritual, and ethnicity. Questions of temporality are particularly salient—from the historical memory evident in evocations of the African diaspora (and the subject's placement therein) to the fleeting nature of embodied motions in ritual (do they have a lasting impact?) and the communitas (á la Turner 1969) created through the gathering's shared (e)motions and reflections.

Deep in the Santa Cruz Valley, among devotees of varying backgrounds I witnessed an expression of embodiment that I identify as both performing and informing spiritual ethnicity. On that day of ancestor ritual, I felt a shift of energies as alternative ritual temporalities and historical memories were invoked, embodied, and performed. Elders spoke one by one, calling on ancestral spirits and conjuring memories of the past. Chief Alagba Baba Erinfolami, a Trinidadian elder and the chief Egungun priest of the shrine, spoke on the power of the ancestors and the need to protect and care for those closest to the spiritual realm—that is, our children.[8] The shrine's leader, an Egungun initiate, Iyalode Loogun Osun Sangodasawande Iya Sangowunmi (also Trinidadian; referred throughout the text as Iya Sangowunmi), spoke on the power of gathering and called on us both to be open to new perspectives and to ask questions. Oba Adejuyigbe Adefunmi II, the African American spiritual and political leader of Oyotunji Village, located in South Carolina, United States, spoke on the deep connection between "the Village" and the IESOM shrine in Santa Cruz, Trinidad.[9] This was his first visit to Trinidad, and he marveled at finding himself onstage there with an Egungun masquerade that shared the same initiatory lineage as the one in Oyotunji Village.[10]

This theme of ancestral connection resonated with the energies being raised and served as a diasporic palimpsest as, one by one, representatives from countries on both sides of the Atlantic Ocean (the United States, Mexico, Colombia, Venezuela, Cuba, Guyana, Nigeria, and Haiti) spoke to the power and importance of the ancestors in their lives and their communities. The devotees spoke on the need for more knowledge to bring back to their communities. And they declared their shared connections—across divisions and distances—through the ancestors, through the African diaspora, back to Africa.[11] As Ivor Miller points out, "Participating in African-derived religions is a method of maintaining historical counter-narratives in which the present generation has direct links to an African past" (2004, 215). And these counternarratives not only extend backward into the past but also pertain to the present; they inform the construction of subjectivities and mobilize agency into our futures and beyond (where perhaps we will one day be ancestors).[12]

In coming together to propitiate Egungun, all those gathered laid claim to shared African ancestry, one not of blood but of Spirit. On that morning the most important marker of identity was not people's nationality, language, or phenotype but their relationship to the spirits of Yorùbá religion, specifically the collective ancestors. Befitting this, our ritual salutations of the ancestors were preempted by an important message from Spirit. Through Iya Sangowunmi, Spirit spoke forcefully to all there of the need to listen to the messages they received from the ancestors and the need to write them down. She emphasized, with her outstretched arm sweeping over us in an embodied gesture of inclusion, that the ancestors speak to everyone. In that moment the ancestors spoke, and we all listened to the different messages that came through (indeed, this piece is an extension of my reflection on those messages).

Our gathering's growing connections were in no small part because the issue of identity and belonging has particular salience among African-descended populations in the Americas (Gomez 1998; Mintz and Price 1976; Scott 1991). The violence of being captured, forcibly transported, sold as goods and labor, and subsequently enslaved attempted to dehumanize the people captured from various African polities. Europeans designed the machineries of colonialism and plantation slavery for control. To that end, they disciplined the cultural and religious expressions of African peoples to eliminate any source of personal or collective power, to varying degrees, across the different empires' colonial projects.[13] This project of dehumanization and control by the slaveholding society and colonial governance aimed to erase the identities of the African people and thus remove the basis for any social solidarity and sources of power (Fanon 1963, 1967; Gomez 1998; Mintz and Price 1976). Nonetheless, despite the centuries-old project of slavery, designed to produce African people in the Americas as tabula rasa, their ingenuity, creativity, and perseverance ensured not only their survival but that of future generations.

These controlling practices went beyond the policing of people's movements to attempt to control their language use, religious beliefs, and cultural expressions.

From the banning of drumming to the deliberate disruption of language communities, the basis for ethnic identity was under assault in the Americas. The extent to which this campaign was successful has been hotly debated over the past century (from E. Franklin Frazier to Melville J. Herskovits) with debates continuing into the contemporary moment (Apter 2017; Yelvington 2001). Many have called our attention to the historical processes and strategies that have resisted and persisted, as well as those that have fallen away (Price 1985; Trouillot 1995). And all the while, as academics debate, "African" people have continued to live their lives, building community and striving for freedom (Robinson 1983; Sharpe 2016; West, Martin, and Wilkins 2009).

Spiritual Ethnicity, Spiritual Affect

The religious subjectivities under examination here are embedded in shared histories of resistance and connected to Black radical traditions integral to the historical fabric of the African diaspora. Here I am referencing resistance to the dehumanizing and exploitative socioeconomic and political systems making up Western "modernity," from slavery and colonialism through to postcolonialism, neoliberalism, and late capitalism. Specific movements include Quilombo dos Palmares and marronage communities throughout the Americas, the Haitian Revolution, Pan-Africanism, négritude, and Black Lives Matter, to name just a few (see Robinson [1983] and West, Martin, and Wilkins [2009] for a framing of the Black radical tradition in the context of Black internationalism). Perhaps more important are all the unnamed ancestors and acts that contributed to the survival of Africans in the Americas and are so central to much of the spiritual work in African diasporic religions.

Further, they exist in a diasporic framework and networks of ritual lineage, initiation, and knowledge transmission crossing borders and boundaries, from Ilé-Ifè to Los Angeles to Bahia, creating transnational spiritual networks (Beliso-De Jesús 2015; Castor 2017; Clarke 2004; Matory 2005). From the ritual practices and spiritual praxis circulating along these networks arise "African-derived mythic histories and identities [that require] their members to assume a transnational identity" (Miller 2004, 199).[14] However, many barriers to unity create obstacles to the institutionalization of the religion and to organizing for collective action. Differences in language, race, ethnicity, class, and in some instances gender and sexual orientation complicate the divisions within branches of the Yorùbá religion and between factions and lineages competing over ritual knowledge and authority. Attempts to unify people across these divisions in recent years have ranged from online organizing for social justice (Castor 2018) to international conferences and symposia.[15] And while there have been visible moments of success, the divisions marking the history of the religions continue to challenge the creation of community.

In this chapter my reflections and explorations of a ritual moment during the Alásùwadà conference raise questions about the impact of spiritual affect, here theorized as the feeling of communitas raised through the ritual circulation of spiritual energy, or in this context àṣẹ.[16] In the coming together and engaging in embodied spiritual praxis coupled with diasporic assertions of belonging, I locate an identity cutting across other forms of organizing difference. In considering this as spiritual ethnicity, I ask: Are there forms of belonging rooted in shared ritual lineages and historical consciousness that challenge (or offer an alternative to) existing forms of belonging such as the nation and ethnicity? In a way that resonates with Youssef Carter's exploration of the African American *fuqara* (in this volume), combinations of historical memory and embodied performance inform forms of belonging in many rituals that recognize and renew spiritual community and its relation to the divine.

Entanglements became visible in the ancestral ritual of the Alásùwadà conference in diasporic testimonies conjoined with a circuit of embodied ritual movements.[17] "These communal practices, sustained by ritualized ties to mythic Africa, lead us to perceive that concepts of 'nation,' history, and identity that differ vastly from those developed in the West are being upheld in communities across the Americas" (Miller 2004, 211). In addition, ties to communities in a contemporary Africa inform the transnational spiritual networks of African diasporic religion devotees. The embodied performances of belonging that are so evident in many African diasporic rituals (and reflected secularly in African American greetings, such as *dap*) inform subjectivities grounded in ties to both an imagined African past and an informed African present.[18] Navigating both Western conceptualizations of the subject (often disembodied) and those rooted in non-Western Indigenous systems (often grounded in the body) has contributed to the resilience, adaptability, innovation, and, yes, brilliance of followers of African diasporic religions (among others) in places like Trinidad and Venezuela and throughout the Americas (Fanon 1967; Gilroy 1993; Hall 2003).[19]

Historical Entanglements

Trinidad and Venezuela are separated geographically by only ten miles at their closest point, yet they are very different historically, politically, and socially. These differences stem from separate colonial histories (British Empire vs. Spanish

Empire) with the resultant legacies of language and political affiliations. The two countries also have commonalities, chief among them the oil and gas reserves fueling their economies. Both countries have strong Roman Catholic communities, an inheritance of a shared Spanish colonial past (Trinidad was under Spanish colonial rule until the early nineteenth century, before it was ceded to the British as part of a treaty negotiation). And they both have strong African diasporic religious communities, including Yorùbá-based religions of Ifá/Orisha. I established in previous research (Castor 2009) that their Ifá/Orisha initiation lineages have separate histories. In Venezuela the Orisha community of the twentieth century was tied to Cuban lineages, with priests (known by the title Babalawo or Babaloricha) coming from Cuba to perform initiations when people did not make the journey to Cuba. This is very different from the Trinidad Orisha religion, which was mostly endogamous in the nineteenth and twentieth centuries.

Even though Trinidad was largely an indirect slave port, the British colony received a large influx of people, relative to its population, from the then Bight of Benin. In the early 1800s, ten thousand or more people were transported as liberated captives during the British naval blockade of West Africa (Adderley 2006). Upon their arrival in Trinidad, they made up a significant portion of the "free colored" population in the British colony, where through a quirk of Spanish law that was on the books, they could own land. This became very important for a religion that is closely tied to the land and that embeds sacred ritual items in the ground. The religion that arose in Trinidad was creolized (at least) twice over, as the people from West Africa represented many communities with distinct, though related, languages, cultures, and histories. Toward the end of the eighteenth century, large numbers of French planters fleeing African freedom fighters in Haiti and other French Caribbean colonies resettled in Trinidad and brought with them a significant African-descended enslaved population in exchange for land grants from the colonial government. While some of the slaves had been born in Africa, many others were generations removed. Those creolized slaves had developed their own religious expressions, similar to what is now associated with Haitian Vodou. When they settled in Trinidad, this complex of spiritual practices was brought into conversation with both the religious expressions of the existing enslaved African communities and those of the newly arrived indentured and freed West Africans. From this complex history of intermixture and dialogue, Trinidad Orisha emerged in the mid-1800s with a spiritual lineage that continues into the present.

In the new millennium, there have been major changes in Trinidad Orisha, as a new Yorùbá-based lineage of Ifá (an oral literature holding the collected history, wisdom, and knowledge of the Yorùbá people, accessed through a system of divination, all under the same name) has emerged locally (Castor 2017, esp. ch. 5). Ifá also served as the impetus for increased levels of communication between Yorùbá devotees in Venezuela and Trinidad. In the early 2000s, an Ifá initiatory lineage and teachings from the Nigerian part of Yorubaland were being established in both countries. This was driven in part by local religious leaders traveling to West Africa for initiations, trainings, and pilgrimages to holy sites and festivals. In doing so, they strove to connect to the historical "source" of diasporic religions and to bring what they learned and experienced back home with them. This religious exchange included a series of festivals and conferences in Trinidad and Venezuela with attendees not only from both countries but also from nations throughout the Americas and West Africa. Within these circulations, Nigerian priests of Ifá and Orisha (male priests—Babalawo or Babalorisa—and female priests, who hold the title Iyanifa or Iyalorisa) have also traveled in both communities, fostering connections between the two countries. For the purposes of this chapter, I focus on one such conference, convened in 2012 under the auspices of Olóyè Solágbadé Pópóolá (a well-known Nigerian Ifá priest who has over a thousand godchildren throughout the Americas). Though the original impetus for the Alásùwadà conference came from Yorubaland, it was held in Trinidad, hosted and organized by IESOM under the leadership of Iya Sangowunmi.

Appeasing the Ancestors: Embodied Memories, Diasporic Time

"Everyone must greet, go and meet every person. First, greet the elders and Egungun. Then greet everyone." This injunction to physically greet all the participants in this conference on the Ifá religion and its application to community building and public policy struck me for its lack of efficiency. My body, keyed into a secular conference with its linear time expectations, was anxious since I was scheduled to present a paper that day from my own research on Ifá.[20] And in this distinctly nonsecular conference, it looked as if my presentation was going to be seriously delayed, if it happened at all. On Saturday morning, instead of hearing people present their papers and then having the scheduled panel discussions, we were all gathered together on the stage, with some people overflowing onto the steps and down the sides. Who were we? This important question informs this chapter: How were identities being constructed through ritual movements and practices of spiritual affect? How were divisions being crossed, communitas being generated, and a feeling of unity being achieved? And if indeed all this happened, how did it then inform the spiritual ethnicity of the participants? What tied the Venezuelan Latina to the Puerto Rican Latino to the African American man from Los Angeles to the Afro-Caribbean woman (me) from Texas to the "Africans" (the local term for African descendants) from Trinidad? This chapter claims that indeed all of these varied gendered bodies, marked by phenotype, geography, nationality, and language into diverse racial and ethnic groups, were brought together in that moment through the ritual movements of their bodies (at the direction of spiritual forces) under the umbrella of a diasporic Yorùbá ethnicity (a spiritual ethnicity).[21]

Ancestor reverence works through a different (alternative, if you will) temporality from the dominant Western capitalistic time form. In calling on these elevated Spirits of those who have gone before—a calling that invokes "direct" hereditary lineages (or blood kinship), ritual lineages, and cultural lineages—the past (that which was) comes into the present moment (that which is) to have an impact on the future (that which is yet to be). In addition to this fairly straightforward linear temporality, in which the past and present impact the future, there are other constructions, such as where our actions in the present moment affect the past. As Deborah Thomas (2016, 183) argues, people have "an experience of time neither as linear nor cyclical, but as simultaneous, where the future, past, and present are mutually constitutive and have the potential to be coincidentally influential," in conditions of exceptional violence (such as slavery, colonialism, and their aftermath). This collapsing of a temporal telos provides a powerful space for spiritual praxis. In this ancestral time, knowledge can be transmitted, skills learned, and vital heritages passed on (see Alexander 2006). In this liminal space, social identities are reimagined as people experience the freedom to reenter their personal narratives—past, present, and future. This movement of subjectivity does not occur solely in an individualistic frame. Rather, it exists in a web of spiritual kinship extending into the multiple temporal registers named above. And in this recentering, communities have the potential to be formed not only across time and space but also across perceived divisions of social identity, be they race, ethnicity, gender, nationality, or language community. For many, this center is conceptualized as an imagined "home," often located as the ancestral Ilé-Ifẹ̀ of Yorubaland. This was evoked in a reflection on Egungun from the Oba Adefunmi II of Oyotunji Village, a guest of honor at the conference.

Oba Adefunmi II spoke of his first time in Trinidad during the Egungun ritual: "I don't feel as if I left home yet. . . . And that is what culture—Yorùbá culture—does for us. Wherever you find it, you are home." (Over the weekend other devotees would echo this sentiment.) Reflecting on this association of shared space with home, I found a grounding in the cosmic realm accessible from many different places. One such pathway is in connecting to the ancestral matrix (others are through engagements with Ifá and Orisha). And in this ancestral connection is an example of a spiritual praxis building community through a collective experience of spiritual ethnicity. As I listened to people from across the Americas situate themselves within the history of the African diaspora and as I experienced the accompanying embodied ritual, questions rose in my mind around the potential of collective Egungun ritual. What were the possibilities for transcending existing socioeconomic, racial, and national divisions? What were the responsibilities to community that came with this subject formation?

This ancestral time/space—or ancestral matrix—exists in the Yorùbá religion within the cosmic realm. And it is through ritual, especially collective ritual, that people in Ilé Aiyé (the Earth) interface with the cosmic realm. The directives of Ifá, under whose guidance we were gathered for the Alásùwadà conference, conveyed the importance of working together, of collectivity, and of unity. In many different manners, these messages had been (and were) delivered throughout the conference in rituals both before and during the conference. On that day, within the Egungun ritual, the hour of testimonials invoked historical and genealogical memories of the diaspora, creating palpable feelings for the possibilities and tenuousness of connection across differences of language, nationality, ethnicity, and race.

As one Ifá initiate from Venezuela testified, "We're calling the ancestors of all those who are present here today to unite." This is notable because it calls on ancestors who may have been enslaved to join together with those who may have enslaved them and their kin. It calls for spiritual reconciliation of historical rifts that in our present moment we have yet to fully face as societies (and as individuals). In thinking through the possibilities and responsibilities of spiritual ethnicity for reconciliation and healing, I am reminded of one moment of the Egungun ritual. Iya Regla Diago-Pinillos, an Afro-Cuban professor who was the most visibly (by phenotype) Afro-Latinx person there, spoke on the issue of skin privilege. Directing her comments toward devotees who had traveled from Mexico, Venezuela, and Colombia, she called out the names of communities of African descendants in each country. Then she spoke of those who are not able to travel internationally for such a conference. She pointed to her outstretched arm, indicating the deep brown hue of her skin. From this she called attention to the reality that many with similar skin tones as her own in Latin America would not have the resources to travel. Iya Regla then said it was the responsibility of the conference's Latinx presenters (largely light-skinned), who had the privilege of travel, to go and share the knowledge they had gained of diasporic history with those communities of Afro-descendants. In recognizing shared positionalities with others from Venezuela, Colombia, and Mexico (Latinx Yorùbá devotees), she also assigned responsibility cutting across racial difference. Thus, the spiritual ethnicity carried with it responsibilities to Blackness tied to a shared African diasporic spirituality.

Crossing the Divide: Spiritual Ethnicity and Latinx Devotees

The call for the Latinx devotees to connect with their Afro-Latinx countrymates drew on a shared connection (spiritual ethnicity) and responsibility to community (spiritual citizenship), raising questions of privilege, access, and belonging. One such question to consider is, Do Latinx who present as Anglo (or light-skinned) have more access to African religious traditions and networks than Afro-Latinx? Drawing on my previous research in Venezuela, I would say that this is so.[22] When looking for a link between Trinidadian and Venezuelan Orisha communities, I had found that working-class and immigrant West Indians in Venezuela were largely involved in Indigenous religions, such as María Lionza. The Orisha community that hosted me in Caracas was largely middle-class (though economically this class distinction may have broken down as the Venezuelan economy has destabilized since 2013 in the post-Chavez era). Throughout Latin America, Afro-Latinx largely live in marginalized communities with lower socioeconomic opportunities. And those communities are largely Christian, with some exceptions (see P. Johnson 2007). These issues of class and color intersect with privilege and access, adding layers of complexity to considerations of spiritual ethnicity and ancestral connections. Honoring the Yorùbá cosmology that has all people originating in old Ilé-Ifè (located now in Nigeria) assists in avoiding a racialized essentialism. Yet the cultural construction of the African diasporic experience is clearly enmeshed in the construction of historical and contemporary racialized systems and subjectivities. These were among the many complexities that swirled through our ritual, informing both narrative and our embodied movements.

On that day we were all gathered there to honor the ancestors, which as constructed created a shared link to the ancestral home of Yorubaland (and more specifically Ilé-Ifè). In part, this draws on the diasporic logics of a shared origin in Mother Africa. This construction of a root with a myriad of branches is certainly not novel, but here the verbal affirmations of a shared source and a shared spiritual heritage set the stage for what was to come. The performative engagements orchestrated by the intervention of Spirit would build on this energy and move it to another level. As aptly put by Yolanda Covington-Ward, "Religious power also comes from conduct, gestures, and other forms of embodiment" (2016, 27). My analysis here focuses on one such raising of power through the ritual movements of the gathered bodies. As if concretizing the tenuous social and ritual relations, the next injunction came from the Spirits of the ancestors, through an Egungun elder who told us, "Everyone is to greet everyone."

Embedded in this simple directive was a series of embodied ritual praxes. First, there was the negotiation of different knowledge levels associated with the embodied protocols of greetings, from casual hugs to more elaborate movements (akin to the African American movement vocabulary codified as dap as previously mentioned; see note 18). These negotiations would have involved translation given the different African diasporic religious spiritual lineages, which have their own distinct greetings, as well as the differing levels of expertise and knowledge among those gathered. In many African diasporic religious branches, notably in Cuban Lucumí or Regla de Ocha (aka Santería), when you greet another practitioner, it is proper to cross one's arms on one's chest and then touch opposite shoulders—shoulder to shoulder on each side.[23] These salutations in Lucumí take place at the start and end of ritual gatherings, often conducted in a specific order of initiatory seniority.

Michael Mason's ethnography of Lucumí rituals in Cuba and the Washington, D.C., area describes how a new initiate named Carter "learns to be a part of the community by using his body in specific ways" (1994, 25). Mason found the movements reflective of the embodied knowledge ingrained during initiations. With regard to the movement of bowing down and extending the right arm to touch the earth, or *dobale* (or in Yorùbá *dòbálè*), and its specific ritual form of full-length prostration, the *moforibale* (or in Yorùbá *iforíbalè*), Mason reminds us that "all initiations include this bodily action of submission and reception of blessings" (29). Through the repetitive motions of the body, meaning and subject making are created and re-created, ordered and reordered. As Mason puts forth, "The moforibale reiterates social order as it exists" (2002, 40). In bringing together people across differences of lineage and spiritual background (layered alongside race, ethnicity, gender, nationalism, and language, to name just a few social categories), ritual greetings became a site of connection and negotiation. One such site of negotiation was navigating the different styles of greeting represented in the gathering.

In Trinidad Orisha the greeting involves first touching alternate shoulders with open arms (though some may cross their arms), followed by placing one's forehead against the forehead of the other person. This last part, the touching of heads, is particular to Trinidad, while the touching of shoulders has a wider circulation through Orisha lineages across the African diaspora. Thus, when

Chief Alagba Baba Erinfolami instructed us all to greet, it was understood this would be the formal ritual greeting of one Orisha practitioner to another. As was to be expected with almost four dozen people, this process of each person greeting every single person took some time. As we each turned to greet the person next to us additional levels of embodiment and àṣẹ (spiritual energy) were added. According to Covington-Ward, in "performative encounters," "the body is used strategically in everyday life to transform interpersonal social relationships in meaningful ways, impacting the social and political positions of the people interacting" (2016, 9). In this instance, as we used our bodies to greet each other, we were recognizing both the àṣẹ held by the other person and our shared positions as holders of àṣẹ, as Yorùbá devotees. The ritual greetings lasted for well over an hour, accompanied by call-and-response singing and drumming. The focused activity of seeing each other, recognizing the other person as spiritual kin, and using our bodies to affirm these relations transformed the social relations from those of strangers and visitors to those of community and family, with the possibility of creating an Ifá community. This latter point had social and political implications if we were, as directed by Alásùwadà, to use our collectivity to make an impact in our societies.

As we greeted each other and prostrated (dobale or moforibale) ourselves to the elders and Egungun, our bodies accessed memories that conflated the present moment with previous ritual actions. The repetitive movement of performing dobale was, as Yvonne Daniel recounts of her own experience in Brazil, a "bending in humility and honouring [of] the knowledge and higher-consciousness of ritual elders" (2005, 32). In doing so, our ritual greetings also created an embodied memory embedding access to the cosmic realm in shared recognition of the divine in ourselves (in the Orí or divine consciousness that each person possesses).[24] These movements also connected us with the Spirit of the Earth (Ilé Aiyé) as we repeatedly touched the ground. In an exchange with me on this topic, a Lucumí priest I will call Baba A. said, "It reinforces my connection to the earth and my respect for the earth. How do I show respect for a deified force of nature on this planet? By trying to put my body as close to it as possible, right?" In our conversation he went on to link the humility of prostration with an expression of love and caring for spiritual forces, elders, and lineage. "How do I show my respect, my love, and my care, even for another person? I put myself as low on the ground as possible. I put myself in contact with the ground as much as possible. I am reinforcing constantly on the level of muscle memory my willingness to humble myself—to the forces of nature, to my elder." This humility is equalizing even as it recognizes hierarchy—equalizing in that there is recognition of the divine in all things, from the Earth to the elder.[25] The prostration also reinforces the connection of lineage and pays tribute to those who go directly before you, the elders.

In speaking on this reinforcement of lineage, Baba A. invoked the temporal: "I also think that it reinforces constantly, and it gets stronger over time, it reinforces our connection to our lineage, right?" This raises an interesting consideration. What are the differences in temporality when people who come together do so for a singular event (as in the Alásùwadà conference described here) versus when they meet regularly in a ritual community? Is there a tension between the ephemeral interactions of a onetime event and the regular repeated motions of prayer (for example, as discussed in chapter 2 in this volume)? I offer that instead of attempting to resolve this tension as part of a binary framework, we should consider a shift in perspective. From this new point of view, the ephemeral and the repetitive are not at odds, vying for the power of transformation. Rather, these different modalities in a cumulative embodiment both hold the potential for significant transformation. Consider that in presenting oneself before the manifestation of an Orisha, say, moforibale in the presence of Oshun, healing is received (with the exchange of àṣẹ being the primary marker of difference, not phenotype, national origin, or even race). Perhaps that healing resolves a potentially dangerous health condition. And that healing was facilitated by the embodied practice over time, with its muscle memory and energy alignments, which allowed for that one moforibale in front of Oshun to be effective. After this, the person may look back and understand their previous dobale and moforibale in a new light, as iterative alignments of body and spirit.[26] If we take the disruption of ritual temporality seriously, then we must consider that a future practice may have an impact on a current or past moment. In fact, that future moment may transform that which has already occurred.

With repetition, the gestures of greeting, prostration, and blessings become ingrained in the body and attached to feelings of connection with both Spirit and community.[27] Thus, they hold resonances with prior moments of ritual fellowship that are accessed anew in new ritual moments. This is reflected throughout African diasporic religions. Mason's observation that "social life, relationships, and ritual knowledge are performed by people as they bow their heads to the ground" (1994, 36) is equally true in Trinidad as in the Cuban Lucumí context. He then gives a description that could have been talking about the Egungun ritual at IESOM in Trinidad, as he called the reader to view dobale or "moforibale as 'a bodily performance' of the relationship between the student and the god-parent, of the uninitiated ori to the ori with ase (or crowned with the Orisha, Ifá or Egungun among other spirits)" (36). In the context described here, relationships were being performed and reinforced among the conference attendees (ranging from newcomers to students to initiates) and then also between the attendees and the elders. This was evident in the next direction we received: "Before greeting, make your way to Iya and Oba, dobale, and receive their blessings."

As is often the case in ritual practice, the instructions continued to come at different times (in local Trini parlance: *piece, piece* or in Yorùbá: *díà díà*) as they were filtered from the spiritual realms to us by the Egungun elders. We were to prostrate ourselves in front of two elders, Iya Sangowunmi (see figure 3.1) and Oba Adefunmi II (see figures 3.2 and 3.3), who were sitting next to each other. First one person and then the next prostrated themselves, head on the ground and hands at their sides, to wait for the blessings not only of the elders but also of the spiritual energies they carried, the blessings of the collective ancestors, and their àṣẹ (see figures 3.1 and 3.2). Mason calls attention to this critical moment where "being raised by the elder completes the 'reciprocal relationship'" (1994, 34) in the act of giving blessings provided through both verbal and bodily expressions. After Iya gave her blessings (and a message from Spirit if there was one), she used her staff to touch the person on the back of one shoulder and then the other. Using two hands (touching the prostrating person's shoulders to indicate that they should rise) and also verbal commands ("dìde" in Yorùbá, meaning "stand up"), she would ritually "raise" the supplicant, who then greeted her again—shoulder to shoulder and head to head—before moving on to do the same process again with the Oba Adefunmi II of Oyotunji Village (see figures 3.2 and 3.3). After these ritual supplications and blessings were complete, we started the process of greeting each other.

Wait! Yet another step was being added—a vital one in the sacred geography being traversed by body and spirit. We were to greet Egungun—in the form of a cloth masquerade that had been fed *orogbo* (bitter kola), *epo* (palm oil), *oti* (clear alcohol), and *obi* (kola nut) at the opening of the ritual—with a moforibale (see figure 3.4). Afterward, we were to dobale (or touch the ground) to greet the elders, Chief Alagba Baba Erinfolami and Awo Ifakolade, who were standing on either side of the Egungun. After this important first step we were directed to move on to greet each other. This circuit from seated elders to Egungun to standing elders created a web of àṣẹ that then moved from person to person as they greeted, raising the spiritual energy. This spiritual affect powered by our motions performed several things, including creating a sense of community and informing our embodied spiritual praxis. Emerging from these two performatives was ultimately a shared identity in the moment, which I have labeled *spiritual ethnicity*. Together, the ritual moments, diasporic declaratives,

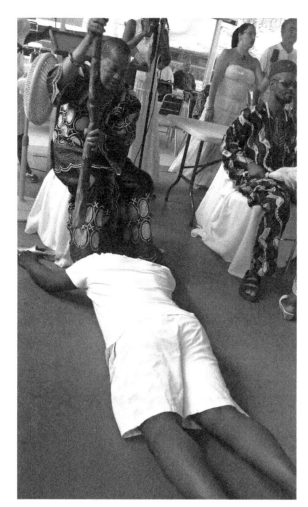

FIGURE 3.1. In response to instructions, a devotee makes *moforibale*, a prostrated greeting, before Iyalode Loogun Osun Sangoda-sawande Iya Sangowunmi and receives her blessing at the Alásùwadà Ifá and Orisha International Conference, hosted by Ile Eko Sango/Osun Mil'osa in Santa Cruz, Trinidad (2012). Photograph by author.

and embodied praxis were strong enough to lay the groundwork for not only a remarkable conference but also a shift of our individual subjectivities toward the collective.[28]

Conclusion

This chapter is a partial answer to Miller's call for scholars to explore "the broader social ramifications of ethnically-based initiation societies involving nonmembers of that ethnic group as found in Brazil, Cuba, Haiti, and other

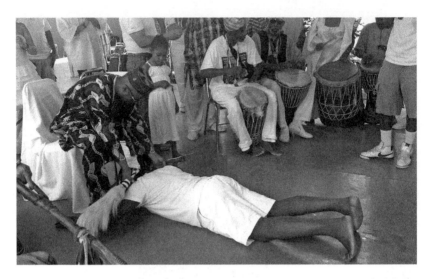

FIGURE 3.2. A devotee receives the blessings of Oba Adejuyigbe Adefunmi II of Oyotunji Village, Sheldon, South Carolina, at the Alásùwadà Ifá and Orisha International Conference, hosted by Ile Eko Sango/Osun Mil'osa in Santa Cruz, Trinidad (2012). Photograph by author.

FIGURE 3.3. As part of the blessing, a message is conveyed to the devotee. Alásùwadà Ifá and Orisha International Conference, hosted by Ile Eko Sango/Osun Mil'osa in Santa Cruz, Trinidad (2012). Photograph by author.

FIGURE 3.4. The devotee (in white) ritually performs *moforibale* in front of Egungun at the Alásùwadà Ifá and Orisha International Conference, hosted by Ile Eko Sango/Osun Mil'osa in Santa Cruz, Trinidad (2012). Photograph by author.

regions" (2004, 211) by looking at the affective means by which ritual can construct a shared belonging, a spiritual ethnicity. Spiritual ethnicity was visible in the Alásùwadà Egungun ritual over the weekend. However, as devotees returned to their homes, one could ask whether the unity created in rituals like the one described here continues to inform people's lives and, as Miller (2004, 196) proposes, assist "them to live better." After the conference, plans to create a working group (utilizing the internet and social media platforms to cross the geographic distances) or to hold an additional conference to continue the dialogue and community building never materialized. This could indicate a fragility in the construction of spiritual ethnicity. As potent as the spiritual affect was in the moment, it seemingly soon dissipated as people returned to their respective homes and everyday lives (often embedded in the linear temporalities of neoliberal labor practices). And yet this should be balanced against the fact that people successfully came together in the moment and formed community, raising the possibility of this happening again. For there exists in the ancestral matrix a temporal fold where pathways continue to inspire visions of community that overcome difference. And from this space, inspiring visions of new subjectivities become available that have the potential to transcend the divisive legacies of slavery and colonialism.

In the unfolding of the Egungun ritual, something was shifted in that moment where together we (each participant, including myself) built community that felt simultaneously ephemeral and transformative. How is it possible for the experience of spiritual ethnicity to be ephemeral yet transformative? As I reflect back on the repetitive motions in the ritual that created an embodied memory, what has become visible to me is the embodiment of spiritual praxis as a link to the spiritual affect and spiritual ethnicity from that day. Every time a devotee performs a dobale, this link could then bring a memory of the past into the future, an evocation that reawakens that energy and affect. This then ties together with the reflections on temporality to create an embodied affective connection with meaning(s) that may shift over time. A future interaction may be shaped by a memory brought forth through a ritual dobale. Alternatively, a future interaction could also reframe the held meaning of the experiences at the 2012 Alásùwadà conference, providing new meanings and relevancies. In this way the embodied practices and spiritual affect that informed spiritual ethnicity exist in potentiality as transformative, ready to be actualized. One experience of shared collectivity, such as that during the Alásùwadà conference, can remain linked to a series of movements available to be actualized.

For example, years after the conference, I entered a new ritual space marked by a diversity of lineages, ethnicities, and phenotypes. I was tense and apprehensive about using the correct ritual protocols for that space. But when I lowered myself to moforibale to the shrine and the elders, my energy shifted. I physically and emotionally relaxed as my body recalled the spiritual affect from previous ritual spaces such as the Alásùwadà conference and the possibility of the collective experience discussed here as spiritual ethnicity. In the space of performing that ritual movement, I accessed both embodied memory and a stored àṣe that shifted my positionality in the new space. I was able to navigate that ritual space successfully and make new connections to people and Spirit. In reflecting on this recent ritual moment, perhaps what appears ephemeral from one point of view may upon further reflection be both/and: both ephemeral and lasting, shifting bodies, temporalities, and energies across horizons of possibility.

ACKNOWLEDGMENTS

The reflections and research for this chapter were informed by generous engagements in multiple realms. I am grateful to the Ifá/Orisha devotees in Trinidad who have accepted me into their community, shrines, and homes. I extend special thanks to the members of IESOM over the years and their spiritual elders, especially Iyalode Sangodasawande Sangowunmi. I appreciate the support and information provided by my elder Olóyè Ṣọlágbadé Pópóọlá. For gathering us together and shepherding us faithfully with both patience and firmness I thank coeditors Yolanda Covington-Ward and Jeanette Jouili. Many thanks to the anonymous readers for their constructive insights and to all of my coauthors in this collection for their engagements during this process, especially Bertin Louis for his fellowship and support. I extend my deep appreciation to Awo Ifásèyítán Taiwo Thompson for his assistance with the Yorùbá tonal markings (all mistakes are my own). I also give thanks to Spirit in its many forms, including Orisha, Egbe, and Egungun. This chapter is dedicated to Chief Alagba Baba Erinfolami; may I continue to listen to the ancestors' messages and, as they ask, "do the work."

NOTES

1. Throughout this chapter I use Orisha as the name for both the priesthood and the sacred forces of nature and deified ancestors that originated in Yorubaland over a thousand years ago. These spiritual forces, be it Oya as an embodiment of the force of the wind and storm or Oshun as fresh water and fertility, were brought across the Atlantic with Africans over hundreds of years of enforced travels during the African slave trade. Ifá is the name associated with the divine word from a high deity, Olódùmarè, and the priesthood and divination system used to access that divine word and wisdom. A shrine is a physical area set aside and consecrated to a specific sacred energy (Orisha, Egbe, or Ifá), often containing vessels and accessories associated with that energy (e.g., brass bells and fans for Oshun).

2. Alásùwadà is a divine energy named and described in an Ifá verse, Ọ̀sá Ògúndá, that watches over both people and things coming together in groups, and groups coming together in collectivities for support, strength, and the collective good (e.g., multiple blades of grass are stronger than a single blade of grass).

3. Trinidad's Egungun should be distinguished from the Egungun rituals of Yorubaland (to which they owe their provenance, via spiritual lineages and communities in Texas and South Carolina), which involve a collectivity of ritual specialists performing specialized roles, as described by John Thabiti Willis: "Egungun may refer to a single Egungun masquerade or to a specific Egungun organization or society, which includes all of the masquerade chiefs and initiated members who may or may not don the mask in a town. An Egungun masquerade named Oya, for instance, includes the person wearing the Oya mask, as well as the drummers, singers, and other ritual specialists who accompany Oya during outings or performances" (2018, 10). While ancestors have been individually venerated in Trinidad's Orisha faith going back to the nineteenth century, the introduction of Egungun masquerade there can be linked to Oloye Aina Olomo, an African American priest, at the end of the twentieth century (Henry 2003; McNeal 2011).

4. Ivor Miller's use of the term *spiritual ethnicity* in the title of his 2004 essay, "The Formation of African Identities in the Americas: Spiritual 'Ethnicity,'" came to my attention after my own independent formulation. Throughout his essay Miller maps out

his conception while never directly introducing the term in the text. In my essay here, I draw from his argument to complement my own thinking and raise some questions about the differences in our conceptualizations. My exploration differs in part by assessing the applicability of spiritual ethnicity to a transnational grouping of people rather than those grounded in a single geographically bounded place or nation.

5. In the Americas, the African diasporic religions of Trinidad Orisha, Cuban Lucumí, and Brazilian Candomblé (to name a few of many) are clearly and recognizably informed by cosmologies, beliefs, and rituals from many groups across West and West Central Africa, as well as drawing (to a lesser extent) from Indigenous and immigrant traditions across the Americas.

6. The quotations are from an Alásùwadà conference invitation.

7. As a Black feminist ethnographer, performances studies scholar, and Ifá/Orisha initiate, I cannot vacate my own body from this analysis. "Ethnography is an *embodied* practice, it is an intensely sensuous way of knowing" (Conquergood 1991, 180). Central to my embodiment is the positionality that my "redness" (a racial attribution local to Trinidad; see Segal 1993), dual nationality (United States and Trinidad), size (on the plus side), gender (cis female, with special connotations in Trinidad of being a red woman), and even hair ("natural") all convey meanings, including varied levels of status, in the ritual space that I explore here. While the calculus of intersectional factors is complex, I exist as both marginal and privileged, both insider and outsider.

8. In 2018 during the writing of this piece, Chief Alagba Baba Erinfolami made his transition to the ancestral realm. This adds a dimension of immediacy to my claims here that there is an ancestral matrix that we can connect to that has a ritual temporality where we can coexist with what has gone, what is, and what will be. And in doing so we can connect with those who have passed from Ilé Aiyé (the Earth). I dedicate this essay to Baba Erinfolami and hope that its energy reaches him in the ancestral realm.

9. For more on Oyotunji Village, see Hucks (2012) and Clarke (2004, 2007).

10. It is important to distinguish the collective Egungun from the more personal or familial ancestors (*egun*) that are individually propitiated (though collective Egungun are often embedded in familial and community lineages). For more on Yorùbá Egungun, see Drewal (1992) and Willis (2017).

11. There is a vast literature on African diasporic circulations, and the mentions in this chapter are not meant as a comprehensive list. Indeed, they merely scratch the surface. Instead, I would call attention to some texts that have informed my own approach to the African diaspora (including Edwards 2009; Gilroy 1991, 1993; Hall 1996, 1999, 2003).

12. Adding another facet to these counternarratives are the direct experiences of devotees from the diaspora as they visit priests and other devotees in West Africa, as well as the experiences of Yorùbá indigenes as they encounter these spiritual visitors in Yorubaland and then become visitors themselves as they travel to places like Trinidad.

13. Many thanks to an anonymous reader for reminding me of the collective gatherings that occurred, largely by ethnicity, in societies, associations, and organizations in Cuba and Brazil. This history is also reflected across the Caribbean, from the Nation Dance of Carriacou to the ethnic groupings in Trinidad's neighborhoods. These col-

lectivities further underscore my point that identity and belonging were important to Africans and their descendants in the Americas, across empires.

14. *Spiritual praxis* is a term that I have adapted from M. Jacqui Alexander's *Pedagogies of Crossing: Meditations on Feminism, Sexual Politics, Memory and the Sacred*, where she speaks of "the cycle of action, reflection and practice as Sacred practice embodied" (2006, 307).

15. These gatherings range in scale from large, open international conferences, such as the International Orisha World Congress (with meetings held in Cuba, Trinidad, Brazil, and Nigeria), to smaller lineage-based gatherings, such as the annual Egbe Obatala symposium in New York in the United States. A series of Ifá conferences in Miami gather more Cuban Lucumí practitioners (though they are open to other lineages). And the newer African and Diasporic Religious Studies Association, founded by Dr. Funlayo Wood, strives to bring together scholars and practitioners from the wide variety of African diasporic religions and communities. This is a larger version of a conference held on Ifá divination in 2008 that resulted in the edited volume *Ifá Divination, Knowledge, Power, and Performance* (Olupona and Abiodun 2016).

16. For more on àṣẹ, see Abiodun (1994) and Boyce Davies (2013, 72–75).

17. I am calling on cultural anthropologist and Caribbean studies scholar Deborah Thomas's definition—"entanglement, for quantum physicists, refers to the notion that two sub-atomic particles, having been initially entangled, will affect each other even when far apart in space and time" (2016, 185)—to speak of the complex and dynamic interplay of embodied ritual practices with forms of belonging (ethnicity, nationality, etc.). In this instance, I am pointing to how expertise in ritual movements becomes an index of belonging to not only the African diasporic religious community but also the larger imagined Yorùbá ethnic community.

18. *Dap* refers to the embodied greetings between two people involving the exchange of bumps between fists, hands, arms, and/or chests, often in a complex combination. While commonly believed to have originated with Black soldiers in the Vietnam War era, the practice has spread throughout the African American community and beyond.

19. My thanks to the anonymous reviewer who questioned (rightly) the use of "the West" as a conceptual construct, especially in the context of largely Global South geographies (Trinidad, Venezuela, Nigeria). While I take this point and embrace visions of decolonial futures where the West as an imperial philosophical and disciplining project no longer occupies significant space politically or philosophically, I feel that projecting this not-yet time onto the contemporary moment would do violence to lived realities that are structured in no small part by negotiating power dynamics with the West, whether through trade agreements, immigration challenges to freedom of movement, Central Intelligence Agency interventions in nearby national and regional spaces, or shared media markets. As Arjun Appadurai (1990) noted (and as is still relevant today), the shape and speed of global forces have created various -scapes (mediascapes, technoscapes, and, of particular relevance here, ethnoscapes) that we are all imbricated in. For more on the project of the West (and the rest), see especially Trouillot (2003).

20. My gratitude to the editors of this volume for calling my attention to the dissonance and tension in my body being located, both literally and metaphorically, in the often-unmarked category of the so-called secular.

21. This differs from the constructions of Yorùbá ethnicity rooted in Black nationalism centered exclusively in an African genealogy (imagined or otherwise) by members of Oyotunji Village, as explored by Kamari Clarke (2004) and Tracey Hucks (2012).

22. David Guss's important work *The Festive State: Race, Ethnicity, and Nationalism as Cultural Performance* (2000)—on the performance of community, ethnicity, and history in an Afro-Venezuelan community—locates this largely in San Juan celebrations, reflective of syncretic Christian and African practices. However, Guss dismisses any relation to Yorùbá religion. Instead, he focuses on a less specific creolized African performative and ritual influence (30).

23. This movement in the Americas, especially throughout the African diaspora, goes back over a century before Wakanda entered the collective consciousness through the Marvel movie *Black Panther*. (Of course, the provenance of this move goes back to at least ancient Egypt, where it is prominently displayed in statue representations of deities and royalty.) The copious images that circulated on social media of people (individuals, families, and large groups) standing with their arms crossed, often dressed in cloth(ing) from various African cultures, evoked a resonance of familiarity among members of African diasporic religions. It is as if everyday people around the world were signaling a secret sign. In addition, social media sites suggest that at least one cast member of the movie (and possibly two or three) is an Ifá/Orisha initiate.

24. The sacred text of Ifá that manifests Alásùwadà, the Odu Òsá Ògúndá, ends with the following lines: "If one Ori is blessed / it will extend to two hundred others / My Ori that is blessed / Has affected you positively / Your Ori that is blessed / Has affected me positively / If one Ori is blessed / It will affect two hundred others." This verse, provided by Olóyè Sọlágbadé Pópóọlá, conveys Ifá's teachings that if one person's life is elevated and improved in alignment with the divine, so the lives of community members ("two hundred others") will also get better (see appendix I, Castor 2017: 169–174).

25. In Yorùbá cosmology the Earth is sacred and divine, referred to as Ilé Aiyé or Onílé.

26. The embodied practices leading to healing and a shift in temporalities (and the relationship between body and spirit) resonate with many of the energy modalities active in the wellness communities of the Americas, with links to practices from yoga to qigong to acupuncture (each of which has its own complicated history with its Asian heritage community). Perhaps the ritualized movements of Yorùbá Ifá/Orisha could be viewed through a lens of energy work and in that way linked to other global practices. This could add a level of understanding of Yorùbá spiritual praxis as a healing/wellness practice, a modality which many in the Americas are more familiar with. This would raise provocative questions with regard to the entanglements of healing and devotion, which depend on shifts from a discrete individualism (an inheritance of European Enlightenment philosophies) to a more collective subject position.

27. This is especially salient when one considers that greetings involve recognizing the divinity of the other person's Orí (spiritual head) and any àṣẹ they have accumulated through initiations. In greeting elders, what is being honored is the divine essence of the Orisha or Ifá that they carry from their initiation.

28. As evidenced here, the "conference" with its ritual components and the active presence of Spirit was beyond the everyday academic understanding of the term. In that moment we felt free and emboldened to dream of new social imaginaries of liberation. Reflecting on this shift I was able to write about the conference's closing ritual, "By late Sunday night, the feeling of unity was palpable. Many hours past the planned end of the conference, people sang and danced together in joyous celebration of that unity. . . . [T]he conference closed with music, dancing, and fellowship as all who were gathered felt the truth of Oshun's message: 'Unity is strength, strength is power'" (Castor 2017, 165–166).

REFERENCES

Abiodun, Rowland. 1994. "Understanding Yoruba Art and Aesthetics: The Concept of Ase." *African Arts* 27 (3): 68–78, 102–103.

Adderley, Rosanne Marion. 2006. *"New Negroes from Africa": Slave Trade Abolition and Free African Settlement in the Nineteenth-Century Caribbean.* Bloomington: Indiana University Press.

Alexander, M. Jacqui. 2006. *Pedagogies of Crossing: Meditations on Feminism, Sexual Politics, Memory and the Sacred.* Durham, NC: Duke University Press.

Appadurai, Arjun. 1990. "Disjuncture and Difference in the Global Cultural Economy." *Theory, Culture and Society* 7 (2–3): 295–310.

Apter, Andrew. 2017. *Oduduwa's Chain: Locations of Culture in the Yoruba-Atlantic.* Chicago: University of Chicago Press.

Beliso-De Jesús, Aisha. 2013. "Religious Cosmopolitanisms: Media, Transnational Santeria, and Travel between the United States and Cuba." *American Ethnologist* 40 (4): 704–720.

Beliso-De Jesús, Aisha. 2014. "Santería Copresence and the Making of African Diaspora Bodies." *Cultural Anthropology* 29 (3): 503–526.

Beliso-De Jesús, Aisha. 2015. *Electric Santería: Racial and Sexual Assemblages of Transnational Religion.* New York: Columbia University Press.

Boyce Davies, Carole. 2013. *Caribbean Spaces: Escapes from Twilight Zones.* Urbana: University of Illinois Press.

Castor, N. Fadeke. 2009. "Invoking the Spirit of Canboulay: Pathways of African Middle Class Cultural Citizenship in Trinidad." PhD diss., University of Chicago.

Castor, N. Fadeke. 2017. *Spiritual Citizenship: Transnational Pathways from Black Power to Ifá in Trinidad.* Durham, NC: Duke University Press.

Castor, N. Fadeke. 2018. "Offerings in the Digital Commons: African Diasporic Religions, Social Media and Social Justice." Paper presented at the American Academy of Religions Annual Meeting, Denver, CO, November.

Clarke, Kamari. 2004. *Mapping Yorùbá Networks: Power and Agency in the Making of Transnational Communities.* Durham, NC: Duke University Press.

Clarke, Kamari. 2007. "Transnational Yoruba Revivalism and the Diasporic Politics of Heritage." *American Ethnologist* 34 (4): 721–734.

Conquergood, Dwight. 1991. "Rethinking Ethnography: Towards a Critical Cultural Politics." *Communications Monographs* 58 (2): 179–194.

Covington-Ward, Yolanda. 2016. *Gesture and Power: Religion, Nationalism, and Everyday Performance in Congo*. Durham, NC: Duke University Press.

Csordas, Thomas J. 1990. "Embodiment as a Paradigm for Anthropology." *Ethos* 18 (1): 5–47.

Daniel, Yvonne. 2005. *Dancing Wisdom: Embodied Knowledge in Haitian Vodou, Cuban Yoruba, and Bahian Candomblé*. Urbana: University of Illinois Press.

Daniel, Yvonne. 2011. *Caribbean and Atlantic Diaspora Dance: Igniting Citizenship*. Urbana: University of Illinois Press.

Daniel, Yvonne. 2018. "Dance Artistry and Bahian Forms of Citizenship: Isaura Oliveira and Malinké." In *Dancing Bahia: Essays on Afro-Brazilian Dance, Education, Memory, and Race*, edited by Lucía M. Suárez, Amélia Conrado, and Yvonne Daniel, 39–70. Bristol, UK: Intellect.

Drewal, Margaret Thompson. 1992. *Yoruba Ritual: Performers, Play, Agency*. Bloomington: Indiana University Press.

Edwards, Brent H. 2009. *The Practice of Diaspora: Literature, Translation, and the Rise of Black Internationalism*. Cambridge, MA: Harvard University Press.

Fanon, Frantz. 1963. *The Wretched of the Earth*. New York: Grove.

Fanon, Frantz. 1967. *Black Skin, White Masks*. New York: Grove.

Gilroy, Paul. 1991. *"There Ain't No Black in the Union Jack": The Cultural Politics of Race and Nation*. Chicago: University of Chicago Press.

Gilroy, Paul. 1993. *The Black Atlantic: Modernity and Double Consciousness*. Cambridge, MA: Harvard University Press.

Gomez, Michael A. 1998. *Exchanging Our Country Marks: The Transformation of African Identities in the Colonial and Antebellum South*. Chapel Hill: University of North Carolina Press.

Guss, David M. 2000. *The Festive State: Race, Ethnicity, and Nationalism as Cultural Performance*. Berkeley: University of California Press.

Hall, Stuart. 1996. "New Ethnicities." In *Stuart Hall: Critical Dialogues in Cultural Studies*, edited by David Morley and Kuan-Hsing Chen, 441–449. London: Routledge.

Hall, Stuart. 1999. "Thinking the Diaspora: Home-Thoughts from Abroad." *Small Axe*, no. 6: 1–18.

Hall, Stuart. 2003. "Cultural Identity and Diaspora." In *Theorizing Diaspora*, edited by Jana Evans Braziel and Anita Mannur, 233–246. Oxford: Blackwell.

Henry, Frances. 2003. *Reclaiming African Religions in Trinidad: The Socio-Political Legitimation of the Orisha and Spiritual Baptist Faiths*. Jamaica: University of West Indies Press.

Hucks, Tracey E. 2012. *Yoruba Traditions and African American Religious Nationalism*. Albuquerque: University of New Mexico Press.

Johnson, E. Patrick. 2006. "Black Performance Studies: Genealogies, Politics, Futures." In *The Sage Handbook of Performance Studies*, edited by D. Soyini Madison and Judith Hamera, 446–463. Thousand Oaks, CA: Sage Publications.

Johnson, Paul C. 2007. *Diaspora Conversions: Black Carib Religion and the Recovery of Africa*. Berkeley: University of California Press.

Mason, Michael Atwood. 1994. "'I Bow My Head to the Ground': The Creation of Bodily Experience in a Cuban American Santería Initiation." *Journal of American Folklore* 107 (423): 23–39.

Mason, Michael Atwood. 2002. *Living Santeria: Rituals and Experiences in an Afro-Cuban Religion*. Washington, DC: Smithsonian Books.

Matory, James Lorand. 1994. *Sex and the Empire That Is No More: Gender and the Politics of Metaphor in Oyo Yorùbá Religion*. Minneapolis: University of Minnesota Press.

Matory, James Lorand. 2005. *Black Atlantic Religion: Tradition, Transnationalism and Matriarchy in the Afro-Brazilian Candomblé*. Princeton, NJ: Princeton University Press.

Matory, James Lorand. 2009. "The Many Who Dance in Me." In *Transnational Transcendence: Essays on Religion and Globalization*, edited by Thomas Csordas, 231–262. Berkeley: University of California Press.

Mazzarella, William. 2009. "Affect: What Is It Good For?" In *Enchantments of Modernity: Empire, Nation, Globalization*, edited by Saurabh Dube, 291–309. New Delhi: Routledge.

McNeal, Keith E. 2011. *Trance and Modernity in the Southern Caribbean: African and Hindu Popular Religions in Trinidad and Tobago*. Gainesville: University Press of Florida.

Miller, Ivor. 2004. "The Formation of African Identities in the Americas: Spiritual 'Ethnicity.'" *Contours* 2 (2): 193–222.

Mintz, Sally W., and Richard Price. 1976. *The Birth of African-American Culture: An Anthropological Perspective*. Boston: Beacon.

Olupona, Jacob K., and Rowland Abiodun, eds. 2016. *Ifá Divination, Knowledge, Power, and Performance*. Bloomington: Indiana University Press.

Price, Richard. 1985. "An Absence of Ruins? Seeking Caribbean Historical Consciousness." *Caribbean Review* 14 (3): 24–29.

Robinson, Cedric J. 1983. *Black Marxism: The Making of the Black Radical Tradition*. Chapel Hill: University of North Carolina Press.

Routon, Kenneth. 2008. "Conjuring the Past: Slavery and the Historical Imagination in Cuba." *American Ethnologist* 35 (4): 632–649.

Scott, David. 1991. "That Event, This Memory: Notes on the Anthropology of African Diasporas in the New World." *Diaspora: A Journal of Transnational Studies* 1 (3): 261–284.

Segal, Daniel. 1993. "'Race' and 'Colour' in Pre-independence Trinidad and Tobago." In *Trinidad Ethnicity*, edited by Kevin Yelvington, 81–115. Knoxville: University of Tennessee Press.

Sharpe, Christina. 2016. *In the Wake: On Blackness and Being*. Durham, NC: Duke University Press.

Stewart, Kathleen. 2017. "In the World That Affect Proposed." *Cultural Anthropology* 32 (2): 192–198.

Thomas, Deborah. 2016. "Time and the Otherwise: Plantations, Garrisons and Being Human in the Caribbean." *Anthropological Theory* 16 (2–3): 177–200.

Trouillot, Michel-Rolph. 1995. *Silencing the Past: Power and the Production of History*. Boston: Beacon Press.

Trouillot, Michel-Rolph. 2003. *Global Transformations: Anthropology and the Modern World*. New York: Palgrave Macmillan.

Turner, Victor. 1969. *The Ritual Process: Structure and Anti-structure*. New Brunswick, NJ: Transaction.

Tweed, Thomas A. 1997. *Our Lady of the Exile: Diasporic Religion at a Cuban Catholic Shrine in Miami*. New York: Oxford University Press.

West, Michael O., William G. Martin, and Fanon Che Wilkins, eds. 2009. *From Toussaint to Tupac: The Black International since the Age of Revolution*. Chapel Hill: University of North Carolina Press.

Willis, John Thabiti. 2018. *Masquerading Politics: Kinship, Gender, and Ethnicity in a Yoruba Town*. Bloomington: Indiana University Press.

Yelvington, Kevin. 2001. "The Anthropology of Afro-Latin America and the Caribbean: Diasporic Dimensions." *Annual Review of Anthropology* 30 (1): 227–260.

PART II

Community, Religious Habitus, and the Senses

4. Faith Full: Sensuous Habitus, Everyday Affect, and Divergent Diaspora in the UCKG

RACHEL CANTAVE

I felt something inside of me telling me to do it. It feels right.
—Author's field notes, anonymous interviewee, March 2014

Q: What do you mean it came from here? [places hand on chest]
A: You know, it's a feeling, like a sensation.
—Author's field notes, interview, April 24, 2014

Collecting empirical data on religious influence is near impossible. However, in 2014 I humbly embarked on this task, initially looking for religious influence by studying religious ideology and texts. I took notes on church sermons. I collected observations on religious identities and ritual practices among Afro-Brazilian Catholics, Neo-Pentecostals, and Candomblé devotees.[1] The information was useful; however, I felt that some core dimension of religious influence and experience was missing. Finally, I began asking adherents directly, through semistructured interviews, what influenced them. I focused on understanding how religious beliefs aid adherents in making important or difficult decisions. I immediately noticed a trend in answers across the religious groups, exemplified by the transcriptions at the start of this chapter.

This chapter is an inquiry into how feelings and sensations guide religious adherents through perilous moral terrain and shape adherents' sense of self. Drawing on data from a 2014 field study examining the diverse religious experiences of Afro-Brazilians in Salvador da Bahia, Brazil, this chapter asks how Neo-Pentecostal "sensational form" and sensuous habitus, or dispositions, impact the individual and collective religious experiences of racialized religious bodies (Klaver and Kamp 2011, 422).[2] I assert that sensing faith is part of affective racialized experiences, and while scholars of critical affective theories have noted that race and racism are constituted through everyday affect and feeling (Ahmed 2005, 2012; Zembylas 2014), few have considered the affective intersection of religious and racial identity and experience (Crawley 2016). As a result, this chapter attempts to bring critical affect theory into conversation with Black religious studies.

In this chapter I explore how the Universal Church of the Kingdom of God (UCKG; Igreja Universal do Reino de Deus) sustains a sensuous habitus that supports individualist and neoliberal goals, including preparing adherents to receive the gifts of the Holy Spirit. I highlight the importance of connection and disconnection in Neo-Pentecostal sensuous relationality and then draw parallels between how UCKG sessions feel and how religious identities are crafted, specifically in the case of Afro-Brazilian members of the UCKG and their corresponding discourses and ideologies of race.

Neo-Pentecostalism: Expansions and Contentions

In 1977 a charismatic Brazilian preached his first UCKG sermon out of an old funeral parlor in Rio de Janeiro (Lima 2008). At that point, the UCKG was a new religious institution headed by two local preachers. However, Edir Macedo and his brother-in-law would eventually expand the influence of the UCKG, building more than six thousand temples in every state of Brazil, opening churches in over two hundred countries, and acquiring the second-largest media company in the nation (Gonçalves da Silva 2007; Lima 2008, 13).

The UCKG is part of the third wave of Pentecostal influence in Brazil, also referred to as Neo-Pentecostalism.[3] The Neo-Pentecostal wave, which took off in the 1970s, coincided with urbanization trends in Brazil. Neo-Pentecostalism has the fastest rate of growth of any religious movement in Brazil since the spread of Catholicism through colonization (Chestnut 2003). Neo-Pentecostal expansion has largely converted poor and Afro-Brazilian populations. Of the many Neo-Pentecostal churches that have been acquiring converts since the 1970s, the UCKG is the richest and the second largest; it comprises primarily Afro-Brazilian women (Chestnut 2003; Rabelo, Ribeiro Mota, and Roberto Almeida 2009, 5).[4]

Defining aspects of Neo-Pentecostalism include ecstatic religious experiences, belief in receiving the Holy Spirit, medical miracles, baptisms, speaking in tongues, tithing, and prosperity theology.[5] In particular, Neo-Pentecostalism is differentiated from preceding Pentecostal waves by its moderate asceticism, business rhetoric, use of media, and emphasis on a spiritual war being fought between believers (*crentes*) and the Devil. Traditional Afro-Brazilian religions have become a primary discursive and religious enemy in this spiritual battle (Gonçalves da Silva 2007, 208). Catholicism, still the most popular religion in Brazil, is often regarded by the UCKG with indifference or shame. The UCKG leadership has blamed Catholicism for allowing syncretic traditions to develop in Brazil, which some see as a result of Catholic idolatry or saint worship, overshadowing the supremacy of Jesus Christ (Chestnut 2003; Selka 2007).[6] The spiritual war between the UCKG and Afro-Brazilian religions has recently intensified, resulting in increased violence against Afro-Brazilian religious devotees and their places of worship (Gonçalves da Silva 2007). Some scholars argue that it is the similarities and not the differences between Neo-Pentecostal rituals and Brazil's preexisting ecstatic traditions that fuel the UCKG's derogatory stance and discourse (Chestnut 2003; Gonçalves da Silva 2007, 208).[7] Many of the affective aspects of Neo-Pentecostal rituals resemble Afro-Brazilian religions and provide services that Afro-Brazilian religions traditionally offered, such as ritual healings, direct access to spirit, and affective ceremonies (Chestnut 2003; Gonçalves da Silva 2007; Rabelo, Ribeiro Mota, and Roberto Almeida 2009). Violent acts like the looting of Afro-Brazilian religious temples can be read as a physical and symbolic demarcation between practices that could otherwise be seen as similar in function and in target populations (working-class Afro-Brazilian women). Ironically, fervent Neo-Pentecostal opposition to traditional African beliefs and practices like Edir Macedo's first book, *Orixás, caboclos e guias: Deuses ou demônios?* (Orixás, caboclos, and guides: gods or demons? [1985]), seem to inadvertently affirm that Afro-Brazilian religions remain powerful and influential in many Brazilians' lives (Comaroff 2012, 50).

Contemporary studies of the spread of Pentecostalism have begun highlighting the role of the senses in religious conversions and experiences of faith, especially in the Global South (Brahinsky 2012; Klaver and Kamp 2011; Rabelo, Ribeiro Mota, and Roberto Almeida 2009; Witte 2011). Analyses of how adherents feel sacred and divine presence both in and through their bodies have highlighted issues of subjectivity and relationality in religion and religious persons' experiences (Brahinsky 2012; Klaver and Kamp 2011; Rabelo, Ribeiro Mota, and Roberto Almeida 2009; Witte 2011). Affective aspects of Pentecostal and

Neo-Pentecostal religious rituals have been described as "creat[ing] a space totally filled by divine presence, a wave of power that spreads and leaves not a soul untouched. But this is also a power that multiplies and individualizes itself, making each body a dwelling" (Rabelo, Ribeiro Mota, and Roberto Almeida 2009, 1). The movement of spiritual influence through multiple individual bodies, as Miriam Rabelo, Sueli Ribeiro Mota, and Cláudio Roberto Almeida (2009, 1) point out, is a defining aspect of group religious experience and its corresponding identity politic. The UCKG is a large religious institution (some argue it functions as a business even) whose influence spans from national politics to local community initiatives (Comaroff 2012, 55; Gonçalves da Silva 2007, 215).[8] As such, UCKG adherents are both the subject and the target of institutional power relations working both on and within the body (Foucault 1977). Studies of embodiment and analyses of sense cultivation continue to bring into focus issues of relationality and the semiotic relationships among people, concepts, and the material and spiritual realms; however, the relationship between race and religion needs to be incorporated into the growing literature on feeling and the senses as well (Beliso-De Jesús 2015; Rabelo, Ribeiro Mota, and Roberto Almeida 2009, 2).

Feeling, the Senses, and the Body

Feeling throughout this chapter refers to physical sensations dependent on the senses that can be experienced on the body (tactile or felt on the skin), as well as sensations felt in the body through the internal organs (e.g., when one's heart is racing), and the cognitive process of knowing that one has a feeling (Miller-McLemore 2014, 690). The senses, which often inform feelings, consist of seven modes of stimuli perception, six of which are linked to specific body parts: sight (eyes), sound (ear), touch (skin), taste (tongue), smell (nose), and motion and balance (inner ear canal); the seventh is unconscious or subconscious perception or intuition (Drewal 2005, 3). However, the senses and the sensations they produce do more than alert individuals to physical stimuli; they act as tools for perception and comprehension. That is, they help people make sense of their physical, emotional, and spiritual worlds (Beliso-De Jesús 2015; Stoller 1989). Contemporary studies of the senses have convincingly argued that our senses are culturally produced. Analyses of sense perception in the Global South have also highlighted that knowledge production, which relies on the senses, must also be culturally constructed (Beliso-De Jesús 2015; Drewal 2005; Geurts 2002; Miller-McLemore 2014; Stoller 1989). The study of non-Western communities and their cultures of perception highlights alternative modes of knowledge and discernment, also known as "indigenous hermeneutics" (Adebanwi et al. 2014, 461).[9] While seeing and hearing may be the basis of Western scientific observation and knowledge production ("see what I mean"), the tactile, olfactory, and gustatory senses can be preferred modes of perception, producing culturally specific forms of knowing in which it would perhaps make more sense to discern comprehension by asking, "You smell me?" In religious research, feeling represents a form of knowing and perception that can be difficult to describe yet particularly salient for discerning esoteric and unknowable matters—matters that require faith or blind conviction (Miller-McLemore 2014, 698).

In this chapter I attempt to portray how UCKG adherents' bodies are disciplined, felt, and observed relationally through the senses. I ground this exploration of the senses in anthropological studies of religious embodiment linking culture to the body, the senses, and consciousness.

> Each culture imbues the body with numerous meanings, which serve as both maps and repertoires for individual experience and expression. This meaning, however, is not merely a cognitive or symbolic overlay. Rather, comparable to how the music of an etude becomes part of the "ways of the hand" (Sudnow 1978) through ritual practice, social meanings become physically embodied. If we accept Bourdieu's thesis about embodiment and social practices, then we can understand how senses—not only moral senses but also religious senses—can be acquired and embedded in our bodily experience. (McGuire 2016, 155)

Not only are the senses at the center of comprehending bodily experience, but the senses can also alter bodily awareness. Studying the Egyptian Islamic Revival, anthropologist Saba Mahmood (2001, 213–214) goes so far as to argue that embodied dispositions, or habitus, are capable of reorganizing and renormalizing consciousness, the will, and desires. Mahmood likens habitus to the Arabic word for religious habit making, or *malaka*, and cites Egyptian Muslim women who teach themselves to become modest and to desire modesty through the consistent practice of veiling as an example. According to Mahmood (2001, 216), religious practices are not solely enacted through the body; they re-form the body by targeting adherents' desires. Religion therefore targets the body, the mind, and the senses. Integrating psychology with anthropology to comprehend religious influence, Steven Parish's (1994) examination of the stimulation of moral consciousness through Hindu prayer demonstrates that religious practices can be generated through conscious exercises that can (attempt to) change an adherent's consciousness from the inside out. Religious rituals can no longer be described as merely embodied repetitive practices meant to express particular religious symbols or ideals; religious rituals are also capable of reconstituting the interior self through body discipline and sensuous habitus (Mahmood 2001; Parish 1994).

Affect, Race, and Religious Identities

Scholars studying identity have noted that religious affiliations are an important part of social identity making that intertwines with other identity influencers like nationality, gender, race, and ethnic background (Goffman, Branaman, and Lemert 1997; Misra 2011). Researchers have also suggested that the relationship between Neo-Pentecostalism and race is shaped by Neo-Pentecostal discourse and ideology centered on individualist and universalist interests. These interests, they argue, often undermine the formation of ethnic group identity (Burdick 1999; Selka 2005). Quantitative studies have shown that Neo-Pentecostal religious affiliations most often correspond with Christian expressions of identity, while race is seen as a less immanent form of self-identification (Driskell, Embry, and Lyon 2008).

In Brazil race-based political and social consciousness have been closely tied to the development of Candomblé and other Afro-Brazilian religions that symbolize, sometimes explicitly and sometimes implicitly, the rejection of slavery, Christianity, heteronormativity, patriarchy, Eurocentricism, middle-class values, and corresponding sensibilities (Bastide and Sebba 2007; de Santana Pinho 2010; Landes 1947). Throughout the twentieth century, Black political organizations advanced the notion of Afro-Brazilians as Black (*negra*), as opposed to brown (*parda*) or mixed (*mulata*), emphasizing a "common oppressor over the last three hundred years in Africa and the Americas, and Africa as a place of common origin" (Selka 2007, 30). The establishment of Afro-Brazilian political and cultural groups in Salvador da Bahia overlapped with the beginnings of Afro-Brazilian cultural commoditization, creating a stronger symbolic connection between Candomblé and Salvador as sites of "authentic" Black Afro-Brazilian identity (Collins 2011; de Santana Pinho 2010; Selka 2005, 2007; Williamson 2012). Despite these forceful connections between Candomblé and Black religious identities, recent ethnographies of religion in Salvador have shown that some self-described Afro-Brazilian evangelicals are pushing for stronger connections between Black and Neo-Pentecostal identities (Burdick 1999; Selka 2007).

Nevertheless, in an era of Neo-Pentecostal expansion, institutions such as the UCKG and their continuous condemnation of traditional African faiths and cultures seem to make it difficult to reconcile Afro-Brazilian racial identity with Neo-Pentecostal ideology. Through an affective lens, however, racial categories can be reexamined according to the "relational construction of identities, in the forces created between people rather than in fixed social categories" (Tolia-Kelly and Crang 2010, 2309; see also Zembylas 2014). In other words, Afro-Brazilian or Black identities in Brazil may be forged through feelings and everyday sensuous experiences that hinge on relational differentiation between faithful/faith-filled bodies (Ahmed 2005; Zembylas 2014). Rethinking race as a technology of affect is a useful method for deconstructing Black ethnic subjectivities (de Santana Pinho 2010), especially in a society where fluid color identification is often preferred and encouraged over a fixed racial binary between Black and White.

Because religion is a consciously crafted site of sensuous experience, Afro-Brazilian Neo-Pentecostals may arguably feel differently about their racial identity in relation to Afro-Brazilians of other faiths. Approaching race as neither biologically nor ideologically constructed but as an affective technology allows space for considering how differentiation is felt and performed among Afro-Brazilian devotees of different faiths, resulting in what I later describe as a divergent diaspora. However, before remarking on the relationship between the UCKG sensuous habitus and Black racial identity, we must consider how ideology informs religious affect and the religious environment.

Neoliberalism, Individualist Discourses, and Drug Narratives

Much of the scholarship on Neo-Pentecostalism has highlighted that populations throughout Latin America, Africa, and Southeast Asia, in particular, are drawn to the movement's individualist ideology and its media-savvy brand of neoliberal ethics (Chestnut 2003; Comaroff 2012). By *neoliberal ethics*, I mean "a philosophy in which . . . the operation of a market or market-like structure is seen as an ethic in itself, capable of acting as a guide for all human action, and substituting for all previously existing ethical beliefs."[10] Neoliberalism encourages market privatization, which emphasizes individualist ideology and entrepreneurial autonomy. Individualist ideology has been described as a social and political idea promoting self-reliance and self-motivation. According to sociologists of religion Marylee Taylor and Stephen Merino (2011, 75), those prone to individualist arguments stress individual responsibility and are less likely to support social policies aimed at bolstering equality.

In interviews, I found individualist rhetoric to be prevalent, especially in narratives concerning why people had converted to the UCKG. Twenty-one out of thirty UCKG men referenced having once been users or sellers of drugs before converting to the UCKG. The frequency of ex-drug narratives suggests that drug rehabilitation is not just a crucial part of UCKG members' social initiatives and religious experience but also an essential part of how the UCKG acquires members. The following are typical conversion narratives shared with me at the UCKG:

> When I arrived, I was a drug addict, I couldn't find contentment in my personal life with anyone, and no one believed in me. For a lot of people, I was a lost case. When I arrived at the UCKG, I met someone who helped me a lot. He was a pastor of the, of the church, and was like a father to me. And *I began to fight*, I dedicated myself to the church. . . . I was able to *free myself* of the vices from the life I lived on the wrong side. The majority of, of the guys that I hung out with in that life, the wrong life, when I was [*pause*] in the criminal world, a lot of them aren't around anymore. They're dead. And I believe that I too, if I hadn't come to the church, would also be dead. (Pastor Paulo, 2013; author's emphasis)

> I was eleven years old when I left home. I used drugs because my family fought a lot. I was also very rebellious and anxious [*nervosa*]. At fourteen years of age, I came into the UCKG, and a pastor there told me, "There's a solution for everything." I began to see that the life of drugs and crime wasn't worth it. I became calmer. (Pastor Gabriel, 2014)

> Look at the work that is done in this church. The UCKG is—outside of Brazil and here in Brazil—important. Why? It's a resuscitation of our youth. They are looking—they come here thinking that they will find support, and, honestly, they find love and daily comfort here. And they find a peace that they don't find outside because many of them are troubled. Força Jovem has a beautiful work doing what? Rescuing Christian youth who are addicted to drugs, who don't have any hope or perspective on life. (Débora, 2014)

Drug rehabilitation services are an integral part of UCKG community work and serve as a visible reminder that the UCKG offers support to community members (like free drug rehabilitation programs) that the Brazilian state has not or cannot manage through social services. A noted feature of neoliberalism in societies is the powerful discourse that moving away from state-run facilities toward private-sector maintenance of public services and contracts will better serve the public. Examples include the privatization of public schools (for example, charter schools) and formerly government-run utility companies, as well as, in this case, support for nonpublic medical services, such as local drug rehabilitation centers. The UCKG is therefore encouraging a neoliberal ethic by urging its adherents, both discursively and through its community presence, to stop relying on local government for support with local and (inter)personal issues; instead, one should manage one's problems alone with support from the church. Interviews showed that many adherents internalized these neoliberal inflected, individualist ideals, restating them in their personal conversion narratives. Furthermore, I found that individualist discourse privileging individual autonomy was often layered with another neoliberal ideal: that people, like markets, should be self-regulating and competitive in order to win. My informants described the benefits of converting to the UCKG accordingly:

> Look, financially, because we teach people in the church [*pause*] *how to win financially* and *not to depend on anyone*. This is the vision that we here pass on to others—to them. That they can, they can, yes, be the head [in charge]. They can be in charge of their own business, *not depending on others*, and that is the vision that we pass on here. That they have potential because there are many people who arrived here at the bottom, people who think that there is no way to overcome their problems. *People who are unemployed, people who are underdeveloped*, people thinking about taking their own life because they think that it's the only solution. It's here that we show them that *they are capable*. That *they can win* and that they *need not depend on anyone to win*. It depends on them alone, in their faith. So you see it's—so many people arrive here homeless, today they are good people, people that are *respected in society, have a good quality of life*. So this is what is taught to people. (Pastor Paulo, 2013; author's emphasis)

> Q: Do you think that the state and community do not offer help but that the church offers this kind of help for people? Help like with work?
> A: Look, there are people [*pause*] who work in the church. There are people who work in the church. But it's the kind of thing where a person arrives here suffering, and *we teach them to win*. *Win both here and outside*, in the world. Do you understand? Because the Universal Church is the kind of thing, we tell people that misery is [*whispered tone*] a thing of the devil. It's because the Bible says that God came to bring life and life with changes, and that is what we believe in the Universal Church. (Pastor Bruno, 2014; author's emphasis)

Discourses that individuals must self-discipline, win, and self-manage were reiterated among the UCKG, its authorities (pastors), and its adherents; in turn, these individualist and neoliberal values shaped ideas of how to be virtuous, how to speak virtuously, and, returning to the topic of this chapter, how to feel virtuous. As one pastor told me, "It depends on them alone" to gain "respect" and a "good quality of life," which, according to the core tenets of the UCKG, can be attained only through baptism and the receiving of the Holy Spirit.

Feeling Inside and Outside the UCKG

The UCKG church I reference throughout this chapter opened its doors approximately twenty years ago directly across from a prominent Candomblé *terreiro* (a Candomblé temple or house of worship) in a working-class neighborhood of Salvador. The historic neighborhood had been a *quilombo*, a maroon community for formerly enslaved Afro-Brazilians. Owing to its prominent role in slave resistance movements, several Candomblé terreiros were established within the neighborhood; over the years, Catholic and other Christian churches began to populate the area as well. The opening of a UCKG there was controversial yet unsurprising. The UCKG had long been engaged in a public campaign to shame Afro-Brazilian religions, and one of its well-known strategies included opening churches across from terreiros in an effort to out Candomblé supporters and devotees who frequented terreiros anonymously (Gonçalves da Silva 2007, 214–215).

The Candomblé terreiro, the UCKG, a Catholic church, a Baptist church, another Pentecostal church, a supermarket, a beauty-supply shop, and a luncheonette lined the commercial street. Cars and buses passed in front of the churches throughout the day; some cars parked haphazardly on the sidewalk, forcing pedestrians to walk in the street while looking over their shoulders for oncoming traffic.

The street saw consistent pedestrian traffic: a mix of residents, churchgoers, *povos-de-santo*, and shoppers.[11] The only quiet moments in the neighborhood seemed to be early Sunday mornings right before Mass and other religious services began. Most afternoons the sounds of car engines and the smell of exhaust gave the neighborhood a distinctly urban feel. The smell of fried foods hung in the air. There seemed to be a steady stream of chatter between neighbors and shopkeepers throughout the day. There was even a community soundtrack consisting of music from the storefronts, music from people's homes, and loud bursts of sound from a passing car or motorcycle. There was also an almost-imperceptible murmur coming from small rectangular speakers tied to the community's lampposts. The music was mostly up-tempo and popular, except for Sunday mornings, when it switched to love ballads. The competing sounds seemed to permeate both public and private spaces, entering homes and returning to the street; the sounds blended together until they reached the tinted glass doors of the UCKG. The doors, often closed but never locked, had the unique ability to let the sounds of Christian ballads seep out into the street while blocking community sounds from coming in. When I reached the UCKG around midday, I would catch a reflection of the terreiro across the street in the glass doors as I pushed them open.

The UCKG doors acted as both a physical and a sensual barrier blocking out the profane sights, sounds, tastes, and smells of the street. From inside, dramatic religious ballads provided a new soundtrack, resounding off the white walls and down each neat row of white plastic chairs. The holy music, as well as the speakers it came from, hung heavy from the high ceilings. The white, pristine appearance was a sharp visual contrast to the chaos, color, and concrete of the neighborhood outside. In fact, the UCKG's sensuous habitus could be described as deliberately crafted in contrast to the literal and figurative outside world.

During my first participant-observation sessions at the UCKG, I felt a stark difference in the sensuous environment and culture between the UCKG and other public, private, and even Catholic and Candomblé spaces I had frequented in Brazil. The difference was not overtly symbolic, iconographic, or architectural (in the way that Catholic crosses and Candomblé altars tended to draw contrast and characterize a space) but more tonal and sensuous. Many religious spaces stimulate symbolic awareness of the sacred through shared and individual sensuous experience, be it through music, decoration, architecture, scents, proprioception, or ritual movements, including dancing, kneeling, and praying.[12] Shared affective experience reinforces an embodied religious culture, which contributes to notions of religious commonality, community, and a corresponding identity. In the UCKG, however, intentional sensuous disconnections and reconnections between profane, sacred, worldly, and ethereal relations reinforced traits of Neo-Pentecostal ideology and, most strikingly, informed adherent bodies to hold a particular sense of self along with corresponding perceptions of the world.

The first disconnection—what I had instantly felt in the UCKG but could not at first pinpoint—was the removal of children from sessions. Families with small children were greeted at the door by women known as *obreiras* (trained volunteers or workers), who then escorted the children to a back room while the rest of the family found seats in the main hall. I asked an obreira why children were removed from the main hall during sessions, and she replied,

"It allows the parents to pray without interruption and connect with the Holy Spirit." The absence of children affected the sensuous culture in a number of ways. First, the visual presence of children and the vulnerability that children and infants exude in their need for adult support were absent from the space, which visually reinforced the importance of individual autonomy. In addition, the sounds of an otherwise family-centric community were silenced as well; babies crying, children giggling, adults hushing their children, and toddlers' footsteps were removed and replaced with only the sacred sounds of adults preaching, praying, and singing.

The removal of children from sessions was the first of a series of sensuous disconnections meant to prepare adherents to receive the gifts of the Holy Spirit. Another immediate sensuous disconnection came from body discipline and tacit emphases on avoiding tactility. While public displays of affection were often enacted in public spaces and in both Catholic churches and Candomblé terreiros, holding hands, hugging, or kissing between family members, couples, or friends was avoided in the UCKG. Tactile disconnections reinforced feelings of independence and isolation. Devotees sat in individual white chairs rather than sharing a pew. Some devotees held a Bible in idle hands, but touch was rarely felt or seen in the sessions, including acts as familiar as a mother-child embrace.

There was a gendered logic to this aversion to touch that reinforced the morally conservative aspects of UCKG ideology as well. Even young married couples would stand side by side throughout a session without holding hands or touching one another. On occasion, a pastor would initiate a special prayer for couples, telling them to hold hands and put their free hand up to God in prayer. These exceptional prayers allowed couples to reestablish their tactile connection momentarily, under the tutelage of a pastor, in order to ask God for protection from jealousy and sin.

Disconnections from children and touch in the earlier parts of UCKG sessions reinforced an introspective awareness of discipline and independence through the body. The body and its capacity for sensuous distractions were moderated by tactile disconnections meant to prepare the body for a greater purpose than mundane physical and sensuous associations; it marked the beginning of re-forming adherent bodies to become sacred vessels for the Holy Spirit.

The UCKG's sensuous habitus, its connections and disconnections, was also experienced audibly. Sessions always began with a pastor leading the church in song over a microphone. Some days, an instrumental CD would accompany the singing; other days, devotees would sing a cappella. Although UCKG members sang the same lyrics and melody in unison, a mode of encouraging collective identity through shared sensuous effervescence, UCKG members also sang as if alone, in their own rhythm and key. That is, there was little effort to maintain a unified or melodious quality to UCKG prayers and songs. Singing in the UCKG felt like a simultaneously individualized and shared sensuous experience.

The sonorous quality of UCKG sessions could be described as a patterned chaos of song, prayer, and preaching expressed through a slowly mounting crescendo. The audible peak consisted of a mix of song and prayer being shouted, cried, whispered, and wailed over other shouting, crying, whispering, and wailing voices. The mix of voices would often become so loud and intense that I could barely hear the pastor's cries over the microphone. The pastors' prayers were accompanied by a staccato refrain of "Amen" and "Yes!" or "No!" The previously disciplined bodies of the adherents were reinvigorated and seemed to react sociably to the sounds and their vibrations. Hands would sometimes accompany prayers and refrains, some gliding slowly from side to side, others frantically waving over a neighbor's head. Some devotees would fall on their knees and begin to weep. Most kept their heads pointed upward and their eyes shut, denying any urge (if it existed) to look around.

As the sessions neared the receiving of the Holy Spirit, the prayers reached an earsplitting volume. At sessions with more than fifteen attendees, the voices yelling over one another made it difficult to focus on any one person; some members' voices seemed to deliberately compete with the intensity of the pastor's prayer and his rhythmic punctuating statements like "Oh Lord!" The intensity of prayer and song would eventually taper off as the pastor transitioned to a quiet sob over the microphone, revealing that a piano instrumental had been playing over the speakers all along. Even with the glass doors closed, passersby on the street could hear the rise and fall of UCKG songs and prayers.

Connections to the Holy Spirit

According to the "What We Believe" section of the UCKG website:

> We believe that those who repent of their sins, receive the Lord Jesus Christ by faith, and hold fast to Him are born again by the Holy Spirit and become children of God.
>
> We believe in the baptism of the Holy Spirit, empowering believers for service with accompanying supernatural gifts of the Holy Spirit, and in fellowship with the Holy Spirit.

Every prayer, action, and feeling in each session and its corresponding disciplinary, individualist underpinning eventually led to the climactic moments when adherents would receive the supernatural gifts of the Holy Spirit.[13] In the presence of the Holy Spirit, previously gendered tactile barriers were obscured as pastors (only men) touched the heads of both women and men to facilitate connections between devotees and the Holy Spirit. Often a pastor would walk up and down the aisle, shouting fervent prayers and holding one hand high to God, as if absorbing power, while the other hand gripped a microphone. As prayers became increasingly urgent, the pastor would eventually stop walking, look into someone's eyes, and place his palm on their forehead; almost instantaneously, the devotee would shake or pass out, a sign they had received the Holy Spirit. Obreiras also broke gendered tactile boundaries to catch and stabilize adherents on the brink of losing bodily control after receiving the gifts of the Holy Spirit.

While tactile experiences among UCKG members had previously been carefully mitigated and disciplined, in the presence of the Holy Spirit touch became a crucial part of each adherent's connection to spirit, be it through the pastor's hand or through the occasional touching of a red mantle.[14] The sudden shift in the UCKG's attitude toward tactility and touch, and the significance of members' previously idle hands, draws attention to the tenuous relationship between the sacred and the profane (Durkheim 1996). Touch, which previously signified the profane and potentially sinful trappings of the body (gluttony, sex, lack of hygiene, vulgarity, all distractions from the sacred), later became the catalyst for spiritual and embodied renewal. The sensuous disconnections from mundane modes of tactility, heightened by prayerful individualization early on in the sessions, later enabled the body to emerge sanctified and host the power of the Holy Spirit (for more on Pentecostal haptics, see Reinhardt 2014).

The centrality of touch to receiving the Holy Spirit is supported theologically as well. When Paul teaches the disciples about the Holy Spirit, he must touch them to make them receptive to the Holy Spirit:

> While Apollos was at Corinth, Paul took the road through the interior and arrived at Ephesus. There he found some disciples and asked them, "Did you receive the Holy Spirit when you believed?"
>
> They answered, "No, we have not even heard that there is a Holy Spirit."
>
> So Paul asked, "Then what baptism did you receive?"
>
> "John's baptism," they replied.
>
> Paul said, "John's baptism was a baptism of repentance. He told the people to believe in the one coming after him, that is, in Jesus." On hear-

ing this, they were baptized in the name of the Lord Jesus. When Paul placed his hands on them, the Holy Spirit came on them, and they spoke in tongues and prophesied. There were about twelve men in all. (Acts 19:1–4, New International Version)

The significance of the tactile sense in highlighting the connections among the body (touching the mantle with your hand), mind (recognizing that touch), and spirit (leading to an altered state of consciousness) is further exemplified in how adherents described connecting with the Holy Spirit. According to a UCKG elder, "[You] sacrifice your body; you cry, you laugh, you pass out. You don't feel anything." By heightening sensations in and on the body, adherents access the Holy Spirit and through this sacred connection transcend sensuous and bodily awareness and constraint. Receiving the Holy Spirit is also described as a rebirth or freedom. As one adherent described it, "You wake up a new person." Personhood (i.e., the body, mind, spirit, and consciousness) is transformed by the Holy Spirit. To understand this process better, rather than explain it in his own words, a pastor referred me to Acts 2:1 of the Bible. The passage reads, "When the day of Pentecost came, they were all together in one place. Suddenly a sound like the blowing of a violent wind came from heaven and filled the whole house where they were sitting. They saw what seemed to be tongues of fire that separated and came to rest on each of them. All of them were filled with the Holy Spirit and began to speak in other tongues as the Spirit enabled them" (Acts 2:1, New International Version).

In this passage feeling again arises as a central part of experiencing the Holy Spirit. Moreover, descriptions of the Spirit are sensuous and obscure normative interpretations of the relationship between the body and its corresponding senses. The Holy Spirit is described as appearing to the men as fiery tongues, an organ traditionally linked to the gustatory and not the visual sense. The fiery tongues then rest on the men, triggering a vulgar conflation of tactile with gustatory functions. Thereafter, the men become "filled" with the Holy Spirit. Upon being filled by the Spirit, the men begin speaking other languages or "tongues," signifying that the Spirit can also penetrate new domains of consciousness.

Not only does the Holy Spirit reorganize the body and its previous modes of sensuous experience (seeing, hearing, feeling, knowing), but once the body has accepted the Holy Spirit, it becomes a vessel for spiritual fulfillment and renewal "enabled" by the Holy Spirit to do things that previously could not be done.

Disconnections and Divergent Diasporas

In this chapter I have attempted to describe how a sensuous habitus acts as a link between ideological and embodied religious experience, shaping modes of perception that both inform and reform the body. My findings suggest that feelings of disconnection experienced during UCKG sessions reaffirm individual autonomy and self-discipline within and between adherents, while feelings of reconnection, enabled by receiving the Holy Spirit, signified the potential for new sanctified relationships within and between adherents.

The removal of children and other tactile distractions, the independent quality of group prayer, and the strategic use of touch to initiate sacred connections to the Holy Spirit constitute an important part of the sensuous habitus that distinguishes UCKG religious meetings from those of other religious communities. Constant reiteration of a sensuous habitus reinforces shared experiences and binds religious adherents in order to fortify group identity politics. Devotees "are made to feel coherently collective" through the time and space they spend in church (Freeman 2010, 8). Maintaining religious identities requires consistent embodying of a particular habitus, of which feeling is an integral part; adherents have to "learn to make the appropriate bodily gestures and facial expressions during religious ceremonies [and] acquire the proper . . . quality of voice for speaking and singing in church or *terreiro*" (Selka 2007, 125), and these embodied and sensuous dispositions are scrutinized openly and implicitly by religious leaders, church members, adherents' own consciences, and, of course, the divine gaze. The UCKG's sensuous habitus serves as an interior and exterior signifier of the UCKG's religious identity, much like the individualist and neoliberal rhetoric of the UCKG's converts.

While UCKG adherents recognize touch as a catalyst to being filled with the Holy Spirit, avoiding tactile intimacy beforehand reinforces each adherent's personal and individualized path to the Holy Spirit. Furthermore, in the UCKG, the loud, dissonant sounds of prayers and songs build a collective emotional and sensuous charge that prepares everyone for the ecstatic ritual of receiving the Holy Spirit. Group identity is informed and affirmed through shared sensuous awareness and a culture of senses produced and reiterated by embodied and ritual practices. Thus, returning to the question of how UCKG devotees assert both a Black and Neo-Pentecostal identity, I argue that these conflicting ideologies are reconciled through the sensuous habitus and affective ideology. For instance, an obreira who proudly self-identifies as *negra* explained her identity to me as follows: "I am Black, but I am baptized in the Holy Spirit and a daughter of God." The *but* in this statement suggests that she is aware that there is a symbolic disconnect between Black identities and Christian identities and that Blackness perhaps does not naturally align with Neo-Pentecostal ideals, but she also asserts that Neo-Pentecostalism is (1) a choice that Blacks can make that (2) is primarily affirmed through baptism and the receiving of the Holy Spirit.

The tensions between race and religious identities and the element of choice that the obreira's "but" highlights were also reinforced discursively through church sermons. For example, a UCKG pastor once remarked during a sermon, "God is negotiating with the devil for our souls. You know the bishop [Edir Macedo] recently went to Angola, to one of the slave ports—you know, where the slaves left from before they came to know Brazil—and he prayed there. He prayed against all the afflictions [*maldições*] that they brought to Brazil." These racial discourses point to an emergent and divergent African diaspora hinging on a temporal shift in racial discourse and politics; the Neo-Pentecostal divergent African diaspora acknowledges its past, in particular, enslavement and the "afflictions" of enslaved ancestors ("I'm Black"); however, it emphatically pronounces its divergence ("but!") by foregrounding one's choice to be baptized and experience a burgeoning future of receiving the Holy Spirit.

The importance of Afro-Brazilians' choice to be Black but children of God is reverberating throughout the public spheres of Brazil as well. In 2012 thirteen evangelical high school students refused to do a school assignment entitled "The Preservation of Ethno-Cultural Brazilian Identity," stating that Afro-Brazilian history promotes sympathy toward "satanism" and "homosexuality." Instead, they submitted a project on contemporary Christian missions in Africa.[15]

Patricia de Santana Pinho's (2010) study of African diasporic identity making in Bahia encourages scholars to take note of the distinct and contextualized "trajectories traced since slave times to this day" (97). To avoid essentializing Black ethnic identities, studies of Blackness should capture and reflect the "location, space, and time they inhabit" (de Santana Pinho 2010, 97). Within the UCKG, I found that there is space to affirm a Black Neo-Pentecostal identity; however, it is not through the privileged contemporary sociopolitical modes such as condemnation of anti-African sentiment or antiracist activism. Instead, what I refer to as the divergent diaspora reframes Africa and its diaspora according to a globalized affective movement looking to proselytize and sanctify Black bodies through the Holy Spirit. I refer to this Black subjectivity as "divergent" in order to emphasize the relationship between choice, affect, and Neo-Pentecostal identity making which is described by the anthropologist Jean Comaroff as ontologically divergent from modern Western notions of self:

A host of born-again believers across the world choose to suspend "free" choice and when convicted by divine authority, manifesting a form of self-hood somewhat different from the deliberate Kantian subject that many see as basic to modern rationalism . . . [I]t may be argued that these idealized selves have had only uneven purchase beyond the West. . . . [T]he born again faiths that flourish across the non-European world at present resonate with local ontologies and senses of being, orientations that defy the dualistic categories of liberal modern orthodoxy. (Comaroff 2012, 44)

Choice is, however, only the first step toward remaking oneself as Black but a child of God. To complete the process, one must be baptized and receive the Holy Spirit. For instance, the same obreira who described herself as "negra but" also remarked, "We [obreiras] received the Holy Spirit, that is, the true spirit of God, to strengthen us and to pass these changes [mudanças] on to others." The "changes" that obreiras pass on are, therefore, bound to the ability to receive the Holy Spirit independently. Receiving the Holy Spirit is a carefully crafted sensuous and transformative experience, as previously described, and it, according to this young woman, allows obreiras to transform others both spiritually and racially. Black racial identities are thus felt, formed, and passed on through relational connections to obreiras and the greater spiritual community, reaching full realization through baptism in the Holy Spirit. What emerges from this analysis of the divergent diaspora is an affective, relational assemblage of Black bodies disconnecting from their African past and afflicted bodily entrapments to be filled with the Holy Spirit and remade in mind, body, spirit, and (racial) consciousness.

Conclusions: Connections and Disconnections

Q: How does it feel when you receive the Holy Spirit?
A: [exasperated sigh] You'll know it when you feel it.

Author's field notes, interview, May 2014

Blackness and the African diaspora are often defined by politics of heritage and shared struggles stemming from colonialism and enslavement (Burdick 1999; de Santana Pinho 2010; Selka 2007). Afro-Brazilian UCKG members, however, are forcefully disassociating from these popular discourses of Blackness and Black identity. From the UCKG perspective, Africa's past is demonic, sick, and most certainly not Christian. Instead, self-identified Black UCKG adherents advance a divergent Black subjectivity, one that shares a present and future in their collective decision to be proselytized through baptism and the Holy Spirit, or filled by faith. The explosive growth of evangelical Christianity, including the UCKG on the African continent, highlights the globalized appeal of a "media-savvy, emotionally hyped, frankly materialistic brand of faith" and the corresponding "force of divine destiny in human affairs" (Comaroff 2012, 42–45). Using an affective lens, it is clear that a divergent diaspora emerges through the strong desire of Black religious devotees around the world (many of whom are converts) to break from fixed notions of a shared African past and redefine Blackness according to modern, universal, and consumerist sensibilities.

As this volume on religious embodiment makes clear, Black religious bodies continue to be the sites through which racial boundaries and their symbolic meanings are negotiated. Receptive bodies' sensuous disconnections from familial and profane bonds (in this case, representative of a shared African past) allow for a direct and redemptive connection to the Holy Spirit; Black bodies surrender to the Holy Spirit and have a renewed perception of and connection to the world through a decidedly individualist and neoliberal religious experience and racial identity. Deep feelings of peace, renewal, and satisfaction following the receiving of the gifts of the Holy Spirit are as far-reaching as the diaspora; feelings stay with adherents long after they leave the church and the scrutiny of their religious community and its leaders. Sensuous dispositions and technologies of affect permeate private and public domains, ending up back in the street with devotees as they walk home and being transported through migration. While feeling alone may not create ideology, religious ideology and experience are certainly colored by feeling.

Feeling and the senses are important to the study of religious embodiment in that they shed light on the aspects of religious habitus that transform racial ideologies and transcend spatial and temporal barriers. According to what they told me, UCKG adherents felt faithful, not just during church sessions, but also at home reading their Bible, in moments of strife, even while riding the public bus. Theorizing from the sensuous aspects of religious experience allows scholars to examine religion as an intuitive, affective, subjective, and interpretive experience. In the words of a UCKG faithful, "You'll know it when you feel it."

ACKNOWLEDGMENTS

I thank the editors of this volume for their supportive and productive engagement with this chapter. I also thank the readers who provided feedback on this chapter's many stages and drafts, including Edeline Cantave, Riddhi Bhandari, Bethany Peak, James Padilioni, and Stephen Selka.

1. Candomblé is an Afro-Brazilian religion that centers on Orixá veneration.

2. This chapter is a result of dissertation fieldwork and analysis (Cantave 2017) comparing civic actions and beliefs concerning community among Afro-Brazilian Catholics, Neo-Pentecostals, and Candomblé practitioners in a working-class, multifaith community of Salvador da Bahia, Brazil.

3. The first wave commenced in 1910 when Protestant missionaries of North American and European descent began their first evangelization attempts in Brazil. The second wave occurred in the 1950s around São Paulo and placed greater emphasis on healing. Some historians attribute low proselytization in these first two waves to the Catholic restoration of the 1930s, in which the Catholic Church was able to expand its membership and reassert its political influence by promoting militant lay figures and supporting the authoritarian political regime of Getúlio Vargas (Premack 2011). Catholic militancy during this period also animated violence against minority religious groups, including both Pentecostals and Candomblé devotees.

4. The largest Pentecostal church in Brazil is the Assemblies of God (Assembleias de Deus).

5. Prosperity theology is the belief that financial success is a blessing from God and that, with faith, piety, and devotion, God may bless adherents with material wealth.

6. *Syncretism* refers to two or more religious belief systems being combined to form a new religious system (Droge 2001). Afro-Brazilian religions such as Candomblé and Umbanda are considered syncretic religions owing to their incorporation of Orixá worship, Indigenous spiritual beliefs, and Catholicism.

7. The preexisting ecstatic traditions are Candomblé, Umbanda, and Kardecian Spiritism.

8. The current mayor of Rio de Janeiro, Marcelo Crivella, and some members of the Brazilian Congress (some of whom form a congressional group referred to as the "Bible Block") are members of the UCKG.

9. I refer to the West as a hegemonic political and epistemic category.

10. Paul Treanor, "Neoliberalism: Origins, Theory, Definition," Paul Treanor's archive, December 2, 2005, http://web.inter.nl.net/users/Paul.Treanor/neoliberalism.html.

11. *Povos-de-santo* is a colloquial phrase that translates as "people of the saint." It is used to refer to the devotees of Afro-Brazilian religions.

12. Proprioception is the perception of multiple bodies united in movement.

13. The epigraph is from Universal Church USA, "What We Believe," n.d., accessed January 17, 2016, http://web.universal.org/usa/about-us/what-we-believe-2/.

14. The red mantle is also known as the "Mantle of Miracles" in the UCKG. It is a red cloth kept on the altar and is used for healing rituals and strengthening of prayers by connecting adherents to the Holy Spirit.

15. Maria Derzi, "Alunos evangélicos se recusam a fazer trabalho sobre a cultura afro-brasileira," *A Crítica*, November 11, 2012, http://www.acritica.com/channels /cotidiano/news/alunos-evangelicos-se-recusam-a-fazer-trabalho-sobre-a-cultura-afro -brasileira.

REFERENCES

Adebanwi, Wale, Laura S. Grillo, Nimi Wariboko, and Jacob K. Olupona. 2014. "Religion and Indigenous Hermeneutics." *Journal of Africana Religions* 2 (4): 457–464.

Ahmed, Sara. 2005. "The Skin of the Community: Affect and Boundary Formation." In *Revolt, Affect, Collectivity: The Unstable Boundaries of Kristeva's Polis*, edited by Tina Chanter and Ewa Płonowska Ziarek, 95–111. Albany: State University of New York Press.

Ahmed, Sara. 2012. *On Being Included: Racism and Diversity in Institutional Life*. Durham, NC: Duke University Press.

Bastide, Roger, and Helen Sebba. 2007. *The African Religions of Brazil: Toward a Sociology of the Interpenetration of Civilizations*. Baltimore: Johns Hopkins University Press.

Beliso-De Jesús, Aisha. 2015. *Electric Santería: Racial and Sexual Assemblages of Transnational Religion*. New York: Columbia University Press.

Brahinsky, Josh. 2012. "Pentecostal Body Politics: Cultivating a Modern Sensorium." *Cultural Anthropology* 27 (2): 215–238.

Burdick, John. 1999. "What Is the Color of the Holy Spirit? Pentecostalism and Black Identity in Brazil." *Latin America Research Review* 34 (2): 109–131.

Cantave, Rachel. 2017. "Serving Faith: A Comparative Study of Religious Influence and Faith-Based Community Service in Salvador da Bahia, Brazil." PhD diss., American University.

Chestnut, Andrew R. 2003. *Competitive Spirits: Latin America's New Religious Economy*. Oxford: Oxford University Press.

Collins, John. 2011. "Melted Gold and National Bodies: The Hermeneutics of Depth and the Value of History in Brazilian Racial Politics." *American Ethnologist* 38 (4): 683–700.

Comaroff, Jean. 2012. "Pentecostalism, Populism and the New Politics of Affect." In *Pentecostalism and Development Churches, NGOs and Social Change in Africa*, edited by Dena Freeman, 41–65. London: Macmillan.

Crawley, Ashon T. 2016. *Blackpentecostal Breath: The Aesthetics of Possibility*. New York: Fordham University Press.

de Santana Pinho, Patricia. 2010. *Mama Africa: Reinventing Blackness in Bahia*, edited by Elena Langdon. Durham, NC: Duke University Press.

Drewal, Henry John. 2005. "Senses in Understandings of Art." *African Arts* 38 (2): 1–96.

Driskell, Robyn, Elizabeth Embry, and Larry Lyon. 2008. "Faith and Politics: The Influence of Religious Beliefs on Political Participation." *Social Science Quarterly* 89 (2): 294–314.

Droge, A. J. 2001. "Retrofitting/Retiring 'Syncretism.'" *Historical Reflections/Réflexions Historiques* 27 (3): 375–387.

Durkheim, Émile. 1996. *The Elementary Forms of the Religious Life*. Translated by Karen E. Fields. New York: Free Press.

Foucault, Michel. 1977. *Discipline and Punish: The Birth of the Prison*. Translated by Alan Sheridan. London: Penguin Books.

Freeman, Elizabeth. 2010. *Time Binds: Queer Temporalities, Queer Histories*. Durham, NC: Duke University Press.

Geurts, Kathryn Linn. 2002. *Culture and the Senses: Embodiment, Identity, and Well-Being in an African Community*. Berkeley: University of California Press.

Goffman, Erving, Ann Branaman, and Charles C. Lemert. 1997. *The Goffman Reader*. Malden, MA: Blackwell.

Gonçalves da Silva, Vagner. 2007. "Neo-Pentecostalism and Afro-Brazilian Religions: Explaining the Attacks on Symbols of the African Religious Heritage in Contemporary Brazil." *Mana* 3: 207–236.

Klaver, Miranda, and Linda van de Kamp. 2011. "Embodied Temporalities in Global Pentecostal Conversion." *Ethnos* 76 (4): 421–425.

Landes, Ruth. 1947. *The City of Women*. Albuquerque: University of New Mexico Press.

Lima, Diana Nogueira de Oliveira. 2008. "'Prosperity' in the 1990s: Ethnography of the Work Commitment between Worshippers and God in the Universal Church of the Kingdom of God." *DADOS: Revista de Ciencias Sociais* 51 (1): 7–34.

Macedo, Edir. 1985. *Orixás, Caboclos & Guias: Deuses ou Demônios?* São Paulo, Brazil: Gráfica Universal.

Mahmood, Saba. 2001. "Feminist Theory, Embodiment, and the Docile Agent: Some Reflections on the Egyptian Islamic Revival." *Cultural Anthropology* 16 (2): 202–236.

McGuire, Meredith B. 2016. "Individual Sensory Experiences, Socialized Senses, and Everyday Lived Religion in Practice." *Social Compass* 63 (2): 152–162.

Miller-McLemore, Bonnie J. 2014. "Coming to Our Senses: Feeling and Knowledge in Theology and Ministry." *Pastoral Psychology* 63 (5–6): 689–704.

Misra, Amalendu. 2011. "My Space/Mi Espacio: Evangelical Christianity and Identity Politics in Mexico." *Bulletin of Latin American Research* 31 (1): 65–79.

Parish, Steven M. 1994. *Moral Knowing in a Hindu Sacred City: An Exploration of Mind, Emotion, and Self*. New York: Columbia University Press.

Premack, Laura. 2011. "'The Holy Rollers Are Invading Our Territory': Southern Baptist Missionaries and the Early Years of Pentecostalism in Brazil." *Journal of Religious History* 35 (1): 1–23.

Rabelo, Miriam C. M., Sueli Ribeiro Mota, and Cláudio Roberto Almeida. 2009. "Cultivating the Senses and Giving In to the Sacred: Notes on Body and Experience among Pentecostal Women in Salvador, Brazil." *Journal of Contemporary Religion* 24 (1): 1–18.

Reinhardt, Bruno. 2014. "Soaking in Tapes: The Haptic Voice of Global Pentecostal Pedagogy in Ghana." *Journal of the Royal Anthropological Institute* 20: 315–336.

Selka, Stephen L. 2005. "Ethnoreligious Identity Politics in Bahia, Brazil." *Latin American Perspectives* 32 (1): 72–94.

Selka, Stephen L. 2007. *Religion and the Politics of Ethnic Identity in Bahia, Brazil*. New World Diasporas. Gainesville: University Press of Florida.

Stoller, Paul. 1989. *The Taste of Ethnographic Things: The Senses in Anthropology*. Philadelphia: University of Pennsylvania Press.

Sudnow, David. 1978. *Ways of the Hand: The Organization of Improvised Conduct*. New York: Harper and Row.

Taylor, Marylee C., and Stephen M. Merino. 2011. "Race, Religion, and Beliefs about Racial Inequality." *Annals of the American Academy of Political and Social Science* 634 (1): 60–77.

Tolia-Kelly, Divya P., and Mike Crang. 2010. "Affect, Race and Identities." *Environment and Planning A* 42 (10): 2309–2314.

Williamson, Kenneth. 2012. "Night Becomes Day: Carnival, Contested Spaces, and the Black Movement in Bahia." *Journal of Latin American and Caribbean Anthropology* 17 (2): 257–278.

Witte, Marleen de. 2011. "Touched by the Spirit: Converting the Senses in a Ghanaian Charismatic Church." *Ethnos* 76 (4): 489–509.

Zembylas, Michalinos. 2014. "Rethinking Race and Racism as *Technologies of Affect*: Theorizing the Implications for Anti-racist Politics and Practice in Education." *Race Ethnicity and Education* 18 (2): 145–162.

5. Covered Bodies, Moral Education, and the Embodiment of Islamic Reform in Northern Nigeria

ELISHA P. RENNE

1. O You, enfolded in your mantle (of reform),
2. Arise and warn,
3. Glorify your Lord,
4. Purify your inner self,
5. And banish all trepidation.
6. Do not bestow favours
in expectation of return,
7. And persevere
in the way of your Lord.
—Qur'an, Sura 74 (The Enfolded)

In the Qur'an and in several hadith, women and men are enjoined to cover their bodies with cloth.[1] As proper Muslims, men should cover their heads with turbans or caps, while women should wear veils. This injunction has been widely observed, but distinctive forms of dress and head coverings are associated with different Islamic reform groups, as in the city of Zaria in northern Nigeria. In Zaria there are numerous Islamic institutions and mosques, which reflect these distinctive affiliations, as well as many schools that support different forms of Islamic education, which include the Abubakar Gumi College of Higher Islamic Studies and the Centre for Islamic and Legal Studies at Ahmadu Bello University.[2] How leaders of different Islamic groups have considered moral bodily comportment and being in the world is reflected in their critical evaluations of the bodily covering of others (or its lack). This critique was evident in the establishment in February 1978 of the Islamic re-form movement Jama'atu Izalat al-Bid'a wa Iqamat al-Sunna—the Society for the Removal of Innovation and the Reinstatement of Tradition, colloquially known as Izala. In Zaria, Izala leaders sought to focus followers' practice on the Qur'an and hadith and to counter the practices of other Islamic orders, such as the reformed Tijāniyya, whose performance of zhikr—ritual commu-nication with the group's founder—they considered to be un-Islamic.[3] Izala leaders, such as Isma'ila Idris in Jos, Sheikh Abubakar Gumi in Kaduna, and Malam Aminu d-Din Abubakar in Kano, also emphasized the importance of Islamic education for both girls and married women, as well as simplicity in dress and demeanor. As discussed later on, these new aspects of comportment for followers of Izala led to a new form of women's body covering, the hijab, which allowed Izala women to leave their family compounds to attend eve-ning classes at local Islamiyya schools for study of the Qur'an. Similarly, Izala men mainly wore simply styled kaftans with caps (hula) or small turbans. Such dress did not encumber them as they moved about town or traveled to Mecca for the hajj. Aside from enabling movement, these body and head coverings conveyed a sense of modesty and simplicity, which have characterized Islamic reform movements in northern Nigeria. Indeed, Shehu Usman dan Fodio, the leader of the nineteenth-century jihad that led to the establishment of the So-koto Caliphate (Last 1967), was said to have had one robe, one set of trousers, and one turban (Hiskett 1973, 31).

This chapter focuses on the significance of cloth coverings in the embodi-ment of Islamic religious practice in Zaria, Kaduna, and, to some extent, Kano, cities in northern Nigeria. Such an approach clarifies how the covering of women's bodies through the use of hijab may represent the distinctive beliefs of one Islamic group but also how cloth coverings may be used to present a uni-fied, international Islamic community, as when the two pieces of white, undif-ferentiated ihram cloth are worn by men, and hijab is worn by women, during the performance of hajj in Mecca. For followers of the reformist Izala move-ment, these embodied practices have been closely related to particular forms of Islamic education—as in Islamic classes for married women—and classes for intending pilgrims, who are required to learn basic hajj prayers and practices before they are given permission by state pilgrimage boards to fly to Mecca (Tangban 1991). The Izala movement's approach, which underscores the inter-connectedness of spiritual, bodily, and material religious practice (Covington-Ward 2016; Meyer and Houtman 2012; Ware 2014), is framed by a particular understanding of moral education that characterized the founding of the Izala movement.

The chapter begins with a discussion of moral education and specifically considers the differences and intersections between the views of Sheikh Abubakar Gumi (1992), one of the founders of Izala, on Islamic education; of Aisha Lemu, former director the Islamic Education Trust; and of Émile Durkheim (1961), the founder of the first department of sociology in France. The implications of religious and secular moral education are then considered. The chapter continues with a brief history of the founding of the Izala movement and its leaders' belief in the importance of teaching knowledge of Islamic texts, including the Qur'an and hadith, as well as proper body techniques in the performance of prayer and ablution. In Zaria City the establishment of Islamic education classes for married women (known as Islamiyya Matan Aure) is examined from the perspective of several Zaria City women who attended these classes when they began in the 1980s. These women explain their experiences when they first attended these classes wearing hijab, as well as the consequences that their acquisition of knowledge of the Qur'an, hadith, and other Islamic texts has had for their lives. Some of these women have gone on to perform the hajj, the pilgrimage to Mecca, which is discussed below.

Abubakar Gumi was also involved in the introduction of registration procedures for Nigerian pilgrimage boards in 1982 (Loimeier 1997, 161). For those registering with the pilgrimage board in Kaduna State, written materials are provided and classes held to prepare pilgrims for proper comportment and prayers during hajj. In Kano State knowledge about performance of the hajj can be acquired in various ways, from classes taught by members of the Muslim Women's Association of Kano to booklets on prayer and performance of the hajj available from local bookshops and state pilgrimage boards, as well as information on the National Hajj Commission of Nigeria website.[4] The experiences of men and women who have performed the hajj suggest the powerful impact of what is referred to by Sunni Muslims as the fifth pillar of Islam.[5] While men's white ihram dress, consisting of two pieces of unsewn cloth, worn with heads uncovered, and women's long, mainly white gowns and hijab, which cover their heads during the ihram period of the hajj, emphasize distinct gender identities, these overwhelmingly white garments nonetheless emphasize Islamic unity. Indeed, during the period of ihram, men and women pray together, unlike the usual separation by gender practiced in mosques in northern Nigeria. The chapter concludes with a consideration of the importance of embodied techniques and the associated use of religious materials such as particular types of cloth in one's comportment as a proper Muslim, practices that "are governed

by education, and at least by the circumstances of life in common, of contact"
(Mauss 1973, 86).

Moral Education and Islamic Reform

The word *moral* derives from *mos*, a way of comporting oneself.
—T. O. Beidelman, *Moral Imagination in Kaguru Modes of Thought*

In his memoir, *Where I Stand*, Abubakar Gumi (1992, 104) recounted his con-
sternation during the 1962 hajj after seeing some Nigerian pilgrims beating the
jamra (the image of Satan) with their shoes, rather than throwing small stones
as is prescribed (see also Loimeier 1997, 136). He consulted with Ahmadu Bello,
then the premier of the Northern Region of Nigeria, whom he had accompanied on hajj, and they determined upon returning to Nigeria to improve Islamic
education in northern Nigeria. Later that year, they brought northern Nigerian
Islamic leaders together in Kaduna to discuss the establishment of a new organization, Jamā'atu Nasril Islam (Association for the Support of Islam), to foster
Islamic unity in the north as well as to provide resources for the building of new
mosques and schools to improve Islamic education in the region. In Kaduna,
Gumi began holding classes in the garage of his house, with teachers initially
paid by him and Bello (Gumi 1992, 105). Through support from local businessmen and Saudi and Kuwaiti donors, Jamā'atu Nasril Islam subsequently was
able to sponsor the building of numerous schools and mosques as well as of its
headquarters in Kaduna. Gumi's insistence on the importance of Islamic education and dress for both women and men reflected his views about countering earlier British colonial intentions: "One has to be taught the inadequacy of
one's language, food or dress, for instance, before one is made to appreciate the
glory of that brought to one by the colonial master" (78). As he noted, "There
had been quite an established intellectual tradition among the Muslims, dating
back several centuries before the coming of the European colonialists. We had
an indigenous form of writing and a developed system of education, based on
our long association with Arabic and Islamic learning. . . . This explains why
European colonialists were regarded with suspicion from the very beginning.
They were considered symbols of foreign conquest and domination, and whatever programme they introduced was seen as another ploy to enhance their
domination and the spread of their religion and culture" (15).

Thus, Gumi viewed Islamic education for women as a means of countering Western intellectual hegemony and as the basis of moral education.[6] In
the book *Tahdhib (Moral Education) and Sirah*, the late B. Aisha Lemu (1986)

provides students with chapters on preparation for prayer, cleanliness, respect for others, Islamic manners, and dress. She concludes that " every Muslim boy or girl, man or woman—who tries in this way to obey Allah and behaves well will be helped and guided by Allah. He will be on the Right Path (as-siratul mustaqim). Allah will give him or her a great reward in life and greater reward in the Hereafter. Thus Tahdhib (Moral Education) is very important for every Muslim. It guides him or her to happiness and peace of mind in this world and in the Hereafter" (15).

This view differs considerably from that of Durkheim, who discussed the importance of developing a new basis of moral education distinct from religion in France in a series of lectures given in 1902–1903. Durkheim sought to replace religion with secular rationalism as the moral basis for the betterment of modern French society, although he recognized that this would not be easy (Durkheim 1961, 20). Essentially, he proposed to uncover the fundamental rules of morality in French society and then to develop them in children through instruction in French primary schools. Three main rules emerged in his conceptualization of moral education: discipline, attachment to society, and autonomy based on secular knowledge, particularly science (264). Such moral education, Durkheim believed, not only was critical to the functioning of the French nation-state but also reflected the particularities of French history and society (Beidelman 1997, 7). Durkheim emphatically excluded religious knowledge and things associated with it, such as the hijab. Indeed, since 2004 it has been illegal for girl students to wear hijab to French public school classes, which continues to be an issue for the children of African migrants in the country. This way of thinking about proper comportment and moral education has also affected educational practice in southwestern Nigeria in particular, where the wearing of hijab in schools continues to be disputed.[7]

Pierre Bourdieu (1967, 338) made a related but somewhat different observation in his discussion of how an educational system not only imparts such "fundamental rules of morality" but, in the process of doing so, also "modifies the content and spirit of the culture which it transmits," an observation with which Gumi would agree. In other words, the mode of transmission of this knowledge (through examinations and competitive grading) and the setting (the presence of desks and chairs, to which some Muslim scholars objected; Bray 1981, 61) affect what is learned in school, aside from the actual curriculum presented there. Thus, one northern Nigerian waziri (vizier), when asked whether he thought Western education was destructive of Muslim morality, told Jean Trevor that "it was not the knowledge which was disruptive but the attitudes and individual competitiveness that went with it" (quoted in Trevor 1975, 250).[8] For Muslim scholars such as Gumi and Lemu, failure to properly cover the body was another aspect of the disruptiveness of Western education.

Islamic education (and later Western education) was not necessarily seen as a moral dilemma for men. However, a complication for urban Hausa Muslim women living in Zaria City centered around the practice of seclusion (*kulle*), which prescribed that married women remain within their compounds and precluded their daily, unaccompanied attendance at Islamic schools. Covering the body with a hijab provided a means for addressing this dilemma.

Yet discussions over whether and how married Muslim women in northern Nigeria should receive an Islamic education have taken place over the past two centuries and have often been associated with various Islamic reformist movements (Ogunbiyi 1969). In the early nineteenth century, the religious reformer Shehu Usman dan Fodio, the founder of the Sokoto Caliphate, wrote about the importance of women's education as part of proper Islamic practice: "Most of our educated men leave their wives, their daughters, and their captives morally abandoned like beasts, without teaching them what God prescribes should be taught them" (1975, 254). His daughter, Nana Asma'u, was instrumental in establishing women's groups for reading the Qur'an in Sokoto in northwestern Nigeria (Boyd 1989; Boyd and Last 1985; Mack and Boyd 2000). (Such reading groups were not available for married women in Zaria City until the introduction of Islamiyya Matan Aure.) Later, during the colonial period, from 1903 to 1960, British education officials were initially loath to encourage girls and women to attend secular government schools because they were concerned about offending local Islamic sensibilities (Boyd 1997; Graham 1966) and because women were not being groomed for the native administration positions (Tibenderana 1985). Thus, Islamic schooling for boys and girls, but not married women, continued through this period in Zaria City. Children's Islamic education consisted of *allo* and *ilmi* schools, the former based on memorization, recitation, and writing of the Qur'an on small boards (allo), the latter based on expository lectures and reading of the Qur'an and hadith, as well as texts that discuss Islamic law and theology (see Hiskett 1975b; Tukur 1963). While young girls often attended allo schools, few continued on to ilmi instruction, because of marriage.

The advent of the Izala movement in the late 1970s led to a reassessment of the importance of education for women of all ages. Indeed, Islamic education for married adult women was an important aspect of the Izala reformers' agenda. For them, basic knowledge of the Qur'an and hadith among married women was critical for raising proper children, which parallels Jean-Jacques

Rousseau's explanation for why he wrote his treatise on education reform, *Émile, or On Education*, for women: "The first education is the most important, and the first education belongs incontestably to women" (1979, 37).[9]

This position on the married women's Islamic education distinguished Izala followers from those supporting the prevailing Qādiriyya and Tijāniyya Islamic Sufi brotherhoods in Zaria City (Muhammed 1997; Renne 2012; Umar 1993), despite a number of sura (chapters) in the Qur'an that emphasize the importance of the pursuit of knowledge.[10] Yet the ability to read the Qur'an and other Islamic texts learned through these Islamiyya classes had other implications, both personally for the women attending them and for marital relations within Hausa households, potentially unsettling them. Thus, Izala leaders and teachers (Gumi 1992) were careful to emphasize the importance of this training not only for Islamic education but also for women's domestic roles as wives and mothers.

While the particular answers of these Izala reformers differed from Durkheim's (they did not want to separate religion and education), they shared a general concern with teaching women to read and understand the texts. Indeed, some Islamiyya schools provided instruction in secular as well as Islamic subjects in order to prepare individuals to work for the material and moral betterment of society. While suspicions persisted about these classes (they were sometimes referred to as "adultery education" in Zaria), such classes have been widely attended in Zaria, Kaduna, and Kano in recent years (Bray 1981; Lawson 1995). Yet the fact that some Islamiyya schools have incorporated subjects taught at Western-style schools (and are taught on these schools' premises) undermines assumptions about a strict shift from religious "traditional" to secular "modern" education and illustrates how local efforts to construct a moral education are culturally and historically grounded.

Islamic Education: Izala and the Introduction of Classes for Married Women in Zaria City

151. Even as We sent a messenger from among you to convey Our messages to you and cleanse you, and teach you the Book and the wisdom, and what you did not know;

152. So, therefore, remember Me, and I shall remember you; and give thanks and do not be ungrateful.

153. O you who believe, seek courage in fortitude and prayer, for God is with those who are patient and persevere.

—Sura 2, Qur'an

In the early 1980s, Izala began to attract followers in Zaria City, the old walled portion of the larger town of Zaria.[11] Izala leaders focused on primary Islamic texts, particularly the Qur'an and the hadith, and rejected "all bid'a [innovations] which are not in concordance with the Sunna of the Prophet" (Funtua 1980, 5, quoted in Loimeier 1997, 229). Initially, Izala teachers (*malamai*) as well as their students faced considerable resistance to the introduction of classes for married women in Zaria City. Owing to this, several schools with classes for married women had their start in the entryways (*zaure*) or garages of private houses whose owners permitted malamai to use the space to teach married women. Some of these classes grew out of allo Islamic schools for young children, which may be seen in the entryways of compounds throughout the old city. One such school was established in the early 1970s in a garage attached to the main compound of the titled royal official, the Magajin Gari Zazzau (the late Alhaji Nuhu Bamalli), in the quarter of Zaria City known as Anguwar Kwarbai. As the school, known as Madarasatul Anwarul Islam, expanded, a separate structure was built to accommodate the school's growing population of primary-school-age children. However, in 1981, with the growth of the Izala movement, the school's teachers introduced classes for married women. A small number of married women, wearing hijab, began attending classes, which focused on portions of the Qur'an and hadith, as well as *fiqh* (Islamic jurisprudence), *tajwid* (recitation of the Qur'an), and *tawhid* (Islamic belief, theology of the unity of God), conducted by teachers at this school. Because of the early opposition to women going outside of their homes to attend Islamic education classes, these women students primarily consisted of the wives of the Islamiyya teachers themselves, who accompanied them to class (see Loimeier 1997, 238).[12]

Initially, some husbands refused to allow their wives to attend classes, arguing that they could learn to read the Qur'an in their homes. However, some married women insisted on attending Islamiyya Matan Aure classes despite their husbands' disapproval, which in some cases led to divorce (Loimeier 1997, 254; Renne 2012; Yandaki 1997, 50). Yet, with time, these classes for married women came to be widely accepted in many *anguwoyi* (quarters or wards) of the old city and consequently led many people to see the value of this new way of thinking about their religion (Umar 2001). By 2002 over twenty-six Islamiyya schools with classes for married women had opened in nineteen different anguwoyi of the city, which reflected both a widespread acceptance of the importance of married women's education and a broader acceptance of the Izala movement there (Renne 2012).[13]

While established to improve women's knowledge of the Qur'an and hadith, seen as beneficial to women themselves, who as better Muslims "will train all society" (Malam Muhammed Bello, quoted in Renne 2012, 55), Islamiyya Matan Aure classes have also provided women in Zaria with the moral authority to challenge domestic strictures associated with seclusion in order to attend classes in the pursuit of Islamic knowledge.[14] Furthermore, some educated Muslim Hausa women's distinctive readings of certain passages of the Qur'an—that all should be educated, including women—have lent ideological support to new behaviors, which included the wearing of a new form of body covering, the hijab, in order to attend Islamiyya classes.

The Introduction of the Hijab

Me ake nufi da hijabi?
Hijabi shi ne shamaki, watau
tufafin da ke rufe jiki duka.

What is the purpose of the hijab?
The hijab is a partition, that is to say, it is
wrapped around a person and covers all the body.
—Sa'idu Yunus Ibrahim, *Matsayin Hijabi a Musulunci*, 1996

The booklet *Matsayin Hijabi a Musulunci* (The place of the hijab in Islam [Ibrahim 1996]), written in Hausa and published in Zaria in 1996, is an excellent example of the so-called ephemeral literature that is sold in market stalls and by itinerant booklet sellers throughout northern Nigeria. In it the author provides readers with an explanation of the importance of Muslim women's wearing of the hijab, followed by specific reasons and references to the Qur'an and other Islamic texts to support the author's position.

Although women had been covering themselves with *gyale* (a long, rectangular cloth used as a veil) at that time and earlier with handwoven *zane* (a large cover cloth or wrapper) when leaving their family compounds (Mahdi 2013, 170; Smith 1954), women began wearing the more body-encompassing and tailored hijab in order to protect themselves and their respectability when entering public spaces to attend Islamiyya classes. Nonetheless, some women faced problems when wearing this form of body covering because of its association with the reformist Izala movement: "When the hijab was first introduced, people said a lot of bad things about it. I can give you an example [from my own experience]. I have a hijab that goes to my feet. When people saw me with it, they said a lot of bad things. Some would say *tazarce* [like the long robes worn by the former president Sani Abacha]; some would say *takunkunmin Gumi* [shackles of Gumi]; some would say *rakata jahannama* [it will escort her to hell], and many bad things. This kind of thing happened to those who are wearing hijab" (interview, Zaria City, June 10, 2001).

As with other aspects of the Izala reforms, which became internalized as proper Islamic belief and practice by the movement's followers, Zaria City women began to reevaluate what was considered proper modest Muslim comportment in their community.[15] Indeed, the Izala malamai (teachers) encouraged the married women coming to their classes to wear the hijab because of their teaching of Qur'anic sura, which instructed women to cover themselves. They also supported the hijab for their students' protection, particularly when schools first began, as one Izala malam explained: "There are some schools, if the women went to school, if they lived nearby, some men used to stop them on their way. . . . The thing was serious. It was at that time that women were asked to wear hijab and to come to school in it. Because at the beginning, [we at] the school didn't care if women were [just] going out—they could wear any cloth they wanted. But if she's coming to school, she must be wearing a uniform— the hijab. But we didn't choose a specific cloth; she must just wear her hijab" (interview, Zaria City, September 1996).

This shift from the gyale veils, which could easily slip off and reveal parts of a woman's body, to the hijab reflects the tendency of religious reformers to represent themselves as purifying past practices (El Guindi 1999). Wearing a hijab allowed married Muslim women to extend their mobility by delineating what constituted a covered moral space outside of their homes so that they could acquire an Islamic education, taught by their Izala teachers (Renne 2013). Indeed, these teachers instructed them on the importance of wearing the hijab as part of Muslim moral practice. These teachings were explained by another Zaria City woman: "The Prophet Muhammad instructed us to wear the hijab because it completes the Islamic religion. . . . Sometimes the parents don't want [her to wear the] hijab. They may accuse the daughter because of the hijab, but if her husband agreed for her to wear it, she should not mind about what the father is saying" (interview, Zaria City, May 9, 2001).

As this woman's comments suggest, women's wearing of the hijab at times led to conflict within families. As the woman cited earlier explained, when she wore a long hijab, she was taunted with the phrase *shackles of Gumi*. By referring to the hijab in conjunction with Gumi, one of the founders of the Izala movement, those belonging to Qādiriyya and Tijāniyya groups expressed their dislike of Izala and its followers. This conflict was sometimes across generations, sometimes between spouses, and sometimes among women themselves. For example, when going to Islamiyya class, one woman was unable to put on her hijab until she had left her house because her father "didn't like hijab." Additionally, some husbands did not want their wives to wear hijab because they did not want them going out unaccompanied to attend Islamiyya Matan Aure classes. One woman who was married began to wear the hijab only when she moved back to her parents' home: "Really, my husband, he didn't like hijab, but since I came back home [to her parents' house], I sewed a hijab and started wearing it. It is three years now since I started wearing it. Nothing happened when I started wearing it. It only improved my respect. Hijab makes a woman appear more respectable [kwarjini]; bad people will not approach her" (interview, Zaria City, May 7, 2001).

Yet despite these initial confrontations, many women persisted in wearing the hijab when in public, when attending Islamiyya classes, and when praying in their houses (figure 5.1). Indeed, as women became accustomed to wearing the hijab, they became less and less comfortable wearing the gyale head covering or veil, with some women rejecting the gyale altogether: "Hijab protects a woman's body because it covers her back and front; any woman who shows her body has no respect. If she wears gyale and puts it on her neck, a small boy can come and talk to her. Everywhere I put my foot, everywhere I am going, I am going with hijab, not only if I am going to school. I don't even know how to use gyale" (interview, Zaria City, May 2, 2001; my emphasis).

For one woman, the idea of proper covering was internalized to the extent that she felt undressed in public if she was not wearing a hijab; she noted, "Wherever I go, I wear hijab because the time I attempted to wear gyale and cover my body, I felt like I was going naked" (interview, Zaria City, June 11, 2001, my emphasis; see also Meneley 2007, 231). This woman's comments also point to the particular gendered dynamics of public space and marriage, which are defused by wearing a hijab. Without proper covering of their bodies, women "invite" men to make sexual advances, which devalue her.

Aside from the shift away from wearing the gyale, which could slide off the head, revealing the neck and arms, to covering oneself securely with the hijab, the different types of gyale and hijab worn by women had different connotations. For example, several women mentioned certain sizes of hijab and gyale as being more proper than others: "If I am going to school, I wear hijab. If I am going someplace and there isn't a definite reason [to wear it, such as school], if I go out with gyale, I wear a big gyale that I think will not attract anyone to me" (interview, Zaria City, November 12, 2001). Thus, while gyale veils were seen at the time as sufficient for protecting women's modesty, they came to be seen as

FIGURE 5.1. Islamic book shop in Zaria City, with wall painting of a Muslim woman wearing hijab. By depicting the woman reading an Islamic text titled *Hijab*, the artist makes reference to the connection between her Islamic education and wearing the head covering in order to attend school. Zaria City, April 14, 2009. Photograph by author.

insufficient covering when women were attending Islamiyya classes and when they were saying their prayers. Eventually, even the short hijab came to be seen as inadequate covering; the long hijab, which covered a woman from head to toe, became required for women attending Islamiyya classes who were practicing modest Muslim comportment: "If you see a respected woman, you will recognize her by the way she dresses and the way she walks. She will dress as is accepted in Islam—she will wear hijab. . . . And she will walk calmly. At home, if she speaks, she will not raise her voice, and she will not talk of things that are not proper" (interview, Zaria City, June 10, 2001).

The women who attended Islamiyya Matan Aure classes described the many benefits of their attendance—for themselves and for their families—and explained why these classes are important to them. Knowing how to pray and knowing how to bathe and to perform one's ablutions properly were important, as was learning how to get along with husbands, cowives, other relatives, and neighbors with patience and without anger, which they also mentioned as benefits of attending Islamiyya classes.

Modesty, Comportment, and Gender

Wearing hijab when attending Islamiyya classes underscored the importance of women covering their bodies, as many, citing the Qur'an, have noted: "Tell the believing women to lower their eyes, guard their private parts, and not display their charms except what is apparent outwardly, and cover their bosoms with their veils and not to show their finery except to their husbands or their fathers" (Qur'an 24:31). Yet the preceding verse in the Qur'an, Sura 24:30, prescribed similar behavior for men: "Tell the believing men to lower their eyes and guard their private parts. There is for them goodness in this. God is aware of what they do."

Men's dress may reflect this admonition as well as other Qur'anic verses such as Sura 33:35, which praises men and women who are modest. For men, this choice of dress is exemplified by Gumi's "taste in clothing": "It was in the Sudan that I learnt to appreciate simple and functional clothing, as against very conspicuous and expensive ones. Since my return from Bakht-er-Ruda my clothes have been simple and inexpensive. I have always strived to wear clothes that, although decent, would never discourage a prospective student from approaching me, because he is scared by their flamboyance" (Gumi 1992, 67–68; see also Renne 2018, 160–161).

Thus, men associated with the Islamic reform group Izala cover their heads with a cap, which may or may not have a small strip of cloth wound around it—a type of head covering known as *hizami*, or "little turban"—while wearing a simple kaftan with pants. The women cover themselves with a hijab over a zane wrapper. As Gumi put it, "In fact, the total rejection of ostentation came to be the hallmark of Izala" (1992, 162). This embodiment of the Qur'anic prescriptions taught in Izala classes, reinforced through simplicity in dress, is also associated with performance of the hajj, particularly when pilgrims are in the state of ihram. As with Islamiyya classes, northern Nigerian Muslims learn new techniques of the body for the proper performance of the hajj through this form of moral education.

Pilgrimage Education, Techniques of the Body, and Dress in Mecca

One of the most important objectives of the Hajj is for us to learn how to do without all the lawful comforts and luxuries that we are accustomed to indulging in. This is why a pilgrim wears the sparest of clothing—a waistcloth and a shoulder cloth without any decoration or embellishment.
—Salman bin Fahad al-Oadah, *Alleviating the Difficulties of the Hajj*, 2006

While the ignorance reflected in some Nigerians' practices while on hajj catalyzed Bello and Gumi's initial establishment of Islamiyya schools in Kaduna (Gumi 1992), they also worked together to organize procedures for northern Nigerians' travel to Mecca (Loimeier 1997; Tangban 1991). After his appointment as *amir al-hajj* (leader of the pilgrimage) in 1975, Gumi sought to improve not only prospective pilgrims' knowledge of Islam but also their preparedness (*istita'a*) through administrative procedures associated with local government pilgrimage boards. "In 1984 the Buhari administration . . . introduced a 'test' for . . . all aspiring pilgrims [who] were required to demonstrate their command of a number of the essential prayers and knowledge of how the prayers were correctly performed" (*New Nigerian*, June 6, 1985, quoted in Loimeier 1997, 161).[16]

In Kano a school was established in 1982 by the Muslim Mothers' Association to train women in preparation for the hajj. Hajiya Rabi Wali, one of the woman founders of the association, explained this program:

One of the things that they were taught was the use of the hijab, especially during hajj. They had been wearing gyale, but the gyale can come off during prayers. The school training hours were as follows: From 8 am to 10 am, the women were given training in the necessary prayers. Then at the time of the Zuhir prayer, we called malamai and people from the Pilgrim Welfare Ministry to come see how we are helping these women and also so that the women would see the difference between men's and women's prayers. (We needed to involve men in the training; otherwise, they might say that we women were doing something radical or feminist.)

The practice Ka'aba we used in the hajj training school was made new every year. We used cardboard boxes to construct it. We also used a small oil drum to serve as jamra, where they learned how to stone Shaitan [Satan]. I continued teaching at the hajj school for women until the former governor Shekarau was elected in April 2007. Then he had the government do it at the transit camp near the Kano airport before they left for hajj. (interview, Kano, June 16, 2011; see also Renne 2018, 145)

With many more people performing hajj, each state provided pilgrims with printed cotton textiles for garments, which along with government flags would identify them, at least when they were not in the state of ihram, when men uniformly wore untailored white *harami* dress and women wore hijab and loosely tailored white *jellabiya* gowns (Okenwa 2016). Beginning in the mid-1960s, intending pilgrims followed a series of steps in order to travel to Mecca. They first obtained medical and vaccination certificates, after which they met with approved hajj agents (or their subagents) to pay and receive receipts for their transport costs (by air or, less frequently, by road). After these documents were obtained, pilgrims were given passports and visas for their travel. When traveling by air, they were expected to come to Kano airport a few days before the flights were to depart, where they stayed in a transit camp located at the airport grounds (Tangban 1991, 246). There they received printed materials and further instruction in hajj procedures.

Pilgrims' dress was one topic covered in this orientation, which had different stipulations for men and women. During the period of ihram, men pilgrims were not allowed to wear sewn garments but rather changed into the two-piece waist and shoulder cloths, also known as ihram (*harami* in Hausa) dress, along with open sandals (figure 5.2; Okenwa 2016). According to the author of a Saudi-produced booklet, *Alleviating the Difficulties of the Hajj*, which was distributed to Nigerian pilgrims: "The basis for the prohibition of wearing of sewn articles of clothing is the hadîth where a man asked the Prophet (peace be upon him) what a pilgrim must wear in the state of ihrām, to which he replied: 'He should not wear a shirt, nor a turban, nor pants, nor a cloak. He should not wear cloth that has been dyed with *wors* or saffron'" (bin Fahad al-Oadah 2006, 35).

Salman bin Fahad al-Oadah goes on to explain that this prescription for un-sewn cloth does not preclude sewing a torn cloth nor even wearing a pair of pants with the seams cut open. He cites "Ibn Taymiyah [who] wrote in *Sharh al-'Umdah*: 'If a pair of pants is cut open, it becomes the equivalent of a waistcloth.' What is most important is that the cloths worn 'are not sewn in the shape and size of the limb'" (36; see also Aḥmad 2000). Indeed, for many men pilgrims, the removal of tailored, sewn clothing and the donning of white ihram dress was "what truly meant hajj for us":

> For both my companions and myself it was the ihram that made the real transition from simple visit to pilgrimage. We helped each other don the two white cloths, the first tight around the hips and reaching the calves, the second thrown over the torso, leaving the right shoulder and arm free. The others helped me to fasten mine with a wide belt, also white, with pockets for keys, money, and papers. My head had to remain bare. On my feet, as prescribed, I put lightweight sandals with neither laces or buckles. After a major ablution of the body . . . I thus entered the state of ihram. (Hammoudi 2006, 120–121)

While the white ihram cloth might consist of several different types of textiles (except silk) in various states of repair, being present in Mecca among Muslims from all over the world dressed in the same simple way was a moving experience for many.

Yet wearing the ihram cloth is not always easy for men accustomed to wearing fitted, sewn garments, as Usman Liman explains with regard to the performance of *tawâf* as they circled around the Ka'aba:[17] "For us males, we were constantly struggling with our wrappers lest they get loose and fall off. One had no pants beneath. To stop moving with the flow of human traffic on the excuse that one want[ed] to retighten his wrapper is very dangerous. One may get knocked down and trampled underneath" (1996, 56).

While he describes the discomfort that he and other pilgrims wearing ihram dress experienced as they approached Mina, he also observed that it was coun-tered by the profound joy of performing the hajj: "Sweat was pouring down our backs and we were still not familiar with wrappers therefore it ought to have been uncomfortable for us. But the religious zeal in us was overpowering. The emotion was choking. The actual Hajj rituals have begun at last. How can one feel any discomfort?"

While women are also exposed to the extreme heat of the Saudi sun, there are no such specific prescriptions for women pilgrims' dress, except that they should cover their heads and bodies, without a veil touching their face. As Saleh

FIGURE 5.2. Nigerian men from Kaduna State wearing ihram during the 2008 hajj. Image courtesy of Alhaji Samaila Nabara (third from right).

Okenwa (2016) noted in his essay "Practical Steps in Performing the Hajj Rites," which is published on the National Hajj Commission of Nigeria website, "A woman can wear whatever she likes as long as it does not display her adornments or resemble men's clothing." The National Hajj Commission of Nigeria and other websites advise women on how to properly perform the hajj and what to wear while at Mecca. For example, in an article by Asma bint Shameem, "Common Mistakes Women Make during Hajj or Umrah," she addresses questions about appropriate dress. Women pilgrims are advised to dress modestly, wearing white garments, often *abaya* (gowns) and hijab, that do not cover their faces.[18]

Once pilgrims are no longer in the state of ihram, they may wear tailored clothing, which includes outfits that are sewn from printed cotton cloth (*atamfa*) given to them by their state Pilgrim Welfare Board (figure 5.3). These outfits represent another aspect of the regularization of hajj procedures for pilgrims as well as the organization for the increasing numbers of Nigerians traveling to Mecca.[19] According to the 2016 Kaduna State Pilgrim Welfare Board overseer, Alhaji Habib Umar Mahmud, earlier *atamfa hajji* (printed hajj) cloths

FIGURE 5.3. Kaduna State *hajiya* pilgrim wearing hijab made from the cloth used during the 2008 hajj in Shika, Nigeria. Photograph by author.

were produced by some of the textile mills in Kaduna, such as Arewa Textiles, Finetex, and United Nigerian Textiles Limited (UNTL) (interview, Kaduna, March 7, 2016). Owing to the closure or reduced productivity of these mills after 2010, the board has ordered these cloths from a textile firm in Kano, the African Textile Manufacturers Ltd. While the date printed on the cloth and the colors differ from year to year, the main patterning for each state is essentially the same, which helps pilgrims from different Nigerian states to identify each other among the many other pilgrims performing hajj.[20]

For both men and women, the performance of hajj can be one of the most significant events of their lives. For men, the donning of ihram dress represents a period of sanctity as well as prohibition of many worldly things: "'Ihram': a noun of action, the root, h-r-m, usually translated as 'sacred.' But it contains the sacred and the forbidden simultaneously. By shedding my ordinary clothes, I was entering into a state of forbidden sanctity" (Hammoudi 2006, 122). This echoes, in a way, Sa'idu Yunus Ibrahim's reference to the hijab as "a partition" (1996, 5). The Nigerian pilgrim Usman Liman explains his own transformative experience this way:

> In less than thirty minutes, we were at Zui-hulaifa. . . . We halted, took our bath, donned the *Ihram* garb, assumed the formal intention of the Umra and in less than one hour rowdy people were transformed into pious look- ing pilgrims. It was white dress upon white dress for everybody. It became difficult to recognise people. There was a strange uniformity. The cry of Labbaika! was all over the place. . . . Everytime I uttered that cry of Lab- baika! I felt an exhilarating feeling run through me, I felt a strange close- ness to my creator, the like of which I had never felt before. (1996, 54)

This sense of being at one with Allah and with one's fellow Muslims through the hajj was materialized through one's bodily movements and dress during the performance of ihram. As Abdellah Hammoudi explains, "*Ihram*, donning *ihram*, entering the state of *ihram*: that was the point. The 'visit' [*ziyara*, initially to Medina] had not required this treatment of my body and my self—surely better to say my body-self. Praying and going to mosque, sanctuary, and cem- etery had required ablutions, but one could wear ordinary dress" (2006, 121). For Muslim men, the two pieces of white cloth worn during ihram—which for some will be used as the shroud when they are buried—materially contributed to a sense of unity.[21]

Embodied Religion and Techniques of the Body in Northern Nigeria

> O, My servants, all of you are naked except for those I have clothed, so seek clothing of Me and I shall clothe you.
> —Hadith 24 in An-Nawawī, *40 Hadith*

> I would never stop if I tried to demonstrate to you all the facts that might be listed to make visible this concourse of the body and moral or intellectual symbols.
> —Marcel Mauss, "Techniques of the Body," 1973

Connections among bodies, cloth (material), and religion have long been made in practice, even while those who distinguish between the things of this world and spiritual beliefs often situate them in different spheres (Morgan 2010). Much as the body and its movements and gestures have often been ignored in the study of religions, which focuses on theological questions and conceptions of belief, there has also been a tendency to disregard associated material things. Yet as Birgit Meyer and Dick Houtman have noted with respect to more recent studies, "the antagonism between religion and things, spirituality and materiality, is a legacy of the 'religious past'" (2012, 2). Indeed, assumptions reflecting "a broader secularist idea of religion as interiorized and private" have tended to discount public expressions of religious belief as inappropriate or disingenuous (Meyer and Houtman 2012, 2; see also Moors 2012, 276). Replicating Durkheim's view of moral education as a secular process in France (known as laïcité), a wider view of state secularism may be seen in the French disapproval of Muslim women wearing the hijab in public.[22] Yet such public expressions and their bodily and material manifestations enable an understanding of the succession of Islamic reform movements in northern Nigeria. Meyer and Houtman suggest that "we can 'know' religion only, though not completely, through its past and present manifestations" (2012, 4). However, they also note the importance of examining "the particular forms and elements through which religion . . . materializes" (2012, 4). Both are useful frames for understanding Islamic reform movements in northern Nigeria. Islamic reformers there, from the nineteenth-century Shehu Usman dan Fodio to Abubakar Gumi in the twentieth century, have been concerned with material things such as veils and turbans, dress and bodily comportment. These things have long been part of the public sphere of religious expression of belief and of moral Islamic education.[23] Even in the distinction between this world (duniya) and the afterlife in Paradise (Lahira da Aljannat)—a critically important matter in the writings of northern Nigerian Muslim scholars—this contrast was represented at times by material things, specifically through textiles, clothing, and the body. Thus, the nineteenth-century Fulani writer Muhammadu Tukur, in his poem "Black Leg-Irons," described both the transience of life in this world and the eternal life in Paradise in terms of cloth. In the former, "the weaver of fine black and white cloth [saki] and the weaver of open-work cloth too, are today no more, only the spider who weaves to give [to] the monkey" (Turkur, quoted in Hiskett 1975a, 33). In Paradise, however, "fine clothes will be bought and will be laid out for the Believers, that we may mount, horses and camels, clothes of silk" (35). This poetic connection among moral states, bodily comportment, and textiles underscores the spiritual and material intersections with which

Islamic reformers in northern Nigeria have historically conceptualized a proper Islamic path.

Such beliefs and actions are learned—intentionally or by imitation. As Marcel Mauss has observed, "The teaching of techniques being essential, we can classify them according to the nature of this education and training" (1973, 78). Mauss makes this point more clearly in his discussion of techniques of the body and moral education: "In all these elements of the art of using the human body, the facts of *education* were dominant. The notion of education could be superimposed on that of imitation. . . . What takes place is a prestigious imitation. The child, the adult, imitates actions that have succeeded, which he has seen successfully performed by people in whom he has confidence and who have authority over him. . . . The individual borrows the series of movements of which he is composed from the action executed in front of him, or with him, by others" (73). Indeed, Mauss noted the relationship between bodies and belief, between moral education and bodily practices, which has implications for observant Muslims, when he remarked that "a pious Muslim can easily be recognized . . . [as] he will go to any lengths to avoid using anything but his right hand" (1973, 78).

In northern Nigeria this connection between learned body techniques and Islamic education may be seen clearly in the practices of men performing hajj and their wearing of ihram dress and in women's attendance at Islamiyya Matan Aure and their wearing of hijab. Furthermore, the importance of modesty of demeanor for both women and men, as prescribed in the Qur'an and in Lemu's introduction to the *Tahdhib (Moral Education) and Sirah*, suggests Mauss's point that particular techniques of the body that subject the body to "tests of stoicism" may serve as a measure of moral education: "I think that the basic education in all these techniques consists of an adaptation of the body to their use. For example, the great tests of stoicism, etc., which constitute initiation for the majority of mankind, have as their aim to teach composure, resistance, seriousness, presence of mind, dignity, etc." (1973, 86).

The many restrictions on body covering, movement, bathing, and intercourse expected of those performing ihram during the hajj pilgrimage would seem to contribute to the internalization of composure and seriousness, as when "rowdy people were transformed into pious looking pilgrims," as Liman (1996, 54) described.[24] Similarly, women who have attended Islamiyya Matan Aure classes in Zaria City associate postures of piety ("she will walk calmly") and modesty with covering their bodies with cloth ("you will recognize her by the way she dresses . . . as is accepted in Islam—she will wear hijab").

Conclusion

The historian Yedida Kalfon Stillman has observed the importance of covering the body in accordance with prevailing Islamic precepts as well as the ways changing beliefs and practices associated with Islamic reform are reflected in Muslim women's veiling practices: "One important force contributing to reveiling in one form or another has been the Islamist movements, both militant and non-militant. These movements . . . represent an alternative to secularism on the one hand and institutional Islam on the other. Irrespective of their political activities, all of these groups advocate a return to a holistic Islamic way of life and to Islamic traditional values, which include inter alia a traditional code of modesty and gender differentiation. One of the primary external markers of the latter is *al-zayy al Islami* or *al-zayy al-Shari'i* (Islamic or Shar'i attire)" (2000, 158).[25]

In northern Nigeria successive Islamic reform movements have supported distinctions in body coverings among their followers. For example, Shi'a Muslim men of the Brotherhood Movement of Nigeria wear round turbans, while Izala men wear "little turbans," caps wound round with hizami cloth. Yet the hijab has become more widely worn by Muslim women from several Islamic reformist groups—both Shi'a and Izala—although they may differ in style and color (Renne 2013). Indeed, the hijab is no longer strictly associated with the followers of these two Islamic movements but is also prescribed as the proper dress for northern Nigerian women during the performance of the hajj pilgrimage. Thus, covering the head and body with the hijab has become an important expression of their identity for many Muslim women from different Islamic groups in northern Nigeria. Similarly, Muslim men from a range of Islamic groups, ethnicities, and national backgrounds cover their bodies with two ihram cloths in particular specified ways during hajj. In both cases, the intimate connection between Muslim bodies and cloth evokes broader embodied meanings, as Hammoudi explains. During his experience of entering "the 'sacred-forbidden' territory" associated with the state of ihram, "the body—when it foregoes its limits, the clear configuration bestowed on it by tailored clothing—projects itself into a transforming time and space" (2006, 123–124).[26] His sense that his body "might be absorbed in bits and pieces, or dissolve," suggests his feeling of being in a space without boundaries and out of time, of merging with his fellow pilgrims of whatever background, while also suggesting the intimate relationship between his body and its cloth covering. However, the gendered differentiation favored by Islamic reformers may be seen clearly in the uncovered heads of men wearing ihram cloths and the covered heads of women wearing hijab and jellabiya gowns. Yet despite these distinctive gendered body coverings, the particular actions performed while in the state of ihram reflect the piety and humility of all human beings before Allah. Learned in hajj preparatory classes, such actions are related to everyday ideals of modest comportment—taught in Islamiyya classes as well as incorporated through "prestigious imitation," as described by Mauss (1973, 73). These bodily practices are prescribed in the Qur'an for both women and men. That leaders of Islamic reform movements, such as Izala in northern Nigeria, frequently aspire to a return to particular forms of moral education that are associated with the fundamentals of the Muslim faith and that support simplicity in dress and comportment suggests the importance of cloth in this process (Schneider and Weiner 1986). By both internalizing and visually expressing these beliefs, the comportment of covered bodies contributes to the material embodiment of Islamic reform, as the verses from Sura 74 (The Enfolded) that began this chapter suggest they should.

ACKNOWLEDGMENTS

I would like to thank the women of Zaria City for their cooperation and helpful interviews and Hassana Yusuf for her assiduous research assistance over the years. I also thank the late Emir of Zazzau, Dr. Shehu Idris CFR, and the present Emir of Zazzau, Ambassador Ahmed Nuhu Bamalli, for their permission to conduct research in Zaria City as well as the vice chancellor of Ahmadu Bello University for research affiliation over the years. Finally, I am grateful for funding from the National Science Foundation for research on women's Islamic education and to the Pasold Foundation for research on the history of head coverings in Zaria.

NOTES

1. According to An-Nawawī (1991, 7), the hadith are a collection of the "recorded words, actions and sanctions of the Prophet Muhammad," which represents one of the two main sources of Islamic knowledge (the other is the Qur'an). The passages from the Qur'an cited in this chapter come from Ali Ahmed's translation, published in 1993.

2. Zaria is also the home of the emir of Zaria, whose palace is located in Zaria City, the old walled portion of the larger city of Zaria. As such, Zaria is a center of both traditional Hausa practices—evidenced by the annual Sallah durbars associated with the Muslim holidays of Eid-el-Fitr and Eid-el-Kabir—and extensive Islamic learning.

3. The Tijāniyya Brotherhood (tariqa) is one of the two main Sufi brotherhoods in northern Nigeria (Mustapha 2014, 4). It was founded by Sheikh Ahmad al-Tijani, who later established a zawiyah (prayer group) in Fez, Morocco, in 1781 (Mustapha and Bunza

2014, 61). Tijāniyya doctrine later spread to northern Nigeria through the teachings of al-Hajj 'Umar al-Futi, who first visited Sokoto in 1825 on his way to and from Mecca (Hiskett 1984, 251). Later, the reformed Tijāniyya leader Sheikh Ibrahim Niass, from Senegal, first publicly visited Kano in 1945. His first large public appearance in Kano then took place in 1951, when "thousands of followers of the Tijāniyya from all over Northern Nigeria had come to Kano to meet him" (Loimeier 1997, 40).

4. The National Hajj Commission of Nigeria website can be found at http://nigeriahajjcom.gov.ng / (accessed April 25, 2016).

5. The five pillars of Islam are *shahāda* (faith), *salāt* (prayer), *zakāt* (charity), *sawm* (fasting), and hajj (pilgrimage to Mecca).

6. This is not to say that Gumi and other Izala officials—unlike later Islamic reformers associated with the group Jamā'atu Ahlus-Sunnah Lidda'Awati Wal Jihād, more commonly known as Boko Haram (translated as "Western education is forbidden")—were opposed to Western education. However, they believed that Islamic education was the basis of a moral education in northern Nigeria.

7. See Jeremiah Oke, "Hijab Crisis Hits LAUTECH International School," *Daily Trust*, January 14, 2019, https://www.dailytrust.com.ng/hijab-crisis-hits-lautech-international -school.html.

8. In a related way, Susan O'Brien (2006, 302) notes that Michel Foucault (in volume 1 of his *History of Sexuality*) "has suggested that modern state power is not so much imposed on populations as absorbed into society through the capillary 'actions' of the human sciences and social techniques that permeate the conduct of everyday life."

9. The connection between mothers' Islamic education and the early training of their children has been a concern in other Muslim reformist communities, as Omnia Shakry notes regarding the moral education of mothers and children in Egypt: "Islamist reformers were able to draw upon resources indigenous to the Islamic discursive tradition that emphasized the proper pedagogy for children, the cultivation of the body, and the constitution of a rightly guided Islamic community" (1998, 128).

10. For example, Qur'an 20:114 reads: "Exalted then be God, the real King; and do not try to anticipate the Qur'ān before the completion of its revelation, but pray: 'O Lord, give me greater knowledge'" (see also Hadith 36, An-Nawawī 1991, 104). The Qādiriyya tariqa, the other main Sufi brotherhood in northern Nigeria, is associated with the founding of the nineteenth-century Sokoto Caliphate (Last 1967).

11. For more detailed accounts of the Izala movement and its founding in Nigeria, see Gumi (1992, 156), Kane (2003), Loimeier (1997, 212), Mustapha and Bunza (2014), and Umar (1993, 167).

12. Some of this resistance reflected the responses of Qādiriyya and Tijāniyya Muslims, who predominated in particular wards of the old city and resented the implicit (and at times scathingly explicit) criticism of their practice of Islam by Gumi and other members of Izala. This tension was evident in control over Friday mosques and the affiliation of imams leading the Friday prayer. Roman Loimeier (1997, 271) notes that control of Friday mosques by Qādiriyya and Tijāniyya leaders within Zaria City led Izala supporters to construct new Friday mosques outside of the old city; see also Kane (2003, 90) and Umar (1993, 174).

13. Elsewhere in northern Nigeria, Muslims are more likely to be associated with Tijāniyya and Qādiriyya groups, while many simply identify themselves as Muslims, according to a poll conducted in 2008–2009 (Ostien 2018, 42–45).

14. Qur'anic literacy also potentially enables alternative readings of this text. For example, one Islamic woman scholar in Jos uses her considerable knowledge of the Qur'an and hadith to support her more liberal view of women's place in public life; see Umar (2004, 117–118) and also Yusuf (1991, 95).

15. Jeanette Jouili (2015) examines the challenges of veiling for Muslim women born in France and living in a secular society that forbids the wearing of headscarves in school and, as of 2011, the full-face veil, niqab, in public. See Scott (2007) and Matthew Weaver, "Burqa Bans, Headscarves and Veils: A Timeline of Legislation in the West," *Guardian*, March 14, 2017, https://www.theguardian.com/world/2017/mar/14/headscarves-and-muslim-veil-ban-debate-timeline. However, some of the same challenges may be faced by Muslim women living in other societies, even those with large Muslim populations, such as northern Nigeria. For example, in March 2009 a controversy arose at Ahmadu Bello University Teaching Hospital, Zaria, when a nurse was dismissed for wearing a hijab that was longer than the prescribed shoulder length. Several people in the Zaria community saw her dismissal as anti-Islamic, while others argued that the hospital had accommodated Muslim women's request to wear a hijab as part of the nursing uniform. In April 2009 the nurse was reinstated and allowed to wear her breast-length hijab. Isa Sa'idu and Aliyu Yusuf, "Hijab: ABUTH to Reinstate Nurse," *Daily Trust*, April 22, 2009, www.dailytrust.com.ng.

16. Abdellah Hammoudi (2006, 41–52) described in some detail his attendance at the "training program for pilgrims of the year A.H. 1419/1999," organized by the Moroccan Ministry of Islamic Affairs in Rabat.

17. The *tawâf al-Ifâdah* is "the second essential pillar of Hajj." According to bin Fahad al-Oadah, "the Qur'ân clearly states: 'Then let them complete the rites prescribed for them, perform their vows, and circumambulate the Ancient House' [Sûrah al-Hajj: 29] The verse makes the tawâf the last of these rites" (2006, 47).

18. Asma bint Shameem, "Common Mistakes Women Make during Hajj or Umrah," Muslim Matters, October 20, 2011. Accessed March 22, 2018, https://www.muslimmatters.org/2011/10/20/common-mistakes-women-make-during-hajj-or-umrah/.

19. One sticking point for Saudi officials was the issue of the many undocumented Nigerian pilgrims (known as *tikari* or *takari*; Liman 1996, 39; Peters 1994, 96) who had overstayed the hajj period and were working in Mecca, Medina, and Jeddah. However, another perspective on the at times fraught relations between Saudi citizens and Nigerian workers is examined in the novel *From Fatika with Love* (Giwa 2012). In Sudan, undocumented Nigerian pilgrims who either chose to remain to work until they could afford the return journey or chose to remain in Sudan are referred to as *fellata*, "a term with some negative connotations used by the Sudanese to denote West African Muslims" (Yamba 1995, 204). (The term *fellata* derives from the names Fula, Fulah, Fulani, or Fulbe, referring to an ethnic group in West Africa.) Bruce Hall (2011) discusses the social hierarchy among Muslims in West Africa and its historical background associated with race.

20. This distinction by state rather than simply by nationality is unusual, as Liman (disapprovingly) observed: "I noticed that we Nigerians come in all colours of uniform. Red, Blue, Brown, Grey, Pink etc. Every state has its own different colour and style of sewing. So much so that we now look at only pilgrims from our own particular state as our 'people'. Whereas all other countries come in one single uniform colour. . . . But we Nigerians . . . carry the issue of stateism to a ridiculous extent" (1996, 42–43).

21. Some men in Zaria told me that they have kept their ihram cloths to be used as their shrouds when they are buried. Hammoudi (2006, 43) quotes the scholar leading the training program for pilgrims in Rabat, Morocco: "'At Arafat you are before God, and *ihram* is your shroud. Between the hands of the All Powerful, the Eternal, nothing can help you, not riches, not prestige!'"

22. For example, in February 2019, plans by Decathlon, Europe's largest sporting goods retailer, to sell a sports hijab were stopped after the company received many negative calls and emails, while some Decathlon salespeople were threatened. Elian Peltier and Aurelien Breeden, "A Sports Hijab Has France Debating the Muslim Veil, Again," *New York Times*, February 28, 2019, https://www.nytimes.com/2019/02/28/world/europe /france-sports-hijab-decathlon.html.

23. Shehu dan Fodio wrote and spoke on several occasions about the evils of ostentatious wealth in his work *Bayān Wujūb al-Hijra ʿala ʾl-ʿIbad* (1978), while Gumi insisted that members of the reform group Izala desist from bowing down "in front of the shuyukh of the turuq because this act of veneration violated the principle of equality among the faithful" (Loimeier 1997, 254–255).

24. Liman (1996, 28) provides a detailed description of the daily activities and interactions of the Nigerians in his pilgrimage group, which included an elderly Izala sheikh: "We had a 'Mallam'—a Shayk [Sheikh] in the room. He was the one we used for translation services when we were looking for the accommodation. He was fairly elderly with more than half his face covered by thick, bushy, grey beard. Always ready and eager to preach, he belonged to the extreme Izala group. Any little thing, they say: 'Ai, wannan kafirci ne' [Ay, that is un-Islamic]. We all unanimously agreed to call him 'Allaramma'" (an honorific form of address to important malams; see Skinner 1993, 1230). Liman's remark provides another perspective on Izala Muslims.

25. See also Ahmed (2011), Jouili (2015), Mahmood (2005), and Tarlo (2010) for discussions of women's increasing use of veils in the United States, France, Egypt, and the United Kingdom.

26. A pilgrim must enter into this state of ihram before crossing the pilgrimage boundary, known as *Miqat*.

REFERENCES

Ahmad, Saʿid. 2000. *Teacher of the Hajj Pilgrims*. Translated by Rafiq Abdur Rehman. Karachi: Darul-Ishaat.

Ahmed, Leila. 2011. *A Quiet Revolution: The Veil's Resurgence, from the Middle East to America*. New Haven, CT: Yale University Press.

Al-Qurʾān. 1993. Translated by Ali Ahmed. Princeton, NJ: Princeton University Press.

An-Nawawī. 1991. *40 Hadith*. Translated by Ezzeddin Ibrahim and Denys Johnson-Davies. Kaduna, Nigeria: Kauran Wali Islamic Bookshop.

Beidelman, T. O. 1986. *Moral Imagination in Kaguru Modes of Thought*. Bloomington: Indiana University Press.

Beidelman, T. O. 1997. *The Cool Knife: Imagery of Gender, Sexuality, and Moral Education in Kaguru Initiation Ritual*. Washington, DC: Smithsonian Institution Press.

bin Fahad al-Oadah, Salman. 2006. *Alleviating the Difficulties of the Hajj*. Riyadh: Islam Today.

Bourdieu, Pierre. 1967. "Systems of Education and Systems of Thought." *International Social Science Journal* 19 (3): 338–358.

Boyd, Jean. 1989. *The Caliph's Sister: Nana Asma'u, 1793–1865, Teacher, Poet, and Islamic Leader*. London: F. Cass.

Boyd, Jean. 1997. "*We Teach Girls That It Is Wrong to Carry Babies on Their Backs!* Or How Inappropriate Policies Damaged Girls' Education in Colonial Era." In *Islam and the History of Learning in Katsina*, edited by Ismaila Abubakar Tsiga and Abdalla Uba Adamu, 105–117. Ibadan, Nigeria: Spectrum Books.

Boyd, Jean, and Murray Last. 1985. "The Role of Women as Agents Religieux in Sokoto." *Canadian Journal of African Studies* 19 (2): 283–300.

Bray, Mark. 1981. *Universal Primary Education in Nigeria: A Study of Kano State*. London: Routledge.

Covington-Ward, Yolanda. 2016. *Gesture and Power: Religion, Nationalism, and Everyday Performance in Congo*. Durham, NC: Duke University Press.

dan Fodio, Shehu Usman [Uthman]. 1975. "Islam and Women." In *Nigerian Perspectives: An Historical Anthology*, edited by Thomas Hodgkin, 254–255. London: Oxford University Press.

dan Fodio, Uthman [Usman]. 1978. *Bayan Wujub al-Hijra 'ala 'l-Ibad*. Edited and translated by F. H. El Masri. Khartoum: Khartoum University Press.

Durkheim, Émile. 1961. *Moral Education: A Study in the Theory and Application of the Sociology of Education*. New York: Free Press.

El Guindi, Fadwa. 1999. *Veil: Modesty, Privacy, and Resistance*. Oxford, UK: Berg.

Funtua, S. A. 1980. "Jama'atu Isalatil Bidia wa Ikamatis Sunna Society in Nigeria." BA thesis, Kano.

Giwa, Audee. 2012. *From Fatika with Love*. Kaduna, Nigeria: Bookmakers International.

Graham, Sonia. 1966. *Government and Mission Education in Northern Nigeria, 1900–1919*. Ibadan, Nigeria: University of Ibadan Press.

Gumi, Abubakar. 1992. *Where I Stand*. With Ismaila Abubakar Tsiga. Ibadan, Nigeria: Spectrum Books.

Hall, Bruce. 2011. *A History of Race in Muslim West Africa, 1600–1960*. Cambridge: Cambridge University Press.

Hammoudi, Abdellah. 2006. *A Season in Mecca*. Translated by Pascale Ghazaleh. New York: Hill and Wang.

Hiskett, Mervyn. 1973. *The Sword of Truth: The Life and Times of Shehu Usuman Dan Fodio*. New York: Oxford University Press.

Hiskett, Mervyn. 1975a. *A History of Hausa Islamic Verse*. London: School of Oriental and African Studies, University of London.

Hiskett, Mervyn. 1975b. "Islamic Education in the Tradition and State Systems in Northern Nigeria." In *Conflict and Harmony in Education in Tropical Africa*, edited by Godfrey N. Brown and Mervyn Hiskett, 134–152. London: George Allen and Unwin.

Hiskett, Mervyn. 1984. *The Development of Islam in West Africa*. London: Longman.

Ibrahim, Sa'idu Yunus. 1996. *Matsayin Hijabi a Musulunci*. Zaria, Nigeria: HudaHuda.

Jouili, Jeanette. 2015. *Pious Practice and Secular Constraints: Women in the Islamic Revival in Europe*. Stanford, CA: Stanford University Press.

Kane, Ousmane. 2003. *Muslim Modernity in Post-colonial Nigeria*. Leiden: Brill.

Last, Murray. 1967. *The Sokoto Caliphate*. London: Longman.

Lawson, Fatima. 1995. "Islamic Fundamentalism and Continuing Education for Hausa Muslim Women in Northern Nigeria." PhD diss., University of Minnesota, Minneapolis.

Lemu, B. Aisha. 1986. *Tahdhib (Moral Education) and Sirah*. Junior Islamic Studies, bk. 3. Minna, Nigeria: Islamic Education Trust.

Liman, Usman. 1996. *Hajj 91: Travel Notes of a Nigerian Pilgrim*. Zaria, Nigeria: Ashel Enterprises.

Loimeier, Roman. 1997. *Islamic Reform and Political Change in Northern Nigeria*. Chicago: Northwestern University Press.

Mack, Beverly, and Jean Boyd. 2000. *One Woman's Jihad: Nana Asma'u, Scholar and Scribe*. Bloomington: Indiana University Press.

Mahdi, Hauwa. 2013. "Invoking *Hijab*: The Power Politics of Spaces and Employment in Nigeria." In *Veiling in Africa*, edited by Elisha P. Renne, 165–185. Bloomington: Indiana University Press.

Mahmood, Saba. 2005. *Politics of Piety: The Islamic Revival and the Feminist Subject*. Princeton, NJ: Princeton University Press.

Mauss, Marcel. 1973. "Techniques of the Body." *Economy and Society* 2 (1): 70–88.

Meneley, Anne. 2007. "Fashions and Fundamentalisms in Fin-de-Siècle Yemen: Chador Barbie and Islamic Socks." *Cultural Anthropology* 22 (2): 214–243.

Meyer, Birgit, and Dick Houtman. 2012. Introduction to *Things: Religion and the Question of Materiality*, edited by Dick Houtman and Birgit Meyer, 1–23. New York: Fordham University Press.

Moors, Annelies. 2012. "Popularizing Islam: Muslims and Materiality—Introduction." *Material Religion* 8 (3): 272–279.

Morgan, David. 2010. *Religion and Material Culture: The Matter of Belief*. New York: Routledge.

Muhammed, A. Y. 1997. "Contemporary Islamic Learning in Katsina: The Contributions of *Riyadhul-Qur'an Islamiyyah* School." In *Islam and the History of Learning in Katsina*, edited by Ismaila Abubakar Tsiga and Abdalla Uba Adamu, 191–199. Ibadan, Nigeria: Spectrum Books.

Mustapha, Abdul Raufu. 2014. Introduction to *Sects and Social Disorder: Muslim Identities and Conflict in Northern Nigeria*, edited by Abdul Raufu Mustapha, 1–15. Woodbridge, UK: Currey.

Mustapha, Abdul Raufu, and Mukhtar Bunza. 2014. "Contemporary Islamic Sects and Groups in Northern Nigeria." In *Sects and Social Disorder: Muslim Identities and Conflict in Northern Nigeria*, edited by Abdul Raufu Mustapha, 54–97. Woodbridge, UK: Currey.

O'Brien, Susan. 2006. "Spirit Discipline: Gender, Islam, and Hierarchies of Treatment in Postcolonial Northern Nigeria." In *Discipline and the Other Body: Correction, Corporeality, Colonialism*, edited by Anupama Rao and Steven Pierce, 273–302. Durham, NC: Duke University Press.

Ogunbiyi, I. A. 1969. "The Position of Women as Stated by 'Uthman b. Fudi." *Odu*, n.s., 2:43–60.

Okenwa, Saleh. 2016. "Practical Steps in Performing the Hajj Rites." National Hajj Commission of Nigeria (NAHCON). Accessed April 25, 2016, http://nigeriahajjcom .gov.ng/.

Ostien, Philip. 2018. "The Muslim Majority in Northern Nigeria: Sects and Trends." In *Creed and Grievance: Muslim-Christian Relations and Conflict Resolution in Northern Nigeria*, edited by Abdul Mustapha and David Ehrhardt, 37–82. Woodbridge, UK: Currey.

Peters, F. E. 1994. *The Hajj: The Muslim Pilgrimage to Mecca and the Holy Places*. Princeton, NJ: Princeton University Press.

Renne, Elisha P. 2012. "Educating Muslim Women and the Izala Movement in Zaria City, Nigeria." *Islamic Africa* 3 (1): 55–86. https://doi.org/10.5192/21540993030155.

Renne, Elisha P. 2013. "The Hijab as Moral Space in Northern Nigeria." In *African Dress: Fashion, Agency, Performance*, edited by Karen T. Hansen and D. Soyini Madison, 92–107. Oxford, UK: Bloomsbury Academic.

Renne, Elisha P. 2018. *Veils, Turbans, and Islamic Reform in Northern Nigeria*. Bloomington: Indiana University Press.

Rousseau, Jean-Jacques. 1979. *Émile, or On Education*. Translated by Allan Bloom. New York: Basic Books.

Schneider, Jane, and Annette Weiner. 1986. "Cloth and the Organization of Human Experience." *Current Anthropology* 27 (2): 178–184.

Scott, Joan. 2007. *The Politics of the Veil*. Princeton, NJ: Princeton University Press.

Shakry, Omnia. 1998. "Schooled Mothers and Structured Play: Child Rearing in Turn-of-the-Century Egypt." In *Remaking Women: Feminism and Modernity in the Middle East*, edited by Lila Abu-Lughod, 126–170. Princeton, NJ: Princeton University Press.

Skinner, A. N. 1993. "Supplement." In *A Hausa-English Dictionary*, edited by G. P. Bargery, 1230. Zaria, Nigeria: Ahmadu Bello University Press.

Smith, Mary. 1954. *Baba of Karo: A Woman of the Muslim Hausa*. New Haven, CT: Yale University Press.

Stillman, Yedida Kalfon. 2000. *Arab Dress: A Short History from the Dawn of Islam to Modern Times*. Edited by Norman A. Stillman. Leiden: Brill.

Tangban, O. E. 1991. "The Hajj and the Nigerian Economy, 1960–1981." *Journal of Religion in Africa* 21 (3): 241–255.

Tarlo, Emma. 2010. *Visibly Muslim: Fashion, Politics, Faith*. Oxford, UK: Berg.

Tibenderana, Peter Kazenga. 1985. "The Beginnings of Girls' Education in the Native Administration Schools in Northern Nigeria, 1930–1945." *Journal of African History* 26 (1): 93–109.

Trevor, Jean. 1975. "Western Education and Muslim Fulani/Hausa Women in Sokoto, Northern Nigeria." In *Conflict and Harmony in Education in Tropical Africa*, edited by Godfrey N. Brown and Mervyn Hiskett, 247–270. London: Allen and Unwin.

Tukur, B. 1963. "Koranic Schools in Northern Nigeria." *West African Journal of Education* 7 (3): 149–152.

Umar, Muhammad. 1993. "Changing Islamic Identity in Nigeria from the 1960s to the 1980s: From Sufism to Anti-Sufism." In *Muslim Identity and Social Change in Sub-Saharan Africa*, edited by Louis Brenner, 154–178. London: Hurst.

Umar, Muhammad. 2001. "Education and Islamic Trends in Northern Nigeria: 1970s–1990s." *Africa Today* 48 (2): 127–150.

Umar, Muhammad. 2004. "Mass Islamic Education and Emergence of Female 'Ulamā' in Northern Nigeria: Backgrounds, Trends, and Consequences." In *The Transmission of Learning in Islamic Africa*, edited by Scott S. Reese, 99–120. Leiden: Brill.

Ware, Rudolph T., III. 2014. *The Walking Qur'an: Islamic Education, Embodied Knowledge, and History in West Africa*. Chapel Hill: University of North Carolina Press.

Yamba, Bawa. 1995. *Permanent Pilgrims: The Role of Pilgrimage in the Lives of West African Muslims in Sudan*. Edinburgh: Edinburgh University Press.

Yandaki, A. I. 1997. "The *Izala* Movement and Islamic Intellectual Discourse in Northern Nigeria: A Case Study of Katsina." In *Islam and the History of Learning in Katsina*, edited by Ismaila Abubakar Tsiga and Abdalla Uba Adamu, 40–52. Ibadan, Nigeria: Spectrum Books.

Yusuf, Bilkisu. 1991. "Hausa-Fulani Women: The State of the Struggle." In *Hausa Women in the Twentieth Century*, edited by Catherine Coles and Beverly Mack, 90–106. Madison: University of Wisconsin Press.

6. Embodied Worship in a Haitian Protestant Church in the Bahamas: Religious Habitus among Bahamians of Haitian Descent

BERTIN M. LOUIS JR.

In 2021 Haitians constitute the largest immigrant group in the Bahamas, where they are highly stigmatized owing to their large representation in Bahamian society and their unique cultural and historical heritage.[1] Many Haitians turn to religious practice as a way to counter normative exploitation, humiliation, and marginalization. Traditionally, Haitians have practiced Catholicism and Vodou. But now Protestant forms of Christianity are flourishing in the Haitian diaspora in the Bahamas (Louis 2014).

The observations and analyses presented in this chapter emerge from ethnographic research conducted in New Providence (Nassau), Bahamas, in 2005 and a research trip to New Providence for two and half weeks in the summer of 2012 (late June and early July), where I collected ethnographic data (through participant observation and interviews) for a project on de facto stateless Haitians.[2] To conduct studies on Haitians in the Bahamas, researchers usually go through Haitian churches to find participants (see College of the Bahamas 2005; Louis 2014; Perry 2017). Haitian Protestantism is on the rise among migrants in the Bahamas, and most Haitians attend Baptist, charismatic, Nazarene, Pentecostal, and other Protestant churches. In a 2005 survey concerning the religion they practiced, 27.7 percent of Haitians interviewed in the Bahamas replied Catholic, whereas 29.1 percent claimed to be Anglican, Baptist, or Pentecostal (College of the Bahamas 2005, 100). These figures suggest a new religious plurality among Haitians in the Bahamas, whereas in 1979 geographer Dawn Marshall (1979, xiii) remarked that the typical Haitian migrant was "almost certainly a Roman Catholic." Haitians attend church to maintain their premigratory religiosity. They also attend church owing to the strong Christian religious culture of the Bahamas and the centrality of church life to Bahamian social life. This, in turn, makes Haitian Protestant and Catholic churches the premier institutions that serve various Haitian needs (spiritual, emotional, financial, and political).

In this chapter I focus on the embodied worship of Bahamians of Haitian descent—people of Haitian parentage born in the Bahamas who are stateless and become Bahamian citizens after the age of eighteen—through the concept of religious habitus: dispositions that are internalized by adherents and reflect particular forms of religiosity. I argue that the development of the religious habitus of Bahamians of Haitian descent through varying forms of embodied worship combines Haitian and Bahamian elements and serves as a key component of an eventual Bahamian identity that partly requires them to be Christians, as the majority of Bahamians identify as Christian. I focus on these sociocultural processes at Victory Chapel Church of the Nazarene, a church founded to minister to the population of Haitian Bahamians. Haitian Protestant hymnody, liturgical dance, and prayer reflect social processes of individual and collective self-remaking through linguistic and embodied practices, which allow Bahamians of Haitian descent to negotiate their different contested identities. In particular, Bahamians of Haitian descent develop a unique, hybrid Christian habitus, both embodied and linguistic, that is developed through bodily and spiritual practices. This, in turn, is part of a dynamic ongoing process that helps them negotiate cultural belonging in the Bahamas (Chong 2015, 109). The religious practices of my interlocutors also demonstrate that religious habitus in practice is more malleable than the late sociologist Pierre Bourdieu's (1977) theoretical conceptualization of habitus as solely unconscious, unalterable behavioral internalization would suggest. As my ethnographic research demonstrates, religious habitus can be altered and can reflect self-conscious changes that differ from traditional expectations of how one is supposed to act, behave, and worship within particular religious spaces (Mahmood 2001).

First, I discuss religious habitus. Then, I cover Haitian migration to the Bahamas, Bahamian identity, and Haitian identity formation in the Bahamas. The chapter concludes with a discussion of Protestant Christianity as a religious choice for Haitians and of the religious habitus at Victory Chapel Church of the Nazarene, a church focused on saving the souls of children of Haitian descent while providing them with a Christian-based sense of dignity to comprehend, combat, and withstand the normative degradation of their Haitian-based identities.

Religious Habitus

This chapter looks at the development of religious habitus through embodied worship at Victory Chapel Church of the Nazarene, where Bahamians of Haitian descent worship within the larger context of the Black, Christian, and xenophobic Bahamas. I use Bourdieu's (1977) work on habitus, which allows us to better understand the processes and effects associated with the internalization of religious experience, with attention to perception and phenomenological experience. In their work on Haitian religion in Miami, Florida, anthropologist Terry Rey and sociologist Alex Stepick (2013, 8–9) add that habitus is also, according to Bourdieu, the "matrix of perception" through which one makes sense of the world and the seat or generator of one's dispositions, inclinations, and tastes. Habitus is also fundamentally about "perception and inclination."

Rey and Stepick also understand religious habitus in relation to a Haitian religious *collusio* (the field within which people interact). Rey and Stepick (2013) argue that this religious collusio is a shared substratum of features that runs beneath the three major religions practiced in Haiti and its diaspora: Catholicism, Protestantism, and Vodou. This religious collusio unites Haitians across denominational and religious differences despite the antagonisms that invariably occur through the interaction of the different religions, their historical interplay, and the subsequent habitus produced from regularized inculcation in each varying religious tradition. Specifically, the Haitian religious collusio "consists in large part of a 'practical sense' that life in this world is inhabited by invisible, supernatural forces that are to be served and which can be called upon and operationalized toward healing ills, mitigating plight, enhancing luck, and achieving goals" (9–10).

How does Rey and Stepick's religious collusio relate to religious habitus? It is first important to understand the importance of religion to the Haitian diaspora of the Bahamas. Haitians are a population that is, for the most part, economically disadvantaged and lives on the margins of "paradise." Religion "functions to provide a sense of *dignity* [my emphasis] that may be otherwise absent—a sense that they are *worthy* [original emphasis] in spite of it all" (Rey and Stepick 2013, 10). Thus, religious habitus "*inclines* people to embrace symbolic systems that pronounce for them their worthiness, systems that are predicated upon the existence of supernatural forces, and thus orient their lives in accordance with them" (10).

Other scholars use Bourdieu's conceptualization of habitus in religious studies because of the concept's potential to foreground the role of the body in religious experience. Sociologists of religion Philip Mellor and Chris Shilling view religious habitus as a set of "embodied predispositions which promote particular forms of orientation to the world . . . [which include] a number of features of embodiment specific to religious life" (2015, 217).[3] As the late anthropologist Saba Mahmood writes in reference to her research about the Muslim act of prayer (ṣalāt) among a women's piety movement in Cairo, Egypt, Bourdieu used habitus as a "means to integrate conceptually phenomenological and structuralist approaches so as to elucidate how the supraindividual structure of society comes to be lived in human experience" (2001, 837). Mahmood also criticizes Bourdieu's conceptualization of habitus as too rigid. In her fieldwork with mosque participants, Mahmood found that although the body served as a "site of moral training and cultivation" (838) there were variations in how Muslims constructed their ethical and religious identities that were influenced by conscious change. In other words, habitus is not solely unconscious but can also be malleable and reflect religious self-fashioning; an individual's part of a larger religious institution and/or collective can use different cultural elements (combining different ways to be Christian, for instance) to become particular kinds of religious entities—not mechanistic cookie-cutter versions of the same type of Christian.

How do subjects, like Bahamians of Haitian descent, use religion to fashion lives of inclusion and dignity within a social context that has at its core a relentless devaluation of Haitianness? How does a person live a life of dignity in a society where there is an incessant assault on their being? How does a person of Haitian descent attempt to be a respected member of a largely Christian society that is fundamentally anti-Haitian?

In relation to my research consultants and the overall situation of Haitians in the anti-Haitian Bahamas, religious habitus is more than the mechanistic inculcation and embodiment of religious doctrine and culture that Bourdieu posits and Mahmood critiques. Religious habitus becomes a tool that Bahamians of Haitian descent use to build a stable sense of self while internalizing secular and religious aspects of Bahamian and Haitian socioreligious life while living between Bahamian and Haitian culture. Religious habitus is more pliable and accommodating when we look at Bahamians of Haitian descent, who use elements from Haitian Protestant culture, Bahamian religious culture, and secular culture to produce unique Christian (Nazarene) religious identities that reflect a hybrid Haitian and Bahamian religious identity as well as producing Christian and, in some cases, eventual Bahamian citizens of Haitian descent. They use hybrid ideas about how Bahamians and Haitians practice Protestant forms of Christianity to fashion a life of self-worth and dignity in a society that violates their basic human rights and racializes Haitians as lower in social status than Bahamians.

In addition to my own conceptualization of religious habitus vis-à-vis Bahamians of Haitian descent, I also draw on Rey and Stepick's discussion of religious habitus to explain why a specific form of Haitian Protestantism (Nazarene Christianity) is so attractive and important to Haitians in the Bahamas, in addition to other reasons that I have outlined elsewhere (Louis 2014). I also draw from sociologist Kelly Chong's (2015) work on religious habitus among South Korean evangelical women to analyze and describe the minutiae of religious practice among Bahamian Christians of Haitian descent that reflects religious habitus. Chong's work focuses on the religious practices of a population that help them negotiate patriarchy and redomestication into a family/gender regime, which helps to maintain South Korean gender arrangements. Chong's work on religious habitus is also useful for providing insights about how Bahamians of Haitian descent access and experience the divine in relation to lives that are shaped by heritage, racism, de facto statelessness, shame, and anger.

Haitian Protestantism, Migration to the Bahamas, and Bahamian Identity

As some religious studies scholars of Latin America and the Caribbean observe, parts of Latin America that were formerly Catholic are becoming Protestant. The growth and success of Protestantism in areas like Colombia (see Brusco 1995) and Jamaica (see Austin-Broos 1997) also extend to Haiti. Since the Wesleyan Missionary Society was established in Haiti in 1817, Protestantism has grown steadily, whereas Haitians traditionally practiced Catholicism and Vodou, all within a historical context of Black revolutionary triumph, poverty, consistent and continued foreign interference (by the United States, France, Germany, foreign nongovernmental organizations, and the United Nations, for example), state repression of the Haitian people, environmental degradation, and the earthquake of January 12, 2010. To illustrate, in 1930 approximately 1.5 percent of Haiti's population practiced Protestant forms of Christianity like the Baptist faith, Pentecostalism, and Methodism. Between 1930 and 1950, the population of Protestants tripled and then doubled again. According to the Haitian sociologist Charles-Poisset Romain (1986, 81), 20 percent of Haiti had converted to some form of Protestant Christianity by 1986. A conservative estimate is that one-third of Haiti's contemporary population is Protestant (Butler 2002, 85).[4]

Haitians tend to leave their home country during periods of intense political and economic turmoil and environmental degradation, migrating to countries throughout the Western Hemisphere and within the surrounding region, such as to the Bahamas. Most Haitians in the Bahamas migrated to the island of New Providence, where Nassau (the capital) and two-thirds of the Bahamian population are located. In 2019 Haitians constituted the largest immigrant group in the Bahamas (approximately thirty thousand to sixty thousand Haitians in a country with a population of just over four hundred thousand). Many, if not most, Haitians are undocumented workers employed as restaurant staff, construction workers, housekeepers, and landscapers. This population has become highly stigmatized owing to continued Haitian migration to the Bahamas, negative media reports concerning Haitians, a lack of research on the Haitian population of the Bahamas, Bahamian xenophobia, and Bahamian governmental policies enacted to limit a Haitian population that is perceived as becoming too large. Haitians are viewed as threatening the sovereignty and social stability of the Bahamas because they are currently regarded as being unassimilable. The people of the Bahamas are very hostile toward Haitians specifically and foreigners in general.

The Bahamas gained political independence from its British colonial master through a relatively peaceful transition of power on July 9, 1973. Tourism became the major economic strategy of modernization after Bahamian independence (Alexander 1997, 67). Tourism accounts for 60 percent of the nation's gross domestic product and employs half of the Bahamian labor force, which makes the per capita income of the Bahamas one of the highest in the Caribbean and Latin America. Although the Bahamas is comparatively more affluent than many of its Caribbean neighbors, the Bahamian economy is subject to moments of uncertainty similar to those other countries experience as part of the global economy. The global financial crisis of 2008 adversely affected the Bahamas. While the economy shows some signs of improvement, the current economic and social realities still make life for the average Bahamian difficult. As of late December 2015, the unemployment rate was 14.8 percent, with unemployment at 30 percent among youth (those between the ages of fifteen and twenty-four). With stagnant wages and the introduction of value-added tax on goods, the cost of living continues to rise. The homicide rate has increased steadily over the years and reached an all-time high of 146 murders in 2015. So the Bahamas is not a paradise, at least not to the average Bahamian and definitely not for its Haitian population. The nation faces the challenges of being part of a larger capitalist economic system in an increasingly globalizing world.

The Bahamas is also a predominantly Black nation, with approximately 85 percent of the population African descended. Bahamian identity is diverse and contains African, American, British, Gullah, and Haitian elements. This hybrid background stems from a history of slavery, migration throughout the Caribbean, and in-migration from other Caribbean areas. Bahamian culture also shares features with other cultures within the region that situate it in a larger African diaspora. The Junkanoo celebration and Bahamian storytelling are examples of a culture that has African origins (Johnson 1991, 17). Another core element of Bahamian identity is the collective practice and observance of Christianity.

The Bahamas prides itself on being a Christian nation where the majority of the inhabitants (96 percent) practice Catholic and Protestant forms of Christianity. Church is arguably more important to the Bahamian social fabric than school, government, or often even the family. As sociologist Dean Collinwood reflects, the most important features of Bahamian life—conscience development, mate selection and marriage, and vital social activities—take place within the confines of the church (Collinwood 1989, 16).

While Christianity plays an important role in contemporary Bahamian identity, another aspect is Bahamians' tendency to be xenophobic. As historian Howard Johnson (1991, 17) observes, resentment of foreigners is a long-standing tradition within Bahamian culture and provides an element of cohesion within a society long divided according to class, color, and race. A historical moment when a distrust of foreigners occurred was the 1920s, when skilled West Indian laborers arrived to work in the growing tourist industry. Bahamian xenophobia during that period culminated in 1926, when flows of West Indian laborers were curtailed owing to a decrease in labor opportunities. This type of resentment has carried over to the contemporary period. As Haitians continue to migrate to the Bahamas, the perceived large size of the Haitian community feeds into xenophobic fears shared by many Bahamians, which are reflected in recent changes to Bahamian immigration policy. In 2014 the Progressive Liberal Party, the ruling party of the Bahamas at the time, made a series of policy changes to establish restrictions targeting Haitian communities in the Bahamas and their progeny (Martinez 2015). Some of these restrictions include the requirement that all people living in the Bahamas have a passport from their country of nationality, which means a passport from their parents' country. Within this context, the identities of Haitians born in the Bahamas develop.

Haitian Identity Formation in the Bahamas

As historians Michael Craton and Gail Saunders (1998) observe, the Bahamian state tends to lump all Haitians together in "an undifferentiated mass" (457) regardless of a person's legal status, birth in the Bahamas, or familial ties. This obscures the internal differentiation within a population that includes Haitian migrants, Haitians born in the Bahamas, people of Haitian descent with Bahamian citizenship (Bahamians of Haitian descent), and Haitians who were born in the Bahamas but have spent part or most of their lives in Haiti and currently reside in the Bahamas. An individual has an automatic right to Bahamian citizenship in the following cases: they are born in the Bahamas, and either of their parents is Bahamian; they are born overseas to a married Bahamian man; or they are born overseas to an unwed Bahamian mother. The progeny of Haitians are thus not granted automatic citizenship, are ineligible for the rights that go with Bahamian citizenship (i.e., voting in local and national elections, being eligible for national and foreign college scholarships, attending college without paying the high fees that foreign-born students pay), and are ascribed the nationality of their parents (Martinez 2015).[5] Regarding the product of a Haitian union, the Haitian Constitution does not recognize children of Haitian parentage as Haitian citizens; they must be born on Haitian soil to obtain Haitian citizenship. Therefore, with the Bahamas following the jus sanguinis law of nationality and Haiti following the jus soli law of nationality, these children are legally neither Bahamian nor Haitian. In other words, they are de facto stateless, which renders their Haitian nationality ineffective. Haitian nationality in the Bahamas provides neither Haitian nor Bahamian citizenship until the age of eighteen, when the children can apply for Bahamian citizenship; some receive it, and some do not (Belton 2010).

In addition to being stateless, the progeny of Haitians are regularly humiliated and marginalized owing to their racialization as Haitian, at the bottom of the Bahamian racial hierarchy. Haitian identities are constructed from their familial heritage as well as from how Haitians are treated by the Bahamian state through the law and in Bahamian public schools. Many of my research consultants from 2005 and 2012 remarked that they were ridiculed and denigrated by Bahamian students and teachers at school, which is the leading site of their interaction and socialization as future Bahamians. In fact, their experiences at school prevented many from publicly identifying as Haitian. Teasing for being Haitian was at times so severe for children of Haitian parentage that they got into physical altercations with bullies, and some did not go to school at all. One young woman I interviewed in 2005 noted that she stayed away from school for most of a year because of the incessant teasing from her Bahamian classmates.

As a result of laws that marginalize them, Haitians utilize various strategies to survive the hostile Bahamian social climate, which include but are not limited to accommodation, ethnocide (passing as Bahamian by changing their names, sometimes legally, to a Bahamian surname, for example), and individual acts of resistance (physically fighting one's tormentors, for instance). Religion and the church, the preeminent institution that addresses Haitian concerns, also play an important role for Haitians. As Rey and Stepick observe, religious congregations "can be a source of social support, solace, and identity formation" (2013, 11). These forms of congregational support "can be conceived of [as] different kinds of 'symbolic capital,'" for example, as resources that can be transformed or "transubstantiated" into material capital and "provide immigrants with an arena for the maintenance of their homeland cultural identity, wherein they also accrue these and other forms of symbolic capital" (11). Haitian church participation also is a collective space that allows Haitian Bahamians, as they are popularly referred to, to learn Haitian Creole and other Haitian customs while developing a hybrid religious habitus (partly Haitian and partly the Christian religious culture found in the Bahamas). Participation in Haitian Protestant denominations also allows Haitians to affirm an identity that at its foundation is evangelical Christian, challenges Bahamian societal stereotypes, and prepares Haitian progeny to become Bahamians of Haitian descent.

Victory Chapel and Religious Habitus: Fet Mwason and Liturgical Dance

Founded in September 25, 1988, as a church to minister to the children of Haitian descent born in the Bahamas, Victory Chapel Church of the Nazarene is a one-level church with a sanctuary that can accommodate at least 250 people. The church moved to its Minnie Street location in 1995. Rev. Dr. Antoine Saint Louis, a charismatic Bahamian of Haitian descent, heads Victory Chapel. He observed in an interview in 2012 that the Haitian children born in the Bahamas were unable to appreciate their two cultures until a church was created where young people could come and be proud of their parents and their place of birth (the Bahamas). Victory Chapel serves as this space, in response to rejection by Bahamian society and culture and, at times, by Haitians and Haitian culture. During my first visit in 2005, the congregation was 50 percent Haitian and 50 percent children and adults of Haitian descent. During my visit in 2012, Victory Chapel's congregation was 60 percent Haitian and 40 percent adults and children of Haitian descent. The congregations at other churches I had studied previously, like New Haitian Mission Baptist Church and International Tabernacle of Praise Ministries (Louis 2014), overwhelmingly consisted of Haitian migrants rather than Bahamians of Haitian descent. A look at a typical church service at Victory Chapel partly illuminates how religious habitus develops.

While a diversity of denominations (Adventist, Baptist, Methodist, Charismatic, and Pentecostal) comprise Haitian Protantism, shared aspects of Haitian Protestant culture provide the burgeoning transnational religious movement with some cohesion. Some of these traits include a rejection of Vodou and the use of a Protestant vocabulary. Other traits include ritualized practices common in Haitian Protestant liturgy, such as the singing of songs and hymns that circulate throughout Haiti and the Haitian diaspora transnationally and are used in church (Louis 2014). Regardless of where Haitian Protestant services are held—Boston Missionary Baptist Church in Massachusetts; the First French-Speaking Baptist Church of Saint Louis, Missouri; Victory Chapel Church of the Nazarene in New Providence, Bahamas; or the Pentecostal Unis of Port-au-Prince, Haiti—many share a similar worship format. Most church services begin with a *culte d'adoration* or *adoration et louange* (worship and praise) portion in which adherents worship and praise God through hymns and prayers led by members of the church hierarchy. Haitian Protestant hymnody is usually drawn from *Chants D'Éspérance* (Songs of hope), a Baptist hymnal used by Haitian Protestant churches within a larger transnational social field.

In my study of Haitian Protestantism, a song I have heard at churches in Brooklyn, New York; at family gatherings in Boston and Washington, D.C.; and at Victory Chapel on several occasions is "Dieu Tout Puissant" (Almighty God), selection 27 from the "Melodies Joyeuses" (Joyous melodies) section of *Chants D'Éspérance*. You would not find this hymn, sung in French or Haitian Creole, at a Bahamian church because Bahamian church services are in English. Thus, Victory Chapel creates a sacralized space where the denigration of Haitians' linguistic hybridity (the ability to speak and understand Haitian Creole and English) is absent, unlike in the anti-Haitian Bahamian society. Singing this song also embodies some of the traditions of Haitian Protestant culture for adherents at Victory Chapel, which in turn enculturates their progeny. Embodied aspects of transnational Haitian Protestant church culture are on full display—such as swaying one's hands in the air, stretching out one's hands reaching to God, and shouting in Haitian Creole "Amen," "Beniswa Letènèl" (Praise the Lord), "Glwa a Dyè" (Glory to God), and "Mèsi Seyè" (Thank you, Lord). Haitian migrants and Bahamians of Haitian descent embody Haitian Protestant culture by kneeling at the altar in fervent, silent prayer while others are standing and singing from memory or their hymnals, like at other Haitian Protestant churches I observed transnationally (in Saint Louis, Missouri; Boston, Massachusetts; and Port-au-Prince, Haiti). When "Dieu Tout Puissant" was sung at Victory Chapel during my fieldwork in 2005, it was done first in French and then in Creole, translating to "Ala w Gran" ("How Great Thou Art").[6]

Sunday morning services at Victory Chapel also reflect how the church ministers to the spiritual and social needs of Haitians born in the Bahamas. Sunday morning services were usually bilingual, conducted in Haitian Creole and English (the official language of the Bahamas), where the pastor would preach in Haitian Creole offering spiritual advice as to how to lean on God and one's Christian character during difficult moments in a person's life. A Bahamian of Haitian descent usually would translate *lapawol de Dye* (the word of God) into English for those Haitian-descended adherents and visitors who did not understand and/or fluently speak or understand Haitian Creole.

When I visited the church in 2012, it was my first time back in the Bahamas since my initial fieldwork in 2005. I was there to conduct follow-up interviews with key informants and new participants about the lived realities of de facto stateless people (Haitian-descended people). During my return, I served as a consultant to David Baluarte, a noted human rights lawyer who is an expert on de jure statelessness. He established a nationality rights clinic called the Nationality Support Unit (NSU) in the Bahamas under the purview of the United Nations High Commissioner for Refugees. On June 24, 2012, David, other members of the NSU, and I went to Victory Chapel. That Sunday was the last day of Fet Mwason (the Haitian harvest [La Moisson in French]). Fet Mwason is celebrated in Haitian churches of various denominations (Baptist, Nazarene, and Pentecostal, for example) in Haiti and in Haiti's diaspora in the Bahamas and the United States. In Haiti it is customary for members of the congregation to bring items from their gardens to the church and place them in front of the altar in a devotional manner. The fruits and vegetables represent the blessings God bestowed upon them through the year. Toward the end of the service, a prayer is said for these blessings, and the items are sold after the service at another location in the church to raise funds for church projects like buying new furniture and replacing other vital items in the church. The biblical source of the meaning of La Moisson comes from a section in the Old Testament: 2 Chronicles 31, which describes the bringing of offerings (food gifts) to the gates of a temple. That day, the church also had a visiting *predikatè* (preacher or evangelist) from a Haitian evangelical church in Fort Lauderdale, Florida, continuing the transnational practice of Haitian Protestant churches in the Bahamas inviting male Haitian evangelists and pastors from Haiti and its diaspora to preach during church services.

That morning, David, the other representatives from the NSU, and I participated in an animated and emotionally charged church service that included a speech from David that declared that the Haitian-descended people born in the Bahamas had a "right to nationality," which caused many of the Haitian teenagers and Bahamians of Haitian descent in attendance to cheer and scream. David also discussed the services of the NSU that could help them through an intake process that could lead to Bahamian citizenship for many of those who were eligible. I delivered a speech that encouraged the Haitian children and teenagers and Bahamians of Haitian descent to draw on their Haitian heritage and to participate in creating a new, fairer Bahamas. I also observed a newer feature in Victory Chapel worship and praise that had been absent during my visits in 2005: liturgical dance. Liturgical dance, an African American church tradition adopted by Bahamian churches, informs the religious habitus of the younger members of Victory Chapel born in the Bahamas. According to one of my research consultants, her use of liturgical dance increased after October 2006 owing to her love of dance (also reflected by other young Haitian women). She recognized that they had adopted the cultural form from Bahamian and international churches. According to her, there was initial resistance to liturgical dance at Victory Chapel partly because, at the time, it was not part of the religious culture of Victory Chapel nor the larger Haitian Protestant community, which tends to be culturally conservative. But according to my research consultant, after some time, people in the church (Haitian migrants mostly) grew to accept and appreciate it (see figure 6.1).

That morning, some of the young women of Victory Chapel danced to a popular African American gospel song by Grammy Award–winning songwriter Pastor Charles Jenkins and Fellowship Chicago, called "Awesome (My God Is)." While standing in place, the dancers pushed their hands down to the lyrics "keep me in the valley" and covered their faces with their hands. They simulated rain falling down through their raised hands coming down, while wiggling their fingers, when the words "hide me from the rain" were sung. Embodied ritual-like liturgical dance demonstrates how Dr. Saint Louis encourages the church's youth to express themselves religiously through popular culture and other cultural forms not readily a part of the Protestant religious traditions of Haiti because he wants them to grow as Christians. Haitian Protestant religious traditions can sometimes be experienced as restrictive by the youth of the church who were born in the Bahamas. But as the dance description describes and figure 6.1 displays, the movements reflect a form of religious worship expressed through their bodies, which helps to reinforce a Christian identity and also resonates with Bahamian cultural identity.

During that service the young women danced with intensity, with the choreographer (dancing with her face covered, to the left in figure 6.1) crying while she danced. The passionate religiosity of so-called Haitian Bahamians is informed by the religious spiritual context but also stems from an effort to cope not only with the individual challenges they face in the Bahamas but with the realities of living in a society that is structured against them. This means not having

FIGURE 6.1. Liturgical dance at Victory Chapel Church of the Nazarene, New Providence, Bahamas, June 24, 2012. Photograph by author.

the same rights as a Bahamian citizen, which include not being able to open a bank account, not being able to vote, and not being able to access the same educational privileges that Bahamian students can. Through these dances and movements that are coordinated with the lyrics of this gospel song, which is popular in the United States and was played over the Bahamian airwaves during my visit, we can see how alternative Christian subjectivities are constituted through ritual dance. We also see how the dancers construct a hybrid Christian identity that draws from an international context (the United States) that is influenced and appropriated by the local societal context (the Bahamas). Victory Chapel Church of the Nazarene, created for Haitian-descended people, informs a hybrid Christian identity that draws from the Protestant religious culture of Haiti and its diaspora in the Bahamas. This example of "praise dancing," as the main choreographer of the routine refers to the ritual genre found in many churches in the African diaspora, also demonstrates how religious culture changes upon finding adequate cultural practices that correspond to the needs of religious practitioners and to the challenges they face in building a stable sense of self, living between Bahamian and Haitian culture.

Religious Habitus: Prayer at Victory Chapel

In 2005 Haitian pastors estimated that there were at least twenty Haitian Protestant churches in the Bahamas. As of 2012 there were at least forty-two churches. So why do Haitian-descended children flock to Victory Chapel? One reason is that the church was created to minister to them. Another reason is the nature of the Nazarene denomination. For Victory Chapel adherents, the intentional choice to attend a Nazarene church is important because this church's doctrine focuses on regeneration, continued growth as a Christian, and the normative repentance for sins. Adherents at Victory Chapel access the divine in part through impassioned prayer, which is part of their religious habitus. A particularly morbid example from my fieldwork that reflects religious habitus as well as the insecurity of people of Haitian descent in the Western Hemisphere illustrates this point.

After the fet mwason service on June 24, 2012, I attended a mass funeral on Saturday, June 30, for eleven Haitians who died when the boat they took to get to the United States capsized and all the people drowned (figures 6.2 and 6.3). Included in the death toll were children.

This tragedy cast a dark cloud over Nassau's Haitian community. That somber feeling was evident at the night service at Victory Chapel I attended the following Sunday, July 1. Toward the end of that service, Dr. Saint Louis held a special prayer for the youth of the church and asked them to assemble in front of the altar. He prayed for protection for the church's youth within Bahamian society. That night, the youth of Victory Chapel prayed fervently for twenty-five to thirty minutes straight, longer than any other time I had observed in all of my transnational studies of Haitian Protestant culture, confessing and surrendering to God as is taught in the Nazarene tradition. Fervent prayer is a ritual that is "linguistic and embodied" and "a way to experience the divine, especially the Holy Spirit," as Chong (2015, 116) describes in her work on South Korean evangelical women. Most of the people assembled knelt in front of the altar and prayed quietly with their eyes closed (see figures 6.4 and 6.5). As a leader of the church, Dr. Saint Louis helps the youth of Victory Chapel interpret the world around them through a Nazarene worldview and also aids them in learning the proper embodied "techniques and methods with which to carry out such prayers, that is, teach[es] them *how* to pray" (Chong 2015, 116).

The young adherents in the church learn how to pray and be Nazarene Christians to counter, among other things, the dehumanizing effects of societal marginalization in the Bahamas because of their Haitian heritage and to resist the evil vices of the secular world (such as premarital sex, drugs, and alcohol).

FIGURE 6.2. Caskets containing adults at a mass funeral for Haitians, New Providence, Bahamas, June 24, 2012. Photograph by author.

FIGURE 6.3. Caskets containing children at a mass funeral for Haitians, New Providence, Bahamas, June 24, 2012. Photograph by author.

FIGURE 6.4. Prayer at Victory Chapel Church of the Nazarene, New Providence, Bahamas, July 1, 2012. Photograph by author.

FIGURE 6.5. Prayer at Victory Chapel Church of the Nazarene, New Providence, Bahamas, July 1, 2012. Photograph by author.

Specifically, Haitian children raised in Bahamian society learn to hate the nationality of their parents because of how it relegates them to the bottom of Bahamian society. Bahamian society rejects Haitian Bahamians so that, among other reasons, the labor of their parents can best serve the Bahamian economy. Bahamians of Haitian descent who attend Victory Chapel enjoy participating in the church partly because it is the church of the eventual Bahamian. That is, many of the progeny of the documented and undocumented migrants who attend the church will eventually become Bahamian citizens.[7] Victory Chapel reflects the liminal, stateless experience of people who were born Haitian, live as Haitians in the Bahamas until the age of eighteen, and then become Bahamian after they are granted Bahamian citizenship. They enjoy attending and participating in activities at Victory Chapel because it is one of the few spaces in Bahamian society where their cultural hybridity is celebrated and normative. Victory Chapel is also active in agitating for citizenship reform through the United Haitian Association in the Bahamas (UHAB). The UHAB president, Dr. Saint Louis of Victory Chapel, has repeatedly recommended to Bahamian government officials that they grant birthright citizenship to people of Haitian descent born in the Bahamas.[8]

Conclusion

In an interview with Victory Chapel member Brother Glodys, a Bahamian of Haitian descent, I asked him about the term *Haitian Bahamian* and whether he considered it to be an indignity, as did some Haitians born in the Bahamas, as a way to describe his identity and, by extension, the identities of other eventual Bahamians.[9] He responded:

> It's not a legal term, so when they say Haitian Bahamian, I'm always asking the question, "Am I a potcake?" because I'm mixed.
>
> A potcake is a dog that has two pedigrees. A pitbull and a German shepherd together that mate, and they just call it a potcake because it's mixed so, and usually you see them type of dogs on the streets without no home and without no owner. So I usually say, "No, I'm not—I am not Haitian Bahamian, I am a Bahamian of Haitian descent." (Nassau, Bahamas, June 26, 2012)

Brother Glodys's mixedness is not a racial mixing but a cultural and national mixing that lies at the heart of many Bahamians' fears for the future—that Bahamians of Haitian descent will threaten the sovereignty of the Bahamas by supplanting "real" Bahamians (primarily Black Bahamians who are Christians and have no recent, observable Haitian ancestry in their background). The only way to distinguish between a Bahamian and a Bahamian of Haitian descent is by learning the surname of the person. Other than that, Bahamians of Haitian descent are similar to other Bahamians, like the people we find at Victory Chapel Church of the Nazarene. Owing to the normative stigmatization and marginalization of Haitian-descended people in the Bahamas, many want to leave the country of their birth as soon as they get their Bahamian passport, which allows them to travel with documents, because of the belief that they can live more dignified lives with more opportunities somewhere else.

As shown by the popularity of Victory Chapel Church of the Nazarene among Bahamians of Haitian descent, the church provides a haven from social marginalization and a dynamic opportunity to become conscious of their humanity. At Victory Chapel, the relationship of religious habitus to the church generates religious practice. Haitians (adults and children) engage in different practices at the church, which help to inculcate certain dispositions and reflect social processes of individual and collective self-remaking through embodied and linguistic practices, which allow Bahamians of Haitian descent to negotiate their different contested identities. As a result, they create a unique, embodied hybrid religious habitus that mixes Haitian and non-Haitian religious and cultural factors and prepares them to become Bahamian citizens because being Christian is a necessary element of contemporary Bahamian identity. By doing so, Victory Chapel creates the adherents it needs not only for the reproduction of the church but also, by extension, for the reproduction of Bahamian society. This is achieved through inculcated dispositions that reside in the hexis: the organization of the human body and the way it operates in the world (Bourdieu 1991). In other words, the hexis resides in embodied practices.

In closing, as long as the Bahamas is structured for those who can be defined solely as Bahamian, gross discrimination against Haitians will persist in the Bahamas, people will leave the country instead of contributing to its development, and the core elements of what it means to be Bahamian will continue to be Blackness, Christianity, and anti-Haitianism. And for those Bahamians of Haitian descent who choose to remain in the Bahamas, many will use their bodies, through liturgical dance and fervent prayer, for example, to shape new ways of being while turning toward a Protestant God. They will do this, partly, by utilizing Protestant Christian religious practices that help to make and remake them into the type of citizens that we find in the Bahamas. Or they can choose to challenge this hierarchy in order to lead dignified lives in "paradise."[10]

1. The term *Haitian* in the Bahamas includes the following groups who have similar, intersecting, and competing interests: Haitian migrants, Haitians born in the Bahamas, people of Haitian descent with Bahamian citizenship (Bahamians of Haitian descent), and Haitians who were born in the Bahamas but have spent part or most of their lives in Haiti and currently reside in the Bahamas. Also, I use "Haitian Bahamian" and "Bahamian(s) of Haitian descent" interchangeably.

2. De facto statelessness refers to when an individual has a nationality that is rendered ineffective owing to the nation they live in. Someone who is de facto stateless can reside outside of the state of their nationality and might have a legal claim to nationality/citizenship in the country of their birth. The situation of people born to Haitian parents in the Bahamas is an example of de facto statelessness. De facto statelessness is in contrast to de jure statelessness, which refers to an individual who is not considered as a national or citizen by any state (Article 1 of the 1954 United Nations Convention Relating to the Status of Stateless Persons). https://www.unhcr.org/ibelong/wp-content/uploads/1954 -Convention-relating-to-the-Status-of-Stateless-Persons_ENG.pdf

3. According to Mellor and Schilling the features of embodiment "have included the existential reassurances and anxieties reflective of human frailty, the stimulation and regulation of emotions relative to the sacred, and the development of rituals, techniques and pedagogics with the aim of stimulating particular forms of consciousness and experience, including those related to transcendence and immanence" (2010, 217).

4. The figure is most likely higher. In the Bureau of Applied Research in Anthropology's *Baseline Study of Livelihood Security in the Departments of the Artibonite, Center, North, Northeast, and West,* Drexel Woodson and Mamadou Baro (1997, 98) observed that Haitian conversion to Protestant forms of Christianity was one of the most significant religious changes in the Adventist Development and Relief Agency's zone of intervention in the past thirty years. In four departments, 20 to 25 percent of the household heads were Protestant, but the figure rose to 38.7 percent in the west (98). A 1996 BARA study on the Southern Peninsula of Haiti yielded similar results (55–56). In fact, there were some areas in Southern Haiti where the percentages of Protestant households were 42.9 percent (Bois La Rue), 55.6 percent (Aréguy), 51.4 percent (Potier), and 100 percent (Boleau). Finally, a study on culture in Port-au-Prince observed that in 1996 approximately 39 percent of Port-au-Prince was Protestant (Houtart and Rémy 1997, 38–39).

5. Bahamian citizenship is legally informed by the Constitution of the Commonwealth of the Bahamas (the 1973 Constitution), the 1973 Bahamas Citizenship Act, and other administrative regulations.

6. For an example in Haitian Creole, go to "Dieu Tout Puissant quand mon coeur considère," HPC Home of Hope, January 21, 2014, YouTube video, 8:35, https://www.youtube .com/watch?v=fL_d2f6U8ts.

7. How do some Haitians born in the Bahamas become citizens of the Bahamas? A loophole that allows some Haitians born in the Bahamas to become Bahamian citizens is found in Article 7 (1) of the Bahamian Constitution:

> A person born in the Bahamas after 9th July 1973 neither of whose parents is a citizen of The Bahamas shall be entitled, upon making application on his attaining the

age of eighteen years or within twelve months thereafter in such manner as may be prescribed, to be registered as a citizen of The Bahamas:

Provided that if he is a citizen of some country other than the Bahamas he shall not be entitled to be registered as a citizen of The Bahamas under this Article unless he renounces his citizenship of that other country, takes the oath of allegiance and makes and registers such declaration of his intentions concerning residence as may be prescribed. https://www.constituteproject.org/constitution/Bahamas_1973.pdf ?lang=en.

8. Although this is important work, UHAB, which consists mainly of Bahamians of Haitian descent, also supports the Bahamian government's current stance on immigration, which adversely affects Haitian migrants.

9. I have changed the name of this research consultant to protect his identity.

10. I am grateful for the assistance of Cassidy Tomlinson and Jasmine Wilson for their interview transcription services and research, which assisted in the completion of this manuscript.

REFERENCES

Alexander, M. Jacqui. 1997. "Erotic Autonomy as a Politics of Decolonization: An Anatomy of Feminist and State Practice in the Bahamas Tourist Economy." In *Feminist Genealogies, Colonial Legacies, Democratic Futures*, edited by M. Jacqui Alexander and Chandra Talpade Mohanty, 63–100. New York: Routledge.

Austin-Broos, Diane. 1997. *Jamaican Genesis: Religion and the Politics of Moral Orders*. Chicago: University of Chicago Press.

Belton, Kristy A. 2010. "Arendt's Children in the Bahamian Context: The Children of Migrants without Status." *International Journal of Bahamian Studies* 16: 35–50.

Bourdieu, Pierre. 1977. *Outline of a Theory of Practice*. Cambridge: Cambridge University Press.

Bourdieu, Pierre. 1991. *Language and Symbolic Power*. Cambridge, UK: Polity.

Brusco, Elizabeth E. 1995. *The Reformation of Machismo: Evangelical Conversion and Gender in Colombia*. Austin: University of Texas Press.

Butler, Melvin. 2002. "'Nou Kwe nan Sentespri' (We Believe in the Holy Spirit): Music, Ecstasy and Identity in Haitian Pentecostal Worship." *Black Music Research Journal* 22 (1): 85–125.

Chong, Kelly H. 2015. "Feminine Habitus: Rhetoric and Rituals of Conversion and Commitment among Contemporary South Korean Evangelical Women." In *The Anthropology of Global Pentecostalism and Evangelicalism*, edited by Simon Coleman and Rosalind I. J. Hackett, 109–128. New York: New York University Press.

College of the Bahamas. 2005. *Haitian Migrants in the Bahamas: A Report for the International Organization for Migration*. New Providence, Bahamas: International Organization for Migration. Accessed April 30, 2009, http://www.iom.int/jahia/webdav /site/myjahi-asite/shared/shared/mainsite/published_docs/books/Haitian_Migrants _Report.pdf.

Collinwood, Dean W. "The Bahamas in Social Transition." In *Modern Bahamian Society*, edited by Dean W. Collinwood and Steve Dodge, 3–26. Parkersburg, IA: Caribbean Books.

Craton, Michael, and Gail Saunders. 1998. *Islanders in the Stream: A History of the Bahamian People*. Vol. 2: *From the Ending of Slavery to the Twenty-First Century*. Athens: University of Georgia Press.

Houtart, François, and Anselme Rémy. 1997. *Les référents culturels à Port-au-Prince*. Port-au-Prince: CRESFED (Centre de Recherche et de Formation Economique et Sociale pour le Développement).

Johnson, Howard. 1991. *The Bahamas in Slavery and Freedom*. Kingston, Jamaica: Ian Randle.

Louis, Bertin M., Jr. 2014. *My Soul Is in Haiti: Protestantism in the Haitian Diaspora of the Bahamas*. New York: New York University Press.

Mahmood, Saba. 2001. "Rehearsed Spontaneity and the Conventionality of Ritual: Disciplines of ṣalāt." *American Ethnologist* 28 (4): 827–853.

Marshall, Dawn. 1979. *"The Haitian Problem": Illegal Migration to the Bahamas*. Kingston, Jamaica: Institute of Social and Economic Research, University of the West Indies.

Martinez, Annette. 2015. "Discriminatory Migration Policies in the Caribbean." Presentation for the Disasters, Displacement and Human Rights Conference, Knoxville, TN, September 27, 2015.

Mellor, Phillip A., and Chris Shilling. 2015. "The Religious Habitus: Embodiment, Religion, and Sociological Theory." In *The New Blackwell Companion to the Sociology of Religion*, edited by Bryan S. Turner, 201–220. Chichester, UK: Wiley-Blackwell.

Perry, Charmaine. 2017. "'It's Better in the Bahamas': The Stigma of Being Haitian, Citizenship and Identity Choices among Second-Generation Haitians in the Bahamas." PhD diss., University of Wisconsin–Milwaukee.

Rey, Terry, and Alex Stepick. 2013. *Crossing the Water and Keeping the Faith: Haitian Religion in Miami*. New York: New York University Press.

Romain, Charles-Poisset. 1986. *Le protestantisme dans la société haïtienne: Contribution à l'étude sociologique d'une religion*. Port-au-Prince: Henri Deschamps.

Woodson, Drexel G., and Mamadou A. Baro. 1997. *A Baseline Study of Livelihood Security in the Department of the Artibonite, Center, North, Northeast, and West, Republic of Haiti*. Tucson: Bureau of Applied Research in Anthropology, University of Arizona.

PART III

Interrogating Sacredness
in Performance

7. The Quest for Spiritual Purpose in a Secular Dance Community: *Bèlè*'s Rebirth in Contemporary Martinique

CAMEE MADDOX-WINGFIELD

"*Bèlè* gives so much to us. It gives socially, politically, even financially . . . but we fail to realize how it gives spiritually. We take, take, take from bèlè, and we never offer anything in return" (interview, May 1, 2014). These words were captured as I interviewed Izaak, a longtime cultural activist in his early fifties, formerly an agricultural laborer and now a music teacher of Martinique's *bèlè* drum-dance tradition.[1] In recounting his testimony of spiritual maturation through bèlè, Izaak confessed that when he first became involved in the bèlè revival movement over thirty years ago, he exploited bèlè's function of protest and resistance to indulge his ego, advance his political ideologies, and establish his reputation as a militant. This former atheist admits that he never gave anything back to bèlè spiritually. He described the years of suffering and psychological turmoil he endured, eventually hitting rock bottom and temporarily abstaining from bèlè activities. Once he acknowledged his relationship to bèlè as a divine connection, he later returned to the bèlè movement with a more profound sense of the drum's spiritual potential and a deeper respect for his Creator and ancestors. It was almost as if through confession, repentance, abstention, and deliverance, he had finally arrived at a place of emancipation.

In contemporary Martinique, a French territory located in the Lesser Antilles, *bèlè* is not simply the name of an ancestral dance practice; the term *bèlè* is used to describe a way of life, or a subculture organized around a rich complex of Afro-Creole drum-dance traditions.[2] The African and European practices that converged in Martinique form the basis of *bèlè linò*, the most popularly performed variation of bèlè, hailing from the northeastern town of Sainte-Marie. Bèlè linò merges the French quadrille square-dancing configuration with African footwork, bent body posture, African percussion, and Creole-language call-and-response singing. It is a communicative dance with courtship-style choreography involving four female-male couples, danced with varying degrees of intensity based on the style of song (Cyrille 2006). During the enslavement era, some Africans would dance bèlè as a sign of status and social integration, to present themselves as equally respectable to their French counterparts. Colonial observers, however, characterized bèlè as Africans' poor imitation of the more elegant and graceful French ballroom styles (Moreau de St. Méry [1796] 1976). Other hypotheses posit that enslaved Africans used bèlè to camouflage different forms of African worship through the appearance of court dancing (Y. Daniel 2009). Therefore, throughout Martinique's colonial history and well into the twentieth century, the practice of bèlè was repressed by the Catholic Church and eclipsed by France's national model of assimilation, nearly erasing the tradition from public life. Throughout its eclipse in the mid-twentieth century, bèlè survived on the peripheries through theatrical folkloric performance by professional troupes, such as the Groupe Folklorique Martiniquais, whose staged renditions catered to the tourist market (Bertrand 1968). Over the past thirty years, however, cultural activists and artist intellectuals have mobilized at the grassroots level to revive bèlè as an honored community tradition and have placed it at the forefront of local struggles around cultural heritage preservation.

In this chapter I use a dialectical approach to analyze bèlè's rebirth as a multifaceted revitalization movement—one with a variety of spiritual interpretations that have evolved in response to the grievances of French national assimilation and neocolonial distress. Although bèlè is commonly understood as a secular/nonreligious dance tradition, debates have emerged among bèlè community members over its spiritual functions in the everyday lives of practitioners. Some dancers, drummers, and singers make claims of numinous experience, emotional transcendence, and ancestor veneration that are facilitated by music and motion and perceived to have a therapeutic healing purpose. These claims contradict the popular notion that bèlè has no sacred significance and that those elements of African religiosity and religious syncretism have dissolved out of Martinique's expressive culture—a perspective that has persisted in the discourse of bèlè until recent times.

Anthony Wallace first theorized a "revitalization movement" as the formation of new or revived religious practices that emerge as a result of deprivation and stress; he defined such a movement as the "deliberate, organized, conscious efforts by members of a society to construct a more satisfying culture" (1956, 265). Though Wallace's framework of revitalization movements has been most salient in studies of American Indian communities grappling with the consequences of assimilation, we can see parallels to such phenomena in France's overseas departments (*départements d'outre-mer*).[3] Epidemiological and anthropological research in Martinique points to increasing rates of depression, suicidal tendencies, and generalized anxiety (Massé 2008). From a comparative perspective, the mental health data in Martinique may not present a stark contrast with mental health in other Caribbean island societies. What is distinctive about the Martinican case, though, is the peculiar set of structural forces contributing to mental and social suffering.

The seminal text *Black Skin, White Masks*, by the renowned Martinican philosopher and psychiatrist Frantz Fanon ([1952] 1967), is a timeless commentary on the intersections of colonization, race, and the psychopathology of Black colonized subjects. Fanon's observations of French colonial racism on his native island pointed to troubles of inferiority and deep-seated feelings of anguish that underpin the dual identity of being Black and French. Richard Price's influential ethnography *The Convict and the Colonel* tells a story of (neo)colonial madness and struggles over cultural memory and identity in the context of Martinique's high-powered modernization and assimilation projects, following the 1946 transition to departmental status (Price 1998). Martinique's subordination to and dependency on France are understood by scholars as a structural cause of psychological distress, mental suffering, and mood disorders among island residents. The ways in which people respond to what medical anthropologist Raymond Massé (2008) calls *détresse créole* (creole distress) are very much rooted in Martinique's cultural specificity, characterized by the perplexing reality of being both French and Antillean. William Miles's neo-Fanonian analysis of Martinique argues that the "political attempts to institutionally repair the fraught relationship with France by redefining Martinique's juridical status will not salve the deeper identity-based grievances" (2012, 10). In other words, the fight for greater autonomy or independence from France will not rectify the widespread psychological imbalances found among islanders.

In my field research conducted from 2009 to 2018, I found that many bèlè practitioners claim to have turned to the tradition to reconcile feelings of alienation, dispossession, and vulnerability associated with Martinique's so-called identity crisis. I argue that despite bèlè's reputation as a secular practice, some bèlè practitioners find sacred meaning in the emotional transformation experienced through bèlè from a range of religious and spiritual orientations. I present a sample of cases that reveal three different types of spiritual engagement gaining ground among bèlè practitioners in recent years. The first involves those who advocate for the increased visibility of bèlè performance in the Catholic Church, a relatively new genre called *bèlè légliz* (church bèlè) that attempts to refashion the Catholic liturgy with Afro-Creole cultural references that were once prohibited by the dominant religious order. The second set of perspectives is found among those practitioners who draw inspiration from the cosmologies of African and Afro-Atlantic religions, such as Haitian Vodou, Cuban Santeria, Brazilian Candomblé, and other traditional African practices. The third dimension is the idea that bèlè is a "*laïque* (secular) spirituality" in and of itself—one that does not rely on any particular theistic religious framework but has a divine quality that encourages holistic wellness, helping to mend the wounds of emotional distress inflicted by Martinique's ongoing colonial subjugation to France. When considered for their liberatory potential, these spiritual interpretations engaged by bèlè proponents challenge the popular conceptions of secularism inherent to French national belonging and offer alternative paths to defining the terms of Martinique's relationship with France.

This research contributes to the body of African diaspora dance and music scholarship that problematizes the sacred/secular dichotomy, demonstrating the fluidity of Black expressive culture across secular and sacred interpretations and performance contexts (Covington-Ward 2015; Y. Daniel 2011; Henry 2008; Tucker 2007; Valnes 2015). Other forms of secular but still spiritual or religiously associated movement traditions have been documented in diasporic sites. For example, in Afro-Cuban rumba, creative synthesis and innovation can be observed through the mixing of secular and religious performance styles and gestures. In making this observation, dance anthropologist Yvonne Daniel writes about the sacralization of rumba with orisha-based movements and argues that "there is little separation between what some would call the sacred and the secular in many Afro-Cuban contexts. The particular mixture of sacred and secular in rumba affirms Afro-Cuban notions regarding spirituality" (1995, 113). In the case of Brazilian capoeira, particularly capoeira Angola, anthropological analyses challenge the notion of capoeira as a nonreligious martial art form and sport, pointing to certain capoeiristas' engagement with the spirit world and supernatural entities and the overlapping logics of capoeira Angola that are shared with, but exist separately from, the Candomblé religion (Varela 2017; Willson 2001).

This research also presents an opportunity to explore debates around *laïcité* (secularism) and French national belonging in a context outside the metropole.[4] Debates around laïcité, and its racist and xenophobic subtexts, typically focus on the contested nature of Islam in France (Fernando 2014; Jouili 2015;

Scott 2007). Rarely do we consider how the demand to embrace secularism as an emblem of French national identity shapes the discourse and practice of Antilleans living in France's overseas departments. Thus, we gain from this research a deeper understanding of Martinique's asymmetrical relationships with the French state, the Caribbean region, and the African diaspora at large. The project aims to pull Martinique from the margins of African diaspora religious scholarship to show how the perception of bèlè as a secular expression is changing and adapting to contemporary desires and demands for spiritual healing.

Bèlè's Rebirth

French national belonging is ideologically premised on a model of assimilation that extends to Antillean citizens living in the overseas departments (Agard-Jones 2009; Bonilla 2015; Browne 2004; J. Daniel 2001). The island's nonindependent political status as an overseas department accords Martinican residents the same rights and privileges afforded under French citizenship in metropolitan France (the vote, parliamentary representation, social security, and public services). Since Martinique's 1946 departmentalization, a strategy for decolonizing through political and economic incorporation into the French state, this island society has witnessed tremendous pressure to assimilate through a heightened valorization of French values and norms, alongside local struggles to define and assert Martinican cultural sensibilities (Beriss 2004; Price 1998). Local traditions, such as those associated with bèlè, *danmyé*, and *kalennda*, were abandoned in favor of European high culture—what Martinican intellectuals Aimé Césaire and Édouard Glissant referred to as "cultural genocide" or "genocide by substitution" (Burton 1995, 5; Glissant 1981, 173).[5]

In the early 1980s, a group of young (mostly male and middle-class) activist-intellectuals returned to their island home following years of university study in Paris. Disillusioned by their experiences with racism, cultural alienation, and second-class treatment in the metropole and newly radicalized by secular Marxist political ideology (a style of leftist *militantisme* that was very popular in France at that time), these activists went back to Martinique with a mission to "culturalize their anticolonial politics" (Geoffrey, interview, July 28, 2014). In collaboration with other local youth organizations, they cultivated relationships with elders and tradition bearers who passed on their knowledge of the bèlè culture, which had nearly vanished from Martinique's public life. Setting themselves apart from professional folkloric performance troupes, the revivalists used a grassroots-oriented approach to challenge exploitative, touristic representations of Martinican culture and promote bèlè through the formation of various community-based cultural associations.

Since the 1980s launch of the bèlè revival movement, cultural activists have worked to reverse negative stereotypes and promote more affirming images of the bèlè tradition. They have created several bèlè schools and developed a rigorously codified dance pedagogy based on the repertoire of bèlè movements and gestures. They maintain the public performance of these traditions through the *swaré bèlè* system—participatory nocturnal ritual events in which "initiated" dancers, drummers, and singers (those who have an advanced command of the repertoire and can perform comfortably to any of the styles improvised by the lead singer) come together on a scheduled date to play bèlè until the early hours of the morning. Unlike professional folkloric troupes, which perform Martinique's traditional culture in staged, choreographed renditions (often criticized by bèlè activists for reinforcing exoticized stereotypes of Antillean culture), the swaré bèlè function through an unscripted rotation of initiated practitioners. For the most part, these practitioners span three generations, categorized by *la jeunesse* (the youth), *les djoubaté* (the revivalists), and *les anciens* (the elders). Most of the elders come from modest, rural backgrounds, having worked as agricultural laborers in the past. Many of them are also Creole monolinguals with low literacy in French. The revivalists and youth who were initiated into bèlè through participation in contemporary class settings, however, come from all social strata and educational backgrounds. Nonmembers of the bèlè community are often surprised to learn that doctors, lawyers, teachers, and other *fonctionnaires* (civil servants) are even remotely interested in bèlè, given the longtime stigma of bèlè as a practice of the rural working class.[6]

Though the swaré bèlè space is not explicitly connected to religious practice, it is ceremonially organized to uphold a distinct set of values and ethics that are instilled in bèlè schools, fostering a unique sense of community belonging and cultural citizenship. These events are typically organized by a coalition of over twenty bèlè cultural associations from across the island that coordinates and governs bèlè activities, called the Coordination Lawonn Bèlè (Coordination around Bèlè).[7] The leaders of this coalition have implemented protocols to ensure the success of bèlè events, citing their moral and ethical commitments to collective work, mutual aid, and solidarity, as well as the values of humility and respect for elders. Devoted practitioners are expected to adhere to this code of honor, especially when it involves the hierarchy of age and skill level in the performance rotation. The swaré bèlè space is enlivened by reverence for the ancestors and protests against the legacies of racism and colonialism. The rituals and ethical codes that shape contemporary bèlè performance inspire in dancers an embodied resistance to oppression and suffering, channeled through the spirit of the ancestors and fervently safeguarded by present-day bèlè activists. Although there are some mild rivalries between bèlè associations, as well as conflicting perspectives around how bèlè should be transmitted, the coalition is generally united in the mission of empowering the people of Martinique.

When I first traveled to Martinique to pursue research on the cultural politics of the bèlè revival, I did not anticipate that my project would evolve to address questions of spirituality and religion. Bèlè had commonly been perceived as a secular/nonreligious tradition and was treated as such in the existing literature. Leaders of the bèlè revival initially focused on the transformative potential of bèlè for refashioning political, economic, and ethical sensibilities; raising social consciousness; empowering the youth in school settings; and promoting solidarity and an ethos of resistance to the French neocolonial presence on the island.[8] Given their radical-left political identities—shaped in Paris and informed by Marxism, socialism, and French liberal ideals of secularism—many militant bèlè activists of the 1980s had more atheistic inclinations and were not motivated by religious or spiritual meaning. Therefore, the scholarship on bèlè's resurgence in Martinique has focused almost exclusively on its secular functions in protest manifestations or folkloric performances for tourists (Cyrille 2002; Gerstin 2000; Pulvar 2009).

In recent years, the bèlè movement has become a stronghold for new sacred meaning-making that emerges through performance rituals, interpersonal communication, and public discourse. When one treats the drum as a divine entity—an instrument that facilitates emotional transcendence through bodily movement—bèlè becomes a tool for self-preservation, as well as a form of devotion and reverence for the ancestors and some deities belonging to African and Afro-diasporic religious pantheons. Many anthropological studies point to the drum and bodily movement as keys for mediating communication with the spirit world, creating the conditions for emotional transcendence, and unifying individuals who share common beliefs and values. However, this scholarship has appeared most prominently in studies of Haitian Vodou (Dunham 1969; Hurston [1938] 1990; McAlister 2002), the Orisha traditions of Cuba and Brazil (Y. Daniel 2005; Hagedorn 2001; Matory 2005), and the Maroon and Kumina traditions of Jamaica (Bilby 2008; Dje Dje 1998). Martinique's drum-dance heritage remains an underanalyzed part of this intellectual conversation, which invites one to question the politics of religiosity and secularism that are at play under French universalist nationalism.

As Greg Johnson (2011) argues in his research on Indigenous religious claims in Hawai'i, the politics of secularism that is intended to restrict religious claims actually stimulates cultural and religious generativity. New religious claims emerge and gain momentum under what Johnson refers to as "friction" (arguably provoked by the state) rather than some "newly achieved cultural consensus" (283). These claims become ever more emboldened, expansive, and variegated among Indigenous stakeholders, leading to the articulation of new religious meaning, expression, and identity—an observation of Johnson's research that can be applied to my analysis of Martinique.

In the French national and overseas contexts, norms of secularism are expected to regulate cultural production and restrict religious expression in the public sphere, defining what is legitimate and acceptable as limited to nonreligious culture. We must therefore consider the contested terrain of legitimizing bèlè as an Afro-Creole spiritual tradition, if its place in Martinique's cultural landscape is to remain devoid of sacred meaning. French republican ideals of laïcité compartmentalize social phenomena, thereby reinforcing particular binaries of sacred/secular or religion/culture, which are perhaps incongruent or in friction with some bèlè practitioners' longing for spiritual connectedness. As my research continues to unfold, it will be important to question whether bèlè can withstand the pressures associated with laïcité as the ancestral dance becomes more integral to contemporary Martinican public life, while also becoming more overtly spiritual. Before getting into the ethnographic data from which my inquiries emerge, I first provide an overview of the place of religion in Martinican society.

Contextualizing Religion in Martinique and Its Meaning in Bèlè

Today Roman Catholicism is the predominant religion of Martinique, although evangelical Protestant denominations are on the rise. With approximately 85 percent of the total population (396,000) practicing Catholicism and an archbishop presiding over sixty priests, Catholic holidays and feasts for the saints are observed regularly on the island, and Catholic adherents make an annual pilgrimage to the island's Sacred Heart Church in Balata (a one-fifth-size replica of the Basilica of the Sacred Heart of Paris). Hinduism came to Martinique with nineteenth-century immigration from South India, although most ethnic Indians in Martinique also identify as Catholic. There are also small Jewish and Islamic faith communities.

The 1685 Code Noir established by King Louis XIV in the French colonies enforced the conversion and baptism of enslaved Africans, and religious educational orders and catechism became especially intense in the years immediately preceding the 1848 emancipation (Ramsey 2011; Schmieder 2014). Despite the success of such orders in converting Martinique's majority Afro-descended population to Catholicism, the *quimbois* conjuring and folk healing tradition went underground and continued to exist alongside Christianity.[9] As William Miles points out, "against the long tradition of Roman Catholicism—nevertheless mitigated by deep-rooted Africanist folk practices (*quimboiserie*)—there is a French cultural overlay of *laïcité*, or secularism" (2014, 121). That is, Martinicans maintain cultural commitments to tradition, such as Catholic observances and the more obscured practices of quimbois, but the French national culture of laïcité also has an influence on the island.[10]

Most people agree that some earlier variant of bèlè dancing served ritual functions in African religious worship during the enslavement era, such as fertility and fecundity rites and harvest dances. However, this belief cannot be substantiated with reliable evidence owing to early colonial-era campaigns to eradicate African religious practices, as well as the racist Eurocentric bias found in written accounts of African dances. Thus, the question of spirituality in bèlè was not taken seriously as a legitimate field of inquiry and has even become a point of contention among some community members. Skeptics find spiritual conceptions of bèlè to be frivolous attempts to construct sacred meaning in a practice that is largely considered recreational, where religion no longer exists or perhaps never existed at all. They tend to criticize spiritual interpretations of the practice as "New Age-y," misguided, or outright exploitative inventions that distort the narrative of bèlè's transmission. It is not my goal to validate or disprove the belief that bèlè has a spiritual purpose. What is more important, and much more interesting to analyze, is how and why ideas about religion and spirituality in the context of bèlè are becoming more conspicuous, as evidenced by the range of sacred notions and embodied practices analyzed in the subsequent sections of this chapter.

Bèlè Légliz: Taking It to the Church

The first point of analysis involves the increasing visibility of bèlè performance in the Catholic Church, a fusion genre called *bèlè légliz*, which aims to refashion the liturgy with recognizable, locally inspired cultural references. Bèlè légliz was initiated at different periods in Martinique's postdepartmental era, dating back to the 1960s, when the Second Vatican Council implemented changes bringing about liturgical reforms that encouraged "inculturation"—the use of local music, dance, and vernacular language in worship services. In 1962 priests in Martinique attempted to restyle the liturgy with Martinique's local heritage and the Creole language, but they were unsuccessful at integrating bèlè into worship activities owing to the drum's negative association with alcohol consumption, Vodou, and *djab* (the devil). Bèlè légliz did not become a marketable genre and achieve wider appeal until around 2009, when albums devoted to the bèlè légliz project were produced, featuring artists such as Victor Treffe, K'zo Jean-Baptiste, and Stella Gonis, and bèlè légliz performance groups began giving concerts.[11] Bèlè légliz music and liturgical dance can now be found during Mass in some churches across the island, even though many Catholics outside of the bèlè community still find it shocking and offensive that the drum now has a place in the church.

Proponents of bèlè légliz define it as a creative adaptation of traditional bèlè, using *lespri bèlè* (the spirit of bèlè) and the repertoire of drum patterns and dance movements as a framework for developing Catholic liturgical expressions. The bèlè légliz team draws their inspiration from Bible verses such as Psalms 96:1–3 and Psalms 150:1–6, which instruct devotees to sing for the Lord and to praise the Lord with dance and the sound of instruments.[12] Because the church historically forbade the drum as a tool of the devil's work, the bèlè légliz team now emphasizes the utilization of the instrument as a tool for glorification. The liturgical movement styles found in bèlè légliz performances are modified (and some might argue sanitized) from the styles of movement found in swaré bèlè contexts, to make them palatable to Catholic audiences.

The bèlè légliz platform asserts that "the inculturation [of the church] must permit Martinicans to truly be themselves in connection with their faith," as articulated by Father Montconthour in a 2006 documentary entitled *Bèlè Légliz*.[13] In his explication of bèlè légliz, this priest employs vocabularies of freedom and liberation, well-being, and faith to envision and articulate a new framework for strengthened Christian identity, where spirituality, expressive culture, and sense of self converge. To quote one of the creators of the bèlè légliz genre: "God asked us to dance for him, so we do it with what we have here: our bodies, our instruments, our culture" (Clerc, interview, July 25, 2014). He argues that Martinique should not have to import gospel expressions from the United States or elsewhere when Martinicans have the cultural resources to develop their own liturgical styles of dance, music, and Creole translations of religious texts, such as hymnals and Bible verses. His emphasis on "we" and "our" suggests a sense of cultural autonomy to creolize Catholic worship with local markers of Martinican identity that historically had been prohibited.

Tracing African and Diasporic Cosmological Thought

The second line of thinking deals with African-inspired philosophical orientations to religion and spirituality that a subset of bèlè activists engage. The cosmologies and traditions of African and Afro-Atlantic religions, including Haitian Vodou, Cuban Santeria, and Brazilian Candomblé, have become important sources of authentic spiritual validation for these individuals who reject the dogmatic nature of the Catholic Church and the church's connection to Martinique's colonial history. It is no surprise, then, that they are inclined to critique or oppose the bèlè légliz project.[14] These practitioners of bèlè chart historical and symbolic connections with Africa and the wider diaspora in how they experience bèlè, embracing extralocal emblems of religious identity to stake their claims of cultural distinctiveness from France.

During my fieldwork I witnessed a number of discrete acts, such as the pouring of libations as an offering to the ancestors in swaré bèlè settings and the smudging of incense to purify the air for the spirits during dance lessons, leading me to question the claim that bèlè is strictly secular and to wonder what spiritual meaning it carried for certain individuals. Over time, my data revealed that very specific elements of African and Afro-diasporic religions held a significant place in the broader imagination of those individuals. Some interlocutors shared narratives that highlighted the sacred relevance of the circular procession that opens the bèlè dance sequence as a physical enactment of the Kongo cosmogram. Some emphasized the spiritual functions of sensual expressivity and flirtatious play in the dance, interpreting bèlè as a fecundity rite that encourages the human life cycle and celebrates the feminine erotic power of women practitioners—notions that overlap with the mythology of Oshun, the Yoruba goddess of fertility and love. Whenever such conversations occurred, I was reminded that these interpretations are deeply personal and that the narratives vary from one individual to the next.

Take, for example, Amadou, a fighter of danmyé (Martinique's martial art combat dance), a drummer, and a dancer in his late thirties who was an outspoken critic of Western Christianity and a vehement defender of both Vodou and Lucumi religious practices. On Amadou's drum, one finds an artistic fusion of both traditions. He describes the image that adorns his drum as a symbol for conjuring, inspired by the vévé (religious symbol) drawings of Vodou, which he has painted in red and white as a way of honoring his orisha Shango, the Yoruba warrior deity of strength, thunder, music, and dance. One also finds a thin rope that stretches across the face of the drum, which, according to his explanation, helps to produce sounds with special frequencies and vibrations that may enable altered states of consciousness among bèlè dancers and danmyé fight-ers. As a fighter of the martial art danmyé tradition, Amadou carries out special rituals to prepare his mind and body for fighting in special danmyé events (in-terview, May 17, 2014).

Another example is Gérôme (in his late thirties), who associates bèlè with the Haitian Vodou lwa (spirit) Kouzen Zaka—the spirit of agriculture and pro-tector of farmworkers in the pantheon of Haitian Vodou. According to elders of the bèlè tradition, bèlè is "une danse de la terre" (a dance of the earth) that was practiced by agricultural laborers to promote land and human fertility; they toiled on plantations to the sound of the bèlè drum and danced as a source of release after a hard day's work. Many of the dance movements in the bèlè reper-toire are representative of movements executed in agricultural field labor, such as grating manioc and cutting sugarcane. Gérôme has spent the past few years researching possible links between Martinican bèlè and the lore of Kouzen Zaka in Vodou. Writing about Kouzen Zaka's dances in Haiti, dance anthro-pologist Yvonne Daniel describes a dance called mayi (from the Mahi nation), which is danced to announce the arrival of Kouzen Zaka's spirit in Vodou cer-emonies: "Mayi . . . is a quick-paced, foot-slapping, agriculturally-rooted dance within Rada rituals and is immensely important in Haiti's agricultural society" (2005, 112). Another dance in Haiti, called djouba, is danced for Kouzen Zaka, and it is performed to a drum that Haitians call the matinik (Cally 1990, 18–19; S. Johnson 2012, 151). This drum is played in the same manner that the bèlè drum is played in Martinique, and the movements of djouba resemble some of the movements found in Martinique's bèlè repertoire: "For playing djouba, the drum is laid on the ground and played with hands and feet, because djouba spirits live in the earth" (Averill and Wilcken 2008, 130).

According to Gérôme, this overlap between Haitian and Martinican folk-lore is not mere coincidence. He implied that this aspect of Caribbean religious heritage has flourished in Haiti, free from the restraints of extended colonial re-pression that caused the disintegration of African-based belief systems in Mar-tinique. In recent years, organizers of the biennial bèlè festival have renamed the four-day festival event Bèlè Djouba to honor this aspect of their culture. At Bèlè Djouba festival gatherings in 2016, I witnessed fruit offerings thrown into the sea and plant offerings installed in the ground while dancers moved with fire torches around the concrete statues of the Anse Cafard slave memorial.[15] Much like the significance of Kouzen Zaka's lore in Haiti, bèlè has become a conduit through which Martinicans can express their spiritual devotion to the earth, land, and soil and memorialize their ancestors, who possessed special systems of knowledge of the natural landscape for their communities to prevail under incredibly harsh circumstances. That spirit of survival, resilience, and solidarity lives on in the collective memory of activists today.

Another perspective, which draws heavily from Egyptian cosmic knowledge, suggests that members of the bèlè performance ensemble are responsible for receiving and carrying solar and/or lunar energy to the spirit world. As my interlocutor Izaak explained, this is why the drummer should position the drum so that its head faces the sun or moon. The dancers open the bèlè sequence by dancing counterclockwise, consistent with the moon's orbit of the earth. The dancers then reverse their circular procession, moving in a clockwise direction, however, because they must go back and gather the positive cosmic energy that descends from the moon as it orbits the earth. Izaak explained that cosmic energy is transmitted through the inverse triangle that is formed by the drummer's foot and two hands as they strike the drum, passing through the body of the drum to the spirit world; therefore, it is the drummer who gives the offering of cosmic energy to the ancestors. I recall that on the day I interviewed Izaak, he responded to my astonishment by concluding, "Our ancestors were so intelligent. . . . These are extraordinary things. *Bèlè is a High Mass, Madame!* You can't have the 'culturel' without the 'cultuel' [worship], and one cannot be a good practitioner of bèlè if they do not integrate worship and devotion into their practice. This means that when I do bèlè, I give worship to the divinities around me, the elements of nature, the stars and the moon—and all of these elements are in bèlè" (interview, May 1, 2014).

Izaak was the only person I encountered in my fieldwork who shared this very specific, riveting interpretation of bèlè as a sacred practice. From our conversation, I got the sense that he had discovered these connections through a combination of research and meditation, reading various sources in an attempt to uncover the origins of bèlè but also praying for clarity and deeply contemplating the stories of the oral tradition he had learned throughout his life, which contained pieces of Martinique's African past. Each of the cases that I have presented here, in fact, speaks to individuals' vested interests in researching, adopting, and valorizing the worship practices and religious beliefs of Africa and its diaspora, particularly those that resonate with bèlè's values and performance elements. This synthesis of spiritual engagement, with Africa at its center, represents a special kind of resistance that is not familiar to or championed by most Martinicans. It demonstrates a commitment to decolonial philosophies and an allegiance to a diasporic religious heritage that was systematically erased from Martinique.

Bèlè as Secular Spirituality

Doktè ka ba la djèwizon, mé bèlè ka djèwi mwen san fason.

Doctors can give the remedy, but bèlè heals me without medicine.
—Noémi, a longtime *danm bèlè* (female dancer), July 25, 2013

One evening in July 2013, I organized a focus-group interview with eight women whom I had most frequently focused on at bèlè classes and in swaré bèlè gatherings over the course of my field research (I had known some of them since 2009). During the four-hour discussion, in which these women revealed the different spiritual and therapeutic aspects of bèlè practice, they shared how the power of the dance and the drum's sounds transport them to higher states of joy and pleasure, especially when the energy is high and the right elements are in place. Most of them agreed that there are times when bèlè is the perfect remedy for relieving stress and tension and making them feel better in emotionally trying circumstances. A friend whom I will refer to as Noémi, a woman in her mid-forties who has danced bèlè since she was a teenager, commented, "Some people prefer to go lay down on a couch in a psychologist's office to find solutions to their problems, but me, I go to bèlè." She went on to describe her process of prayer while in the swaré bèlè dance space: "When I'm dancing in my *carré* [square formation of four dancers], I find my Father, Son, and Holy Ghost, and while I'm doing my *monté o tanbou* [salute to the drummers], I pray. . . . I either give thanks, or I deposit my problems" (interview, July 25, 2013).[16] Noémi's statement suggests that bèlè in secular swaré bèlè performance contexts has the same transcendental healing effect as Christian praise and worship, outside of the formal institutional framework of the church.

Here I examine the third perspective, which conceptualizes bèlè as a laïque (secular) spirituality. Ideas about spirituality and religion in the bèlè revival movement have evolved over time as many of today's practitioners discover sacred meaning in what has long been treated as a secular practice. Beyond the realm of political mobilization and economic solidarity, bèlè is said to have a tremendous impact on participants' emotional health and spiritual growth, which are treated as interdependent variables affecting a person's well-being, rather than mutually exclusive categories. Some bèlè practitioners seem to legitimize or make sense of their transformative experiences by mapping different spiritual narratives onto a performance practice that does not have an explicit connection to any particular religious heritage. The designation *laïque spirituality*, an expression that is gaining popularity among members of the bèlè community, seems suitable for encompassing the range of spiritual and emotional journeys one might undertake through participation in bèlè.

Though the idea of a secular spirituality may seem like an oxymoron, it is currently undergoing serious discussion and exploration among certain leaders of the movement. This term exposes the extent to which the practitioners who endorse the term are shaped by French liberal ideals of secular modernity and are perhaps uncomfortable with the idea of religion in the bèlè context. In using the term *laïque spirituality*, are they subconsciously seeking to gain recognition for bèlè through a framework of French secular normativity? Or do they consciously reject the idea of religion owing to its association with hierarchical organization, dogma, and doctrine, in favor of liberal concepts (such as "self" and "freedom") offered by spirituality (Mitchell 2011)? The term allows them to challenge the idea that bèlè is purely a cultural product or recreational activity that has no sacred meaning but to do so by employing a concept that renders bèlè legitimate in the context of laïcité. On numerous occasions, my interlocutors told me that bèlè is not religious but is without question spiritual, and I was frequently advised not to get the two categories confused in my analysis. In unpacking the distinction between religion and spirituality, Kerry Mitchell (2011) draws from Michel Foucault's definition of spirituality, which locates personal transformation and "care of the self" within larger operations of power. Mitchell argues that the proclivity to focus on (and even celebrate) the concepts "self" and "freedom" in spirituality discourse obscures our understanding of the social constructedness of spirituality—that it is shaped by fluid social relations and power dynamics (see Foucault 2005).

Conclusion

Actors in the bèlè movement have done tremendous work in encouraging its followers to uphold a system of values, morals, and ethical guidelines rooted in the ancestral heritage of Martinique. The tradition is said to comprise its own set of convictions and principles, and participation in bèlè has helped to craft an alternative worldview, diverging from that which has been imposed through French colonial hegemony. Participants congregate for weekly, monthly, and annual rituals and ceremonial gatherings to rejoice, socialize, give reverence, and promote the spirit of bèlè as it was inherited from generations past. Occasionally, I came across bèlè practitioners who claimed to have experienced trance while dancing bèlè, and for many, bèlè performance is an emotional release that serves as a healthy alternative to talk therapy, meditation, or yoga. A woman once explained to me how she cried during her entire *carré bèlè* and *monté o tanbou* sequence at a swaré bèlè as she grieved the loss of a loved one. As we can see, the bèlè dance space has the capacity to become one's altar or prayer bench, where one can give grace, offer prayers of invocation, and release feelings of pain and tension.

Although spiritual experiences in bèlè are indeed personal and vary from one individual to the next, the spaces where these experiences occur are very much social, relational, and community oriented. The inclination to resist larger structures of colonial power is a political one, which reinforces Mitchell's call to read spirituality through a Foucauldian lens. Bèlè as a sacred practice, experienced at the individual and group levels, cannot be detached from its political implications, whether it is interpreted through Catholic liturgical expression, Afro-syncretic cosmology, or laïque spirituality.

The quest for sacred purpose in the bèlè tradition, with both Christian- and African-inspired religious interpretations, as well as notions of secular spirituality, represents a new form of subversion of the legacy of French colonialism. One could argue that these different orientations to spirituality are incompatible or in conflict with one another in the struggle for legitimacy. Some skeptics deny the spiritual function of bèlè altogether and choose to engage bèlè for strictly social and recreational purposes. Perhaps rival perspectives about how the tradition is to be developed and transmitted could hinder the larger objective of empowerment. But rather than debating the legitimacy of these perspectives, I see this as an occasion to situate Martinique's drum-dance heritage and spirituality politics in an ever-expanding intellectual conversation about the complex anthropological subject we call Afro-Atlantic religion. This examination contributes to our understandings of laïcité in a nonmetropolitan context, from the contested field of bèlè performance, where the binary of religion/culture is unsettled from a range of perspectives.

This research is influenced by the recent scholarship on Afro-Atlantic religion and spirituality that critically examines how ethnographers *and* practitioners of African-inspired religions in Latin America and the Caribbean conceive, construct, reframe, and write about religious expression in the quest to recover "pure" or "authentic" African origins (Capone 2010; P. Johnson 2007; Matory 2005; Palmié 2013). These interventions problematize the essentialization of Black religiosity and call attention to how religious economies and the "commerce of memory making" (Johnson 2007, 45) shape the complexity of Black religious experience. My research, particularly the examination of bèlè légliz, also confronts the tendency in anthropology to dismiss or overlook Christian-based cultural movements in Caribbeanist and Latin Americanist scholarship. The "disciplinary bias" against Christianity (Louis 2014, 10) is most likely due to overarching generalizations of Christianity as a tool of oppression and domination. This tendency ignores new currents pointing to the region's increasing religious pluralism and spiritual diversity, shifting religious markets, and the influence that other religious orientations are having on Christianity, and vice versa.[17]

This project is further enriched by the body of scholarship that interrogates the French tradition of militant laïcité for its role in marginalizing religious minorities. How are French Antillean bèlè activists, as overseas subjects of the French state, impacted by the republican ideals of secularism in their search for sacred meaning in an African-derived ancestral practice? French Antilleans of African descent have always had to wrestle with the double consciousness of their Blackness and Frenchness, and research shows that French Antilleans in metropolitan France are divided on which identity holds greater importance (Constant 2012). Even though French Antilleans, in theory, meet all the conditions for successful assimilation through their devout practice of Catholicism or their allegiance to the liberal ideals of secularism, they continue to face discrimination, marginalization, and poor treatment as second-class citizens.

To revisit Wallace's theory of revitalization movements, conceptualized as new or revived religious practices that emerge in response to widespread distress, bèlè activists are indeed making "deliberate, organized, conscious efforts . . . to construct a more satisfying culture" (1956, 265). One could go so far as to argue that bèlè is a new syncretic religious practice in the making, but it may be too early to tell. If we envisage bèlè's rebirth as a revitalization movement, it is one that is uniquely multifaceted, transmitting a variety of spiritual interpretations with the unified mission of healing and unshackling the psychological chains of colonialism in Martinique.

NOTES

1. Throughout this chapter I use pseudonyms in place of real names to protect the anonymity of my interlocutors.

2. The *tambour bèlè* (bèlè drum) is made from a repurposed rum barrel and a goatskin drumhead.

3. For further reading on American Indian revitalization movements, see White (2009).

4. *The metropole* refers to metropolitan France, or the part of France in mainland Europe, in contrast to the overseas territories of France.

5. Danmyé, also known as *ladja*, is a combat/martial art tradition danced by two combatants in the center of a circle, musically accompanied by the bèlè drum and call-and-response singing. One version of kalennda involves competitive interplay between a drummer and a solo dancer in the center of a circle. Another variation of kalennda (*kalennda lisid*) is a group dance with an unlimited number of participants dancing in playful harmony with each other while accenting steps in sync with the rhythmic sequences of the drum.

6. Most of the bèlè revivalists' parents prohibited them from practicing bèlè when they were children (assimilation was quite strong in the 1960s). Bèlè practice was long stigmatized as *bagay vyé nèg* (a pejorative Creole expression for old, rustic, unsophisticated aspects of Black rural life) or *bagay djab* (devilish, associated with evil).

7. Although each member organization of this coalition maintains its own identity and governing structure, the Coordination Lawonn Bèlè has an executive committee of elected leadership posts (the *komité lézalié*), consisting of a coordinator, secretary, treasurer, and so on. The Coordination Lawonn Bèlè and its member organizations are all registered as *associations loi de 1901* (nonprofit organizations).

8. For example, during the thirty-eight-day general strike and political unrest of 2009, bèlè street performance was used as a medium for igniting the public in protest repertoires and demonstrations. See Maddox (2015) and Gilbert Pago, "The Time of Anti-capitalist and Anti-colonial Contestation," *International Viewpoint*, April 14, 2009, http://www.internationalviewpoint.org/spip.php?article1648.

9. Quimbois is Martinique's tradition of conjuring and folk healing. It is comparable to American hoodoo or Jamaican obeah and is largely dismissed in public life as old superstition and witchcraft.

10. As Vanessa Agard-Jones (2009) articulates in her work, the French liberal rights framework and the norms of laïcité ostensibly protect LGBTQ communities in the French Antilles from homophobic attacks that are founded on conservative Christian principles and tend to restrict and/or criminalize homosexuality in other Caribbean island societies. However, tensions persist among elected officials of the socialist party in Martinique on the issue of gay marriage, with religious conviction at the root of the discord (5).

11. These albums were produced by Fred Jean-Baptiste of Mizik Label in Martinique.

12. The *Bèlè Légliz* (2009) album liner notes refer to 2 Samuel 6, about King David dancing before the Lord and playing instruments with the Israelites.

13. Father Montconthour, "Donner la chance à Jésus d'être Créole" [Give Jesus a chance to be Créole], 3:17, *Le Jour de Seigneur* video, excerpt from *Bèlè Légliz*, dir. Philippe Fusellier and Eric Pailler, 26 mins. (CFRT, France2, RFO, 2006), accessed May 15, 2015, http://bcove.me/hnvpdvos.

14. Bèlè associations do not officially endorse or reject bèlè légliz or any particular African-inspired religious interpretation of bèlè. Competing perspectives and critiques are mostly a matter of one's personal opinion and experience. Views and commitments regarding bèlè's sacred elements tend to vary across youth, activists, and elders.

15. Anse Cafard is a slave memorial located off the Caribbean coast of Diamond Beach in the southern town of Diamant. The monument consists of twenty concrete statues standing eight feet tall, overlooking the sea, memorializing the enslaved Africans who lost their lives when a slave ship capsized in 1830.

16. In the choreography of bèlè from Sainte Marie developed from the quadrille, the *carré bèlè* is the square-dancing segment of the sequence, whereby two female-male couples dance face-to-face in the formation of a square and swap positions so that the dancers may exchange partners. The *monté o tanbou* is the segment of the dance se-

quence following the square dancing, whereby each couple takes a turn dancing together in a moment of playful display, and they accompany one another dancing toward the drummer as a way of greeting and giving thanks to the drummer.

17. John Burdick shows, for example, how progressive Catholics (Burdick 2004) and evangelicals (Burdick 2013) in Brazil are implicated in contemporary struggles around Black identity politics. Expressions that are traditionally associated with the African presence in Brazil (such as samba, capoeira, and the instrumentation of Candomblé music) have had a considerable influence on contemporary liturgical performance in Christian settings. Bertin Louis's (2014) work on the Haitian Protestant diaspora is also useful in understanding contemporary Caribbean religious diversity.

REFERENCES

Agard-Jones, Vanessa. 2009. "*Le Jeu de Qui*? Sexual Politics at Play in the French Caribbean." *Caribbean Review of Gender Studies*, no. 3: 1–19.

Averill, Gage, and Lois Wilcken. 2008. "Haiti." In *The Garland Handbook of Latin American Music*, edited by Dale Alan Olsen and Daniel Edward Sheehy, 126–142. New York: Routledge.

Bèlè Légliz. 2009. Martinique: Mizik Label. Compact disc.

Beriss, David. 2004. *Black Skins, French Voices: Caribbean Ethnicity and Activism in Urban France*. Cambridge, UK: Westview Press.

Bertrand, Anca. 1968. "À propos des ballets folkloriques Martiniquais." *Parallèles* 26: 74–77.

Bilby, Kenneth. 2008. *True-Born Maroons*. Gainesville: University of Florida Press.

Bonilla, Yarimar. 2015. *Non-Sovereign Futures: French Caribbean Politics in the Wake of Disenchantment*. Chicago: University of Chicago Press.

Browne, Katherine. 2004. *Creole Economics: Caribbean Cunning under the French Flag*. Austin: University of Texas Press.

Burdick, John. 2004. *Legacies of Liberation: The Progressive Catholic Church in Brazil at the Start of a New Millennium*. Aldershot, UK: Ashgate.

Burdick, John. 2013. *The Color of Sound: Race, Religion, and Music in Brazil*. New York: New York University Press.

Burton, Richard D. E. 1995. "French West Indies à l'heure de l'Europe: An Overview." In *French and West Indian: Martinique, Guadeloupe and French Guiana Today*, edited by Richard D. E. Burton and Fred Reno, 1–19. Charlottesville: University of Virginia Press.

Cally, Sully. 1990. *Musiques et danses afro-caraïbes: Martinique*. Gros-Morne, Martinique: Sully-Cally/Lezin.

Capone, Stefania. 2010. *Searching for Africa in Brazil: Power and Tradition in Candomblé*. Durham, NC: Duke University Press.

Constant, Fred. 2012. "'Black France' and the National Identity Debate: How Best to Be Black and French?" In *Black France/France Noire: The History and Politics of Blackness*, edited by Trica Danielle Keaton, T. Denean Sharpley-Whiting, and Tyler Stovall, 123–144. Durham, NC: Duke University Press.

Covington-Ward, Yolanda. 2015. *Gesture and Power: Religion, Nationalism, and Everyday Performance in Congo*. Durham, NC: Duke University Press.

Cyrille, Dominique. 2002. "Sa Ki Ta Nou (This Belongs to Us): Creole Dances of the French Caribbean." In *Caribbean Dance from Abakuá to Zouk: How Movement Shapes Identity*, edited by Susanna Sloat, 221–244. Gainesville: University Press of Florida.

Cyrille, Dominique. 2006. "Imagining an Afro-Creole Nation: Eugène Mona's Music in Martinique of the 1980s." *Latin American Music Review* 27 (2): 148–170.

Daniel, Justin. 2001. "The Construction of Dependency: Economy and Politics in the French Antilles." In *Islands at the Crossroads: Politics in the Non-independent Caribbean*, edited by Aarón Gamaliel Ramos and Angel Israel Rivera, 61–79. Kingston, Jamaica: Ian Randle.

Daniel, Yvonne. 1995 *Rumba: Dance and Social Change in Contemporary Cuba*. Bloomington: Indiana University Press.

Daniel, Yvonne. 2005. *Dancing Wisdom: Embodied Knowledge in Haitian Vodou, Cuban Yoruba, and Bahian Candomblé*. Urbana: University of Illinois Press.

Daniel, Yvonne. 2009. "A Critical Analysis of Caribbean Contredanse." *Transforming Anthropology* 17 (2): 147–154.

Daniel, Yvonne. 2011. *Caribbean and Atlantic Diaspora Dance: Igniting Citizenship*. Urbana: University of Illinois Press.

Dje Dje, Jacqueline Cogdell. 1998. "Remembering Kojo: History, Music, and Gender in the January Sixth Celebration of the Jamaican Accompong Maroons." *Black Music Research Journal* 18 (1–2): 67–120.

Dunham, Katherine. 1969. *Island Possessed*. Chicago: University of Chicago Press.

Fanon, Frantz. (1952) 1967. *Black Skin, White Masks*. Translated by Charles Lam Markmann. New York: Grove.

Fernando, Mayanthi L. 2014. *The Republic Unsettled: Muslim French and the Contradictions of Secularism*. Durham, NC: Duke University Press.

Foucault, Michel. 2005. *The Hermeneutics of the Subject: Lectures at the Collège de France, 1981–1982*. New York: Picador.

Fusellier, Philippe, and Eric Pailler, dirs. 2006 *Bèlè Légliz*. 26 min. CFRT, France2, RFO.

Gerstin, Julian. 2000. "Musical Revivals and Social Movements in Contemporary Martinique: Ideology, Identity, Ambivalence." In *The African Diaspora: A Musical Perspective*, edited by Ingrid Monson, 295–328. New York: Garland.

Glissant, Édouard. 1981. *Le discours antillais*. Paris: Seuil.

Hagedorn, Katherine. 2001. *Divine Utterances: The Performance of Afro-Cuban Santería*. Washington, DC: Smithsonian Institution Press.

Henry, Clarence Bernard. 2008. *Let's Make Some Noise: Axé and the African Roots of Brazilian Popular Music*. Jackson: University Press of Mississippi.

Hurston, Zora Neale. (1938) 1990. *Tell My Horse: Voodoo and Life in Haiti and Jamaica*. New York: Perennial Library.

Johnson, Greg. 2011. "Courting Culture: Unexpected Relationships between Religion and Law in Contemporary Hawai'i." In *After Secular Law*, edited by Winnifred Fallers Sullivan, Robert A. Yelle, and Mateo Taussig-Rubbo, 282–301. Stanford, CA: Stanford University Press.

Johnson, Paul Christopher. 2007. *Diaspora Conversions: Black Carib Religion and the Recovery of Africa*. Berkeley: University of California Press.

Johnson, Sara E. 2012. *The Fear of French Negroes: Transcolonial Collaboration in the Revolutionary Americas*. Berkeley: University of California Press.

Jouili, Jeanette. 2015. *Pious Practice and Secular Constraints: Women in the Islamic Revival in Europe*. Stanford, CA: Stanford University Press.

Louis, Bertin M., Jr. 2014. *My Soul Is in Haiti: Protestantism in the Haitian Diaspora of the Bahamas*. New York: New York University Press.

Maddox, Camee. 2015. "'Yes We Can! Down with Colonization!': Race, Gender, and the 2009 General Strike in Martinique." *Transforming Anthropology* 23 (2): 90–103.

Massé, Raymond. 2008. *Détresse Créole: Ethnoépidémiologie de la détresse psychique à la Martinique*. Quebec: Presses de l'Université Laval.

Matory, J. Lorand. 2005. *Black Atlantic Religion: Tradition, Transnationalism, and Matriarchy in the Afro-Brazilian Candomblé*. Princeton, NJ: Princeton University Press.

McAlister, Elizabeth A. 2002. *Rara! Vodou, Power, and Performance in Haiti and Its Diaspora*. Berkeley: University of California Press.

Miles, William F. S. 2012. "Schizophrenic Island, Fifty Years after Fanon: Martinique, the Pent-Up 'Paradise.'" *International Journal of Francophone Studies* 15 (1): 9–33.

Miles, William F. S. 2014. *Scars of Partition: Postcolonial Legacies in French and British Borderlands*. Lincoln: University of Nebraska Press.

Mitchell, Kerry A. 2011. "The Politics of Spirituality: Liberalizing the Definition of Religion." In *Secularism and Religion-Making*, edited by Markus Dressler and Arvind-Pal S. Mandair, 125–140. New York: Oxford University Press.

Moreau de St. Méry, M. L. E. 1796. *Danse: Article extrait d'un ouvrage de M. L. E. Moreau de St. Méry ayant pour titre: Répertoire des notions colonials. Par Ordre Alphabétique*. Philadelphia: Printed by the author.

Palmié, Stephan. 2013. *The Cooking of History: How Not to Study Afro-Cuban Religion*. Chicago: University of Chicago Press.

Price, Richard. 1998. *The Convict and the Colonel: A Story of Colonialism and Resistance*. Durham, NC: Duke University Press.

Pulvar, Olivier. 2009. "Le bèlè en Martinique, défense du patrimoine et promotion de produits culturels." In *Communication et dynamiques de globalisation culturelle*, edited by Alain Kiyindou, Jean-Chrétien D. Ekambo, and Ludovic-Robert Miyouna, 39–48. Paris: Harmattan.

Ramsey, Kate. 2011. *The Spirits and the Law: Vodou and Power in Haiti*. Chicago: University of Chicago Press.

Schmieder, Ulrike. 2014. "The Teaching Religious Orders and Slave Emancipation in Martinique." *Journal of Caribbean History* 47 (2): 153–183.

Scott, Joan Wallach. 2007. *The Politics of the Veil*. Princeton, NJ: Princeton University Press.

Tucker, Linda G. 2007. *Lockstep and Dance: Images of Black Men in Popular Culture*. Jackson: University Press of Mississippi.

Valnes, Matthew. 2015. "Taking It Higher: The Spirituality of Sensuality in Funk Performance." *African and Black Diaspora: An International Journal* 9 (1): 3–15.

Varela, Sergio González. 2017. "The Religious Foundations of Capoeira Angola: The Cosmopolitics of an Apparently Non-religious Practice." *Religion and Society* 8 (1): 79–93.

Wallace, Anthony F. C. 1956. "Revitalization Movements." *American Anthropologist* 58 (2): 264–281.

White, Phillip M. 2009. "Researching American Indian Revitalization Movements." *Journal of Religious and Theological Information* 8 (3–4): 155–163.

Willson, Margaret. 2001. "Designs of Deception: Concepts of Consciousness, Spirituality and Survival in Capoeira Angola in Salvador, Brazil." *Anthropology of Consciousness* 12 (1): 19–36.

8. Embodying Black Islam: The Ethics and Aesthetics of Afro-Diasporic Muslim Hip-Hop in Britain

JEANETTE S. JOUILI

Over the past fifteen years, hip-hop has grown slowly but steadily within the British Islamic cultural sphere, a trend spearheaded mainly by British Muslims of African descent. In a religious scene that, when it came to music, was long dominated by Islamic devotional music (*nasheed*), hip-hop has struggled with a legitimacy problem. For Muslim hip-hop artists, however, this music genre justifies itself for its significant contribution to forging a Black Muslim identity and the specific ethical commitments that are germane to this project.

For the artists in question, hip-hop's potential Islamic legitimacy is rooted in the ethics and politics of "original" hip-hop (connected to contesting racism and neocolonialism and promoting Black consciousness). It is this commitment that Muslim hip-hop artists generally seek to uphold. Much has been written about the ethico*political* commitments of "Muslim" hip-hop, especially in the United States but also in parts of western Europe, Africa, and the Middle East.[1] However, little attention has been paid to another dimension of Muslim hip-hop that is central to the artists' efforts to authenticate hip-hop as Islamic— the particular *aesthetic* styles that Muslim hip-hop culture has adopted and that are intrinsically linked to the ethics of hip-hop.[2]

In this essay I attend to the central role of the body within the ethics and aesthetics of Islamic hip-hop as conceived by Afro-descendant British Muslim hip-hop practitioners.[3] I use the term *Islamic hip-hop*—a term that is endorsed by some practitioners but rejected or used only with caution by others—to talk about hip-hop music made by Muslim performers who regularly perform at Muslim community events and consciously aspire to produce hip-hop that enjoys a certain Islamic legitimacy. And I argue, more particularly, that the body—its performance, portrayal, and agency, whether onstage or in its lyrical representation—is pivotal for rendering the genre a legitimate form of Islamic expression and, in turn, for fashioning an *authentic* Black Muslim cultural space. In this context, body representation and performance cannot be reduced to mere symbolism, a politics of authenticity (thus representing something that is already there), or a politics of identity flattened by liberal multicultural politics (McNay 2008). Rather, the body, with its attending ethical potentialities, serves as a *conduit* for cultivating pious Muslim subjectivities and shaping ethical communities. Muslim piety, according to my interlocutors, is understood as already incorporating, next to a deep God-consciousness, an ethicopolitical sensibility that commits to combating all forms of oppression, including (anti-Black) racism, in order to promote the Islamic virtue of justice ('*adl*). This commitment, I illustrate here, is grounded within a broader ethics of intersubjectivity, defined by responsibility, compassion, and care.

After briefly situating British Muslim hip-hop artists within the Muslim music scene in Britain, I describe the discursive strategies through which Muslim hip-hop performers authenticate hip-hop as a Black Islamic art form. The arguments in this authentication narrative have important consequences for (en)sounding and performing Islamic hip-hop and thus impact its sensory and corporeal experience; I discuss here more particularly the sartorial styles and forms of bodily comportment onstage. In the last section, I consider the case of Poetic Pilgrimage, a Muslim female hip-hop duo, which is an interesting example for studying the (embodied) ethics and aesthetics of Black British Muslim hip-hop in its distinct female articulation. Embedded in a rich tradition of Black diasporic women's expression through literature and music as well as in Islamic spiritual traditions, these two female hip-hop artists center the body, not only within their performances but also within their lyrics, in ways that push forward the reflection on intersubjective ethics as an embodied endeavor.

Shaping Black British Islam through Hip-Hop

Until quite recently Islamic hip-hop has been among the most contested music genres within the Islamic culture scene in Britain. While the legitimacy of music and more particularly of musical instruments is a subject of Islamic theological debates, which reverberate especially in Islamic revival circles (see, for instance, Otterbeck 2008), debates among British Muslims have often crystallized around hip-hop, a secular music culture conceived by many pious practitioners as most opposed to an Islamic ethos. According to many hip-hop musicians themselves, this is mainly due to hip-hop culture's general notoriety (associated with sexual promiscuity, drugs, and violence) but also to what Su'ad Abdul Khabeer (2016, 3), who writes for the US Muslim context, calls the "ethnoreligious hegemonies of Arab and South Asian communities," which determine that one could not "engage Black expressive cultures *as* Muslims." This certainly holds true for the ethnically diverse British Muslim community, which is numerically and institutionally dominated by Muslims of South Asian and, to a lesser extent, Middle Eastern background (South Asian Muslims constitute more than two-thirds of the British Muslim population). African-descendant Muslims in Britain, whether hailing from sub-Saharan African countries or from the Caribbean (usually converts), are a quickly growing community but still make up a relatively small proportion of the overall population, and they have generally been overlooked in discussions on British Islam (see Curtis 2014).[4]

In a context where "authentic" Muslim culture is, especially among the older generations, presumed to be located within Middle Eastern and South Asian traditions, Islamic hip-hop in Britain explicitly challenges these ethnoreligious-based understandings of religious authenticity.[5] As several Muslim hip-hop artists of Afro-Caribbean background told me, just as Muslims all over the world had initially adapted their pre-Islamic local cultural traditions to the requirements of the new religion, they today claim the right to do so as well. This point was powerfully brought home to me during a conversation in July 2011 with Tanya Muneera Williams and Sukina Douglas, two women of Jamaican descent who make up the hip-hop duo Poetic Pilgrimage, at Sukina's home in North West London. Muneera said, "The culture should not override Islam. If there is something in your culture that is adverse to Islam, of course, we won't practice it, but if it is healthy and something . . . that helps us to breathe Islam, then this is definitely necessary. There have been problems with people's identity; they think they have to act like they are of South Asian culture or that they have to act as if they are from Saudi Arabia, all these things. But actually our culture is fine, we just need to find ways to make it compatible." Sukina here intervened and added, "Muneera hit the nail on the head. It's like, until we have an identity which is native, from where we are, it will be someone else's interpretation, someone else's commentary. It will never be real, it won't be us."

Becoming Muslim, for these artists, consisted not in adopting anything Arabic or Indo-Pakistani as the authentic Islamic way but in maintaining and furthering those elements from their own cultural background that they considered to be aligned with the ethics of their new faith, while at the same time also resituating themselves within a global Muslim heritage. This ambition, translated into an artistic/musical project, has in turn given rise to a variety of styles under the umbrella of Islamic hip-hop. Each of the African-descendant performers or bands I met throughout my fieldwork in London and other British cities drew in a unique way on what they understood to be their own "musical heritage." In recent years, these artists have succeeded in gaining greater access to stages in mainstream Muslim spaces. Nonetheless, events in these spaces rarely give hip-hop a dominant place, and thus these artists continue to have something of an underground status. Unlike some nasheed artists, they do not work with the known "Islamic" record labels but are completely independent, promoting their music on social media and, if they produce CDs, self-distributing them. In spite of a certain feeling of marginalization, many of the artists also appreciate this situation. True to their ideal of authentic hip-hop, being underground artists is a status they do not necessarily seek to escape, even if they simultaneously struggle for acceptance of their art form within mainstream British Muslim scenes.

Authenticating Hip-Hop

To fully comprehend my interlocutors' particular engagement with the hip-hop tradition, one has to take into account how Islamic traditions have engaged with practices of *listening* as a mode of "ethical attunement" (Hirschkind 2015, 168), thereby delineating something like a specific Islamic acoustemology. This acoustemology (as for other religious traditions) is embedded in a broader sensory epistemology that acknowledges the role of embodied and perceptual experiences in the shaping and "molding of the human senses in accord with a religious tradition" (166). Consequently, Islamic scholars throughout the ages have reflected extensively on how to discipline the ear (and the gaze) so as to hone specific ethical dispositions. While these scholars have never succeeded in circumscribing the multifarious music traditions produced in Muslim contexts throughout the ages, the traditions of ethical cultivation have been reworked within contemporary Islamic revival circles across the globe. Popular culture, and especially music, has been hesitantly but gradually included in the realm of pious activities, with the acknowledgment of art's and music's potential to strengthen Muslim subjectivities (see, for instance, Winegar 2009).

In this sense, my interlocutors were all, without exception, conscious that, in addition to their own aspiration to piety and virtuous conduct, they as musicians are in a position to promote, through their music but also through their accompanying conduct, pious dispositions within their audience. These considerations that acknowledged a strong ethical relation between performers and listeners infused my interlocutors' efforts to redefine hip-hop in terms of being simultaneously an explicitly claimed Black art form and an authentic Islamic music genre.

Throughout my fieldwork I have encountered two distinct but intertwined tropes that the artists articulated to authenticate hip-hop, both establishing a hip-hop genealogy leading back to a certain Muslim identity—which also had important consequences for dovetailing Islamic hip-hop to earlier Islamic acoustemologies. The first trope created a link between African American music traditions and African Muslim culture by stressing the influence of West African (Muslim) griot music that enslaved West African Muslims had brought along to the Americas.[6] Connecting hip-hop to griot music as an important oral or storytelling tradition enabled these practitioners to define the genre as a *spoken-word art* that is about transmitting social commentary and memory. In their discussions of hip-hop, they thereby clearly downgraded danceability, one of the prime objectives of mainstream hip-hop, while foregrounding listening practices. To my interlocutors, beats then seemed secondary, understood to be merely supportive, allowing the message to better enter the listener's ear. In other words, they considered the spoken-word art, not the beats, to prove hip-hop's correspondence with the sonic-linguistic practices of Islam's pronounced oral tradition. For this reason, many artists often switched easily between instrumental hip-hop/rap and spoken-poetry pieces, which points to the proximity they perceived between these two performance styles.[7] Interestingly, this focus on hip-hop as a spoken-word genre has triggered a thriving spoken-poetry scene in the larger British Muslim community.

The second trope that my interlocutors employed to authenticate hip-hop was related to an effort to disconnect "authentic" hip-hop from commercial mainstream hip-hop in order to emphasize the genre as a tool for transmitting ethical messages.[8] In this regard, British Muslim hip-hop artists regularly pointed out that hip-hop's origins were grounded in a Black political consciousness with an aspiration toward *social justice*. They directly linked this awareness to the fact that many of the hip-hop pioneers either were Muslims or were inspired by Islam-derived philosophies (see also Abdul Khabeer 2016; Aidi 2004; McLarney 2019).[9] Consequently, according to the artists I talked to, Islamic hip-hop had to stay committed to producing messages in line with hip-hop's original ethics, thereby also staying true to Islamic ethical principles. Mohammed Yahya, a Mozambican-British Muslim rapper based in London, explained this to me when describing his own transition from mainstream to Islamic hip-hop during one of our first conversations, in late July 2008: "A lot of [contemporary] hip-hop is very egotistical, is very like, I'm the greatest rapper . . . very braggin', you know; and Islam came to strip away your ego. . . . So I had to constantly look at my lyrics, to make sure the sincerity was there, and I was writing from the heart and always tried to propagate a positive message." Because of this pronounced message-based tradition inherent in hip-hop, pious performers and listeners frequently stressed hip-hop's unique potential to convey ethical content. In this context, I found it particularly interesting that performers and event organizers valued the genre for its ability to reach out to urban Muslim youth who are alienated from the conventional spaces of Muslim piety.

The articulation of these two tropes, of hip-hop as a spoken-word art form in the tradition of West African Muslim griot musical storytelling and of African American Muslim hip-hop pioneers concerned with an ethics of social justice, proved for my interlocutors not just hip-hop's compatibility with Islam but even its inherent Islamic character. A comment Sukina made during an early conversation I had with her in 2008 summarizes this twofold argument well and reflects my interlocutors' general take: "I don't regard hip-hop as that contemporary art form that you see on TV. I look at it as coming from West African griots, right through the plantation, and that social commentary, and that is what hip-hop is to me. . . . Within the history of hip-hop you will always find, like in the US, people who are Muslim or who are strongly influenced by Islam, because I think Islam always played a role. It wasn't just a faith; it was about Black consciousness. The faith is affiliated with African American history, African American identity."

These different arguments all point to my interlocutors' particular understanding of Islamic hip-hop in terms of an ethical endeavor, where the aspirational cultivation of piety, political consciousness, and community building interweaves considerations of content (messages) with considerations of sound (spoken words surpassing beats).

Performing Islamic Hip-Hop

The narratives that foreground hip-hop as an ethical spoken-word art also bear crucially on the performance style of the Muslim hip-hop artists I studied. As I address in this section, it is by *embodying* the ethics of hip-hop that the artists seek to fully actualize the authenticity and legitimacy of hip-hop within pious Muslim spaces—relatively small-scale live shows at Muslim community events being generally the main venue for this art form.[10] What I found striking when attending these events was how the hip-hop performers brought a body politics reflective of conscious (that is, "authentic") hip-hop together with one reflective of Islamic ethical traditions, in an apparently natural way. These performers employed styles that simultaneously expressed an urban, cosmopolitan understanding of Black or African dignity and also Muslim etiquette and piety. Performing conscious hip-hop entailed, for my interlocutors, enacting political consciousness and Black awareness rather than sexualized identities. And these performance styles seemed to cohere well with their understanding of Islamic etiquette, which demands a certain bodily restraint. Such embodied restraint was furthermore facilitated by foregrounding hip-hop as a spoken-word art rather than as dance music. Many performers spoke to me openly about how they monitored their own body movements and gestures in line with these considerations. Such a reflexive approach sought to uphold embodied modesty, ensuring that sexuality was not displayed publicly. But it also meant expressing humility, something that—as the artists recognized (exposed in Mohammed Yahya's comment quoted earlier)—was often opposed to understandings of mainstream hip-hop.

The British-Nigerian spoken-word poet Rakin Fetuga, a former member of the now-defunct Mecca II Medina, the pioneering group of Islamic hip-hop in the United Kingdom, related his own perspective about embodied restraint and rap during one of our more recent conversations, in the summer of 2016. He himself had made the transition from mainstream rap—he was an up-and-coming artist in the UK hip-hop scene in the 1990s—to Islamic hip-hop:

> As a Muslim male rapper, you still have to be modest. For example, we could not behave like how the mainstream rappers behave, they are rating their private parts, you wouldn't be doing that. . . . Also, the way to behave with women in the mainstream . . . , but as a Muslim artist, you keep far away from that. You are just [*with a smile and changes into a very soft, melodic voice*], *Salam alaykum, masha' Allah* [*puts his hand on his heart, as in a greeting*]; perhaps sign a thing for them, *Jazak Allah kheir*, that's it.[11]

Rakin's overly soft, melodic voice and his adoption of a different body posture as he talked to me indicated how he consciously *performed* for his female listeners a different kind of masculinity, and thereby also his adherence to an Islamic code of modest conduct, in order to avoid any possibility of misunderstanding and inappropriate interaction. Indeed, I have seen him many times at Muslim events interacting with female audience members in exactly this way. For many of my female interlocutors who wear hijab, the hijab itself becomes a crucial bodily technique that promotes particular types of bodily conduct, as Sukina made clear in the following statement: "In regard to conducting ourselves onstage, I think these things . . . come naturally, in a way. . . . You know, it's like if you dress a certain way, your body kind of follows you. . . . If you are dressed modestly, you just do conduct yourself in a certain way." Sukina's comment clearly exposes how dress, as a material object, is an important part of many body techniques, as it contributes to what Jean-Pierre Warnier calls a "sensory-motor experience" (2001, 7).[12] Another strategy to guarantee modesty was to perform in a seated position. Pearls of Islam, for instance, a band consisting of two sisters of Afro-Caribbean descent who call their music *rhythm and nasheed* rather than *hip-hop* (adapting the name from R&B), usually performed this way, especially in front of mixed-gender audiences, so to avoid, they explained to me, any dance movements the music might incline them to do.

In a context where Black people have often been represented as oversexualized, with unruly bodies and a pathological sexuality (see, for instance, Hammonds 1999; Jackson 2006), one could argue that these forms of conduct enact a "politics of pious respectability" (Abdul Khabeer 2016, 144). However, given that these artists, as pious Muslims, adhere to a normative understanding of virtuous conduct (which may vary from stricter to less strict interpretations, as there is no doctrinal unanimity in this respect) and aspire to embody it, I do not want to view the adoption of an embodied pious habitus in hip-hop exclusively through this lens. Black respectability politics is usually understood to stand in tension with ideas of Black authenticity, because this politics aspires to prove Black people's conformity with (white) mainstream values and thus downplays its own difference (see, for instance, White 2001). My interlocutors, on the contrary, unabashedly promoted a Black Muslim authenticity that did not shy away from Afrocentric aesthetics and Black-power symbols. Through their music and their performances, they introduced this message as well as the ensuing critique of anti-Black racism into the larger British Muslim community. Simultaneously, they claimed, against many Afrocentric arguments, that Islam has a central and legitimate space in a Black cultural-political space.[13]

Thus, at Islamic hip-hop events, I witnessed a performance style being forged with a specific set of gestures and phrases combining, again seamlessly, hip-hop and Islamic elements. Key in the repertoire of hip-hop gestures I observed regularly were hand movements, which help communicate the lyrics, provide emphasis to the words (such as waving hands in the air or waving the hands, palms down, from side to side, in the rhythm of the rap), and facilitate maintaining the flow. A basic bouncing movement highly characteristic of hip-hop—produced by stepping back and forth with bended knees, with the torso bending slightly to each step—was adopted by many performers as well. Apart from that, I rarely saw hip-hop artists engaging in more extensive dance movements.[14] Indeed, the corporeality espoused onstage seemed to me much more in line with early political hip-hop, in which the performance of sexuality was not central and which instead involved an embodiment of the social narrative of emancipation, and resistance. Therefore, during Muslim hip-hop performances, a raised, clenched fist was a prominent gesture onstage (also invoked in many lyrics). The fist, interestingly, was frequently interchanged with another hand gesture, the raised right-hand index finger, which, within an Islamic context, signifies *tawhid* (oneness of God). Onstage, this principle of oneness was often explained to the audience—in an allusion to Islamic mystical teachings on tawhid in terms of unity of being—as connoting unity among all people.[15] Call-and-response routines included shout-outs to various local identities (for instance, East London, West London, and so on) or "Takbir," with the crowd answering "Allahu akbar" (God is the greatest), which could alternate with pious invocations such as "Wave your hand if you love Allah"; performances started with the obligatory "Salam alaykum" (Peace be upon you) and "bismillah" (in the name of God).[16]

My interlocutors' performative mode, which enacted this specific fusion of Muslim and hip-hop elements in order to embody an Afro-Islamic authenticity, was, of course, most immediately apparent through their sartorial styles onstage. The hip-hop artists I worked with have all developed over the years their own quite distinct ways of dressing that produce and display a Black Muslim aesthetic. As some explained to me, it took them much reflection and experimentation to figure out their own styles. Muneera and Sukina from Poetic Pilgrimage talked to me extensively about the matter of dress, on- and offstage. During our first conversation in 2008, Sukina related to me her initial difficulties in acquiring an ensemble of clothes that reflected not only Muslim principles of modesty but also her own personal tastes: "So, there was a long period where we would perform, and we have clothes on, and we are like, this is not anything about us. . . . We cringe when we see pictures, oh, what the hell are we wearing? But you know, *hamdulilah*, it takes time to start to build up a wardrobe, and you start to get different pieces from places you are traveling to." During our conversation at her apartment in 2011, she returned to that topic. Interestingly, here she pointed to the communal relevance of individual dress choices: "It's another big thing I am interested to work on, how we as Black Muslims relate to our community as well. When we walk through neighborhoods like Harlesden or Willesden and they see Black women covering their heads, they are Muslims, but they still wear African colors, African hijabs."

During Islamic hip-hop performances, I usually noticed urban wear, sweatpants, hoodies, and sneakers alternating or combined with *thobes*, African blouses (wax-printed or embroidered), and Moroccan slippers; also popular were T-shirts and baseball hats with self-designed themes or slogans that reflected a Muslim or Afro-Muslim identity (often in Arabic script).[17] For women, skirts in various ethnic designs, whether African, Indian, or Middle Eastern, were combined with fashion items bought in London's high streets, often worn in layers. Accessories, in general, were key in these outfits: kufis for men and hijab for women, often (but not always) made out of African textiles, along with chains of prayer beads (*tasbih*) in the West African style (large wooden beads) wrapped around the wrist or worn as necklaces. Shawls, again out of African textiles but also Palestinian keffiyeh scarves and shawls from Yemen, were very popular among men and women alike. For the women, heavy bangles and chunky earrings in wood or silver, often with Afrocentric symbolism or other accessories coming from different regions of Africa (very popular, too, was Tuareg silver craft) completed the wardrobe.

Dress in this performance context therefore became an interesting technology of the self, where individuality was created and performed through fashion but clearly embedded within a *communal* perspective. As Sukina made clear in her statement, it was about maintaining old ties with the Black community, about creating new communities around a Black Muslim identity and transforming the broader Muslim community by making space for a Black narrative. The embodied practices I discuss here rendered the body a crucial tool to produce community by inculcating communal ethical dispositions based on an Islamic piety infused with Black awareness and confidence. As I show in the reminder of the chapter, the central role accorded the body in producing particular kinds of dispositions could also resonate within hip-hop lyrics.

Writing the Body of the Black Muslim Woman

As mentioned earlier, Poetic Pilgrimage is a female Muslim hip-hop and spoken-word duo, consisting of Sukina and Muneera. They are today the most well-known Muslim female rappers from the United Kingdom. They have been featured in a widely seen *Al-Jazeera* documentary and have performed extensively in Europe and overseas. Poetic Pilgrimage offers an interesting example for discussing Muslim hip-hop and embodied ethics, not only in performance but also with regard to the lyrics.

Their lyrics span from spiritual and very pious to socially engaged, with no clear dividing line between these topics; many artists fuse both elements, given that they are so much part of their understanding of what their Muslimness entails in terms of Islamic ethics—ethics that my interlocutors perceived not

FIGURE 8.1. Poetic Pilgrimage at the Dishoom Eid Festival, King's Cross, London, July 17, 2017. Photograph by author.

only as commensurable with Black consciousness but even as requiring it. Poetic Pilgrimage's lyrics capture well their personal experiences as Black Muslim women in Britain having to navigate historical misrepresentations of Black and Muslim female bodies as well as the spiritual struggles of converts, believers, seekers, and politically conscious beings.

Within all their lyrics, there is a consistent concern with spiritual flourishing, female agency, female restorative power, and self-worth, themes that situate them within a broader Black feminist tradition articulated through music and writing (see, for instance, Bennett and Dickerson 2001). In line with this tradition, which has claimed the right to define and represent the Black female body on its own terms, Poetic Pilgrimage unapologetically set out to define and represent the Black Muslim *hijabi* female body. They moreover lay claim to their own *voices*, here especially in response to more conservative (often labeled as Salafi) interpretations of Islam that prohibit women from singing in mixed-gender public spaces. Poetic Pilgrimage has received much condemnation from some conservative Muslim circles for this reason. Their lyrics consequently respond to multiple forms of marginalization: as Muslim women in an increasingly Islamophobic Europe, as Black women in a white-majority society defined by racial hegemonies that have historically misrepresented and devalorized the Black body, as Black Muslims in a Muslim community with "ethnoreligious hegemonies" that favor South Asians and Middle Easterners, and finally as women in a heterogeneous Muslim community where certain currents endorse strict gendered norms that exclude women from public spaces and the performing arts.

Against these multiple forms of exclusion, Poetic Pilgrimage celebrates through their words and their stage presence the proud Black and devout Muslim woman. The following lines from the track "Star Women" (2010) exemplify this key message, with a language that situates the body at the center of this message:

We female MC avant-gardes
refuse to flaunt our body parts,
pump your fist, this world is ours. (Sukina)

In these hard days
you're amazed
how my tongue stays ablaze,
the *x* in my DNA
that makes me rhyme for better days,
inspired by women who are victims
of corrupted systems,
channeling this energy
that is pimped up inside of me,
from victims to victors to victorious
how glorious
you can see in my stride,
in the way that I ride.[18] (Muneera)

In what follows, I discuss two spoken-word pieces written and performed by Muneera and Sukina respectively: "White Lilies" and "I Carry." These pieces epitomize Poetic Pilgrimage's effort to reclaim and represent the Black female body in ways that integrate Black body politics into Islamic understandings of the body. I demonstrate how both pieces powerfully put the performers' bodies at the service of cultivating among their listeners an intersubjective ethics grounded in care, responsibility, and compassion.

I first saw Sukina and Muneera perform these two pieces in February 2009 when attending the "I Am Malcolm X" tour organized by the Muslim organization Radical Middle Way at the Drum in Birmingham, a major Black cultural venue.[19] The hall was fully packed; the majority of attendees were Muslims from a range of different ethnic and racial backgrounds. Unlike in Poetic Pilgrimage's highly energetic hip-hop performances, here both performers adopted the more collected body postures of spoken-word poets. Both arrived silently onstage, and each situated herself in front of a microphone. While Muneera got ready to speak, Sukina clasped her arms together and closed her eyes, adopting a still posture.

Muneera: "White Lilies"

Muneera recited with a powerful and passionate voice her poem "White Lilies," which affirms the importance of denouncing the systemic violence inflicted on Black bodies. The importance of speaking out is framed within a context where being silenced is a real possibility:

> The thought of a butterfly wingless or a bee honeyless
> Is like me not being able to express
> Lungs expanding allowing me to get things off my chest.

In "White Lilies" the desire to speak out is not merely a matter of individual self-expression. It is a physical, bodily need. But this need, as Muneera makes clear immediately afterward, is linked to a primordial condition of humanness, which for her refers to the innate knowledge of God's existence and the social responsibilities that issue from that knowledge:

> I must confess I do get some form of satisfaction from the request of my
> Lord
> . . . .
> You see, before I was born I took two oaths
> One to testify in the name of He
> And the other to write in the name of He the most righteous
> Until the souls of the voiceless can be set free.

The duty to speak in order to set free the "souls of the voiceless" requires talking about hard and painful truths, about the evil that exists, which is so much connected to humans' moral fragility and thus to the potential to commit evil. The objective is a shock effect that rouses in the listener a reaction, compassion or dread:

Not just beyond yellow meadows and blue streams
But into the deepest, darkest depths of your heart
Until you choke on the horrors that I've seen
That I've been.

Muneera's frank speech does not stop at exposing personal experiences of (sexual) violence inflicted on her own body, which she related that evening in an increasingly emotional voice:

I've shared alleys with crack fiends, slept in backstreets
As rats and rodents rode all over me
Cold and exposed to vulnerability
. . . .
Welcome to the birth of the death of my chastity
Desperately seeking to fill my once womb, now tomb, with love.

"White Lilies" does not foreground or isolate her personal pain but immediately and explicitly connects it to a collective condition, juxtaposing her own bodily suffering with a broader experience of social and physical violence that affects her community. In this sense, perpetrators and victims are both casualties of the same structural conditions that affect Black communities. But "White Lilies" makes clear that the effects of violence are gendered, particularly impacting women, who are often left behind in the vicious circle of violence and the carceral system:

So I use these words to mediate
Yet still they can't alleviate
Mother's tears when her son has just been gunned down by his own
    peers
Or a mother's tears
When her son has just pulled the trigger, end another's years

While recognizing the gender-specific effects of violence within her community, Muneera nonetheless mitigates these differences by highlighting a relational self, thereby cutting short any notion of the individual(ist) poet. In the following lines, her body transforms into the body of the young man, the perpetrator of the killing, adopting his body postures that signify allegiance to his locality—and Muneera performs these gestures onstage:

So he being me, we, to transferably react
And every action can be my last breath
My last nothing left

Banging on my warrior chest with no valour in my heart
Repping my manor on my parts
With my swagger or street smarts

Then, assuming once again a silent posture and reducing the volume of her voice, she steps out of his body in the lyrics, just before he, too, finds a brutal end:

Cross' my path now he's marked
As a chalky white figure

Here the (feminine) "I" has transmuted into a "he" and then melts into a "we." The poem thereby highlights the collective vulnerability of the "we" within a context of structural violence. In spite of this vulnerability and the omnipresence of death, Muneera celebrates her own strength, her resilient body that survives and continues to speak out, depicting—in the tradition of Black feminist writing—the woman's body as a source of power, restorative, maternal, nurturing, and therefore uncomfortable, even menacing, to the status quo:

But there will be no white lilies left
There will be no white lilies left
Because I still have a fire in my chest
Substance in my breath
Like babies' milk in a mother's breast
Yes, they call us end-time women

And, again, she insists on the necessity of speaking out, even in the face of efforts to silence her, speaking out about taboo topics such as sexual violence against women. Muneera now turns her gaze from her immediate environment of urban Britain to a more global perspective:

And others say that we should be forbidden
From speaking about the rape of Sudanese women
And remind people of the responsibility of this world that we live in
But the blood keeps dripping
And as their blood keeps dripping they want me to stop singing
As their blood keeps dripping they want us to erase the lines that we've
    written

As the poem draws to a close and her voice begins to slow, she reiterates her determination to denounce injustice and suffering, with an understanding that her passionate commitment to do so itself results from an ontological condition that leads back to an ultimate divine agency. Thus, speaking out is a commitment, her mission, a promise:

> So until He fancies me and leaves my white lilies to rest
> Or physically and emotionally removes the pain that I feel deep inside
> my chest
> Until my lord leaves my white lilies to rest
> I pray my last words would sound and feel something similar to this,
> Amin.

Sukina: "I Carry"

In contrast to Muneera's poem, which was performed with strong gestures, reflecting the personal and emotional involvement of the poet, Sukina employed mostly a minimalist performance style, with a calm, collected body posture. She began in a slow cadence, carefully articulating each word and using only a few hand gestures. Now it was Muneera's turn to settle into a silent pose, eyes closed, to let Sukina take center stage:

> I carry the decrepit legacy of the wretched casualties
> Who lost the faculty to fathom what it means to be free
> I carry the weight like mothers dashing desperately across borders
> becoming refugees
> With their blessed seeds tied to their backs
> Under attack from bombs dropped, limbs hacked, by devils on horseback
> I inhale the scent of mutilated corpses tossed in a mass grave
> I am a slave awaiting emancipation day
> I am a believer preparing my soul for judgment day.

Sukina speaks in a slow, quiet, and even voice. Her first verses set the stage for a poem that uses Sukina's body as the locus for remembering and feeling with the "wretched of the earth" across time and space. It is a piece of remembrance and resistance to a history and ongoing present of oppression, suffered by Black and brown bodies, enslaved, colonized bodies, and by those bodies who today have inherited this history and who continue to endure the ongoing structural neo-imperialist conditions. Throughout her poem Sukina names the destinies of Africans in the Western Hemisphere, in sub-Saharan Africa (Sierra Leone, Sudan/Darfur) and of people in the Middle East (Iraq, Iran, Palestine), with their histories of enslavement, colonialism, and war. At the same time,

"I Carry" is, like "White Lilies," attentive to how these conditions play out in gendered ways, and denounces all forms of patriarchy:

> The tears of war widows roll down my cheek, and when another bomb
>   drops
> That could be me wrapped in a white sheet
> I'm an Iranian woman marching for equality
> I rather die standing up than live on my knees
> It seems they didn't get the memo that my soul was born free.

Sukina explicitly puts her capacity to write and perform in the service of these forgotten victims, whose memory she wants to perpetuate:

> Lyricist slash activist is my vision of viewpoint
> The ink of my (ball) point turns from blue to red
> I write with the blood of the *shuhada* [martyrs]
> So that they can use my breath to sing freedom lullabies
> To those who sleep in warm beds
> And they, please, can be heard beyond death.

At the same time, and similar to "White Lilies," in "I Carry" Sukina's body does not merely stand for suffering but also personifies resilience, resistance, and ultimately redemption. At this point, Sukina's body posture changes; she becomes more expressive, raising her fist, standing tall:

> You see me, hijab tied tight, black-gloved fist raised high
> Chanting the war cry, no justice no peace, no justice no peace
> To the day I lose life . . .

In the next verses, Sukina regrets the passivity of a society where listeners are exposed to mass-mediatized news but desensitized to human suffering that does not affect them directly. This is a society that prefers to be distracted by amusement, fantasy worlds, rather than confronting the hard reality of life around us:

> We suffer the tragedy of apathy, no time even for sympathy
> See, we prefer the fallacy of fantasy
> To the morning light we call reality

Sukina concludes her poem with a pious invocation for the resurrection of all those deceased victims at the end of times, ending, like Muneera, as one does a prayer, with "Amin" (amen).

Writing Embodied Ethics, Relational Selves, and the Body as a Conduit

Both of Poetic Pilgrimage's pieces espouse a poetics of embodiment, where references to corporeality are recurrently employed in ways that render the human body a crucial site for producing connectivity and relationality. Embodied language here is meant to enable the listener to directly experience relations to an Other who is geographically or socially distant and to render present and immediate—through involving the senses—the Other's personal or collective (embodied) suffering.

"White Lilies" is especially concerned with Black suffering related to structural racism and war. Through her regular Islamic references, Muneera solidly integrates an Islamic identity into a collective Black imaginary (local and global) that often excludes this particular identity from its core. "I Carry," by contrast, significantly enlarges the space of the Islamic *umma* (community) as it is often imagined in British Muslim circles. In her critique of imperial and neo-imperial wars and postcolonial violence, Sukina connects the "centers" of the Muslim world to the "peripheries" not conventionally imagined to be relevant to its center, such as sub-Saharan Africa (Sierra Leone, Sudan). She thereby challenges the hierarchies of suffering often established in non-Black Muslim discourses based on these (racialized) geographies. But she also incorporates into this space what one might call the "Islamic Black Atlantic" and invokes the suffering of those who are understood to have been lost to the umma. Together, these two pieces present interesting reconfigurations of the commonly imagined geography of the Islamic umma. The umma, as a "collective moral project" (Hirschkind 2006, 118), is here reimagined through new types of spatial connections, thus also expanding the ethical obligations that are germane to these connections.

The suffering addressed in these poems—the denunciation of suffering and the call for compassion and ultimately resistance against the structures that produce suffering—becomes the ultimate reason for Sukina's and Muneera's desire to write, sing, and perform. Suffering in both poems is captured repeatedly through the terms *blood* and *tears*, the two bodily fluids that evoke physical and emotional pain. And the shed blood makes their work a moral obligation: "as their blood keeps dripping they want me to stop singing" ("White Lilies") and "I write with the blood of the *shuhada*" ("I Carry"). At the same time, both poets identify within their own bodies the (specifically feminine) force that allows them to use their lyrics as an act of and call to resistance. Muneera's violated body is resuscitated through the "fire in [her] chest" and the "substance in [her] breath like babies' milk in a mother's breast," while Sukina's body, "hijab tied tight, black-gloved fist raised high," is "chanting the war cry."

Both poets explicitly want to rouse us from our "apathy" that allows us to sleep calmly ("in warm beds" ["I Carry"]) and want to physically disturb us ("until you choke on the horrors that I've seen" ["White Lilies"]). By doing so, they seek to tear down what Allen Feldman (2015) calls the "political apperception" or "anesthesia" induced by sovereign state power and its media apparatus in blanking out and/or banalizing the violence of contemporary warfare. Through these poems, then, they aim to reactivate our numbed sensory skills to perceive and react to violence. In "I Carry," Sukina makes us experience the distant suffering by experiencing phenomenologically the agony of those she invokes. We feel with Sukina, who makes directly accessible to us the otherwise-invisible and forgotten suffering. In "I Carry," compassion—not pity but cosuffering—is produced and mediated by the performer's body, which "carries," "inhales," "bleeds," and "weeps" for the victims who are rarely publicly mourned, so that we can feel via her body. Muneera, through her experiences of growing up in impoverished neighborhoods in urban Britain, reveals to us from the most personal vantage point possible the effects of structural and endemic racism but also of a still-patriarchal society (Britain) where sexual violence against women is too often normalized: her own body turns, through rape, from "womb" to "tomb." Yet, as already noted, she immediately grounds her own painful experiences within a collective experience. Like Sukina, she wants to use lyrics to mediate the suffering of Others for her listeners. This is most powerfully expressed in her poem when her violated female body switches into a male body from her neighborhood who ultimately finds a violent end.

In their lyrics, the performers' bodies—Black Muslim female bodies that are the locus of multiple forms of oppression—transgress boundaries of gender and race, locality and time, and become conduits for relating to Others, for producing compassion for all the forgotten histories of suffering endured by Black and brown bodies. Hence, their bodies come to transcend their own particularity in order to denote a broader *moral geography*. By doing so, both poets expose an understanding of bodies as elastic and nonbounded, able to connect to and fuse with others, endowed with a sort of transcorporeal perceptivity. Such understandings have also been richly utilized within Islamic spiritual traditions (see Kugle 2007; Mittermaier 2011; Ware 2014) and nourish these poets as well. Both poems, then, present a form of embodied epistemology where the body produces a knowledge that allows the listener to make the suffering of the Other accessible to the self.

Judith Butler, in a piece where she reflects on the possibilities of feeling moved and acted upon by events outside of one's own immediate surroundings, argues, "If I am only bound to those who are close to me, already familiar, then my ethics are invariably parochial, communitarian, and exclusionary. If I am only bound to those who are 'human' in the abstract, then I avert every effort to translate culturally between my own situation and that of others. . . . But ethical relations are mediated . . . and this means that questions of location are confounded such that what is happening 'there' also happens in some sense 'here'" (2012, 104).

"I Carry" and "White Lilies" are two examples where the poets employ their bodies and bodily perception to *mediate* these ethical relations, creating the "here" to which everyone can relate. Both "summon the other" to themselves by making "the flesh . . . word" (Dickerson 2001, 196) and turn their bodies into a "site of love, compassion, understanding" (Bennett and Dickerson 2001, 11). The poems depend on bodies' capacities to produce affect, to affect and be affected through "intensities that pass body to body, . . . resonances that circulate about [and] between bodies and worlds" (Seigworth and Gregg 2010, 1). Thereby, they strive to overcome the limitations of a reductive physical existence, enclosed in individual material bodies, so as to enable us to reach out to the other over time, space, and difference (Hamington 2004). Gail Weiss (1999) describes this capacity of bodies to produce connections with others as "intercorporeality," which, she insists, has important ethical entailments. Thus, Weiss urges recognition of "the body's role in calling us to respond ethically to one another" (Weiss 1999, 5) and to "attribute moral significance not merely to intellectual but also to concomitant physical and emotional responses that arise out of our complex, concrete relationships with other bodies" (5).

More specifically, the emotional responses these poems seek to elicit stem from relations that are established through an invitation to cosuffer, a capacity that relies centrally on recognizing our shared sense of embodied vulnerability. In this sense, these poems acknowledge the ethical obligations that are produced by the ontological vulnerability of the human body. While this resonates in certain ways with Butler's (2009, 2) call for a "new bodily ontology," which invites us to rethink notions around "precariousness, vulnerability, injurability" in conjunction with the importance of "interdependency," these poems also point to the fact that the "current distribution of precariousness on a global scale is wildly out of balance" (Murphy 2011, 582), with the "wretched of the earth" (Fanon 2004) bearing the brunt. Indeed, these poets expose a pronounced awareness of the workings of the "racial ontologies" that Frantz Fanon (2008) has extensively critiqued, which postulate an "ontological order of value" (Wynter 1984, 42).[20] Echoing these decolonial critiques, these poems implore an understanding of the ethical obligations that connect the promotion of an ontological embodied interdependence with a radical undoing of racial ontologies (Maldonado-Torres 2007; Wynter 1984).

At the same time, however, Muneera's and Sukina's understanding of the ethical obligations produced by embodied connectivity and intersubjectivity is not merely social, humanist, or materialist. It is also metaphysical, because it is intrinsically connected to the divine, from which, according to their understanding, all originates—therefore embedded in a quite different episteme. The care that they perceive and that is cultivated through these bodily perceived relations derives from the ultimate covenant with God and triggers a fundamental, existential responsibility. And as Sukina furthermore makes clear, this struggle on earth for social and political justice is embedded within an eschatological perspective; if she offers herself to become the spokesperson of the oppressed, this also partakes in an eschatological striving. And, similarly, it explains these performers' understanding that the oppressed, whose suffering must arouse a reaction in us in order to correct injustice in this world, will find absolute justice only in the *akhira*, the afterlife.

Conclusion

I have argued in this chapter that Islamic hip-hop, as my interlocutors defined it, was a deep and multilayered ethical endeavor. It was committed not only to promoting a vibrant and thriving Black Muslim community in Britain but also to contributing to reshaping and educating the broader British Muslim community. By doing so, it aimed to fully participate in the subject-fashioning projects of Islamic ethical traditions, to instill piety that includes a central commitment to social values, especially social justice. It was in this latter sense that the hip-hop practitioners of my research saw hip-hop as a particularly apt tool. The body, as I showed in this chapter, took center stage in the ethical labor these practitioners engaged in and thus became a key site for these community-shaping efforts. The body, its deportment and its stylization, was not just a tool for proving hip-hop's Islamic legitimacy but a conduit through which a Black Muslim habitus was shaped and cultivated. These particular body politics made Islamic hip-hop look a certain way and shaped its particular aesthetic styles. Especially intriguing for me was how this potential of the body to build community—through its simultaneous potential for cultivating interior dispositions—was actively harnessed within certain hip-hop lyrics. Building on the example of lyrics by Poetic Pilgrimage, I showed the possibility of writing the body in a way that produces affective responses with the objective of establishing ethical connections defined by compassion, care, and obligation.

Most central here was the exposure of bodily vulnerability—an ontological condition that does not affect everyone in similar ways but is connected to broader structural conditions. Building on this recognition of embodied vulnerability, these lyrics not only appealed to communal ethics but opened up possibilities for ethical attachments that transcend particular group identities in a quest for broader justice.

ACKNOWLEDGMENTS

I want to thank my interlocutors in London, especially Muneera Williams, Sukina Douglas, and Ismael Lea South, for all their contributions and assistance during more than a decade of fieldwork. My appreciation goes also to Yolanda Covington-Ward and to the anonymous reviewers for their important and thoughtful feedback on the chapter.

NOTES

1. See, for instance, Abdul Khabeer (2016), Aidi (2014), Hill (2017), and Swedenburg (2002).

2. A notable exception here is the recent work by Su'ad Abdul Khabeer (2016), who has paid meticulous attention to Muslim hip-hop culture as a sartorial phenomenon.

3. Between 2007 and 2018, I conducted fieldwork with pious British Muslim culture and arts practitioners, mainly in London and to a lesser extent in other British cities. Among these practitioners, who came from a variety of different ethnic and racial backgrounds, were a substantial number who were of African descent. In this chapter I focus specifically on this group.

4. Scholarship on Black Muslim communities in the United Kingdom is almost completely absent, with the exception of recent studies on British Somali communities (see especially Liberatore 2017). An interesting monograph has been written by Richard Reddie (2009), a Black British pastor interested in understanding the growing phenomenon of Black British Christians converting to Islam.

5. Elsewhere (Jouili 2019), I have discussed the complicated articulations of the relationship between religion and culture among British Muslim art practitioners.

6. An Afro-Atlantic space that unites Black American and African aesthetic and musical experiences has been proposed by some music scholars but criticized by others as "romantic Afro-Atlanticism" (Perry 2004, 17). I am not so much interested in the historical veracity of this argument as in the ethical possibilities that this argument opens up for the artists who engage in it.

7. Furthermore, there are those who proclaim themselves "no-music" rappers, who follow the more restrictive theological interpretations that proclaim the illegitimacy of musical instruments (with the exception of drums).

8. The trope of the opposition between authentic and corrupted hip-hop has been debated among scholars; some view the distinction between a "golden age" and a "cor-

rupted" hip-hop as a too-normative vision that does not take seriously the aesthetic as an independent category (Perry 2004).

9. On the strong Muslim identity (whether Sunni Islam, Nation of Islam, or Five Percenters) of early hip-hop, see Abdul Khabeer (2016), Perry (2004), and Winters (2011). Ellen McLarney (2019) furthermore points to the broader significance of the "Black Muslim language" for giving voice to the Black experience and critiquing white supremacy, a language that has become central in Black cultural production.

10. The question of choice of performance venue is another interesting aspect that I cannot address here.

11. *Salam alaykum* is the traditional Muslim greeting, which translates as "Peace be upon you." *Masha' Allah* is used when someone is being complimented and translates as "God has willed." *Jazak Allah* is an expression of gratitude, meaning "May God reward you."

12. I have elaborated more on the role of the hijab as a material object with inherent sensory effects in the cultivation of embodied modesty in Jouili (2015).

13. Abdul Khabeer (2016) refers to this way of being as "Muslim cool," where piety intertwines with a self-conscious Blackness.

14. There are, of course, different understandings of modesty, and at times any hip-hop gestures might be seen as lacking modesty. It is in this sense that Abdul Khabeer argues, "Black music stands in for Black lack/excess" (2016, 84).

15. In Sufi metaphysics, the principle of tawhid is expanded into the doctrine of the "unity of being" (*wahda al-wujud*), which postulates that God and the entire creation are one. See, for instance, Chittick (2010).

16. *Takbir* is an exclamation that invites others to call out "Allahu akbar" (God is the greatest).

17. *Thobes* (an anglicized version of the Arabic term *thawb*) are ankle-length garments for men, worn in a variety of styles in many parts of the Muslim world.

18. "Poetic Pilgrimage—Star Women (R.I.P. J-Dilla)," pilgrimgrace, October 27, 2010, YouTube video, 2:22, https://www.youtube.com/watch?v=JrHturd8mOo.

19. The two performances during the "I Am Malcolm X" tour can be watched on YouTube: for "White Lilies," go to "Poetic Pilgrimage Spoken Word: I Am Malcolm X Tour," GlobalFaction, March 15, 2009, YouTube video, 3:55, https://www.youtube.com/watch?v=i-PEG-VRlNM. For "I Carry," go to "Poetic Pilgrimage Spoken Word 2: I Am Malcolm X Tour," GlobalFaction, March 17, 2009, YouTube video, 3:44, https://www.youtube.com/watch?v=uFgI5xcDQpE&t=11s.

20. These racialized orders of value go from negating being Black life to declaring it disposable (see, for instance, Marriott 2018; Rana 2016).

REFERENCES

Abdul Khabeer, Su'ad. 2016. *Muslim Cool: Race, Religion, and Hip Hop in the United States.* New York: New York University Press.

Aidi, Hisham. 2014. *Rebel Music: Race, Empire, and the New Muslim Youth Culture.* New York: Random House.

Bennett, Michael, and Vanessa D. Dickerson. 2001. Introduction to *Recovering the Black Female Body: Self-Representations by African American Women*, edited by Michael Bennett and Vanessa D. Dickerson, 1–17. New Brunswick, NJ: Rutgers University Press.

Butler, Judith. 2009. *Frames of War: When Is Life Grievable?* London: Verso Books.

Butler, Judith. 2012. "Precarious Life, Vulnerability, and the Ethics of Cohabitation." *The Journal of Speculative Philosophy* 26 (2): 134–151.

Chittick, William C. 2010. *The Sufi Path of Knowledge: Ibn al-Arabi's Metaphysics of Imagination*. Albany: State University of New York Press.

Curtis, Edward E., IV. 2014. *The Call of Bilal: Islam in the African Diaspora*. Chapel Hill: University of North Carolina Press.

Dickerson, Vanessa D. 2001. "Summoning SomeBody: The Flesh Made Word in Toni Morrison's Fiction." In *Recovering the Black Female Body: Self-Representations by African American Women*, edited by Michael Bennett and Vanessa D. Dickerson, 195–217. New Brunswick, NJ: Rutgers University Press.

Feldman, Allen. 2015. *Archives of the Insensible: Of War, Photopolitics, and Dead Memory*. Chicago: University of Chicago Press.

Hamington, Maurice. 2004. *Embodied Care: Jane Addams, Maurice Merleau-Ponty, and Feminist Ethics*. Urbana: University of Illinois Press.

Hammonds, Evelynn M. 1999. "Toward a Genealogy of Black Female Sexuality: The Problematic of Silence." In *Feminist Theory and the Body: A Reader*, edited by Janet Price and Margrit Shildrick, 93–104. New York: Routledge.

Hill, Joseph. 2017. "A Mystical Cosmopolitanism: Sufi Hip Hop and the Aesthetics of Islam in Dakar." *Culture and Religion* 18 (4): 1–21.

Hirschkind, Charles. 2006. *The Ethical Soundscape: Cassette Sermons and Islamic Counterpublics*. New York: Columbia University Press.

Hirschkind, Charles. 2015. "Religion." In *Keywords in Sound*, edited by David Novak and Matt Sakakeeny, 165–174. Durham, NC: Duke University Press

Jackson, Ronald. 2006. *Scripting the Masculine Black Body: Identity, Discourse and Racial Politics in Popular Media*. Albany: State University of New York Press.

Jouili, Jeanette. 2015. *Pious Practice and Secular Constraints. Women in the Islamic Revival in Europe*. Stanford, CA: Stanford University Press

Jouili, Jeanette. 2019. "Islam and Culture: Dis/junctures in a Modern Conceptual Terrain." *Comparative Studies in Society and History* 61 (1): 207–237.

Kugle, Scott A. 2007. *Sufis and Saints' Bodies: Mysticism, Corporeality, and Sacred Power in Islam*. Chapel Hill: University of North Carolina Press.

Liberatore, Giulia. 2017. *Somali, Muslim, British: Striving in Securitized Britain*. London: Bloomsbury.

Maldonado-Torres, Nelson. 2007. "On the Coloniality of Being: Contributions to the Development of a Concept." *Cultural Studies* 21 (2–3): 240–270.

Marriott, David. 2018. *Whither Fanon? Studies in the Blackness of Being*. Stanford, CA: Stanford University Press.

McLarney, Ellen. 2019. "James Baldwin and the Power of Black Muslim Language." *Social Text* 37 (1): 51–84.

McNay, Lois. 2008. *Against Recognition*. Cambridge, UK: Polity.

Mittermaier, Amira. 2011. *Dreams That Matter: Egyptian Landscapes of the Imagination*. Berkeley: University of California Press.

Murphy, Ann V. 2011. "Corporeal Vulnerability and the New Humanism." *Hypatia* 26 (3): 575–590.

Otterbeck, Jonas. 2008. "Battling over the Public Sphere: Islamic Reactions to the Music of Today." *Contemporary Islam* 2 (3): 211–228.

Perry, Imani. 2004. *Prophets of the Hood: Politics and Poetics in Hip Hop*. Durham, NC: Duke University Press.

Rana, Junaid. 2016. "The Racial Infrastructure of the Terror-Industrial Complex." *Social Text* 34 (4): 111–138.

Reddie, Richard. 2009. *Black Muslims in Britain: Why Are a Growing Number of Young Black People Converting to Islam?* Oxford: Lion Books.

Seigworth, Gregory J., and Melissa Gregg. 2010. "An Inventory of Shimmers." In *The Affect Theory Reader*, edited by Melissa Gregg and Gregory J. Seigworth, 1–25. Durham, NC: Duke University Press.

Swedenburg, Ted. 2002. "Hip Hop Music in the Transglobal Islamic Underground." *Black Arts Quarterly* 6 (3): 12–21.

Ware, Rudolph T., III. 2014. *The Walking Qur'an: Islamic Education, Embodied Knowledge, and History in West Africa*. Chapel Hill: University of North Carolina Press.

Warnier, Jean-Pierre. 2001. "A Praxeological Approach to Subjectivation in a Material World." *Journal of Material Culture* 6 (1): 5–24.

Weiss, Gail. 2013. *Body Images: Embodiment as Intercorporeality*. London: Routledge.

White, E. Frances. 2001. *Dark Continent of Our Bodies: Black Feminism and the Politics of Respectability*. Philadelphia: Temple University Press.

Winegar, Jessica. 2009. "Culture Is the Solution: The Civilizing Mission of Egypt's Culture Palaces." *Review of Middle East Studies* 43 (2): 189–197.

Winters, Joseph. 2011. "Unstrange Bedfellows: Hip Hop and Religion." *Religion Compass* 5 (6): 260–270.

Wynter, Sylvia. 1984. "The Ceremony Must Be Found: After Humanism." *Boundary* 2 12–13, no. 3 (Spring–Autumn 1984): 19–70.

9. Secular Affective Politics in a National Dance about AIDS in Mozambique

AARON MONTOYA

Imagine an hour-long dance performance where an African nation is represented by dancers playing the roles of lovers, schoolgirls, playboys, military men, businessmen, sex workers, intravenous drug users, traditional healers, peasants, and pastors. Then, throw onto the stage four dancers in full-body tights and masks that cover their faces. The tights are made using a batik wash technique that mixes many colors, but red and yellow dominate to symbolize blood and infection. Attached to the tights are strange spikes and nodes, calling to mind grotesque growths and sores. These four HIV/AIDS virus dancers threaten the unsuspecting characters from African social life, such as romantic partners who are dancing ballroom style in elegant suits and dresses.[1] The virus dancers infect more complicit, even villainous characters such as sex workers and traditional healers, who then transmit AIDS to others in society. Finally, a lone hero dancer enters wearing white tights and covered with white elastic fabric that forms a tip on the head and a circular rim around the dancer's knees. This condom dancer is backed by ten other character dancers wearing condom "hats" on their heads. Together they banish the virus dancers from the stage. It is a wacky performance but seemingly effective at communicating the national message to use condoms in the struggle against AIDS.

The preceding is a description of a dance called *Amatodos* (1998), produced by the Companhia Nacional de Canto e Dança (CNCD; Mozambican National Song and Dance Company). For at least five years, the CNCD consistently performed *Amatodos* in their tours around the country and abroad. This constant reproduction made *Amatodos* one of the most widely circulated dances about AIDS that emerged out of the industry of information, education, and communication (IEC) campaigns about the epidemic. Early in the history of IEC campaigns, the industry recognized that dance, music, and theater were effective media for communicating to the Mozambican people about the dramatic spread of AIDS (ARPAC 2004).[2] The IEC campaigns were part of much larger AIDS-related programs that involved epidemiological surveillance systems, laboratory support, treatment, and the introduction of retroviral therapy. Under the recent push for multisector governance by powerful institutions such as the World Bank and the Clinton Foundation, AIDS communication projects have been prioritized in every sector of Mozambique, not just the health sector. Thus, Mozambicans have witnessed a lot of IEC campaigns and a lot of art about AIDS. Dance performances were constant features of these campaigns, and *Amatodos* was the most widely circulated and influential of all the performances.

Most IEC campaigns focused on seemingly simple messages about abstinence, condom use, and safe sex. *Amatodos*'s message, for example, was explicitly presented through the character of the heroic dancing condom and the final scene where the condom-wearing populace expels the viruses from the stage. Yet studies of IEC campaigns have identified how audiences interpret campaigns in surprising ways that diverge from the aims of health agencies (Bastos 2002; Carrillo 2002; Galvão 1997; Kalipeni, Flynn, and Pope 2009; Martin 1997; Matsinhe 2008; Parker 2000; Prolongeau 1995). In fact, the studies show that while many campaigns are ineffective at changing behaviors, they are good at disseminating powerful political discourses about the nation, race, class, gender, sexuality, and religion that stigmatize and marginalize social groups and regulate populations. The studies advocate for more ethnographically grounded understandings of how IEC campaigns are interpreted, how they circulate and gain signification, and how people respond to them through their daily cultural practices and behaviors.

This chapter examines how *Amatodos* was experienced and interpreted by audiences as well as CNCD members: the very people who choreographed and performed the dance.[3] My interlocutors' experiences of *Amatodos* diverged significantly from its message about condoms and safe sex; they saw and felt scenes that pitted restraint against excess, reason against passions, where the clear aberrant behaviors and sensibilities were more closely tied to the body, and the superior ones were cerebral; the more appropriate behaviors were Christian faith based, and the more dangerous ones were African derived. For many, this split between rational, controlled citizens and unruly, backward subjects resembled Mozambicans' experiences of Portuguese colonialism, which constructed racialized ideologies about nonnative citizens and nativized subjects (Cabaço 2010; Mamdani 1996) and set the stage for the centrality of performing racialized subjectivities through daily cultural practices, habits, and dispositions that were seemingly beyond colonial race discourses.[4] My examination of *Amatodos*, then, is concerned with how the secular sensibilities and dispositions that were performed in *Amatodos* echo a longer history of secular-modern rule in Mozambique that instituted the secular relationally through other social formations of religion, race, class, gender, and geography (urban, rural, peri-urban). To illuminate *Amatodos* as a performance of secular-modern rule, I take an approach that investigates closely the kinesthetic and affective experience of dancing and watching dance. This embodied approach helps identify the racialized elements of *Amatodos* that mobilize antidance and anti-African aesthetics.

Amatodos communicated an overly simplistic and sappy message about AIDS, which many shrugged off; nevertheless, it became an important cultural hub for the Mozambican state, and other entities steeped in Christian and secular sensibilities, through which it attempted to regulate what counted as properly religious through making negative gestures toward ecstatic bodies, skilled dancing bodies. Therefore, one consequence of *Amatodos*, and the numerous campaigns that followed, was that Mozambican society fashioned an AIDS-free subjectivity that was tied to the daily cultural practices, habits, and dispositions of secular-modern rule. While AIDS dances like *Amatodos* did make immediate positive impacts with their messaging about condoms and safe sex, AIDS dances were limited in their ability to convince audiences, to win them over about how to positively change behaviors, because the dances' secular sensibilities toward the body were incompatible with how many Mozambicans experience movement and spirituality. Instead, my study of audience responses revealed how many people rejected IEC messaging about AIDS because it promoted a proper AIDS-free subjectivity bounded by secular-religious binaries. As an alternative, they frequently embraced AIDS dance choreographies for their ecstatic energies and spiritual experiences that emerged through heightened aesthetic states—the very thing that supposedly caused the spread of the epidemic.

The Antecedents to *Amatodos* and the Political Background

The CNCD is one of Mozambique's proudest cultural institutions in an oceanic panorama of dance groups and dance cultures. While the history of dance in Mozambique is incredibly diverse and has yet to be sufficiently examined and documented, one theme that recurs is how Mozambicans mobilize dance as a journey of transformational states. Dance summons ancestors, excites emotions, creates psychological release, and brings people together. Dancing promotes heightened emotions from the social to intimate relations that are highly valued by people. Because of the significance of transformational states, the other theme in Mozambican dance history is that the nation-state, from Portuguese colonialism to the current neoliberal regime, has attempted to regulate dancing and direct dances for the benefit of its own political discourses. Skilled dancing bodies and the ecstatic scenes they invoke are the nexus of state-society engagement over what bodies best represent Mozambican identity. For more than three decades, the CNCD has been producing and circulating dance choreographies with the objective to move audiences and shape their behaviors. By the time the CNCD created and toured *Amatodos* in the late 1990s, performers and audiences were already accustomed to dance being used by the state to compel and educate, as well as being used by ordinary people as a platform to perform their own embodied knowledge and values. Simply put, the CNCD was a central hub in Mozambicans' contestation over the politics of representation.

The CNCD's aesthetic and pedagogical conventions were in large part forged through the struggle for decolonization. Dance was a significant medium for education and inspiration during the armed struggle (1962–1975), and dance ascended as one of the favorite state-sponsored cultural practices during the brief socialist period (1975–1986). Mozambique gained independence from Portugal only in 1975, after more than a decade of armed struggle organized by FRELIMO (Frente de Libertação de Moçambique, or Mozambican Liberation Front), which conducted a guerrilla war from its military bases in northern Mozambique and neighboring Tanzania. Its military camps were extremely diverse places that consisted of rebellious missionary-educated men, dispossessed peasants from the north, and disaffected migrant laborers from the south, as well as Africans and foreigners from other revolutionary causes and socialist movements across the continent and globe. Music and dance happenings were routine in FRELIMO's military camps as entertainment and intercultural exchange, as instruction about FRELIMO's nationalism, and as part of military training and strategy. Upon independence, FRELIMO established a Marxist-Leninist government that was determined to reverse the legacy of apartheid and capitalist exploitation by Portuguese colonialism. One of the first actions of the new government was establishing cultural institutions, such as the Centro de Estudos Culturais (Center for Cultural Studies) in Maputo as well as community centers called *casas de cultura*, which would educate and animate the Mozambican people about FRELIMO's decolonizing revolution. The military camps of FRELIMO, and their use of dance music for mass mobilization and education, were the models for these cultural centers.

When the CNCD was officially established in 1983, the dance company instituted aesthetic and pedagogical conventions that had been forged through the armed struggle and then further developed movement, musical, and theatrical techniques to engage audiences, drawing them into its performances and inspiring a massive following on its tours within the country and abroad. The CNCD's most iconic choreographies often reproduced aspects of dances from ceremonial contexts that joined ancestral and material worlds to produce transformational states. The CNCD also drew on popular dances in other contexts of community participation, such as harvest festivities and coming-of-age rituals, to evoke moments of extreme rapture and fascination. Then, using techniques from modern theater, the CNCD skillfully integrated the aesthetic building of dance and music with narratives that were frequently linked to, or at least in dialogue with, political discourses. Thus, the CNCD was consistently producing choreographies where dancing bodies and the transformational states they induce instructed audiences about Mozambican history and citizenship.

For example, the CNCD's first productions—*Em Moçambique o sol nasceu* (1983), *As mãos* (1984), and *N'TSay* (1986)—displayed FRELIMO's revolutionary goals of transcending colonialism. *Em Moçambique o sol nasceu* (The sun is rising in Mozambique) was a versatile compilation of multiple dances easily identified as "traditional" but more accurately described as "neotraditional" because they were the CNCD's representations of folklore dances. The choreography ran through a list of Mozambique's most iconic folklore performances that were associated with particular ethnolinguistic groups and regions. The choreography invited audiences to valorize Mozambican culture and rituals that had frequently been marginalized and brutally repressed during Portuguese colonialism. It also implored Mozambicans to transcend regional and ethnolinguistic differences to form a nation united through its diversity. Another choreography, *As mãos* (The hands), was the CNCD's first dance to fuse the neotraditional dances that were its bread and butter with the internationally recognized genres of ballet and Cuban modern, which were the other two main techniques that CNCD members trained in. In *As mãos*, the lead male dancer, who was Black, specialized in African dance, and the lead female dancer, who was mixed race (*mestiça*), specialized in ballet and Cuban modern. *As mãos* is a love story based on a legend about the origins of humanity from the Makonde people in Mozambique. The two lead dancers performed together on stage, showing a mutual respect for the multiple dance cultures present in Mozambique. FRELIMO hailed the dance for its message of nonracialism, and audiences largely understand *As mãos* as a dance about how Mozambican society would surpass the legacy of racial segregation. Another choreography, *N'Tsay*, is a dance about a mythic goddess of the same name, who was also a deity for many people in central Mozambique. The choreography is an allegory of the armed struggle, telling the story of a mythic queen, N'Tsay, who saved her people from the foreigners who had corrupted the king and enslaved the population. *N'Tsay* encourages audiences to understand Mozambican nationalism as an epic struggle against foreign invaders and a corrupt male comprador class that sold out the people for temporary personal wealth. *Em Moçambique o sol nasceu, As mãos,* and *N'TSay* were the CNCD's first well-received choreographies. They folded audiences into embodied experiences of moving beyond colonial society. These dances fused the aesthetics of transformational states, abundantly performed onstage, with political narratives about transcending the colonial mentalities of tribalism, racialism, patriarchy, and classism that were instituted by the Portuguese and continued to be relevant in the postcolonial wake.

The decolonizing goals of FRELIMO, however, were thwarted by harsh realities and mired in the party's own internal contradictions and failures. Mozambique's brief socialist experiment lasted only from 1977, when the government declared itself a Marxist-Leninist state, until 1986, when the government agreed to the first round of the International Monetary Fund's structural adjustment programs to deal with its ballooning debt from the civil war. During this period Mozambique was destroyed by a "war of destabilization," in large part propagated by apartheid South Africa and its Cold War allies, who supported a rebel army called RENAMO (Resistência Nacional Moçambicana, or the Mozambican National Resistance; Hall and Young 1997; Hanlon 1986).[5] While the civil war raged and FRELIMO's fiery rhetoric of rupture was contradicted by its policies of continuity with the colonial economy (Dinerman 2006; Pitcher 2002), the CNCD staged new choreographies embodying unity and hope for change. *A grande festa* (A great celebration; 1988) staged several festive scenes where dancers progressively built on each scene and enveloped themselves in feelings of high spirits. The piece was choreographed to honor Mozambicans' capacity to be resilient during crisis and find joy through their communal collaborations to make dance music. While *A grande festa* did not have one message that unfolded through its performance, it was amply framed by publicity and political discourses that urged Mozambicans to keep faith in the government, its war, and its party and argued that Mozambique would survive the injustices of Western capitalism's policy of "rolling back" socialist governments through fomenting armed insurgency.

In the 1990s the CNCD also played an important role in the transition to peace, a new era of multiparty elections, and massive national reconstruction projects funded by the international donor community. In 1992 peace accords were signed by FRELIMO and RENAMO. While the armed conflict had halted, peace and security remained an unfulfilled goal (Cabrita 2000). The CNCD's *Ode à paz* (Ode to peace; 1992) addressed the country's fragility and people's aspirations for stability. The choreography culminated in an intense scene with two groups of dancers battling it out on the stage, each trying to outdo the other in agility, strength, and wits. Neither group was able to overcome the other. Instead, the choreography locked the dancers and audiences together in an anguished repetition of pulls, tugs, and leaps that devolved into disorder and exhaustion. Both CNCD performers and audiences reported how the dance brought them to tears with its reproduction of the energies of the war and feelings of being fed up with endless cycles of violence.

In sum, since independence, the CNCD has designed choreographies that astutely assembled aesthetic stimulation, folklore, and politics to communicate physically compelling journeys of transcendence. *Amatodos* was among the CNCD's next major choreographies in this lineage of dances that engaged the public in epic tales of strife, national struggle, and resilience. Like its predecessors, *Amatodos* mobilized kinesthetic and other sensory involvements and relations to draw audiences emotionally and physically into formations of citizenship.

Theoretical and Methodological Approach to *Amatodos*

Thus far, I have given a brief history of Mozambique and Mozambicans' aspirations for change through a few iconic choreographies produced by the CNCD. Rather than only recounting history through dance, I now move to an embodied approach to *Amatodos* to show how the CNCD choreographies performed secular sensibilities for dramatic effect. By the time of *Amatodos*, performers and audiences were accustomed to CNCD choreographies. They were used to making a material correspondence between the medium of the choreography itself (the dancing body) and the embodied subject (the audience and the larger public). Following the ideological framing of CNCD choreographies, Mozambicans were to embrace and mimic the aesthetic transcendences onstage, thus bringing about desired behavioral changes that would become diffused throughout society. Mozambicans themselves would take up the dance routines of transcendence as disciplinary techniques working in the body to then transform their society (Foucault 1975). However, dancers and audiences did not necessarily invest their performances of transcendence with the same normalizing techniques that the FRELIMO patrons of the CNCD would have intended. The embodiment of FRELIMO discourses was a slippery, unstable process.

My approach to power and embodiment is inspired by scholars in dance studies who have developed methodologies for studying the energies and agencies created by moving bodies (Castaldi 2006; Chakravorty 2008; Giersdorf 2013; Manning 2006; O'Shea 2007; Shea Murphy 2007). Dance scholarship has been dedicated to writing histories of dances and/or recounting history through dance. Many have focused extensively on the role of state agencies and elites in appropriating dances to shape nationalist ideology and to create national subjects (Daniel 1995; Handler 1988; Kaeppler 1993; Ramsey 1995). Their studies of dance have countered the Eurocentric and logocentric biases that privileged written texts and audiovisual media. Instead, they demonstrate the significance of performative genres in nation making, and they document histories of people who have frequently been absent from or marginalized in official histories. In addition, dance studies have addressed how ordinary people and the most disadvantaged populations have been able to defend themselves and even hijack and reconfigure nation-state processes through their dance practices (Meduri 2008; Nájera-Ramírez 1997; Reed 2010). They argue that it is not enough to examine how dance is a vehicle for discursive practices. Studies must account for the experiential significance of the body as a responsive and creative subject, in contrast to the longer tradition in scholarship that "posited the body as an object, manipulated by external forces in the service of something" (Novack 1995, 179). Thus, critical and ethnographic approaches to dance emphasize the importance of kinesthesia and of somatic awareness in movement practice as a learning and transformative experience (Ness 1992). They emphasize a mobile model of subjectivity to examine how communication and sociality are derived from the body rather than exclusively from language (Godard 1996). They show how dancing bodies are not isolated from linguistic expression or bounded only to ephemeral moments; instead, dancing bodies are intelligent somatic practices that inform and are informed by other sensorial experiences and signifying practices. The dancing body gets "written upon" by discursive practices but also writes on discursive and equivalent social processes (Browning 1995; Foster 1995).

These critical and ethnographic approaches to dance have contributed theoretical ideas about power and embodiment that I apply to *Amatodos* to illuminate the social effect of the choreography for the CNCD and audiences. I became skeptical about the effectiveness of *Amatodos* because in my interviews people were not that interested in the messages about condoms, other than saying that such messages depicted the obvious about AIDS transmission but failed to address the difficult issues of love and desire and the familial, social, and economic pressures that make sex and condom use so vexing (Manuel 2008).

However, they were keenly interested in describing the choreography and the sensorial and kinesthetic processes that made a particular consciousness about AIDS possible. *Amatodos* provoked strong sensations and sentiments about sex, about dancing at a nightclub, about dancing at a communal event that induced spirit possession. *Amatodos* had a profound personal and social effect that, on the one hand, evoked intense experiences of rapture and spiritual transcendence while, on the other hand, using these sexual and sacred emotions as foils to project negative characterizations of intimacy and spiritual life. This back-and-forth in *Amatodos* between excess and constraint, the dancing body and the controlled subject, caused an affective experience of the secular. It drew audiences emotionally and physically into formations of secular citizenship by dancing excesses and then negating the value of ecstatic, heightened states.

Scholars (Asad 2003; Hirschkind 2011; Mahmood 2005) have shown how despite the discursive efforts to construct public life into secular-religious binaries, secularism is in fact not necessarily in the business of eliminating religion from public life; rather, it delineates and fashions religious domains in ways that are conducive to liberal rule. Their scholarship frames my somatic analysis of *Amatodos*. I argue that *Amatodos* worked to promote a proper religiosity that was conducive to neoliberal rule by performing contrasts between proper AIDS-free subjects who were restrained, disembodied, and interiorized and complicit and downright criminal subjects who were unrestrained, ecstatic, and African. *Amatodos* participates in a secular-religious domain by performing a full sensorium of positive and negative behaviors to communicate its national message about condom use and safe sex.

Still, *Amatodos*'s performance of secular sensibilities was slippery and unstable. Many people discussed how they immersed themselves in *Amatodos* with little regard for its secular politics. To judge from my interviews, the dance failed to compel audiences with its secular message. That a secularist dance would fail to convince audiences is also consistent with what we know of history. Studies of dances in Africa and its diaspora have documented and analyzed dances considered sacred by the participants. Scholars document how sacred dances are participatory realms where interactions among dance movement and instrumental and vocal movement generate heightened aesthetic stimulation, experienced by the participants as transcendent or transformational states of being (Daniel 2011, 129–158). They analyze how sacred dances that produce heightened states of aesthetic stimulation can occur at many places along a secular-spiritual continuum (Daniel 2011; Gottschild 2003; Israel 2014; Welsh Asante 1985). They have taught us that while Africanist religious dance ritual is frequently absent for many Africans and descendants, African ancestral heritage and sacred African legacies nevertheless resurface in numerous performative forms—not just in distinct African religious structures. Despite the history of compulsory Christianity and secular modernism, Africanist sacred ethical and aesthetic sensibilities are expressed through dance in many contexts, including popular, theatrical, ceremonial, and even official state ceremonies and tourist venues (Covington-Ward 2016; Daniel 2005; Israel 2014). *Amatodos* was celebrated for its ecstatic moments and sensuality, even though it was supposed to convince audiences to negate the sensuous body and promote a "secular sensorium" (Hirschkind 2011, 637).[6]

Thus, sacred sensibilities are powerful modes of social action in Mozambican politics and social life that are frequently in play with secular affective projects but also must be understood on their own terms. Furthermore, because the affective experience of secular politics depends on a negative gesture of othering embodied sacred practices, the secular politics is always unstable and emerges in the mode of failure.[7]

I now turn to how *Amatodos* promoted a secular sensorium and how this sensorium offended many participants because, in order to enact a proper AIDS-free subjectivity, *Amatodos* mobilized colonial structures of separate and unequal performative social formations. Then, in the final section, I investigate how many participants celebrated the spiritual experiences that emerged through ecstatic dancing bodies, thus immersing themselves in *Amatodos* with little regard to its secular politics. Both sections work to illuminate the relationality of secular and sacred embodied practices in Mozambique. Together, the sections show how IEC projects, and the biomedical and development projects that fund them, play the "secular game" (Asad 2003) in Mozambique and how many Mozambicans mobilize their bodies for alternative spiritual experiences.

Amatodos as Secular Dance

I studied *Amatodos* through my fieldwork experience when I helped create a professional development program at the Escola Nacional de Dança (END; National Dance School).[8] For this program I cotaught the courses Documentation of Dance and History of Mozambican Concert Dance. In these classes we guided the students on how to do interviews, collect data, write field notes, and interpret interviews. We passed on these skills through action-oriented classwork in which students and teachers researched Mozambican dance history together. We brought in weekly guests to talk about their participation in the founding of the CNCD and END. Together we studied these institutions and performances from 1975 until the present. *Amatodos* was one of the performances we examined more closely.

Initially, the class dismissed *Amatodos* as a crude and silly dance. Frequently, they would refer to it as "just an AIDS dance" (é só a dança do SIDA). The CNCD members would say it was just "something to show we are with FRELIMO" (para mostrar que estamos com a Freli) or "dances we do for the donors" (as danças que fazemos para os doadores). But, with time, the teachers and students demonstrated that they cared more about the dance than they initially let on. They zealously discussed each of *Amatodos*'s eight scenes, describing how sonic, visual, and kinesthetic elements created character types and debating what effect these theatrical elements had on their own experiences.

The choreography starts with a comforting prelude of traditional percussion, which is how the CNCD starts most of its performances. The prelude calls to mind an idyllic, rural setting that most audiences would expect in CNCD performances. This idyllic ambience gradually fades to the first scene, which depicts an urban environment with the stage lights illuminating dancers dressed in tuxedos and evening dresses accompanied by synthesized sounds. Even pulses and steely beats provide the rhythm for the performers, who are dancing a waltz. The heterosexual couples are elegant and dance romantically. One couple sits on a box at center stage under a light with their backs toward each other, as if they were held in suspension. The couple exists in their own bubble while around them swirl other dancers also dressed up for a night on the town. Then enter aggressive and agile virus dancers accompanied by icy, crisp techno sounds like water freezing. The viruses dance in Afro-modern dance patterns with grounded, low positions and heavyweight efforts—like slashing and punching. They fill the stage space with expansive arm and leg attacks and sudden, athletic jumps. Their faces are covered, resembling the masquerade dancers that are common in secret societies and coming-of-age ceremonies. The scene takes place against a carmine backdrop that amplifies the sense of a love affair as well as ominous trouble.

For this first scene, *Amatodos* presents the romantic couples as allegories of Mozambican citizens who must navigate this new world of AIDS. This allegory is made explicit by having a female and male dancer sitting on a box at center stage. This scene is a reproduction of the image from the "think about life!" ("pense na vida!") campaign, an IEC publicity campaign produced by the Ministry of Health through the National STD/AIDS Control Programme. The image shows the silhouette of a man and a woman seated, apparently naked, back to back, and in a thoughtful pose. Above the image is written "think about life!" and below the image is written "avoid AIDS!" ("evite o sida!"). In the 1990s through the 2000s, the "think about life!" poster was the most iconic of IEC campaigns.

In the second scene, a condom dancer enters the stage accompanied by the sound of a wooden flute that lightens the menacing atmosphere. This condom dancer executes a series of balletic moves around the couple. The dancer performs a *couru* and a *soutenu* and swiftly ends in front of the couple in an arabesque.[9] Finally, the condom disappears from the scene by executing a *chaînés*, leaving the couple at center stage sitting reflectively on the box.[10] The light wind-instrument sound and the balletic dance patterns present the condom as the hero of *Amatodos*, in contrast to the African aesthetics of the villainous virus dancers.

In the third scene, schoolgirls fall victim to a male dandy, who judging from his suit, which matches the schoolgirl uniforms, might be a teacher. Traditional percussion and wind instruments, similar to the prelude, accompany the schoolgirls, while the mischievous playboy/teacher dancer moves to the clashes of sharp cymbal shots on a drum kit, as played by a heavy metal band.

The fourth scene displays three drug-addicted thugs experiencing heroin-induced elation, set to heavy rock drum-kit sounds. They wear costumes such as ripped denim jeans, a Tupac Shakur T-shirt, and an unbuttoned sleeveless vest that bares the dancer's chest. As the scene develops, the male dancers move clumsily to the drum instruments and meander around the stage in drug-induced highs.

In these first four scenes, *Amatodos* leads audiences through scenarios where romantic partners, schoolgirls, playboys, and intravenous drug users are confronted by villainous AIDS virus dancers. *Amatodos*'s message was simple for many of those who participated in our class. Unprotected sex is risky. Men exploit younger women. Intravenous drugs are dangerous. Condoms save lives. Be smart and think about life is a sensible message. But for other participants the scenes established an accusatory tone and crude characterizations that they were uncomfortable with. The most suspect behaviors in *Amatodos* are presented by characters who are absorbed in the euphoric sensations of the body, such as the thugs and the romantic couples. The more ecstatic dancing bodies represent negative acts of flirtation, copulation, and drug-induced euphoria. Urban rhythms such as synthesized sounds and jazz-rock percussion ensembles accompany these riskier states, which have tragic consequences. The villainous viruses perform moves typical of Afro-modern dance, and they dress like masquerade dancers. In contrast, the hero condom dancer performs balletic moves. Those who were uncomfortable with these characterizations pointed out that from the start *Amatodos* presents hierarchical distinctions between "thinking about life" and "feeling life," or even "dancing to life." *Amatodos* communicates a message about how people can avoid AIDS through somber, reflective "think about life" bodies, while those who are absorbed in their senses are at risk, or even at fault. As the next scenes of *Amatodos* unfold, its accusatory narrative increases. Proper citizens are portrayed as cerebral and restrained. Those who overindulge in sensual pleasures are responsible for the spread of the disease.

The fifth scene depicts urban African nightlife, driven by recorded South African pop and house music by Boom Shaka and then Brenda Fassie. The female dancers are dressed as sex workers, wearing miniskirts, crop tops, and brightly colored wigs. In contrast, the male dancers are dressed as sailors, soldiers, truck drivers, and businessmen. The women circulate around the stage while approaching the men, caressing them, and asking them for cigarettes. The men respond approvingly and stroke them on their shoulders, waists, and buttocks. Boom Shaka pounds with a pulsing African house bass beat. The dance music initiates collective joy among the dancers and the audience, who for the first time in the performance respond with hoots, hollers, whistles, and clapping. The dancers engage each other in playful bravado, showing off their dance moves. Men and women provoke each other with their sensuous sagittal hip pivots, bending ever lower to the ground as their legs touch and torsos grind together. Who can bend lower? Whose pelvis can pulse more strongly? The sensual stimulation continues to build as other dancers diverge from hot to cool sensuality that is expressed more subtly through soft hip gyrations that move through vertical, horizontal, and sagittal planes, which is common in popular partner dances such as *zouk*, *passada*, and *kizomba*. Adding another layer to the scene, many dancers perform quirky simulations of sexy movements. Bent low to the ground, knees flexed, and keeping their torsos fixed horizontal to the stage, the dancers make awkward leg kicks and flailing circular arm swings, all the while beaming goofy smiles. Together the dancers' provocations border on competitions as each tries to outdo the other. Who can be raunchier, who can be sultrier, who can be more eccentric?

The class identified strongly with *Amatodos*'s representation of popular nightlife dancing as a participatory, communal event. The development of hot, cold, and eccentric sensuality accurately displayed what they valued most about popular nightlife dancing. When done well, such dance events promote collaboration among participants, who play off of each other's unique dancing styles to collectively build aesthetic stimulation and create ecstatic moments. The students' discussion confirmed what scholars have identified about how transcendence is the upmost sensibility for many African and African diaspora dance communities across secular and sacred contexts. The dance scholar Yvonne

Daniel, for example, in her book *Caribbean and Atlantic Diaspora Dance: Igniting Citizenship*, finds transcendent states to be paramount throughout many genres in the circum-Atlantic world:

> Dances encourage performers to become totally at one with the movement such that the corporeal becomes the ecstatic, so that the ancestral world joins the present and transformational states of being preside, or so that dancers reach heightened levels of excitation where aesthetic responses overflow. . . . Performers and observers feel glimpses of the human/ spirit connection and are inevitably affected; they are consequently transported to a realm of extreme fascination, engagement, and rapture. . . . Repeated transcendent experiences over time give the dancing community form and solidarity, and dancing itself encourages a virtual journey that makes the ephemeral moments of the dance usual, normal, the ideal. (2011, 38)

The *Amatodos* dancers create a transcendent experience by collaboratively adding layers of corporeal expression and building off each other's skilled body isolations and polyrhythmic movements. As the dancers' hot, cool, and eccentric sensualities boil over, *Amatodos* takes performers and audiences on a journey that makes the ephemeral behaviors in an urban nightlife dance the ideal.

Yet the scene takes a puritanical turn in the next song by depicting the sensuality performed in the nightlife scene as "lascivious" behavior, a depiction that is all too familiar in colonialist discourses about African dance. The second song in the fifth scene is a ballad called "Too Late for Mama," by Brenda Fassie. The performance changes from playful provocations to representations of raunchy multipartner heterosexual sex. The lyrics are heavy with a message of inevitability as Fassie repeats the refrain in English: "It's too late for mama, too late, too late." A mood of tragedy is also created because of the details of Fassie's fame and eventual death, which were widely known, as she was considered the most popular Afropop star at the time. Fassie was both a loved and controversial figure because of her erotic performances onstage and outlandish public persona. Fassie's life was tragically plagued with alcohol and drug abuse. When she died of a cocaine overdose in 2004, it was revealed that she was HIV positive. *Amatodos*'s hypersexualized performance to Fassie's song "Too Late for Mama" renders the nightlife dancing as hedonism. All the lavish work to transport the musicians, dancers, and audience to a realm of rapture is quickly short-circuited by a scene that equates ecstatic dancing with promiscuous sex. For the group of Mozambicans who participated in the class, this scene provoked intense debate about why it was necessary in *Amatodos* to demean the

African body, popular dance forms, and African forms of transcendence. The next scene helped many resolve this question through a closer analysis of dance and colonial history.

The sixth scene focuses on mother-to-child transmission of AIDS and the role of Christianity in warning and caring for people.[11] The scene is introduced by a women's choir who sing in Changana "AIDS ends life" and "AIDS does not have a cure."[12] A woman who participated in the orgy in the "Too Late for Mama" scene has contracted AIDS, which is symbolized by abject growths on her costume. She carries a doll wrapped in cloth with virus outgrowths protruding. The choir creates a somber mood, but it turns more hopeful as a single male performer dressed in a brown habit with a large cross on the front comforts the mother. The pastor receives the infected child, who is rejected by a group of female dancers who retreat backstage, repulsed by the child. The pastor is a heroic character, similar to the condom who displayed balletic moves, wore white costuming, and danced to ethereal music. The pastor holds up the baby to the community of women onstage and to the audience to show them the consequences of the nightclub scene. In contrast to the nightlife dancing, the pastor is controlled and calm, standing erect and walking. His body movements are the opposite of the low-to-the-ground body positions, the flexed joints, the polyrhythmic body isolations, and the curvilinear body forms of the virus dancers and nightlife crowd. The spectacular dancing that induces transformational states in the nightclub scene now appears quite sinful. This sixth scene presents a different kind of transcendence that is cerebral, lyrical, and faith based. In this scene, transcendence—as in accepting the child and mother and coming to terms with AIDS—occurs through a steady belief in God and a pious following of his principles as written in the Bible. Unfortunately, *Amatodos* frames these two forms of transcendence as mutually exclusive. Only one promotes HIV-free lives, while the other spreads the disease. We are now deep into a secular sensorium as well as approaching white supremacist attitudes about African expressive culture and embodied spirituality, which emerged through the history of colonialism and compulsory Christianity.

Our classroom conversations evolved into heated debates regarding the different presentations of secular Christianity versus African aesthetics. Many students were emotionally taken by the sorrow in the scene of mother-to-child transmission. The sadness was enhanced by the beautiful women's choir, the shaded lighting design, the stillness after the excitation in the previous scene, and the empathetic paternal figure of the pastor who cared for the rejected child. This scene depicted terrible social problems, such as how women have been infected at higher rates and have borne the heaviest tolls and how infected children have been abandoned or orphaned. The scene also recalled how faith-based charities have built orphanages to meet the rise in children infected with AIDS; in Mozambique the role of the Catholic Church in this has been particularly noteworthy. Many participants noted the effectiveness of this emotionally impactful scene. Others were more ambivalent and even demonstrated anger toward the scene. While agreeing with their colleagues about the importance of the social problems that *Amatodos* raised, they wished *Amatodos* could have raised these issues without mobilizing the history of racialized discourses about African dance and the superiority of faith-based practices over practice-based religious traditions. They described how *Amatodos* echoed this colonial history.

The Portuguese frequently used dancing bodies as markers of an inferior "native" (*indígena*) identity. Many dances were prohibited, and performers were subject to criminal penal codes that imprisoned them and justified the use of violence against them. The Portuguese believed that dancing excited aggression and violence.[13] They described "Indigenous" dances (*danças indígenas*) as messiah crazed, idolatrous, libidinous, and lewd. Dances that performed healing ceremonies were seen as satanic or as promoting irrational false belief. Colonial perspectives on dance were foils against which colonialists created their own imagined identities as superior, civilized people. Ecstatic bodies symbolized abjection, and based on this, the colonialists projected their own positive understandings of themselves as still, rational, industrious people. Thus, such negative descriptions of dance cultures were crucial to European understandings of themselves as citizens ready for the demands of civil life, while nativized subjects had to prove themselves by working, paying taxes, and adopting nuclear families and secular Christian values before they could be considered as citizens of the Portuguese nation.

The Portuguese's ethnocentric preoccupation with Mozambicans' dancing illustrates the colonialists' own struggles to turn themselves into a superior citizen class. While the citizen status of the Portuguese and other settlers was legally protected, the elaborate system of hierarchical categories for the people in the Portuguese Overseas Province of Mozambique in fact took enormous cultural and material resources to bring into being (Cabaço 2010). Secular sensibilities about the body contributed to the settler population's attempts to shape themselves into a separate race deserving of privileged citizen status. Secular Christianity promoted a distanced relationship with the body. It favored faith-based practices that centered on the reading and recitation of scriptures and sermons about the "word" of God. Clergy led public worship in specific locations (churches and cathedrals), while at home practitioners continued to strengthen their faith through reflective scripture studies and solemn prayer.

Colonialists understood their faith-based practices as antithetical to the African embodied practice-based ceremonial traditions (Honwana 2002), and they used dancing bodies as the primary symbol of this difference. White settlers, and sometimes "assimilated" Africans (*asimilados*), confined their religious practices and maintained a "reserved" and "orderly" decorum, which meant ridding themselves (their souls and daily behaviors) of corrupting bodily influences. In contrast to the mind-body obsessions of Christian faith-based practices, African religious structures were experienced and expressed through the body, and worldviews, ideologies, and histories were transmitted through embodied rituals (Honwana 2002). Dancing promoted a special relationship with spiritual practices such that dance became a connection to the ancestors and cosmic entities. African dance practices moved people into the spiritual realm.

Dance was therefore a significant site for performing durable citizen-subject identity formations that naturalized a system of different modes of rule, different application of laws, different categories of humans, and different forms of divine transcendence. Despite the violence that the Portuguese colonial state directed toward dance cultures and people who danced, Portuguese colonial rule never eliminated African dance and religious practices, not just because the Portuguese state was weak but because dance was vital for the colonial state's own project of shaping a proper religious domain of secular Christianity. Many decades later, secular liberalism, in the form of *Amatodos* and other IEC campaigns, continued making negative gestures toward African dance and popular aesthetic and spiritual traditions for its own project of fashioning properly religious subjects. *Amatodos* remained an important link in the chain of cultural production and signification that has fashioned a performative system of citizen-subjects.

For many class participants, *Amatodos* was a contemporary revision of this ugly history of using the dancing body to define and regulate what can be considered religious. Up through the sixth scene's Christian chorus, *Amatodos* made negative gestures toward those dance cultures that were most impassioned, ecstatic, communal, and transformational. These negative gestures were foils for an imagined responsible, AIDS-free citizen. Through this visual, aural, and kinesthetic material, *Amatodos* advocated for Mozambicans to be reasonable, to be orderly and not give in to corporeal pleasures. Secular emancipation from religion—understood as the error of irrational, emotional, unscientific belief and corporeal passions—was implicit in *Amatodos*; it was the visceral reasoning that gave *Amatodos* dramatic effect. Yet, just as scholars have challenged the idea of secular-religious binaries (Asad 2003; Mahmood 2005) by arguing that secular rule did not eliminate religion but delineated and refashioned it in ways conducive to liberal rule, so too *Amatodos*'s illusory binary between the secular body and ecstatic bodies was bound to fail. *Amatodos*'s secular sensorium propelled into motion the imaginary of an AIDS-free subject and an AIDS-guilty subject, an imaginary that mobilized older separate and unequal performative social formations to enact neoliberal rule. The class participants used their own knowledge of Mozambican history and politics to identify how few Mozambicans would have benefited from such secular imaginaries; only those with historically accumulated privileges were well situated to articulate themselves through secular-religious binaries to solidify their status as proper citizens. Only FRELIMO, ex-patriots living in Mozambique, the well-educated and well-connected, were able to forge ahead using the ecstatic moving body as prime material to fashion their own imaginary of a future-oriented thinking subject. Still, the class participants had their own sensibilities about the ideal subject, which generated an alternative reading of *Amatodos*.

Amatodos as Sacred Dance

Despite *Amatodos*'s accusatory narrative, audiences perceived the power of the dancing body as an ideal beyond the secular, as an energy with its own social action and effects that were on a different register of human experience from the secular. In the last two scenes of *Amatodos*, the class participants critically studied *Amatodos* for its ability to "go beyond"—to produce transcendent states. They were emotionally moved by these moments of aesthetic excess that approached the spiritual, even though such moments were intended to be interpreted as negative behaviors that ought to be reformed. Their alternative readings of *Amatodos* confirmed that audiences valued *Amatodos* for how the dancing encouraged the "journey to make the ephemeral the ideal," as Yvonne Daniel wrote, no matter the simplistic characterizations, the accusatory tone, and the secular sensorium to "think about life." *Amatodos*'s failure to elicit the proper emotional response among audiences illuminates the insecurity and indeterminacy of secular projects (Hirschkind 2011, 643).

The seventh scene of *Amatodos* is an accolade to the CNCD—it appears precisely to display the dancers' skills and choreographic acumen. Eighteen dancers perform choreographic combinations that create geometric shapes onstage. The combinations build into a final apotheosis of solos and duos accompanied by seven musicians on traditional percussive instruments who produce an immense buzz, train-like energy charging forward. Collectively, the dancers and musicians push themselves to the brink, as if the train will fly off the tracks. Finally, the scene does derail when one male dancer slows down, his movements falter, his timing is off, and eventually he falls to the ground. In silence, the other dancers gather around him. From stage right emerges a woman dressed in a long black sarong. She has upper-arm cuff bracelets made of shells with black ostrich feathers. She is wearing a blonde wig. She places herself above the fallen dancer and shoos away the other dancers who are standing over their colleague. She stares at him, stretches out her arms, and makes sweeping arm circles around the dancer on the floor. The other dancers and audience members shout cheers and ululations. We have now moved into the eighth scene. The mood has shifted from festive to ceremonial, from heighted aesthetics to religious energy. The lead dancer is a traditional healer, or *nyamusoro*, who guides the community in a healing ritual.

As the nyamusoro dancer executes the scanning and sweeping arm movements around the fallen dancer, she starts to travel in a stomping motion. Eight male and female dancers join the nyamusoro dancer. They repeat the same movements through several rotations, adding hand claps at the end of each cycle. The audience responds with increased wailings and cheers. Then the dancers drop to the ground to execute bowed kneeling positions. Their backs are vertical and their heads bowed slightly downward. The solemn moment is broken by a female singer offstage who sings a repetitive high-pitched chant. She cycles through two measures, and then on the third the dancers join the chanting refrain as they add hand claps, cupping the hands instead of leaving the palms flat, to produce a hollow sound. The percussion joins with a timbre that is lower, heavier, as if closer to the ground, than the percussion during the festive scene, which was higher, airier, and cleaner. Dancers stomp and clap, singers chant refrains, and musicians create deep percussive grooves; they all collaborate to produce the rise and fall of cyclic ground-heaven rhythmic movements that build like oceanic currents.

As the scene nears its culmination, the dancers continue executing highly repetitive, simple sitting and kneeling movement patterns, bouncing up and down, which causes their heads to flop and their hair to fly around. The nyamusoro, however, travels freely on the stage and varies her movement patterns frequently. She holds a flat metallic object, a gigantic razor blade, as she stomp-travels through the bowed-kneeling dancers, twirling as she holds her healing instrument in the air. She stands over the ill dancer and drops the razor blade down on him for four counts; then she raises the razor blade high in the air for another four counts. She repeats the pattern several times, traveling, twirling, cutting, and raising the razor blade high. The intensity continues to build. Finally, another dancer, who was the playboy/teacher in the schoolgirl scene, enters the stage with sores on his suit and walking in a discombobulated way.

He falls to the ground. The nyamusoro dancer slices down on him with the prop razor blade and then travels to other patients to do the same cutting action on them. The scene continues with the nyamusoro infecting other dancers with the cutting ritual until finally three female dancers enter and stop the healer. They take her razor blade and smash it on the floor, bringing the ceremony to a crashing halt, like an ocean wave breaking on a shore.

The scene depicted a traditional healer performing a cutting ceremony that aimed at curing the ailment of the fallen dancer but unwittingly contributed to the spread of AIDS. No matter this negative framing, the class participants thought the eighth scene was the most sublime for its reproduction of a healing ceremony. For the class participants, the seventh and eighth scenes replaced the message of "think about life!" with "dance life." No matter what *Amatodos* had communicated earlier about sex, drugs, alcohol, promiscuity, and the importance of refined, restrained Christian values, the energetic and rhythmic bodies in the last scenes were perfection. Their energies neared the celestial. Even though the whole discursive field for *Amatodos* was the negation of the sensuous body and the promotion of a secular sensorium to overcome rapturous religious bodies, the class participants cut across secular sensibilities to register their own experiences of the sacred.

Scholars of dance and religion in Africa and its diaspora have consistently documented how sacred sensibilities have been registered in secular contexts. Religious values and practices have been preserved and reinvented through performances in seemingly nonsacred genres (Askew 2002; Covington-Ward 2016; Daniel 2005, 2013; González 2010; Straker 2009). Many Africans and African descendants participate in sacred practices of ancestor veneration, mediumship, food offerings, animal sacrifice, divination, herbalism, libations, and bloodletting and hold entrenched beliefs in mystic powers (Stewart 2005). Yet what is most obvious, but too frequently overlooked or underanalyzed, is that the dancing body, the intelligent moving body—in conjunction with song and music and all produced through communal participation—is the source of knowledge for these practices and cultivates the sensibilities that reproduce the practices. Dancing is not simply an ephemeral manifestation of more durable cultural structures. The dancing body speaks ritual practices, expresses spiritual states, and communicates knowledge in corporeal sequences and simple or virtuoso displays.

Ritual practices are "spoken" through specific movement characteristics, which have been analyzed by scholars such as Robert Farris Thompson (1974), Kariamu Welsh Asante (1985), Brenda Dixon Gottschild (2003), and Yvonne Daniel (1995, 2005). Sacred sensibilities start with the essential body positions of soft, flexed knees and divided torsos (when the body moves independently from the waist down) that create the "grounded," low, or readied stances that are necessary for enacting and receiving the spiritual. The natural bends are essential body mechanics from which participants can mount elaborate body isolations that create aesthetic stimulation. Sacred rituals create the compounding of aesthetic stimulation through skilled body isolations reproduced polyrhythmically both in movement and in music. One body isolation pulses to a specific beat pattern, while another body part is synced to another sequence. Or, as often occurs in highly skilled performances, a dancer will play with the musicians by syncopating or counterpointing with the musicians. Thus, sacred dances encourage, and even enforce, a hierarchy of the senses where the kinesthetic and sonic are closely associated with the divine. Corporeal intimacy with musical complexity is something celestial and therefore is frequently one of the most valued sensual experiences. Dance therefore plays a significant role in constituting the sacred and the self-fashioning attitudes, embodied dispositions, visceral reasonings, patterned hierarchies of the senses, and beliefs of religious people. Corporeal intimacy and complexity can call forth deities and evoke transcendent or transformational states of being at many places on the secular-spiritual continuum.

The last scenes in *Amatodos* exemplified how the sacred was registered in a secular venue. The context was not just a theatrical venue but a dance that was highly committed to a secularist affective experience of AIDS. The sacred was registered both by the performers onstage and also by the audiences. Onstage, the performers displayed something similar to what Nathanael Homewood (in this volume) calls "embodied resistance," where the performers' bodies resisted the modernist state's negative scripting of African performances. Offstage, audiences also demonstrated resistance to the scripting in a way that resembled what the dance scholar Priya Srinivasan (2009) calls the "unruly spectator," where audiences, in the context of the Indian dance Bharata Natyam, refused to view performances from the discourses of authenticity that falsified history and concealed labor. The participants in our class, many of whom were also performers, refused to be fashioned into a proper religious domain scripted by secular sensibilities and bounded by secular-religious binaries. Instead, they immersed themselves in the aesthetic and spiritual elation performed by the unruly bodies. Like the nightlife dancing and festive scene, the rhythmic and energetic body elevated them beyond the narrative framing of "think about life!" In these scenes, they understood that other knowledge was being enacted and transmitted. In the context of *Amatodos*, the participants identified how these kinesthetic elements took them beyond the secular rhetoric and instead made the ecstatic energies the ideal.

Conclusion

In this chapter I have discussed how our classroom inquiries into *Amatodos* revealed how the choreography embodied the affective experience of secular politics. I analyzed the visual, aural, and kinesthetic elements in the performance to understand how *Amatodos* created sensibilities that shape a secular body, or what Charles Hirschkind (2011) called the *secular sensorium*. *Amatodos* engaged the performers and audiences in a progressive amplification of heightened states of sensual pleasure—flirtations, copulation, mood-altering elation, compounding body rhythms, religious trances—while contrasting such heightened states with more restrained, cerebral actions. Its affective force relied on continually producing a contradiction: it displayed intelligent moving bodies, and the lush energetics and rhythms they produced, while then inscribing these bodies as sinful and threatening. This was the secular sensorium that *Amatodos* pulled audiences into and that caused many to react ambivalently to the choreography. Therefore, *Amatodos* was a much more complicated dance than it would seem just judging from its message about condoms and "think about life!"

Amatodos provoked favorable, ambivalent, and ireful responses from the participants. Performing *Amatodos* gave CNCD members and others opportunities to engage in social action as representatives of national and international projects and to contribute to raising awareness about social problems associated with the epidemic. The CNCD dancers were proud to tour and raise awareness about these problems among audiences, especially since such conversations had not yet started in many communities in the late 1990s and early 2000s. The CNCD members were also pleased about gaining employment, which offered relief from a harsh environment of prolonged austerity.

However, most also agreed that the secularist hierarchies were inappropriate and counterproductive to the task of creating awareness about AIDS. The negative gestures toward African dance cultures and spiritualities were cheap moves that reflected the long history of colonial attitudes toward African dancing bodies and religious practices. *Amatodos* mobilized racialized music and dance elements to create characterizations of heroes, victims, and villains in Mozambican social life. The sonic and kinesthetic elements added dramatic effect by rendering African aesthetics and spirituality as dangerous in an era of AIDS. Audiences were presented with a secular ideal, which was interpreted as representing FRELIMO and donor ideals about citizenship. These ideals were fundamentally incompatible with how many Mozambicans lived and worshipped. Thus, *Amatodos*'s narrative created a gap between secular ideals and most Mozambicans' spiritual and aesthetic lives.

Through this case study of *Amatodos*, this chapter shows how dance, since colonialism, has been an important cultural hub for linking together formations of the secular and state modernizing projects within a larger chain of body politics that included social formations of race, class, gender, ethnicity, geography, and sexuality, to construct who counted as citizens in Mozambique. *Amatodos*'s secular narrative failed to convince audiences, which demonstrates how IEC campaigns have betrayed their informational, educational, and communication goals and what kind of unplanned effects the campaigns have had (Bastos 2002; Carrillo 2002; Galvão 1997; Kalipeni, Flynn, and Pope 2009; Martin 1997; Matsinhe 2008; Parker 2000; Prolongeau 1995). *Amatodos* also demonstrated the instability of the modern neoliberal state, which has failed to foster secular sensibilities through its projects.

Instead, *Amatodos* gave many people opportunities for social action through performing sacred sensibilities that were not necessarily subject to the play of secularism. The sacred sensibilities had an affective force of their own that promoted other corporeal and spiritual dialogues. While *Amatodos* was a failure in many respects, performers and audiences were able to feel proud of the choreography for its scenes of heightened aesthetic states, which joined performers and audiences together in spiritual convergences.

In 2011 a different dance project emerged, called *Pós-Amatodos* (Beyond *Amatodos*), which involved many of the same CNCD dancers but with ten years of IEC campaigns behind them. *Pós-Amatodos* was organized differently, with a focus on dancers' experiences of living in an era of AIDS. *Pós-Amatodos* supported artists to experiment with how to express their experiences and ignore the heavy didactic and evangelical scripts pushed by donors and FRELIMO. As a result, *Pós-Amatodos* performances explored other aesthetic and ethical experiences of the body that were worthy of attention, such as the significance of intimacy and touch in corporeal/human relationality as well as the significance of the moving body in cultivating compassion and maintaining relations with the immaterial world.

NOTES

1. While HIV is the virus and AIDS is the condition or syndrome, for brevity and in keeping with the way most people in Mozambique speak about the disease, in this chapter I use the term AIDS to refer to both. I rely on the reader's knowledge that HIV (human immunodeficiency virus) is the specific virus that may cause severe damage to the immune system and lead to the condition of AIDS (acquired immunodeficiency syndrome).

2. In 1986 the prevalence of AIDS in Mozambique was believed to be below 1 percent of the adult population, although there was no way to measure rates yet (Matsinhe 2008, 38–39). A decade later, infrastructure was in place to measure how the rate reached a countrywide average of around 10 percent of the adult population between the ages of fifteen and forty-nine, with rates much higher, at around 25 percent, in the central provinces (38–39). The most recent studies show that by 2016 the prevalence hovered at 13 percent of the adult population, 15 percent among women and 10 percent among men, with an estimated 1.9 million Mozambicans living with AIDS (USAID 2021).

3. I studied *Amatodos* while working with Maputo dancers, artists, and educators, many of whom were CNCD members, in educational and performance projects between 2009 and 2012.

4. For a discussion of the legacy of the citizen-subject system in dance during Mozambicans' dramatic shifts between colonialism, socialism, and neoliberalism, see my dissertation, "Performing Citizen and Subject: Resistance and Dance in Mozambique" (2016).

5. By the 1990s, the two warring factions, FRELIMO and RENAMO, had created an environment where, out of a total population of 16.3 million, an estimated 2 million Mozambicans were refugees in neighboring countries, 3 million were displaced within Mozambique, and 800,000 had perished (Finnegan 1992).

6. Charles Hirschkind describes the secular sensorium as the "sensibilities that give shape to a secular life" (2011, 637).

7. Hirschkind (2011) argues that we need to keep the relationality of secular and sacred embodied practices within our methods of analysis. Attention to sacred and secular sensibilities helps us understand how the secular is always subject to instability and indeterminacy. As Hirschkind argues,

> The analysis of the secular I am developing here directs us less toward a determinant set of embodied dispositions than to a distinct mode of power, one that mobilizes the productive tension between religious and secular to generate new practices through a process of internal self-differentiation. The boundaries of our categories religious and secular do not preexist this process but are continuously determined and reciprocally redefined within it. Moreover, insomuch as the identity of a secular practice owes to a particular dynamic relation established between these two categories—that every secular practice is accompanied by a religious shadow as it were—then the secular will always be subject to a certain indeterminacy or instability. This instability, ensured by the in principle impossibility of bordering off the secular from the religious, is not a limit on secular power but a condition of its exercise. (643)

8. I worked with my partner, Yula Cisneros Montoya, who is a Mexican-born dancer and educator with experience in Mozambique, as well as faculty and dancers at the CNCD and END to create a professional development program called Programa de Apoio à Dança (Program for the Support of Dance) with funding from a Mozambique/Norwegian Professional Development Grant, through the Norwegian embassy in Maputo, Mozambique. I cotaught the Documentation of Dance and History of Mozambican Dance classes with Lúcio Chumbitico, a dancer and educator from Grupo Milhoro and a graduate of the Universidade Pedagógica (Pedagogical University). In addition, I helped in the creation of the dance project *Pós-Amatodos*, which organized a dance contest,

production, and tour with support from the US embassy of Mozambique and the President's Emergency Plan for AIDS Relief. Through this experience, I came to know more about how *Amatodos* came into being, both practically as a CNCD dance work and also as a complex performance that participates in state ideologies, displays secularist sensibilities, and gives opportunities for sacred social action as well.

9. Couru is a ballet "running" step in which the dancer stands high on the balls of the feet and underpart of the toes. It can be done in place or used to travel in a swift running motion. *Soutenu* is a classical ballet term meaning "sustained" and describes a ballet dancer turning in fifth position *en pointe* and ending up with the opposite foot in front. The arabesque is one of the basic poses in ballet. It is a position of the body, in profile, supported on one leg, which can be straight or bent, with the other leg extended behind and at right angles to it, and the arms held in various harmonious positions creating the longest possible line from the fingertips to the toes. The shoulders must be held square to the line of direction.

10. Chaînés is a ballet "link" step that involves a series of rapid turns on the points or demi-pointes. It is done in a straight line or in a circle.

11. The CNCD members reported that as they toured in the north, where Islam is more prominent, they added symbols of Islam in *Amatodos*. Therefore, in some performances Islam was presented as the proper religious form.

12. Changana is one of the most widely spoken languages in the south of Mozambique. It is part of the Xitsonga language group in southern Africa. The CNCD changed the verses of the choral group from Changana to other languages as they traveled to other areas of Mozambique.

13. My summary of Portuguese and European colonial attitudes toward dance cultures and communities in Mozambique is drawn from personal interviews with Mozambicans who lived under colonialism. I also draw from numerous published resources in Mozambique, of which I mention only a few here, such as nationalist writings by lusophone Africans (see Andrade 1997), biographies (see Jesus 2010; Matuse 2004), Mozambican poetry (see Craveirinha 1980; Santos 1984; Sousa 2001), and colonial texts preserved in archives and libraries (see Pereira 1966). In addition, descriptions of colonial perspectives toward African dance cultures can be gleaned from works by contemporary Portuguese scholars (see Matos 2013).

REFERENCES

Andrade, Mário de. 1997. *Origens do nacionalismo africano: Continuidade e rupture nos movimentos unitarios emergentes da luta contra a dominação colonial portuguesa, 1911–1961*. Lisbon: Dom Quixote.

ARPAC. 2004. *Impacto das mensgens sobre o HIV/SIDA nos programas de informação, educação e comunicação*. Maputo: ARPAC (Arquivo do Património Cultural).

Asad, Talal. 2003. *Formations of the Secular: Christianity, Islam, Modernity*. Stanford, CA: Stanford University Press.

Askew, Kelly. 2002. *Performing the Nation: Swahili Music and Cultural Politics in Tanzania*. Chicago: University of Chicago Press.

Bastos, Cristina. 2002. *Ciência, poder, acção: As respostas à SIDA*. Lisbon: Imprensa de Ciências Sociais, Universidade de Lisboa.

Browning, Barbara. 1995. *Samba: Resistance in Motion*. Bloomington: Indiana University Press.

Cabaço, José Luís. 2010. *Moçambique: Identidade, colonialismo e libertação*. Maputo: Marimbique.

Cabrita, João M. 2000. *Mozambique: The Tortuous Road to Democracy*. New York: Palgrave.

Carrillo, Héctor. 2002. *The Night Is Young: Sexuality in Mexico in the Times of AIDS*. Chicago: University of Chicago Press.

Castaldi, Francesca. 2006. *Choreographies of African Identities: Négritude, Dance, and the National Ballet of Senegal*. Urbana: University of Illinois Press.

Chakravorty, Pallabi. 2008. *Bells of Change: Kathak Dance, Women, and Modernity in India*. Calcutta: Seagull Books.

Covington-Ward, Yolanda. 2016. *Gesture and Power: Religion, Nationalism, and Everyday Performance in Congo*. Durham, NC: Duke University Press.

Craveirinha, José. 1980. *Xigubo*. Lisbon: Edições 70.

Daniel, Yvonne. 1995. *Rumba: Dance and Social Change in Contemporary Cuba*. Bloomington: Indiana University Press.

Daniel, Yvonne. 2005. *Dancing Wisdom: Embodied Knowledge in Haitian Vodou, Cuban Yoruba, and Bahian Candomblé*. Urbana: University of Illinois Press.

Daniel, Yvonne. 2011. *Caribbean and Atlantic Diaspora Dance: Igniting Citizenship*. Urbana: University of Illinois Press.

Dinerman, Alice. 2006. *Revolution, Counter-Revolution and Revisionism in Postcolonial Africa: The Case of Mozambique, 1975–1994*. New York: Routledge.

Finnegan, William. 1992. *A Complicated War: The Harrowing of Mozambique*. Berkeley: University of California Press.

Foster, Susan Leigh. 1995. "Choreographing History." In *Choreographing History*, edited by Susan Leigh Foster, 3–24. Bloomington: Indiana University Press.

Foucault, Michel. 1975. *Discipline and Punish: The Birth of the Prison*. London: Penguin.

Galvão, Jane. 1997. "As respostas das organizações não-governamentais brasileiras frente à epidemia de HIV.SIDA." In *Políticas, instituições e AIDS: Enfrentando a epidemia no Brasil*, edited by Richard Parker, 69–108. Rio de Janeiro: ABIA (Associação Brasileira Interdisciplinar de AIDS) and Jorge Zahar.

Giersdorf, Jens Richard. 2013. *The Body of the People: East German Dance since 1945*. Madison: University of Wisconsin Press.

Godard, Hubert. 1996. "Singular, Moving Geographies." In "The French Issue." *Writings on Dance*, no. 15: 12–21.

González, Anita. 2010. *Afro-Mexico: Dancing between Myth and Reality*. Austin: University of Texas Press.

Gottschild, Brenda Dixon. 2003. *The Black Dancing Body: A Geography from Coon to Cool*. New York: Palgrave Macmillan.

Hall, Margaret, and Tom Young. 1997. *Confronting Leviathan: Mozambique since Independence*. London: Hurst.

Handler, Richard. 1988. *Nationalism and the Politics of Culture in Quebec*. Madison: University of Wisconsin Press.

Hanlon, Joseph. 1986. *Beggar Your Neighbor: Apartheid Power in Southern Africa*. Bloomington: Indiana University Press.

Hirschkind, Charles. 2011. "Is There a Secular Body?" *Cultural Anthropology* 26 (4): 633–647.

Honwana, Alcinda Manuel. 2002. *Espíritos vivos, tradições modernas: Possessão de espíritos e reintegração social pós-guerra no sul de Moçambique*. Maputo: Promédia.

Israel, Paolo. 2014. *In Step with the Times: Mapiko Masquerades of Mozambique*. Athens: Ohio University Press.

Jesus, José Manuel Duarte de. 2010. *Eduardo Mondlane: Um homen a abater*. Coimbra: Almedina.

Kaeppler, Adrienne L. 1993. *Poetry in Motion: Studies of Tongan Dance*. Tonga: Vava'u Press.

Kalipeni, Ezekiel, Karen Flynn, and Cynthia Pope, eds. 2009. *Strong Women, Dangerous Times: Gender and HIV/AIDS in Africa*. New York: Nova Science.

Mahmood, Saba. 2005. *Politics of Piety: The Islamic Revival and the Feminist Subject*. Princeton, NJ: Princeton University Press.

Mamdani, Mahmood. 1996. *Citizen and Subject: Contemporary Africa and the Legacy of Late Colonialism*. Princeton, NJ: Princeton University Press.

Manning, Susan. 2006. *Ecstasy and the Demon: The Dances of Mary Wigman*. Minneapolis: University of Minnesota Press.

Manuel, Sandra. 2008. *Love and Desire: Concepts, Narratives and Practices of Sex amongst Youths in Maputo City*. Dakar: Saint Paul.

Martin, Denise. 1997. "Mulheres e AIDS: Uma abordagem antroloógica." *Revista USP*, no. 33 (March–May): 88–101.

Matos, Patrícia Ferraz de. 2013. *The Colours of the Empire: Racialized Representations during Portuguese Colonialism*. New York: Berghahn Books.

Matsinhe, Cristiano. 2008. *Tabula Rasa: Dynamics of the Mozambican Response to HIV/AIDS*. Maputo: Kula.

Matuse, Renato. 2004. *A paixão pela terra*. Maputo: Macmillan Moçambique.

Meduri, Avanthi. 2008. "The Transfiguration of Indian/Asian Dance in the United Kingdom: Contemporary Bharatanatyam in Global Contexts." *Asian Theatre Journal* 25 (2): 298–328. https://doi.org/10.1353/atj.0.0017.

Montoya, Aaron. 2016. "Performing Citizen and Subject: Resistance and Dance in Mozambique." PhD diss., University of California, Santa Cruz.

Nájera-Ramírez, Olga. 1997. *La Fiesta de Los Tastoanes: Critical Encounters in Mexican Festival Performance*. Albuquerque: University of New Mexico Press.

Ness, Sally Ann. 1992. *Body, Movement, and Culture: Kinesthetic and Visual Symbolism in a Philippine Community*. Philadelphia: University of Pennsylvania Press.

Novack, Cynthia Jean. 1995. "The Body's Endeavors as Cultural Practices." In *Choreographing History*, edited by Susan Leigh Foster, 177–184. Bloomington: Indiana University Press.

O'Shea, Janet. 2007. *At Home in the World: Bharata Natyam on the Global Stage*. Middletown, CT: Wesleyan University Press.

Parker, Richard. 2000. *Na contramão da AIDS: Sexualidade, intervenção e política*. Rio de Janeiro: ABIA (Associação Brasileira Interdisciplinar de AIDS) and Editora 34.

Pereira, Alberto Feliciano Marques. 1966. *A arte em Moçambique*. Lisbon: n.p., 1966.

Pitcher, M. Anne. 2002. *Transforming Mozambique: The Politics of Privatization, 1975–2000*. Cambridge: Cambridge University Press.

Prolongeau, Hubert. 1995. *Une mort africaine: Le SIDA au quotidien*. Seuil L'Histoire Immediate. Paris: Seuil.

Ramsey, Kate. 1995. "Vodou and Nationalism: The Staging of Folklore in Mid-Twentieth Century Haiti." *Women and Performance: A Journal of Feminist Theory* 7 (2): 187–218. https://doi.org/10.1080/07407709508571216.

Reed, Susan Anita. 2010. *Dance and the Nation: Performance, Ritual, and Politics in Sri Lanka*. Madison: University of Wisconsin Press.

Santos, Marcelino dos. 1984. *Canto de amor natural*. Maputo: Associação dos Escritores Moçambicanos.

Shea Murphy, Jacqueline. 2007. *The People Have Never Stopped Dancing: Native American Modern Dance Histories*. Minneapolis: University of Minnesota Press.

Sousa, Noémia de. 2001. *Sangue negro*. Maputo: Associação dos Escritores Moçambicanos.

Srinivasan, Priya. 2009. "A 'Material'-ist Reading of the Bharata Natyam Dancing Body: The Possibility of the 'Unruly Spectator.'" In *Worlding Dance*, edited by Susan Leigh Foster, 53–75. New York: Palgrave Macmillan.

Stewart, Diane. 2005. *Three Eyes for the Journey: African Dimensions of the Jamaican Religious Experience*. Oxford: Oxford University Press.

Straker, Jay. 2009. *Youth, Nationalism, and the Guinean Revolution*. Bloomington: Indiana University Press.

Thompson, Robert Farris. 1974. *African Art in Motion*. Berkeley: University of California Press.

USAID. "Controlling the HIV/AIDS Epidemic," accessed January 6, 2021, https://www.usaid.gov/mozambique/fact-sheets/controlling-hivaids-epidemic.

Welsh Asante, Kariamu. 1985. "Commonalities in African Dance: An Aesthetic Foundation." In *African Culture: The Rhythms of Unity*, edited by Molefi Kete Asante and Kariamu Welsh Asante, 71–82. Westport, CT: Greenwood.

PART IV

Religious Discipline and the Gendered and Sexual Body

10. Wrestling with Homosexuality: Kinesthesia as Resistance in Ghanaian Pentecostalism

NATHANAEL J. HOMEWOOD

Their bodies, exhausted and finally worn down by the physical intensity of deliverance, were propped up as the church chairperson took a photograph to memorialize the experience. The three women, two of them still uncertain what had just transpired, sat in the middle, surrounded by a dozen male pastors, all grinning. The deliverers embraced them as bodily trophies after a two-hour deliverance event defined by bodies in contact and in conflict. The clothes of the two women were still disheveled, but most of the flesh that had been revealed during the throes of deliverance was no longer laid bare. Their faces were covered with sweat and tears, wearing looks of bewilderment and pain. The crowd of thousands who had cheered throughout the lengthy ordeal remained. A crush of people continued to push forward, trying to get their own pictures for posterity, each person's movement creating a syncopated wave that rippled through the crowd. The pictures—frozen vignettes and digital tableaux—all failed to capture much of what had transpired, however.

The bodily stillness in the photo taken by the chairperson contrasted starkly with the persistent, frenetic, and unremitting bodily motion of the deliverance experience. Bodies had jolted, punched, danced, spasmed, and screamed. The central claim of this chapter is simply that in deliverance, bodies and bodily movements matter. To illustrate the extent to which this is true, I interpret an act of deliverance from the spirits of "lesbianism" in a Ghanaian Pentecostal church by watching bodies in motion, in contact, and in convulsion.

This chapter does not intervene directly in the discussion about homosexuality and charismatic churches, instead proffering an argument about bodily resistance. In doing so, this chapter transposes arguments about the publicity of sexuality in Pentecostal settings into the register of ritual. Homosexuality is made public not only through discourse but also through the violence of rituals whereby sexuality is wrested from its privacy and thrown onto a public stage. Careful attention to both scripted and nonscripted kinesthetic movements reveals much about persistent and hoary Pentecostal scripts concerning sexuality. While each violent action from the pastorate delineates which bodies are forcibly disciplined—which is a harrowing experience for lgbtq believers—attention to the variety of kinesthetic movements throughout deliverance by all participants illuminates a crack in those rigid and vicious scripts.[1] In the case explored here, the movement of two lesbian women creates a clamoring resistance to exclusionary Pentecostal sexual mores.

Asserting the moving body as the central analytic requires sweeping descriptions of the way that bodies move in deliverance since the beliefs of the religious do not rest solely or primarily on theological strictures or cognitive understandings. Instead, religious beliefs are assemblages that include affect and motor movement. Pentecostalism in particular is animated by striking bodily experiences and kinesthetic participation. Evidence of the supernatural—good and evil—is felt in the body. Pentecostal convictions may include preexisting beliefs, but these convictions are enforced by "a deeper structure of religious feeling that can tie together disparate, even contradictory, experiences, bodily sensations, feelings and thoughts" (Pellegrini 2007, 918). Thus, the thick description of bodies in motion utilized in this chapter is an argument for taking bodily movements and sensations seriously for the way they structure religious experiences and beliefs about sexuality. Bodies simultaneously succumb to churchly scripts and resist those very norms.

The ritual of deliverance requires that bodies be a primary subject of analysis. Deliverance is defined by bodily movement. The spasming, contorting, excessive body is the undelivered body or, in other words, the possessed body. The ambition of the prophet or pastor—the one doing the delivering—is to turn the frenetic jolts and movements of the undelivered body into bodily stillness. The docile, unmoving, and still body is the delivered body. Docility is the most important embodied message of deliverance choreographed by the prophet, a sign of the prophet's power over both the ethereal and the material. As such, bodies that refuse docility and continue convulsing resist the religious choreography and its attendant scripts.

The Deliverance of Morowa and Kifah

The deliverance at the center of this chapter was an attempt to deliver two women—Morowa and Kifah—from the spirit of lesbianism. In the act of deliverance, each bodily action by Morowa, Kifah, the prophet, and the pastors revealed a potent story of sexuality and hardened the congregation's assumptions about nonnormative sexuality. Since the spirit involved in this deliverance act was the spirit of lesbianism, the whole performance communicated a plethora of ideas and beliefs not only about women, lesbianism, and women's bodies but also about the church's control of bodies, patriarchal fantasies, and violent denial of nonnormativity.

The church I discuss here—an often-frequented but much-maligned church in Ghanaian popular discourse—was the focus of a significant portion of my participant-observation research on Ghanaian Pentecostalism and sexuality for nine months in 2015 and 2016.[2] Owing to the sensitivity of my research, I use pseudonyms throughout this chapter. I will call the church, which is located on the outskirts of Accra, God's Global Path Church and will refer to the prophet as Emmanuel. The deliverance service of God's Global Path Church occurs every Wednesday and is attended by more than three thousand people and many more spirits. The deliverance services are attended by church members as well as a diversity of people in desperate need of deliverance, who often come from other churches and occasionally from different religious traditions. The centrality of deliverance at God's Global Path Church is not unique. Among a large swath of charismatic Christians in Ghana, deliverance is the central ritual that forms the climax of the church service. All the other rituals are subsidiary or understood in relation to deliverance. Paul Gifford in his analysis of the role of Pentecostalism in Ghanaian society sees deliverance as "perhaps Ghanaian Christianity's most pressing issue" (1998, 108). What is unique, however, about Emmanuel and God's Global Path Church is the manner in which they push the limits of charismatic Christianity. Accordingly, the church is often scorned by traditional Pentecostal pastors and prophets for a variety of extremes, most notably for its troubling use of violence within deliverance rituals.

Deliverance is a physical ritual that points to the presence of evil spirits in those being delivered. As Adriaan van Klinken (2013) pointed out through his research in Zambia, homosexuality is often portrayed as an enchanted battlefield littered with evil spirits and, at times, the devil. For Emmanuel, homosexuality is always an enchanted battleground that influences and impacts material bodies. The evil spirits of nonnormative sexualities possess human bodies, a problem solved only after the prophet physically wrests these evil spirits from the body. This is a battleground of problematic power dynamics. The prophet wields spiritual authority, which allows him to reign not only over spirits but also over the bodies that house those spirits.

There were four primary bodies involved in this particular deliverance experience. The first body was that of the prophet Emmanuel, a young man who is controversial and extraordinarily well known among the constellation of charismatic superstars in Ghana. Ghana's popular media are obsessed with Emmanuel and the outrageous nature of his claims, which are often turned into memes. However, the excessive and brutal violence of Emmanuel's deliverance rituals—for example, against a couple who conceived outside the bounds of marriage and in another instance toward a pregnant woman—receives widespread condemnation. While the deliverance discussed here received no such public condemnation, it was, to my eye, more brutal and sustained in its violence.

The three women conscripted in this event—Morowa, Ethel, and Kifah—were all tangentially aware of each other before being thrust together into this religious drama. All three women were in their twenties. Kifah and Morowa lived in a busy industrial community near Accra. Morowa lived alone in a run-down hotel, isolated from her family, who remained in Nigeria. Kifah lived nearby, along with her family. Ethel lived with her family in greater Accra, in a neighborhood that is a thirty-minute *tro tro* (minibus taxi) ride from God's Global Path Church. She was the only family member who regularly attends Emmanuel's services. Ethel, who knew Morowa from a film they were involved in, invited Morowa to the service because Morowa wanted deliverance from something that was bothering her. Kifah came on her own volition but already knew Morowa because they worked at the same club in their community. This would be the only time that Kifah and Morowa attended Emmanuel's church. After the events of this day, they actively, and angrily in Morowa's case, avoided anything to do with Emmanuel, even shunning his televised appearances. Morowa, however, did not give up on Pentecostalism. She still firmly believed in the power of Pentecostal rituals and immediately traveled back to Nigeria to visit her "spiritual father," the famed T. B. Joshua.

On this particular day, my own body watched the violent and sexualized deliverance from a position of privilege. Earlier during this deliverance service, I had been identified as *obroni* and called on by the prophet to account publicly for my presence.[3] I awkwardly stumbled through some answers to the prophet's queries, my voice cracking at one point, but was spared bodily contact. Instead of performing deliverance, the prophet prophesied to the congregation's delight that I would one day write a book—a prophecy that has yet to materialize. After the prophecy, Emmanuel asked me to watch the remaining deliverance episodes from the comfortable couches on the stage where his acolytes sat. My placement on the stage clearly demarcated my body as subservient to the prophet but also as privileged.

I was admittedly confused by the whole performance, both my own performance and Emmanuel's feigned ignorance. The anxiety I experienced, the immediate and unquestioning capitulation to Emmanuel's instructions, and the comfort I felt when moved to a place of honor each left me distressed to varying degrees. I wondered, why did Emmanuel purport not to know the reason for my presence? Although I had not met the prophet himself until this very public moment, I had spent a considerable amount of time at his house and had, through his intermediaries, received his approval to conduct research among his church and had been attending his services for some months.

My position at the front of the church also implicated my body in a particular way, one that became increasingly uncomfortable after the deliverance began. It would be the only time my body inhabited this particular position, as in quieter moments away from the pandemonium of deliverance I was able to discuss with the church's pastor why I preferred to participate as a congregant. Nonetheless, to my great discomfort, my bodily presence was complicit in what occurred afterward. My quiet, still body among Emmanuel's acolytes—my bodily refusal to intervene—was interpreted as an embodied statement of assent to all that occurred. When the service ended, I eschewed the tro tros and walked the entire distance to my apartment. On my walk, I replayed the scene over and over again in my mind, wondering about my participation and even the viability of the entire project. I rehashed these concerns later that week when a condensed version of the event was replayed on the prophet's television station. I concocted all sorts of reasons—many reasonable—about why I had not intervened. Although no amount of hindsight absolved me of my embodied complicity, I concluded that, given the chance to replay the day's events, I would not have done anything differently. It seems to me that ethnographic fieldwork is often marked by these paradoxical tensions.

As Emmanuel prowled around the congregation picking out unsuspecting persons and delivering them from their demons, he eventually became fixated on Morowa. He asked her in the most oblique terms if she wanted deliverance from "that thing." She answered in the affirmative as if she knew what "that thing" was. From the very beginning, there was unspoken confusion. Morowa later told me that she had a specific issue—not lesbianism—that she thought the prophet was going to solve. She described her thought process in this moment:

"I was like, which of the spirits is that? I was so happy. I was like, my problems are over." Kifah similarly was not present to be delivered from lesbianism but had hoped for a financial windfall from attending Emmanuel's church.

The confusion and ambiguity about the deliverance vanished when Emmanuel publicly referred to her issue as "girl-girl." When the congregation seemed confused by this, he added other examples to make it clear that he was invoking a category of sexuality, girl-on-girl sex. Morowa's body was discursively made in this moment, in particular by the context of Ghanaian and Pentecostal social attitudes toward lesbianism. It is impossible to extricate the material body—that is, the physical dimensions of being human—from the discursive body, in this case a discursive body of antiqueer animus (Thoreson 2014). However much one wishes to focus on the material body, it is necessary to admit that bodies are never free from the cultural constraints already written onto them. In this deliverance from the spirits of lesbianism, from the moment deliverance commenced, these rigid antiqueer scripts were operative, written into and onto various bodies. Henceforth, each bodily action was read as confirming the congregation's worst suspicions about homosexuality.

In her work on lesbianism in Ghana, Serena Owusua Dankwa argues that lesbianism in Accra is mostly secretive, hidden, and disguised. Or it was. Dankwa uses the term *discretion* to describe the situation of women who love women. Lesbianism was marked by privacy and secrecy rather than explicit discussion or public displays of affection (Dankwa 2009, 194). Nonnormative sexualities were not necessarily condemned or condoned but existed in "the realm of the unspoken" (194). That silence is being overtaken by a Pentecostal cacophony, however, and Astrid Bochow remarks that Pentecostal churches in Ghana have created "sexuality as a subject of public discourse, if only in its negation" (2008, 353). Charismatic churches spend a great deal of time imagining various sexual demons, placing restrictions on sexual relationships, and condemning nonheteronormative sexualities, which has moved sexuality from the private to the public, from silent acceptance to deafening denouncements. The antiqueer animus of Ghanaian Pentecostal churches has reached deep into the wider society. As one of my interlocutors, a gay man, stated, "I asked a traditional healer about homosexuality. He told me it was wrong. I asked, why? And he said, because the Bible says so."

Occasionally, Pentecostal discourse refers to this culture of sexual discretion, but any signs of tact are obliterated through ritual. For example, before uttering any details concerning Morowa's sexuality, Emmanuel apologized profusely for revealing such a private issue. He even tried to shift the blame to the Holy Spirit, arguing that without the spirit's prompting he would never reveal such information. Further, before enacting the deliverance ritual, Emmanuel continued to speak of her sexuality obliquely, using phrases like "the issue," "that thing," and "girl-girl." However, once the ritual of deliverance began, the terms *lesbian* and *lesbianism* were thrown around with vitriolic repetition.

Elsewhere I have pointed out the creative use of religious spaces by lgbtq Christians, whereby some lgbtq Christians find safety in performing their queerness under the cover of religious heteronormativity (Homewood 2016). Deliverance at God's Global Path Church is clearly a different case. Despite the tentativeness in Emmanuel's language, he outed Morowa as a lesbian. Morowa's sexuality immediately became public and problematic, even though she was never asked whether she considered herself a lesbian or wanted such information to be public. She does in fact identify as a lesbian, but she did not want this to be public. This kind of outing is not uncommon among Pentecostal churches. I spoke with a handful of gay men who have been forced to craft a multitude of ways of avoiding such outing. Oftentimes they purposefully avoid prophets and prophetesses like Emmanuel who traffic in this kind of prophetic outing and sexual deliverance.

Emmanuel did not immediately attempt to deliver Morowa. Instead, he sent four of his pastors to deliver her from this sexual spirit. After the first pastor touched Morowa, she instantly changed from her demure disposition, hands clasped in front of her and eyes cast down, into a much more aggressive posture. No longer intimidated or nervous, she twisted, turned, and moved her arms in an effort to elude the pastors' grip. The first bodily contact instigated an embodied conflict in a manner that Emmanuel's rhetoric did not.

It was from the first touch an odd haptic experience for Morowa. Morowa had experienced the laying on of hands by many pastors and prophets in the process of healing and deliverance. In the past, she had experienced the touch in a particular way: "If a good man of God touches me, I will feel cold, and it will go right from my forehead all the way down, cold!" This is not unique; Pentecostal ritual feelings are often described as sensations of warmth and coolness (Csordas 1988, 125). But in this deliverance, unlike in all of her previous experiences, Morowa felt differently: "But in this case, I want to tell you the truth, when he touched me, I didn't feel anything cold." Morowa's thermoception reflexively provided clues that this deliverance might not be like anything else she had experienced. Her body sensed and interpreted cues from this world and beyond. Only in hindsight was she able to articulate this fact consciously, curating it as evidence that the deliverance was not real. Her body, though, felt and engaged in a kind of bodily resistance to the touch of the pastors. While it may have remained unconscious, such deeply embodied sensing set off a whole host of embodied reactions to the force of the pastorate, as Morowa exhibited throughout the deliverance episode. I term this type of bodily knowledge *embodied perception*. Embodied perception is the acquiring of knowledge through the moving and feeling body. Embodied perception is not about sudden, cognitive bursts but the oftentimes unconscious ways in which bodies communicate. In this case, through embodied perception Morowa felt resistance. She could not immediately identify the bodily meanings but over time reflexively realized that her body had been providing signposts of a narrative far different than the prophetic script.

The area around Morowa was quickly cleared of other congregants and the plastic lawn chairs on which they sat. Two pastors pulled Morowa's arms taut behind her back at an awkward angle while she tried to move forward toward the prophet. As they held her arms and tried to control her body, it became clear that this was an attempt to discipline Morowa's lesbian body. One pastor put a handkerchief between his hand and her flesh as a buffer, a move that another pastor would emulate later as Morowa's convulsions became stronger. It was a very purposeful move for the pastors, as Morowa's flailing made procuring the handkerchief and applying it to her flesh a difficult move to execute. There was something about this particular deliverance body and its flailing limbs that the pastors wanted to communicate; they inculcated fear, disgust, and horror around the lesbian body.

Another pastor held a microphone toward Morowa's face to amplify what she was yelling. Morowa repeated into the microphone, "I am a beautiful Morowa," "I am beautiful," and the like. While Morowa was demanding people pay attention to her beauty, the physical conflict between her and the pastors was ongoing. As they twisted and turned, Morowa yelled that she liked to dance. Emmanuel instructed the pastors to let go of her. He invited her to come to the front and dance. The pastors released her arms, and she sauntered up to the front of the church. As the band struggled to find a tune that suited Morowa's tastes, she paced back and forth. Her body never stopped moving. She would walk in one direction, turn on her heel, and walk back the other way. Eventually the band gave up, and an iPad was secured. Morowa began to dance in a manner that could be described not as provocative but certainly as sensual. She enjoyed her body. Her eyes looked up and down her body, and her hands moved around her body. No longer angrily pulling away from the pastors or yelling into a microphone, Morowa smiled. She recounted later, "I really enjoyed the dancing so much." Morowa shook her backside toward the congregation. They vociferously shouted their disapproval, waved her off with their hands, or turned away in disgust. With a simple hand gesture, Emmanuel had the music cut off.

The whole scene was marked by things that the prophet allowed deliverance bodies to do, things that deliverance bodies must be stopped from doing, and things that the prophet forced deliverance bodies to do. To dance and touch one's own body did not cross the church's limits of modesty, but when Morowa bent over at the waist at a nearly ninety-degree angle, pushing her backside out to emphasize the space it occupied and shaking it with the music, the prophet stopped the deliverance body. These interstices certainly seem to confirm a Foucauldian interpretation of the pastorate's role in disciplining the body. As Michel Foucault writes, "the pastor . . . is in a position to watch over [the flock] and to exercise with respect to them, in any case, a surveillance and continuous control" (quoted in Carrette 1999, 24). Deliverance is an act of both surveillance (the pastorate and entire church inflict their curious, judgmental, and voyeuristic gaze on the moving body) and control (ultimately the body is forced to do or not do exactly as the prophet desires). It is set as a battle between the cosmic forces of good and evil for possession of the body, but deliverance is always an attempt to write churchly and cultural scripts—that is, narratives of power, ecclesiastical and otherwise—onto the material bodies of believers. Deliverance allows for the pastorate to control and discipline the sexual body, as confession did and continues to do in some other Christian traditions.

After stopping the body from dancing, Emmanuel introduced another body to the drama. He summoned Ethel, the friend who had invited Morowa to the church, to join them up front. As soon as Ethel appeared, Morowa spoke about her relationship to Ethel and how "she like[d] her very much." There was a distinct disparity in how Ethel's and Morowa's bodies occupied space. For the entirety of the episode, Ethel offered only one-word answers. Her body was downtrodden, with slumped shoulders, eyes looking downward, and a dour facial expression. Morowa was given most of the front of the church to pace, while Ethel stood still among the pastors. Ethel's inaction contrasted with Morowa's incessant bodily movements. In every bodily way, Ethel made it clear that she did not need deliverance, that her body was not to be treated in the same way as Morowa's body. She wanted her body to be read as straight and free of spirits.

The introduction of Ethel's body was followed by a sonic disruption. The anguished screams of a woman near the back of the sanctuary pierced through the production occurring at the front of church. It quickly became obvious that these were not merely screams but a bodily disruption. From the crush of individuals four ushers emerged carrying Kifah's flailing and shrieking body. Each usher held a limb so that every time she convulsed, her torso bounced up and down, her head hanging dangerously close to the ground. They set her on the ground, and she began rolling around while groaning. Kifah's body remained in a repetitive loop; her rolling around was punctuated by groans and screams and accompanied by the persistent rubbing of her abdomen. Toward the end of the service, her fingers determinedly and purposefully moved around her genitals, clearly imitating or engaging in an autoerotic act.

The introduction of Kifah's deliverance body was very different from that of Morowa's deliverance body or Ethel's body. The first two women—Morowa and Ethel—were selected by Emmanuel and constructed in a particular way: the insatiable lesbian body that must be delivered and the chaste nonlesbian body. Kifah's deliverance body reacted more spontaneously, responding to the stimuli of the experience and the affective atmosphere, rather than the instructions of the prophet and pastors. The pastors quickly wrote their discursive sexual script onto her, with one pastor informing me privately before exclaiming to the congregation that she was "a lesbian who liked licking others' vaginas." While the crudeness of his description would shock some church congregations, sexualized and explicit rhetoric is relatively standard fare at God's Global Path Church and very much in line with the impetus of evangelical and Pentecostal churches to describe all sins that may befall congregants in as much detail as possible. Each of her bodily actions was interpreted to fit these scripts despite the lack of obvious embodied correlation. In doing so, Emmanuel and his cohorts imposed an affect of disgust on Kifah's body. As she rolled around the floor, she was given a wide berth; nobody came near her body. Her body—like Morowa's body—was to be avoided except for the violent pastoral outbursts intended to reorient the body into a straight and dispossessed one.

Eventually, the two camps—Emmanuel and his pastors on one side and the possessed women on the other—came into bodily conflict. Most of the pastors began delivering Morowa, while Emmanuel focused on Kifah. Kifah repeatedly touched her genitals and moved her fingers as if she was pleasuring herself. Every time she touched herself, Emmanuel hit her hand. This was the first time Emmanuel touched either woman, and it appeared to have little impact. Emmanuel asked his wife to come and hold Kifah's crotch. The role of his wife's hand in the process was not viewed as a delivering touch but as a pragmatic way to stop the autoerotic imitation. Her hand formed a barrier so that Kifah could no longer touch herself. Emmanuel replaced his wife's hand with his foot and repeatedly kicked Kifah. With each kick he made a pfff sound into the microphone. Kifah continued to wiggle and writhe on the ground and never acceded to Emmanuel's desire that she become docile.

While Emmanuel spent all of his time with Kifah, six of his pastors physically tried to rip the demon out of Morowa. As they held her, she managed to drag them around the front of the church. Even amid the violence Morowa tried to dance, shaking her backside at the pastors who had her in their grasp. Whenever the pastors' bodies came in contact with Morowa's backside, she would determinedly rub her body on theirs. Some of them held her while others punched her in the stomach. One pastor ripped off a bracelet she was wearing. Her face and head were hit repeatedly. One tried stomping on her feet. Another repeatedly pulled her head down toward his crotch, miming a heteronormative oral sex act. She described to me months later that the assault was painfully etched on her body for days: "[I was] feeling headache, pains all over my body, everything. I couldn't even sleep that night because of my headache." While deliverance is always physical and often includes a violent element, this was the most vicious deliverance display I witnessed in my fieldwork. This ritual rending of lesbianism from the body was a bodily beating, yet despite the ferocity Morowa never spoke of her experience in terms of physical or sexual abuse. She understood all of the physical contact within the context of Pentecostal rituals, namely, deliverance. The pastorate may have been wrong in their diagnosis of what plagued her, but in all our conversations she never condemned or objected to their means.

This saga lasted over two hours, and yet it ended inconclusively. Docility, that ever important marker of pastoral victory, never occurred. Morowa and Kifah never stopped moving, though exhaustion overtook everyone involved and the movements slowly became less and less determined. Emmanuel hurriedly herded his pastors and the women together for the photo described at the onset of this essay. The photo finally made still bodies that had been in continual motion throughout the drama. The photo stood in as an act of victory, attempting to articulate a comprehensive deliverance that simply had not occurred, an act of celebration that did not correspond with the many varied bodily movements that had made up the deliverance drama.

Resistance through Embodied Perception

Bodies matter. Bodies tell stories. Bodies in rituals—their emotions, movements, and dynamic bodily interactions—shape the way people perceive the world and act in it. In this case, the movement of bodies was used by Emmanuel to tell a story of lesbianism as a difficult demon to part with, to vilify lesbianism, and to demonize women's bodies, among a host of other patriarchal scripts. The violent movements of ecclesiastical power made the body something to be feared, loathed, and ultimately disciplined. The poignant image here of the pastors using their handkerchiefs illustrates an unwillingness to touch the material body for fear of its disgusting nature. The way touch was used, the way bodies writhed, and the manner in which violence and intimacy were enacted reinforced Pentecostal norms about sexuality. For the attentive congregation, the brutality imposed on Morowa's and Kifah's bodies added to any prior beliefs about the demonic sinfulness of lesbianism and concretized homosexuality as something to be truly abhorred.

There was, however, something more, something different from these churchly scripts of antiqueer animus, that captured my attention throughout the whole ordeal. I witnessed an alternative way of being through the bodies of Kifah and Morowa. It is vital to look to the body because bodies offer something different from doctrine and rhetoric; they are more capacious in their storytelling. The movement of bodies is opaque. Bodies are inherently ambiguous, pliable, and indeterminate. In her stunning book *Terrorist Assemblages: Homonationalism in Queer Times*, Jasbir Puar quotes Amit Rai's argument that the body's indeterminacy "promotes 'affective confusion' that allows for new affects, and thus new politics, to emerge" (2007, 208). The indeterminacy of bodily affects can be read in multiple ways. In those slippages, movements neither completely adhere to nor completely resist religious force, but they do at least offer partial resistance to the religious refusal to recognize lgbtq persons as human. Bodies can find the gaps in the scripts of antiqueer animus and push against them, literally.

Bodies are resilient against efforts to inscribe them. In spite of Emmanuel's dogged determination to elicit disgust, there were multiple kinesthetic movements that told another story. Morowa, yelling determinedly about her bodily beauty and dancing as a performance of this embodied beauty, resisted the ways in which Emmanuel and the other pastors attempted to impose—by word and physical force—disgust and heteronormativity on her body. Owing to such embodied resilience, I would like to consider the possibility of reading Morowa's and Kifah's bodies as sites of resistance. Bodies may have cultural scripts written onto them, but those same bodies are capable of writing resistance. As Susan Leigh Foster ventures, scholars should "approach the body's involvement in any activity with an assumption of potential agency to participate in or resist whatever forms of cultural production are underway" (1995, 15). I apply these instructions to this story of deliverance: Kifah's and Morowa's bodies resisted crushing cultural and religious impositions.

I want to consider two ways of theorizing this resistance. The first is a Foucauldian approach to exorcism, which regards kinetic activity as always and already constructed by regimes of power. The second, as previously mentioned, is embodied perception. Embodied perception is, in part, an effort to move beyond the Foucauldian paradigm. Embodied perception allows for a certain bodily agency that is absent in Foucault's reading. It allows for the body—in this case Morowa's and Kifah's bodies—to be read in all of its capacious and polyvalent beauty. In embodied perception, bodies create meaning as they move, inculcating a kind of corporeal learning. The actual bodily movements are not necessarily entirely innovative or new—all movements are to some extent conditioned and acquired—but one can "gain knowledge as a result of performing" these movements (Noland 2009, 7).

A Foucauldian Response to Exorcism

Foucault in his lectures on the abnormal provides fodder for reading bodies as a site of resistance to discipline. I am limiting the discussion to these lectures as they provide the clearest example of Foucault dealing with something akin to deliverance. In his lectures Foucault (2007, 208) discussed *The Possession at Loudun*. The possession and concomitant exorcisms were a popular event at an Ursuline convent in the 1630s. Large crowds watched the nuns as they convulsed, were constrained, and were eventually exorcised. Theologian Mark Jordan describes the exorcisms in terms that could easily apply to the deliverance described here: "At Loudun, large crowds gathered for the exorcisms and measures were taken to ensure a good show. It was an approved pornography: the nuns were mostly young women, constrained and taunted" (2015, 87–88). From the archive of these possessed women and their exorcisms, Foucault extracts a number of lessons but primarily one about bodies and resistance (Jordan 2015, 87–88).

Foucault looked at the convulsing possessed body with its "indefinite multiplicity of movements, jolts, sensations, tremors, pains and pleasures" (2007, 207) and noted that in possession the struggle for and against power is centered in the body. The body becomes the canvas on which power encounters resistance to its attempts to dominate. As we saw in Morowa's and Kifah's deliverance, the body controlled is the unmoving body, but the convulsing body is a site of struggle. The convulsions are the resistance: "the plastic and visible form of the combat within the body of the possessed" (212). Such combat is primarily between the body and the exorcist. When the surveillance and discipline of the exorcist are too extreme, exceed certain limits, the body cries out in convulsions, or as Jordan eloquently describes it, the spasms of convulsive bodies are "a somatic refusal of script" (2015, 89). The role of the exorcist is to ultimately deny this "somatic refusal of script," that is, to render the women's material bodies docile and in doing so to rescript the convulsion as something ultimately acquiescent to power.

Foucault's theorizing fails to describe the experiences of Morowa and Kifah in a multitude of ways. Two issues in particular are worth noting for the manner in which they silence the radicality of what occurred within that Ghanaian church. First, Foucault's (2007, 213) approach to the nuns' convulsions silences bodily agency. Morowa and Kifah experienced bodily agency, regardless of the intentionality or lack thereof attached to their motor movements. One need not be cognizant of the decision to move for it to have meaning. Movement unto itself creates meaning. That is, so long as one is aware of the body moving—but not necessarily the decision to move—and so long as one feels the corporeal actions, then the body creates meaning. It cultivates meaning that may never be consciously cognized but meaning that is embedded deep within. To claim bodily agency is merely to claim that Kifah and Morowa move and learn, broadly defined, through that movement. Both Morowa's and Kifah's convulsing bodies were not merely the effect of resistance; they were *resistance*.

Second, Foucault's account is really, unsurprisingly, an extended description of the genius of power. Resistance is merely another opportunity for power to reinvent, adapt, or modify. As Jordan writes, "If every extension of power elicits resistance, every resistance incites the rhetorical genius of power" (2015, 90). With the possessions at Loudun, Foucault is dealing with an archive where deliverance was successful, where—as is always the case with Foucault—power ultimately reasserts its control. In the words of Jordan, ecclesiastical power "keeps writing its curious poetry, keeps changing its scripts at any sign of surprising resistance. Power tends not toward true science but toward more cunning poetics" (91).

In many ways, this was also the story of the deliverance bodies of Morowa and Kifah. Their convulsing bodies, their dancing bodies, and their bodies in pain were a sort of material resistance, and yet, at the same time, they were not. Their resistance, their fight, and their out-and-out refusal to become docile startled the prophet, the pastors, and the congregation. And yet, even in resistance, the deliverance bodies were rescripted when Emmanuel quickly and perfunctorily proclaimed victory through verbal exhortations of praise toward his spiritual father, Jesus, without any corroborating bodily evidence. Such a proclamation is a right that ecclesiastical power bestows on his office. The resistance was rescripted as evidence of an extremely powerful prophet who controls even the most resistant bodies. This is what the congregation witnessed in the case of Morowa and Kifah. It was, however, not the entire story, as Morowa, Kifah, and Ethel informed me over time. Indeed, the bodies of Morowa and Kifah revealed something far different from Emmanuel's rushed conclusion.

Ecclesiastical power, even with its polyglot nature, is not necessarily the end of the narrative. Morowa's and Kifah's deliverance worked, yet, at the same time, it did not work. Morowa and Kifah—despite the insistence of these churchly scripts—were not delivered, at least not from their lesbianism. In the story of Morowa and Kifah, there exists at least the possibility that power, though dominant, can be resisted. I argue that this resistance—which took months to be articulated fully in a conscious sense (I interviewed the participants multiple times over three months)—was learned through motor movements. Theirs is a story of embodied perception.

Morowa's and Kifah's responses were slow in coming, as initially they were unsure how to process the pandemonium and madness of the deliverance event, but after three months of conversation with me, the two women explicitly rejected their deliverance. As Morowa stated, "Nothing really happened." Yet it strikes me that unconsciously this conclusion was drawn first from the motor movements during the deliverance encounter. Their bodily movements were a form of resistance that need not necessarily be accompanied by a discourse of assent to be powerful.

Embodied perception is rooted in a particular understanding of embodiment as bodily being-in-the-world. It is an analytic that emphasizes the body as the fleshy entity by and through which the world is encountered. Embodiment must, then, consider the discursive body "generated in connection to power relationships" and the way it is or is not felt immediately within the material, fleshy body (Pinn 2010, 5). Embodiment is neither merely the material body nor only the discursive body but the exploration of those bodies in tension. Taking the visceral, felt movements of the material body seriously challenges the overwhelming discursive or cultural constructivist view of the body as always and already constructed. More eloquently, embodiment is, in the words of Carrie Noland, "that ambiguous phenomenon in which culture both asserts and loses its grip on individual subjects" (2009, 3). Embodiment, thus articulated, allows for resistant possibilities, meaningful even in their smallness. Meanwhile, *perception* refers broadly to a capacity to learn, to develop, to acquire, and to feel. It is not something that necessarily happens immediately in a conscious burst but instead through the perpetual moving of the human body.[4]

Embodied perception is the gaining of knowledge through movement and feeling—knowledge about the cultural pressures that attempt to define the body and the capacity to resist those cultural and churchly impositions. While Emmanuel and others attempted to discipline the bodies of Morowa and Kifah, the women learned of their bodies' capacity to respond to and reject antiqueer scripts about the inhumanness of nonnormative sexualities.

Embodied perception is affective; that is, it is a preconscious kinesthetic experience, transpersonal and noncognitive. It is an awareness that is rooted in the senses without necessarily having a reflexive, conscious correspondent. In the words of Noland, it is a "somatic affect." Noland adds that kinesthetic sensations are "a particular kind of affect belonging both to the body that precedes our subjectivity (narrowly construed) and the contingent, cumulative subjectivity our body allows us to build over time" (2009, 4). Likewise, Deidre Sklar refers to the incredible amount of knowledge generated through bodily moving as "not only somatic, but affective" (1994, 11). The power of this intimate connection between the affective and the somatic is helpful in understanding how Morowa's and Kifah's kinetic, moving bodies resisted in ways that transcended consciousness. The kinesthetic affect can recursively, experimentally, and unconsciously cultivate new politics. Regardless of the motivation for the movement, or its intentionality, moving bodies can and do resist.

Of the three women we met at the beginning of this chapter, only Ethel continues to attend Emmanuel's church. The other two avoid it as a mode of rejection. "I am not going there again," Morowa told me, adding, "I told Ethel, 'I am not going to your church again.' . . . [It is] not as if the church is a bad church or a fake church because, no, it's not fake, it's good, very good, but me, I don't like the church." That ambivalent denunciation is centered solely on rejecting the deliverance event they were part of. Morowa and Kifah do not reject the office of the prophet or even necessarily the efficaciousness of the prophet Emmanuel. Morowa in particular believes that prophets hold the answers to all of her issues in life. She just does not think lesbianism is the issue—or an issue—that Emmanuel should have been worried about. To be clear, she does identify as a lesbian: "Yes, I am a lesbian. I am a lesbian, no doubt. . . . I enjoy making love to a girl." Note the present tense; part of her rejection of the deliverance is to continue making love to women. She added, "Lesbian spirit is not my problem. I have a bigger problem that is after my life, what is lesbian then? Lesbian is nothing. I have a bigger problem that is after my life. What are we talking about? When there is a bigger thing in front of the prophet? What is lesbian?"

Sometimes when I was talking to her, she became extraordinarily angry, grabbing my recorder and yelling into it in order to communicate better her affective register concerning the event: "I've been angry ever since Emmanuel delivered me." Describing the amount of money she had spent on counseling and prophetic accoutrements such as stickers, oil, and water at Emmanuel's church, she added, "I am angry so I won't say anything good. Four hundred Ghana cedis, gone! I am angry. What did I use four hundred Ghana cedis to do? Nothing. What did I use four hundred Ghana cedis to do? I came back from

Emmanuel's church with no money with me. So, what have I used four hundred cedis to do? Is that not nonsense? . . . The more I remember of that morning, I am very angry."

But, most important, she was not delivered. She described it as such: "I cannot see a difference. Because if the Holy Spirit has healed me, what has gone from my life [lesbianism] wouldn't have come back. I am not saying there is no holy spirit in his [Emmanuel's] church. But if the holy spirit was used on me, what left my life [lesbianism] would not have come back." Disappointed, Ethel admitted the deliverance had not worked: "She [Morowa] isn't ready to change. She has made up her mind about that act [lesbianism], she still does it." She added, "Morowa doesn't want to stop it [lesbianism], so she has closed the doors of her heart not to be delivered. You can't force someone to be delivered." This statement is rich, as deliverance is defined by the imposition of force— physically and spiritually. It is the attempt, often violent, to force a body to abide by the prophet's worldview. Nonetheless, Ethel's statement indicates that both Kifah's and Morowa's bodies have cracked open—at least for Ethel—the power of deliverance, revealing a gap in its efficaciousness. Looking back on the deliverance, Ethel wishes she had realized earlier that the deliverance was not taking hold. She said that the extraordinary length of time the deliverance took was not a sign of a stubborn spirit that would eventually be ousted (as it was rescripted by the prophet); instead, "it took hours because she [Morowa] was not ready to be delivered."

Conclusion

Kifah and Morowa ultimately rejected and resisted deliverance consciously by (re)claiming their lesbianism, but the argument here is that the rejection and resistance existed long before Morowa said that "nothing happened" and long before Kifah rejected Emmanuel's church. Instead, that resistance occurred within the experience of deliverance. The motor decisions these women made during deliverance challenged Emmanuel and a variety of power constructs in meaningful ways, and through these motor decisions, the women cultivated resistance.

These bodies resisted by refusing to obey the bodily discipline that was so brutally enacted on them. Kifah refused to stop touching herself despite persistent efforts by the prophet Emmanuel and his wife to detach her hand from her genitals. Kifah refused to stop moving even when the pastors and ushers held her body down. Morowa fought back with immense force, at times dragging four pastors around the front of the stage. She refused to dance in a way deemed acceptable. She refused to fall down when force was applied, instead applying equal force against the pastors to ensure that she remained standing. Repeatedly, the women resisted with their bodies. Each of their movements, screams, and refusals pushed against the conditioning of the churchly scripts.

Perhaps the most prominent way these bodies resisted those scripts was in their refusal to become docile, rendering Emmanuel's touch, and that of his acolytes, ineffective. The bodily goal of deliverance is to turn a convulsing body into a docile body, and these bodies resisted that effort. Both bodies, in their commitment to move without ceasing, resisted deliverance and, accordingly, all of its attendant cultural scripts. The commitment to move and to fight in the face of extreme force was an act of radical resistance. Repeatedly throughout this particular deliverance service, and many like it, bodies obeyed the demand for docility. Emmanuel often reserved his touch until the end of the deliverance encounter and then with a swift slap watched the bodies fall to the ground. That did not occur in the case of Morowa and Kifah; their bodies refused to accede to the bodily demands of the prophet.

Noland (2009, 1–17) argues that variations in bodily movement can resist by producing behavioral effects, effects that can move from the affective register to conscious decision-making. This is what occurred when, months later, Morowa and Kifah consciously chose to reject their deliverance experiences. This rejection resulted in part from reflection on what their bodies did during the episode; consider Morowa reflecting on how her body felt differently when she was touched in Emmanuel's church compared with how it normally felt when she was touched by a good man of God. They cultivated embodied resistance. I do not, however, want to overextend this claim about the movement from affect to consciousness to imply that such a development is necessary in resistance. Morowa's and Kifah's bodies resisted in meaningful ways without conscious assent: their pushing, punching, denouncing, and unyielding bodily movements were resistance in and of themselves.

The story of Morowa and Kifah is unique and yet common. Many in the lgbtq community in Ghana shared with me their stories of sexual deliverance that did not alter their sexual identities, practices, or worldviews. They told me of prophets unsuccessfully trying to push them to the ground, prophetesses attempting desperately to deliver them, and prayerful exhortations screamed at them. In the end, they always rejected the deliverance. The ultimate proof of that rejection was almost always participation in nonheteronormative sex. Resistance is deeply and intimately embodied, and I imagine that, as for Morowa and Kifah, careful examination of the ways that these bodies interacted during these deliverance sessions would reveal many stories of embodied perception. Over and over again, ecclesiastical scripts appear dominant, but in small movements—really any movement—the body of the delivered is "afforded a chance to feel itself moving through space" (Noland 2009, 1) and to experience embodied perception of a resistance politic. Kinesthesia is a powerful force, a somatic way of knowing, that illuminates how the lived, moving body can act as resistance to even the most violent patriarchal and heteronormative regimes.

NOTES

1. Throughout this chapter I, like many others, do not capitalize the acronym lgbtq (lesbian, gay, bisexual, transgender, and queer) to indicate the fluidity of these categories.

2. Along with being dismissed by other Pentecostal prophets, the church is the frequent target of memes and other critiques through social media, is regularly adjudicated in the media, and is used in many ways as the example par excellence of Pentecostal excesses.

3. *Obroni* is a Twi word for a white person or foreigner.

4. I use *perception* rather than *learning* to avoid being too cognitive or too epistemologically inflected.

REFERENCES

Bochow, Astrid. 2008. "Valentine's Day in Ghana: Youth, Sex and Secrets." In *Generations in Africa: Connections and Conflicts*, edited by Erdmute Alber, Sjaak van der Geest, and Susan Reynolds Whyte, 333–356. Berlin: LIT.

Carrette, Jeremy R., ed. 1999. *Religion and Culture: Michel Foucault*. Manchester, Manchester University Press.

Csordas, Thomas J. 1988. "Elements of Charismatic Persuasion and Healing." *Medical Anthropology Quarterly* 2 (2): 121–142.

Dankwa, Serena Owusua. 2009. "'It's a Silent Trade:' Female Same-Sex Intimacies in Post-colonial Ghana." *Nora: Nordic Journal of Women's Studies* 17 (3): 192–205.

Foster, Susan Leigh, 1995. "Choreographing History." In *Choreographing History*, edited by Susan Leigh Foster, 3–24. Bloomington: Indiana University Press.

Foucault, Michel. 2007. *Abnormal: Lectures at the Collège de France, 1974–1975*. New York: Picador.

Gifford, Paul. 1998. *African Christianity: Its Public Role*. London: Hurst.

Homewood, Nathanael. 2016. "'I Was on Fire': The Challenge of Counter-Intimacies within Zimbabwean Christianity." In *Public Religion and the Politics of Homosexuality in Africa*, edited by Adriaan van Klinken and Ezra Chitando, 243–259. Oxford: Routledge.

Jordan, Mark. 2015. *Convulsing Bodies: Religion and Resistance in Foucault*. Stanford, CA: Stanford University Press.

Noland, Carrie. 2009. *Agency and Embodiment*. Cambridge, MA: Harvard University Press.

Pellegrini, Ann. 2007. "'Signaling through the Flames': Hell House Performance and Structures of Religious Feeling." *American Quarterly* 59 (3): 911–935.

Pinn, Anthony B. 2010. *Embodiment and the New Shape of Black Theological Thought.* New York: New York University Press.

Puar, Jasbir K. 2007. *Terrorist Assemblages: Homonationalism in Queer Times.* Durham, NC: Duke University Press.

Sklar, Deidre. 1994. "Can Bodylore Be Brought to Its Senses?" *Journal of American Folklore* 107 (423): 9–22.

Thoreson, Ryan Richard. 2014. "Troubling the Waters of a 'Wave of Homophobia': Political Economies of Anti-queer Animus in Sub-Saharan Africa." *Sexualities* 17 (1–2): 23–42.

van Klinken, Adriaan S. 2013. "Gay Rights, the Devil and the End Times: Public Religion and the Enchantment of the Homosexuality Debate in Zambia." *Religion* 43 (4): 519–540.

11. Exceptional Healing: Gender, Materiality, Embodiment, and Prophetism in the Lower Congo

YOLANDA COVINGTON-WARD

Ngunz'a Nzambi weti niakisa
Yaya wo-o-o-
Ngunza lulendo weti katula mpeve
Yaya wo-o-o-
Sola Ngunza-yakuniakisa
Yaya wo-o-o-
The Prophet of the Lord heals
Yaya wo-o-o-
The [powerful] prophet exorcizes the spirit
Yaya wo-o-o-
Choose the prophet [who] can heal you,
Yaya wo-o-o-
—Efraim Andersson, *Messianic Popular Movements in the Lower Congo*, 1858

During the early to mid-twentieth century in colonial-era Belgian Congo, a number of related religious movements disturbed the immense African colony.[1] Known interchangeably as *kingunza* ("prophetic movement" in KiKongo) or Kimbanguism, the movements began in 1921 with the activities of a Christian prophet named Simon Kimbangu.[2] Kimbangu was MuKongo, a member of the BisiKongo (also known as BaKongo or Kongo) ethnic group, a KiKongo-speaking group living in the modern-day Democratic Republic of the Congo, Republic of the Congo, and Angola, located in or near the area where the precolonial Kongo

Kingdom existed. The verses in the epigraph (first displayed in KiKongo and then translated into English) come from a song created by *bangunza* (prophets) in the mid-1930s in the province now known as Kongo Central[3]—a majority-BisiKongo province—in the Democratic Republic of the Congo. The lyrics demonstrate the importance of healing as part of prophets' repertoire of gifts and as an attraction for potential followers. In the larger contemporary religious landscape in the DRC healing continues to play an outsized role in motivating church attendance, especially considering the prohibitive cost of hospital-based medical treatment. But in the contexts of modern-day churches born from the kingunza movements, how is healing practiced, and how has it changed since the time of kingunza? Who can heal? And in what contexts?

This chapter centers on the gender politics of healing as part of the religious practices of modern-day bangunza in a small Protestant AIC (African independent church) located in Luozi, a town on the north bank of the Congo River in Kongo Central province. Known as the Dibundu dia Mpeve Nlongo mu Afelika (DMNA) in KiKongo, the Communauté de Saint Esprit en Afrique in French, or the Church of the Holy Spirit in Africa in English, this Kongo church was founded in 1961 during the immediate postcolonial period, breaking away from a Swedish Protestant mission.[4] It was one of many churches that emerged from the kingunza religious movements. One of the distinguishing characteristics of this and other kingunza churches is the emphasis on the embodiment of the Holy Spirit in the bodies of members. The vigorous trembling that occurs during these experiences, which DMNA members describe as the Holy Spirit descending into their bodies, is called *kuzakama* (or *zakama*) in KiKongo. There is a belief that everyone may receive the Holy Spirit, which can be seen as almost a democratization of spiritual power. Conversely, however, only selected people may channel the Holy Spirit to heal and bless others; thus, in the DMNA church women are currently excluded from healing and holding major leadership roles. This marginalization of women, which occurred when the church was formally founded in 1961, stands in stark contrast to a long history of female prophets and healers in this region and in the kingunza movement from which the church emerged.

This chapter seeks to address this conundrum by highlighting the unique role of materiality, the Holy Spirit, and embodiment in both restricting and expanding the access of women to exercising spiritual powers. While the process of routinization—the creation of religious institutions from religious movements—usually leads to the establishment of a hierarchy and a lack of gender equity (Crumbley 2008, 23), such a process is never complete—meaning that there are ways around these restrictions. Building on the work of key religious studies scholars who study lived religion—everyday practices of religiosity—I argue that a focus on embodiment enables two types of analyses: first, examination of the eroding and porous boundaries between lived religion inside and outside of religious institutions and, second, investigation of the processual emergence of a hardening line between men and women in relationship to healing activities. My research shows that, contrary to the proscriptions of the church leadership, women in the DMNA church do heal others in some instances. Using interviews conducted in the Democratic Republic of the Congo in 2005 and 2010 with DMNA church members, I analyze three such incidents to argue that lived religion is a continuously unfolding and incomplete process.

To understand how and why the roles of women transformed so drastically when the DMNA church was founded, I outline the history of the founding of the church, the importance of the Holy Spirit in the visions and dreams of the church's founder, and the subsequent adoption of material practices, and I contrast the current roles of women in the church with their past roles in the region's religious movements. I then analyze a number of justifications given for the exclusion of women from positions of spiritual authority, focusing especially on menstrual blood and sacred white cloth. Last, I address how women with spiritual gifts continue to practice healing in ways that circumvent institutional restrictions, harkening back to the colonial era, when women's healing activities were less restricted within the context of the kingunza religious movements. Overall, this chapter pushes scholars of African and African diaspora religions to explore the nuances and intricacies of the relationships between materiality and embodiment and the ways they may impact religious beliefs and practices. For the women of the DMNA church, embodied trembling and a shared belief in continuous revelation and prophetism allow them to evade restrictions put into place based on their founding prophet's inspired vision of sacred white cloth that women may potentially pollute with menstrual blood. This case shows that scholars need to pay more attention to instances in which materiality and embodiment may in fact have an ambivalent relationship with one another as lived religion unfolds in a dynamic process.

The Intricacies of Lived Religion

In her influential book *Lived Religion: Faith and Practice in Everyday Life*, Meredith McGuire defines lived religion as "useful for distinguishing the actual experience of religious persons from the prescribed religion of institutionally defined beliefs and practices" (2008, 12). McGuire focuses on everyday practices of religiosity, emphasizing attention to materiality, embodiment, and the senses for capturing how religion is lived outside of institutional settings. Such an approach has been widely lauded throughout religious studies and has led to scholars studying religious practices of often marginalized or less powerful groups. However, scholars such as Nancy Ammerman warn that "lived religion does often happen on the margins between orthodox prescriptions and innovative experiences, but religion does not have to be marginal to be 'lived.' What happens inside religious organizations counts, too" (2014, 190). She identifies lived religion as "the material, embodied aspects of religion as they occur in everyday life" (190). By pointing out that lived religion occurs both inside and outside of religious institutions, Ammerman complicates notions of lived religion as occurring in any one type of space or context and blurs boundaries between sacred and profane worlds.

Extending the work of these authors even further, in this chapter I argue that a focus on embodiment, specifically healing practices, allows us to see lived religion as an unfolding and incomplete process, one in which religious practices are enacted and redefined outside of, within, and then once again outside of religious institutions. In this instance, the spiritual embodied practices that are most important in the DMNA church—what we can call Kongo lived religion—originated in persecuted colonial-era religious movements, were redefined and codified as a part of new churches immediately after independence, and are being redefined and redeployed once again by women in a number of settings outside of the walls of the church.

Moreover, this chapter also seeks to complicate the relationship between material and embodied religion. In much of the existing scholarship, material culture and embodiment are discussed as being brought together in the religious practices that make up everyday lived religion. For instance, prayer shawls and rosary beads are used as part of Jewish and Catholic prayer practices, just as devotees of Yoruba orishas in Ifá religions wear clothing in colors that are particular to each orisha (Ammerman 2013, 85; Castor 2017). Even consumption practices can form a part of everyday religion (Rouse 2006). However, materiality and embodiment may not always work toward the same ends in religious contexts. What happens when materiality and embodiment conflict?

Women Spiritual Leaders in the Lower Congo

Women have held positions of spiritual authority for centuries in the Kongo region, as prophets, healers, diviners, ritual specialists, and a number of other roles. One very important example is Dona Beatrice Vita Kimpa, a young MuKongo woman who led the most famous precolonial religious movement in the region, the Antonian movement of the early 1700s. After becoming gravely ill and recovering, she claimed to be possessed by the spirit of Saint Anthony, a male Catholic saint, a claim that had particular salience in the Kongo Kingdom as a sovereign state that had converted to Christianity in 1491. Dona Beatrice said she would reunite the fractured kingdom, which had been torn apart by power struggles after the Kongo king was killed by the Portuguese in the mid-1600s. Notably, her movement was also reformist and advocated for a Kongo-centered Christianity by saying that Jesus was born in Mbanza Kongo (the capital of the Kongo Kingdom), arguing for the existence of Black saints, and challenging the hegemony of Italian Capuchin missionaries. She gained so many followers that her influence and power threatened both European Catholic missionaries and multiple claimants to the throne. Dona Beatrice was burned alive at the stake as a heretic on July 2, 1706 (Thornton 1998b). Moreover, women *banganga* (traditional healers and ritual specialists) were quite common even before Dona Beatrice's movement and continued to exercise their professions well into the colonial period.

Moving forward to the colonial period, women were also prominent figures in the kingunza movements (Mahaniah 1975, 1988; Vellut 2005). Two of the seven disciples who were closest to Simon Kimbangu were women, Telezi Mbonga and Mikala Mandombe (Irvine 1974, 38; Pemberton 1993, 220; Raymaekers 1971, 36). Many women were also arrested and sent to penal labor camps along with men for participating in the kingunza movements. While I explore the stories of colonial-era Kongo women prophets in greater detail in my other work (see Covington-Ward 2014), suffice it to say that women had many opportunities to exercise healing abilities, to prophesy, and to engage in a wide range of activities of spiritual leadership during the kingunza movements. This, however, was to change for those women who became members of the DMNA church.

Overview of the Origins and Creation of the DMNA Church

Founded in 1961 by Masamba Esaie, a prophet who had returned from forced exile in a penal labor camp, the DMNA church is one of many that developed directly out of the kingunza movements of the colonial period.[5] The DMNA church was trying to forge a different path from European and American mission-led churches in the Lower Congo, which included British and American Baptists, missionaries from Swedish Mission Covenant Church, Catholics from Belgium, and others. As previously mentioned, the most notable embodied practice in the DMNA church in relation to its theology is an emphasis on healing and/or blessing through ecstatic trance, most often signified by bodily trembling as an embodiment of the presence of the Holy Spirit.[6] This trembling, however, originates in the embodiment of *banganga*, who were active during the precolonial era and persecuted during the colonial period. Their bodies would tremble vigorously when inhabited by territorial or other nature spirits, although this type of trembling is called *mayembo* rather than *zakama* (Covington-Ward 2016, 84). Thus, nonmembers of the DMNA church referred to its members as "the people who tremble" or "the tremblers," among other terms. People in Luozi also often referred to the DMNA church itself as the church of bangunza, or prophets.

Esaie and his followers determined the overall character of the DMNA church on February 12, 1961, when the church was founded at a huge gathering. This meeting was called after their form of prayer and healing (which embraced trembling caused by the Holy Spirit) had been rejected by the Swedish mission-led church of which they had been members. According to Pastor Malala (the legal representative for the DMNA church and the son of Esaie), Esaie told him and it also appears in Esaie's writings that "he [Esaie] had a vision, because he was a visionary, this man. . . . In a vision he saw the worship of angels. Angels in worship service. He saw that much of that which was in secret, in the *pendele*, was also practiced by the angels. . . . [7] If you are going to pray, all the men, you put on your hats. All the women, you put on your headscarves. . . . Similarly, the prayer in bare feet, he saw that in his vision, the manner of dancing, and so on" (interview, Luozi, DRC, November 14, 2005).[8]

Thus, Esaie's vision had revealed to him how he and his followers should worship, dress, and pray. The implication seemed to be that by emulating the worship of angels, he and his adepts would become closer to the angels and, by extension, to God. Revelations through visions and dreams such as these play a large role in the kingunza tradition. Kimbangu himself was called to become a prophet through voices he heard, as well as a number of dreams and visions (Mackay 1987, 124; Mackay and Ntoni-Nzinga 1993, 241; Pemberton 1993, 204). Because he believed in the divine source of these visions, Esaie was inspired to re-create the worship of the angels through dress and worship practices in the new DMNA church that he established.

The prophet Esaie's vision of angels revealed not only certain forms of worship but also a particular type of dress (Pastor Malala, Luozi, November 14, 2005). Thus, one of the most distinguishing characteristics of the DMNA church members is that they dress in all-white clothing. Although this attire is not obligatory and people can still enter the church without it, it is the preferred form of dress for the church. In relating the white cloth to the Esaie's vision, the white dress represents and embodies a spiritual connectedness to God. In the church, the color white is also connected to honor and worthiness, with pastors and deacons pointing me to the biblical passage of Revelations 3:4: "Yet you have a few people in Sardis who have not soiled their clothes. They will walk with me, dressed in white, for they are worthy" (New International Version). Moreover, church documents further state that "to be clothed in white signifies being prosperous . . . honored, happy."[9] Pastor Kasambi, the primary pastor of the Luozi DMNA church at the time of the interview, added that the color white also signifies purity and cannot be worn if you have sinned (Luozi, November 12, 2005).[10] This is another reason that wearing the color white is important in the church.[11] Thus, in the DMNA church, the wearing of white cloth has become a visual sign of one's congregational membership and, moreover, one's spirituality and moral standing.

While the color white has particular meaning in biblical verses and Christian theology, the color white and white clothing have salience in other ways for many congregants in the DMNA church. White (*luvemba*, plural *mpemba*) is also an important color in Kongo cosmology, where it is associated with the spirit world and the land of the dead. This is opposed to the color black (*kala*), which is associated with the land of the living, with both worlds separated by red (*tukula*), the color of transition between the two worlds (Fu-Kiau 1969; MacGaffey 1986b, 45).[12]

Overall, the DMNA church came to define itself through a combination of distinctive material culture and embodied practices. The white cloth—supported through biblical scripture, inspired visions, and traditional Kongo beliefs about the land of the dead—marked the bodies of DMNA adherents in a larger religious landscape while also serving as a material means of accessing the spiritual realm and the Holy Spirit. Kuzakama/zakama, the embodied trembling caused by the Holy Spirit, signaled a direct connection to God without the need for missionaries as intermediaries and redefined the worship practices of the DMNA as a distinctly Kongo form of Protestant Christianity. Through a shifting contrapuntal dialogue, both materiality around white cloth and spirit-induced trembling come to play a huge role in the larger discourse around women, their bodies, and their roles in the DMNA church and in healing practices more generally.

Women in the DMNA Church and Their Rejection as Spiritual Leaders

When the church was officially established on February 12, 1961, decisions were made not only about the form of dress and worship but also about the role and status of women in the church. The routinization of religious movements into established churches has had similar outcomes throughout Africa and across the world. Religious movements that were originally egalitarian, especially in regard to gender, are often codified into hierarchical religious institutions in which women are marginalized. As Deidre Crumbley observes in her study of Yoruba AICs, "During this routinization process . . . the radicalism of the original vision is often dramatically domesticated. . . . Gender equity yields to the emergence or reemergence of male domination" (2008, 23). This also applies in the DMNA church. Women cannot act in the role of pastor, deacon, healer, or *ntwadisi*, nor can they preach the word of God to a mixed-sex congregation.[13] Preaching is allowed only if those present are all women. Women can, however, pray for the sick as well as participate in the service as church members. There is also a women's organization within the church headed by the pastor's wife, who also heads a similar, yet larger organization (Protestant Women) for all the women of the local Protestant churches in Luozi. In our conversation about the roles of women in the church, Pastor Kasambi admitted that some women do have the gift of healing and that the fact that it cannot be practiced in the church can be seen as a form of discrimination (Luozi, November 12, 2005). However, Pastor Malala would probably disagree, as he said that although women's roles are limited, women are very important in the church and "are not marginalized" (Luozi, November 14, 2005).

Women play a vital role in the DMNA church as members of the congregation (see figure 11.1 for a photo of the women and girls of the DMNA church). Often females made up the majority of the congregants that I observed in the church over the course of my research. The gender makeup of the congregation was made even more evident through the spatial separation of the sexes, since the men's side of the sanctuary often looked empty, while the women's side was often filled to overflowing. Moreover, women are also essential to the singing that takes place in the church owing to a gendered call-and-response pattern in which the men sing a verse and the women answer in response.

Regardless of their numerical majority, women's roles are circumscribed in the DMNA church in Luozi. At this point I would like to consider two questions: First, what roles and positions of spiritual authority did women have in the kingunza movement and Kongo religious history before the founding of

FIGURE 11.1. Women, girls, and several small boys next to the DMNA church in Luozi, Democratic Republic of Congo, July 18, 2010. Photograph by author.

the church? Second, on what grounds were women excluded from positions of spiritual authority and from enacting certain rituals in the DMNA church?

That the process of routinization leads to the exclusion of women from positions of spiritual and political authority within the church is not unique to the DMNA church. Rosalind Hackett's (1987) study of female religious leaders in AICs in Calabar, Nigeria, reveals a recurring pattern in which the leadership of female-founded churches is either willingly handed over to or usurped by men, with some exceptions. Brigid Sackey's (2006) study of the status of women in AICs in Ghana reveals that gender relations and the status of women depend on the social and historical context in which the churches emerge, so that in some cases female leaders are replaced by men. Bennetta Jules-Rosette's (1975, 1981, 1996) studies of the roles of women in Maranke and Marowe churches in Zambia, Malawi, and the Democratic Republic of the Congo show that women in these churches have access to ceremonial leadership through their roles as singers, subgroup leaders, and midwives but "are formally excluded from the groups' major decision-making processes" (1981, 193). Moreover, Crumbley's (2008, 96) extensive study of three Yoruba Aladura churches reveals the diversity of women's roles in churches within the same system of spiritual beliefs: in the Christ Apostolic Church, female ordination is prohibited, but women can be evangelists and head ministers; in the Celestial Church of Christ, women can neither be ordained nor preach and are excluded from almost all ceremonial leadership; and in the Church of the Lord-Aladura, women can be ordained alongside men.

But how is the exclusion of women (who often make up the majority of the congregation in AICS) from positions of spiritual and political authority justified in different AICS? Based on her research in Ghana, Sackey (2006, 65–68) reveals a number of reasons for the usurping of women's authority in newly established AICS. These include the desire to uphold the status quo set by European missionaries, the higher literacy rates of men (making them better equipped to deal with administrative matters), restrictions on women based in biblical scripture, negative stereotypes about women's "disorders" (lack of mental capabilities, menstrual uncleanliness, etc.), and attempts by men to secure whatever powerful positions were not taken by Europeans in African colonial societies.

In my own interviews about the DMNA church, two main narratives were highlighted when discussing the reasons for not allowing women to hold leadership positions or to heal, both of which fit within Sackey's discussion of negative women's disorders: sexual impropriety and menstrual blood. Both of these justifications invoke the body in different ways: as a tool of seduction and forbidden pleasure and as the source of a tangible, biological fluid that not only threatens to contaminate but may also cause spiritual harm.

In regard to sexual impropriety, Pastor Kasambi stated that in the past, when deacons, deaconesses, and other leaders left their respective homes to evangelize together, there were cases of adultery. For this reason, women as a group were prohibited from becoming pastors and deacons (Luozi, November 12, 2005). One notes, however, that the punishment of an entire sex was one-sided; men were not excluded from these positions although they were also involved in cases of infidelity. Paul Nyuvudi, a Kongo evangelist who himself became active in the bangunza movement, also mentions in his 1928 account prophets and prophetesses living in the same house and having relationships that led to pregnancy (Mackay and Ntoni-Nzinga 1993, 251–253). What emerges in both the interview and Nyuvudi's text are concerns about sexual impropriety when women and men in positions of spiritual power work together. However, the burden for such illicit sexual relations is placed on the women, so the encumbrance of moral weakness is borne by them alone. Like other essentialist biblical discourses that present women as temptresses who ultimately lead men astray (Bach 1997; Higginbotham 1993), in the case of the bangunza movement the women once again shoulder the brunt of responsibility for mutual adultery, and such reasoning is used to curtail opportunities for spiritual advancement that other women after them may seek.

Another type of women's disorder that seems to attract significant attention in discussions of the exclusion of women from spiritual leadership is menstruation and menstrual blood. Crumbley (2008) has thoroughly explored the discourse and practice surrounding menstrual blood and women's status in three Yoruba Aladura churches. Thus, for example, while women can be ordained in the Church of the Lord-Aladura, both ordained and unordained women are excluded from the sanctuary when menstruating (77). It is such an important rule that it has been written into the church's constitution. Moreover, in the Celestial Church of Christ, women cannot preach, must avoid the altar at all times, and cannot enter the church while menstruating. It is believed that the angels are offended by the smell of menstrual blood (81).

Materiality emerges as a key factor when, in considering the justifications for the blanket exclusion of women from positions of spiritual and political authority in the DMNA church, the most compelling reason likewise centers on the flow of menstrual blood and its potential contact with the dress of angels—the white cloth. Before the meeting that led to the formation of the DMNA church, women were important members of the kingunza movement who also laid their hands on people to heal and bless them. According to Pastor Malala, however, this was prohibited after February 12, owing specifically to concerns about menstrual blood:

YOLANDA: Can women become pastors in the church?
MALALA: In our church, at first, women did this. They even laid on hands. . . . All of these things, they were prohibited. What happened? There is a principle, or rather I don't know whether it is a taboo or what, a woman, in the state of menstruation . . . is seen as a certain impurity, [she] can't come into the church. No . . . when she finishes her cycle, she washes herself, after three days, she goes to return to the church. But before this was done . . . we observed women who didn't know how to keep their body hygienic. In America it is different . . . but here it is deplorable, the hygienic consciousness, and is regrettable. Women don't even know to cover themselves with underwear and to put everything there that is necessary to avoid the blood

escaping. So she comes to the service, as she has the habit of putting on her white dress, then with the economic forces, she doesn't even have underwear, nothing, and you see, there are some women who stain. We saw a certain woman who was laying on hands, and it began to run down her leg. Thus, when this happened, this thing, we said, no. . . . It is in this way, we said to prohibit this, on February 12. (Luozi, November 14, 2005)

Several themes emerge from this explanation of the exclusion of women from spiritual power in the church. The first is the idea of a woman's menstrual blood as impure and unclean. A menstruating woman's presence is prohibited in the space of the church itself, and she is allowed to return only after a prescribed period of time has passed after the end of her cycle. As the menstrual blood is seen as impure, the moral and spiritual purity symbolized by wearing the white cloth of the angels is thus sullied by the menstrual blood that escapes the woman's body and comes into contact with the white cloth. This need to control menstrual blood lest it contaminate or pollute echoes similar gendered conceptions about women and their bodies present in the seminal work of Mary Douglas ([1966] 2002) and, more recently, in research among widows in southern Africa (see Golomski, this volume).

Conceptions of menstrual blood as impure predate the formation of the DMNA church. In his early twentieth-century ethnographic study of Kongo customs, John Weeks notes, "During menstruation a woman must not cook her husband's food nor any other man's, neither touch anything belonging to men, and must not return the salutation of any man. . . . [S]he is unclean during these days" (1908, 418). Swedish missionary Karl Laman's own ethnographic study, based on notes written by Kongo informants between 1910 and 1918 (Janzen 1972, 320), mentions similar ideas about menstrual blood: "A woman staying in a house for menstruating must not plant manioc, for it will be no good. Nor may she pass the tobacco plantation of another, or this too, will be adversely affected—the tobacco will have a pungent taste. She may not, either, enter a house in which there is a *nkisi*, for a menstruating woman is unclean" (Laman 1962, 3:207).[14] After the DMNA church was founded, a house for menstruating women was among the structures erected at Nzieta, the headquarters of the DMNA church. The women must reside there until their menses ends and they are purified from their condition (Fu-Kiau 1969, 152). A. kia Bunseki-Lumanisa Fu-Kiau, a preeminent MuKongo scholar, refers to this women's menstruation house as a representation of "impurity in the Church of the Holy Spirit" (Fu-Kiau 1969, 152).

A second theme that emerges in Pastor Malala's discussion of the decision taken on February 12, 1961, is a concern about women's lack of hygienic consciousness in their white dresses. This he attributes to both larger social financial problems and a general lack of knowledge about hygiene and maintenance. However, how widespread were such incidents? Is the pastor underestimating women's ability to cope with their monthly menstruation? I question the assumption that women lacked the knowledge to take care of their bodies, since they had to deal with menstruation each month and had the knowledge of mothers, grandmothers, and other women in the community at their disposal. I also wonder if my presence as an American researcher encouraged Pastor Malala to articulate the exclusion of women within a larger discourse of underdevelopment and hygiene. This view is not so different from the ideologies of the Belgians and other European colonizers in their judgments of African cultural practices as inferior. Here, however, the alleged lack of hygienic containment of menstrual blood is problematic because of the contact between that which is impure and the sacred white cloth.

A third theme that is latent here but more pronounced in other discussions and interviews is the belief in a type of force in menstrual blood. According to Fu-Kiau (1969, 119), blood, or *menga*, is one of many powerful bodily fluids (along with saliva, urine, and tears) and has a type of neutral force that can be used for either good or bad, depending on the intention. To understand the significance of this life force, we must place it within larger Kongo conceptions of body and soul. Although there are variations throughout the Kongo cultural region, some understandings of body and soul are shared in many groups, while the names may be different. Traditionally, there was a belief in a "double person" concept, in which there is an inner person and an outer person, with each of these people consisting of two parts (Jacobson-Widding 1979, 309–324). The outer person, often called *nitu*, consists of an outer body or shell, *vuvudi* (which physically rots upon death), and the inner invisible and perishable aspect of the soul, called *moyo*. "Among the Kongo proper . . . the destructible aspect of the soul is called *moyo* or *mvumbi*. This is the life-essence or the life-force, which resides in the blood (*menga*). . . . *Moyo* is destroyed by death, but not immediately. It does not cease to exist until all the liquids of the body have dried up" (307).[15] Thus, Kongo conceptions of body and soul reveal that blood is thought to have some sort of power based on the life essence that inhabits it. In fact, this life essence, moyo, is believed to be eaten by witches as part of witchcraft (308). Blood (usually from animals) is also used in sacrifices and in composing an nkisi (sacred medicine) "in order to imbue it with power" (Laman 1962, 40).

There is also evidence that women's menstrual blood is perceived to be powerful not only in a general sense but more specifically as an active force. In his interview Pastor Kasambi also supported the exclusion of women from the church when menstruating through the belief that their condition and their presence in the church take away the ability to enter into trance (Luozi, November 12, 2005).[16] Mama Ntima, the wife of Pastor Kasambi and a DMNA church member, confirmed a belief in the active force of menstrual blood, saying, "When I was young, my mother said, 'If you get your menstruation, you have to tell me because since ancient times, according to our ancestors, this blood is an impure blood, very bad. Because if you are menstruating, if you cook for your father, which he eats and then goes to [the] fields, he is at risk for an accident" (Luozi, July 27, 2010). Thus, women's blood is believed to have the power to both sap the ability to receive the Holy Spirit and cause harm or "bad luck." Menstrual blood, then, is not just material but active in its own right. Thus, for the founders of the DMNA church, the "potential impurity" of women's menstrual blood invalidates their full participation as spiritual leaders in the DMNA church.

Kongo Women in the DMNA Church and the Prophetic Tradition

For Kongo people living in the Lower Congo, the constant presence of prophetism as articulated through zakama, trembling caused by the Holy Spirit, shapes people's sense of themselves and self-definition as Christians in very particular ways. Here zakama is not just an individual experience; it is also couched within a historical lineage of shared embodiment. In his analysis of trends in Kongo religious thought before, during, and after European colonialism, John Janzen (1977) associates trembling with the concept of mpeve and its relevance for spiritual belief and action: "Mpeve specified the vital principle or attribute of every individual. Its verbal root, veeva, meant to blow, to breathe, or implied the breeze responsible for the fluttering of a cloth or flag" (107). The manifestation of mpeve in the expression of the Holy Spirit through embodied trembling thus aligns with this preexisting belief system and, notably, is available to all, regardless of sex. Women, then, can also tap into this prophetic tradition and thus navigate some of the restrictions that emerged in the postcolonial period.

A number of questions can be asked about the disconnect between the official doctrine of the DMNA church and the moments of slippage where there lie possibilities for women's spiritual leadership. While the DMNA church sought to redefine the role of women in its organization on February 12, 1961, based on a discourse of sexual impropriety and menstrual blood that polluted sacred cloth, what happened to women who healed with the Holy Spirit? Did the practice just disappear altogether? Moreover, what happened with postmenopausal women? Or pregnant women who were not menstruating? In the interviews that I conducted in the town of Luozi during the summer of 2010, I began to observe an interesting trend in the responses of my interviewees. Women are banned from healing; however, in actual practice, women continue to heal, mostly in private but also in public in some exceptional instances. Through their own trembling bodies, animated by the Holy Spirit, women are able to circumvent the restrictions that emerged from the prophet Esaie's revelations.

The first example occurred when Pastor Kasambi was still enrolled in school to complete his training to become a pastor. He became sick and had a serious pain in his ribs, which increased whenever he took a deep breath. He went to be healed in the DMNA church, but according to Mama Ntima, "the miracles were powerless." After not receiving relief in the church or from the doctor at the local hospital, they were visited by two older women, Mama Sedima and Mama Leni. The women said that God had told them to come and heal him and that his illness was caused by a jealous classmate who would come to check on him. They prayed over Pastor Kasambi, and Mama Sedima trembled, full of the Holy Spirit, while Mama Leni sang. Mama Sedima also used water, her Bible, and a short stick called an *nkawa*, which she shook over Pastor Kasambi's body while saying "in the name of Jesus" three times. Soon thereafter, his classmate did in fact visit their home to inquire about Pastor Kasambi's health. He asked, "How were you healed?" and the two women responded, "It is the Holy Spirit that healed him" (Mama Ntima, Luozi, July 27, 2010).

This was a private healing, away from the church and away from the prying eyes of others. However, these women used the same tools and the same embodied characteristics that male prophets use in the church. Moreover, they healed a man training to become a pastor in the same church where they themselves were excluded from practicing their gift of healing. This healing, as an expression of lived religion, embodied several characteristics already recognized and incorporated into the religious practices and beliefs of the DMNA church. The belief in spiritual causes of illness that can be traced to particular people, the presence of the Holy Spirit as evidenced through embodied trembling, the use of singing to help invoke the Holy Spirit, and the use of blessed water and the nkawa—all of these elements are part of the religious practices and beliefs of the DMNA church. What is different here is that the prophecy about the jealous classmate was not checked and approved by any male church leader and that these were extraordinary circumstances in which all other options had been exhausted. Mama Sedima and Mama Leni were able to accomplish what male DMNA church leaders had not: healing Pastor Kasambi of his ailments and fending off the spiritual attack of his jealous classmate. This case study allows us to see how the activities that define the lived religion of DMNA church members exist both within and outside of the church walls and are redefined as appropriate for women when the circumstances have become drastic.

The second example is another private healing away from the church but in a more public space. Mama Ntima recalled the following story. She and her teenage son were working on one of their family fields in 2006, quite a few miles away from Luozi. It was common practice for local inhabitants to live in the town of Luozi and farm on plots of land that were several hours away on foot. Mama Ntima and her son had walked to their family's plot, which was located in a very isolated rural area. They were the only people there, and there was no one else around to assist them. Suddenly, her son fell to the ground, complaining of a headache, clutching his legs, and crying. He said he could not walk. She ran to him and said she heard a voice telling her to "niakisa yandi," which means to remove the bad spirits from him. She prayed and prayed to remove the bad spirits and began to tremble with the Holy Spirit (zakama). After some time, he stood up and walked, and they went home.

As in the previous example, Mama Ntima found herself in an extreme situation. While under normal circumstances she would not be allowed to try to heal anyone under the rules of the DMNA church, in this situation no one else was present to assist in fending off the perceived spiritual attack that had temporarily disabled her son. Using prayer and embodied trembling, she was able to help her son to recover. It is noteworthy that she mentioned hearing a voice. Hearing voices is part of the experience of continuous revelation that defines the Kongo prophetic tradition in this area. Indeed, Kimbangu himself heard voices that pushed him toward becoming a prophet: "But from day to day I heard a voice that told me I would do the work of Peter and of John. I would be an apostle" (quoted in Pemberton 1993, 204). By heeding the spiritual voice and enacting the prayer and zakama that worked to chase away bad spirits, Mama Ntima placed herself firmly within the Kongo prophetic tradition, joining many other men and women who have acted as prophets in the region. This larger prophetic tradition, based on a number of embodied practices and beliefs, has shaped not only lived religion in the DMNA church itself but also lived religion outside of its walls.

The third and final example is the story of a woman named Mama Lutatamana, as told by Mama Luzola, another DMNA church member. This story came up after I had finished an earlier interview with Mama Luzola and had turned off the recorder. My research assistant, Marie, reached out to Mama Luzola to ask if we could interview her about this particular incident, verify the details, and record it, and she agreed. According to Mama Luzola, there was a large DMNA revival meeting in the town of Luvuvamu in 1998 or 1999.[17] This meeting was attended by people from many DMNA churches throughout the Lower Congo, as well as some members from across the border in the Republic of the Congo, specifically from Point-Noire. I have reproduced the interview at length to try to fully capture how embodiment and healing drove a public confrontation about women and healing:

> MAMA LUZOLA: I can speak very well about that, and I also was there that day, I was at Luvuvamu. There were people from Pointe-Noire who came to Luvuvamu, and then there was a woman named Mama Lutatamana, and precisely then a woman from the mission who really got sick in her house, suddenly just like that. She was even going to die. Her children were crying. The husband wasn't there, he had left to welcome the people from Point Noire who were coming, and others had left to look for an animal; there were only women. Mama Lutatamana did her work, and the sick woman woke up immediately, and then when they arrived, the people from Pointe Noire weren't happy to see that a woman could heal another woman. She had encircled the woman who was nearly half-dead.
>
> YOLANDA: How?
>
> MAMA LUZOLA: She gave the *lusakumunu* [benediction/blessing], she had circled around the sick woman three times with a handkerchief, she also gave water to the sick woman. She shouted aloud, PLEASE!
>
> YOLANDA: With kuzakama?
>
> MAMA LUZOLA: With kuzakama also, full of the Holy Spirit. Then the woman woke up also. She found her healing.
>
> YOLANDA: She had also . . .
>
> MAMA LUZOLA: Yes, she had also laid hands on her . . .
>
> YOLANDA: What happened with Mama Lutatamana afterward?
>
> MARIE: The people were angry.
>
> MAMA LUZOLA: Why? The church itself said, Why did a woman heal, because it is not authorized? Now, the leader who is there, the revival camp leader, said it is the Holy Spirit who authorized it. Since the woman was guided by the Holy Spirit, leave it alone then! It is God that wanted her to do this . . .
>
> YOLANDA: What is the name in KiKongo?

MARIE: *Kupupula* [creating a violent current of air in order to make something fall—she imitates the gesture of vigorously flapping a cloth as she explains]. If it is for a sick person, it is *vayikisa mpeve zambi* [make the bad spirits come out]. You say, *Vayika!* Get out! *Kupupula*, it is to do the action to make the bad spirits leave, which the bangunza do with their handkerchiefs/cloths. *Vayika* is a verbal action, and *kupupula* or *kububula* that accompanies it is a physical action. (Luozi, July 30, 2010)

This example presents a compelling set of practices and beliefs that highlight multiple dimensions of embodiment within the context of spiritual healing in the DMNA church—spiritual forces making bodies tremble, flapping cloths affecting spiritual forces within bodies, an unsanctioned woman running around and touching sick bodies to foster healing and protection. To start, I want to address the lusakumunu. This is a special ritual blessing in the DMNA church (created by a woman in fact; see Covington-Ward 2014) in which male leaders of the church run counterclockwise around lines of kneeling church members three times to bless them and protect them against spiritual harm. Women do not normally give the lusakumunu, only men. However, in this instance Mama Lutatamana enacted this blessing to ritually protect the sick woman. Before we assume that this act is just an appropriation of church ritual, we should acknowledge the possibility of nonchurch influences on the origins of the lusakumunu itself, as making three circles also existed historically in other spiritual traditions in the area, such as Lemba, a therapeutic healing and trade association that emerged in the region in the seventeenth century (Janzen 1982, 193). With this, the lusakumunu that was created in the DMNA church may have also been drawing on non-Christian lived-religion traditions in the area. The same can be said of the embodied trembling caused by the Holy Spirit, which harkens back to the kingunza (prophetic) movements but also references banganga (traditional healers and ritual specialists) simultaneously. Mama Lutatamana also used her handkerchief to try to force bad spirits out of the woman's body. As I have witnessed it, this is done as a flapping motion that is made near the body using the handkerchief, creating a sudden current of air (kupupula). Moreover, Mama Lutatamana laid her hands on the woman, openly healing her in a public space with many other women watching.

In response to this healing, many male DMNA church members were angry, while the revival leader eventually supported the healing event. The situation of this healing echoed previous circumstances: men were not around or available, a person was gravely ill, and the situation called for prompt action. What differed was the incredibly public nature of this healing; many women were watching, rather than a dyad or small group. The stakes were definitely higher in this case because during the colonial era, it was often public healing that attracted followers to Kimbangu and other prophets. I read this situation as certain members of the DMNA church seeing Mama Lutatamana as a threat to the hegemony and authority of their church. In seeking to proscribe her activities, the DMNA church reclaimed the embodied practices that composed the lived religion of their members as a form of DMNA worship specifically. However, the male revival leader recognized Mama Lutatamana's claim on the larger Kongo prophetic tradition that shaped her healing practices; "the Holy Spirit . . . authorized it." All of this shows the ongoing dialogue between lived religion within and outside of the church walls and a circulating body of knowledge, beliefs, and embodied practices that have been shaping this region for centuries.

Together these three examples emphasize the importance of the body as a conduit (Covington-Ward 2016) between the natural and supernatural realms, where spiritual forces are acting on the women in the DMNA church, leading to a circumvention of the restrictions on women's roles. The women are not claiming to be acting intentionally but rather responding to the embodied callings of the Holy Spirit. People in this region have historically believed in continuous revelation—that God continues to interact with humans into the present day (Thornton 1998a, 257). The presence of God, through being filled with the Holy Spirit, hearing voices, having visions and revelations, and experiencing embodied trembling, continues to happen for Kongo people regardless of gender. Thus, while Esaie's vision shaped the importance of white cloth, material practices, and the restriction of women's roles in the DMNA church, it was not the last word (or gesture) on the matter. The lived religion of women in this church (and the men and women they heal) contests these restrictions in many ways.

Conclusion

In closing, this chapter has argued for renewed attention to the contrapuntal dialogue between materiality and embodiment in African and African diasporic religions. Rather than assuming that material objects, material practices, and embodiment are always working together to further spiritual aims, I have extensively examined a discourse based on materiality that both enables and restricts women's participation in the DMNA church and that is challenged (and is always open to be potentially challenged) by Holy Spirit–induced embodied trembling. Women healing in different contexts outside of the DMNA church (both privately and publicly) reveal the tenuous claims on spiritual authority that derive from the materiality of the sacred white cloth. With or without the constrictions tied to menstrual blood and potential contamination, Kongo women in the DMNA church always possess the potential to wield prophetic gifts, like their male counterparts and their ancestors before them. Indeed, this prophetic heritage is open to all in the region, regardless of religious affiliation or gender. Mama Ntima clearly confirmed this when she said, "Whether you are a member of the church or not, you can do this miracle" (Luozi, July 27, 2010). This realm of spiritual possibility, grounded in the body, enables the exceptional healing of DMNA women.

ACKNOWLEDGMENTS

I would like to thank Professor Mahaniah Kimpianga for his hospitality during my time in the Congo. Thanks also to the Luyobisa family (Marceline, especially) and to Mama Jacqueline for taking care of me during my stay. I express my deepest gratitude to all of my interlocuters, who agreed to be interviewed. Thank you also to Ne Nkamu Luyindula for his amazing work on the interview transcriptions and KiKongo translations. My 2010 trip was funded by a Bowman Faculty Research Grant from the Nationality Rooms and an African Studies Course Development grant from the African Studies Program, both at the University of Pittsburgh. I would also like to thank my coeditor, Jeanette S. Jouili, for her feedback and support.

NOTES

1. In the epigraph I have more accurately translated two words from the original translation provided by Efraim Andersson.

2. *Ngunza* in KiKongo is defined as "someone who speaks in the name of a chief; hero, prophet" (Laman 1936, 696). In the context of the religious movements and churches that this essay is based on, *ngunza* is generally understood to mean "prophet" (the plural is *bangunza*).

3. Kongo Central is the current name for the province that was known as the Lower Congo (Bas-Congo) during much of the colonial and postcolonial period. The name of the province was changed to Kongo Central in 2015.

4. Before independence, the church it had belonged to was led by missionaries of the Svenska Missionforbundet (Swedish Mission Covenant Church).

5. Hundreds of Kongo men and women were arrested for engaging in prophetic activities and sent to penal labor camps in other parts of the vast colony. Kimbangu was imprisoned in one such camp for thirty years and died there in 1951. This long-term confinement was the most common approach used by the Belgians to try to suppress the movements.

6. Trembling as a sign of contact with the spiritual realm played a crucial role in healing, divination, and initiation in the traditional religions of precolonial Congo as well. The spirits involved were usually nature spirits, ancestors, or others who were no longer in the world of the living; there was also widespread belief in a larger, more powerful god known as Nzambi Mpungu (see Bockie 1993; Brown 2012).

7. According to Pastor Malala, *pendele* was the name for the secret meeting places where kingunza prayer and healing sessions were held, often in the forest, during the persecution of the prophetic movements during the colonial period.

8. All of the names of interviewees in this chapter are pseudonyms. I have followed the practice of using Tata (Father), Mama, Pastor, or other titles when referring to my interviewees because these titles of respect were used to address older men and women in Luozi when I did my research.

9. I was given a copy of "Les Grandes lignes doctrinales" (2005) while I was in Luozi. This is an internal church document laying out the larger beliefs and practices of the DMNA church.

10. In my discussions of whiteness as representing purity, I do not want to ignore the racial hierarchies that emerged out of slavery and colonialism, which equated moral superiority, cleanliness, and all that is good with people of European descent and moral inferiority, slovenliness, and all that is bad with people of African descent (see Kim Hall [1995] for some of these juxtapositions in English literature and travel narratives and Yolanda Covington-Ward [2016] for a brief discussion of racial ideas of whiteness in the larger Congo). However, further research needs to be done on the particular expression of such beliefs in the DMNA church in particular.

11. Many of the same associations can be found in Elisha Renne's study of the meaning of white cloth in traditional Yoruba religious worship and the Cherubim and Seraphim Church in Nigeria, in which she explores "the process of progressive distinction by which religious groups express new beliefs through material objects" (2005, 141). Like in the DMNA church, white cloth came to play an important part in the Cherubim and Seraphim Church, based on visions of angels dressed in white seen by founders of the church (2005, 146) and the association of white garments with morality and spiritual purity.

12. Moreover, in traditional Yoruba religious beliefs, white cloth was and is used for "protection, as medicine, and as a representation of spiritual connections" (Renne 2005, 143).

13. The *ntwadisi* is the person who weighs the spirit of congregation members during a ritual known as the *bascule*. The bascule is a part of the weekly worship practice and involves each church member approaching the ntwadisi, who is filled with the Holy Spirit, and trying to grasp his hand. If the church member is successful, the ntwadisi usually "jumps" the person in the air three times. The person's purity of spirit is determined by the height of the jumps. For more on the bascule, see Covington-Ward (2016) or MacGaffey (1983).

14. A *nkisi* is a special object or group of objects that hold a sacred medicine and are imbued with spiritual power.

15. Such beliefs about a life force present in blood clarify why the process of drying out or mummifying a body, in particular the bodies of chiefs and kings, was so important

in the past. The body was dried out over a fire until all of the internal liquids disappeared (Jacobson-Widding 1979, 307), a process that took from several months to a year. Not until this process was complete was the body officially dead, and the now-mummified body wrapped and buried, sometimes in a large figure made out of cloth, called a Niombo. For more information about Niombo figures and mummification, see Widman (1967).

16. Much has been written about menstrual taboos in different contexts, including in religious spaces and worship. *Purity and Danger: An Analysis of the Concepts of Pollution and Taboo*, by Mary Douglas (1966), examines menstrual blood as well as many other substances considered polluting and dangerous in different societies.

17. While at the time I did not ask where Luvuvamu was located, there is a village called Luvuvamu in Songololo Territory in Kongo Central/Lower Congo.

REFERENCES

Ammerman, Nancy. 2013. *Sacred Stories, Spiritual Tribes: Finding Religion in Everyday Life.* New York: Oxford University Press.

Ammerman, Nancy. 2014. "2013 Paul Hanly Furfey Lecture: Finding Religion in Everyday Life." *Sociology of Religion* 75 (2): 189–207.

Andersson, Efraim. 1958. *Messianic Popular Movements in the Lower Congo.* Uppsala: Almqvist & Wiksells Boktryckeri.

Bach, Alice. 1997. *Women, Seduction, and Betrayal in Biblical Narrative.* Cambridge: Cambridge University Press.

Bockie, Simon. 1993. *Death and the Invisible Powers: The World of Kongo Belief.* Bloomington: Indiana University Press.

Brown, Ras Michael. 2012. *African-Atlantic Cultures and the South Carolina Lowcountry.* Cambridge: Cambridge University Press.

Castor, N. Fadeke. 2017. *Spiritual Citizenship: Transnational Pathways from Black Power to Ifá in Trinidad.* Durham, NC: Duke University Press.

Covington-Ward, Yolanda. 2014. "'Your Name Is Written in the Sky': Unearthing the Stories of Kongo Female Prophets in Colonial Belgian Congo, 1921–1960." *Journal of Africana Religions* 2 (3): 317–346.

Covington-Ward, Yolanda. 2016. *Gesture and Power: Religion, Nationalism, and Everyday Performance in Congo.* Durham, NC: Duke University Press.

Crumbley, Deidre Ann. 2008. *Spirit, Structure, and Flesh: Gendered Experiences in African Instituted Churches among the Yoruba of Nigeria.* Madison: University of Wisconsin Press.

Douglas, Mary. (1966) 2002. *Purity and Danger: An Analysis of the Concepts of Pollution and Taboo.* London: Routledge Classics.

Fu-Kiau, A. kia Bunseki-Lumanisa. 1969. *N'Kongo ye nza yakun'zungidila; nza-Kôngo/Le Mukongo et le monde qui l'entourait.* Kinshasa: Office National de la recherche et de développement.

Hackett, Rosalind. 1987. "Women as Leaders and Participants in the Spiritual Churches." In *New Religious Movements in Nigeria*, edited by Rosalind Hackett, 191–196. Lewiston, NY: Edwin Mellen.

Hall, Kim. 1995. *Things of Darkness: Economies of Race and Gender in Early Modern England*. Ithaca, NY: Cornell University Press.

Higginbotham, Evelyn Brooks. 1993. *Righteous Discontent: The Women's Movement in the Black Baptist Church, 1880–1920*. Cambridge, MA: Harvard University Press.

Irvine, Cecilia. 1974. "The Birth of the Kimbanguist Movement in the Bas-Zaire, 1921." *Journal of Religion in Africa* 6 (1): 23–76.

Jacobson-Widding, Anita. 1979. *Red—White—Black as a Mode of Thought: A Study of Triadic Classification by Colours in the Ritual Symbolism and Cognitive Thought of the Peoples of the Lower Congo*. Uppsala, Sweden: Almqvist and Wiksell International.

Janzen, John. 1972. "Laman's Kongo Ethnography: Observations on Sources, Methodology, and Theory." *Africa: Journal of the International African Institute* 42 (4): 316–328.

Janzen, John. 1977. "The Tradition of Renewal in Kongo Religion." In *African Religions, A Symposium*, edited by Newell S. Booth Jr., 69–115. New York: Nok.

Janzen, John M. 1982. *Lemba, 1650–1930: A Drum of Affliction in Africa and the New World*. New York: Garland.

Jules-Rosette, Bennetta. 1975. *African Apostles: Ritual Conversion in the Church of John Maranke*. Ithaca, NY: Cornell University Press.

Jules-Rosette, Bennetta. 1981. "Women in Indigenous African Cults and Churches." In *The Black Woman Cross-Culturally*, edited by Filomena Steady, 185–207. Cambridge, MA: Schenkman.

Jules-Rosette, Bennetta. 1996. "Privilege without Power: Women in African Cults and Churches." In *Women in Africa and the African Diaspora: A Reader*, 2nd ed., edited by Rosalyn Terborg-Penn and Andrea Benton Rushing, 101–119. Washington, DC: Howard University Press.

Laman, Karl Edvard. 1962. *The Kongo*. Vol. 3. Uppsala: Studia Ethnographica Upsaliensia.

MacGaffey, Wyatt. 1983. *Modern Kongo Prophets: Religion in a Plural Society*. Bloomington: Indiana University Press.

MacGaffey, Wyatt. 1986a. "Ethnography and the Closing of the Frontier in Lower Congo, 1885–1921." *Africa: Journal of the International African Institute* 56 (3): 263–279.

MacGaffey, Wyatt. 1986b. *Religion and Society in Central Africa: The BaKongo of Lower Zaire*. Chicago: University of Chicago Press.

Mackay, D. J. 1987. "Simon Kimbangu and the B.M.S. Tradition." *Journal of Religion in Africa* 17 (2): 113–171.

Mackay, Donald, and Daniel Ntoni-Nzinga. 1993. "Kimbangu's Interlocutor: Nyuvudi's *Nsamu Miangunza (The Story of the Prophets)*." *Journal of Religion in Africa* 23 (3): 232–265.

Mahaniah, Kimpianga. 1975. "The Background of Prophetic Movements in the Belgian Congo." PhD diss., Temple University.

Mahaniah, Kimpianga. 1988. *L'impact du Christianisme au Manianga*. Kinshasa: Editions Centre de Vulgarisation Agricole.

McGuire, Meredith. 2008. *Lived Religion: Faith and Practice in Everyday Life*. New York: Oxford University Press.

Pemberton, Jeremy. 1993. "The History of Simon Kimbangu, Prophet, by the Writers Nfinangani and Nzungu, 1921: An Introduction and Annotated Translation." *Journal of Religion in Africa* 23 (3): 194–231.

Raymaekers, Paul. 1971. "Histoire de Simon Kimbangu, prophète, d'après les écrivains Nfinangani et Nzungu (1921)." *Archives de Sociologie des Religions* 31 (1): 15–42.

Renne, Elisha. 2005. "'Let Your Garments Always Be White': Expressions of the Past and Present in Yoruba Religious Textiles." In *African Religion and Social Change: Essays in Honor of John Peel,* edited by Toyin Falola, 139–163. Durham, NC: Carolina Academic Press.

Rouse, Carolyn. 2006. "Shopping with Sister Zubayda: African American Sunni Muslim Rituals of Consumption and Belonging." In *Women and Religion in the African Diaspora: Knowledge, Power, and Performance,* edited by R. Marie Griffith and Barbara Dianne Savage, 245–265. Baltimore: Johns Hopkins University Press.

Sackey, Brigid M. 2006. *New Directions in Gender and Religion: The Changing Status of Women in African Independent Churches.* Lanham, MD: Lexington Books.

Thornton, John. 1998a. *Africa and Africans in the Making of the Atlantic World, 1400–1800.* 2nd ed. New York: Cambridge University Press.

Thornton, John. 1998b. *The Kongolese Saint Anthony: Dona Beatriz Kimpa Vita and the Antonian Movement, 1684–1706.* Cambridge: Cambridge University Press.

Vellut, Jean-Luc, ed. 2005. *Simon Kimbangu 1921: De la predication à la deportation; Les Sources. Vol. 1. Fonds missionaires protestants (1), Alliance missionaire suédoise (Svenska Missionsförbundet, SMF).* Brussels: Academie Royale des Sciences d'Outre Mer.

Weeks, John H. 1908. "Notes on Some Customs of the Lower Congo People." *Folklore* 19 (4): 409–437.

Widman, Ragnar. 1967. *The Niombo Cult among the Babwende.* Stockholm: Ethnographical Museum of Sweden.

12. Dark Matter: Formations of Death Pollution in Southeastern African Funerals

CASEY GOLOMSKI

Dark matter is an evocative percept for an embodied religious phenomenon called *sinyama*, *sintima*, or *umnyama* in southeastern African deathways and an example of what anthropologists have called *symbolic pollution*.[1] Symbolic pollution is a phenomenon reflective of power inequalities, gender ideologies, and sociocultural systems of classification. The substance of bodily pollution—blood, hair, mortal remains—has been a standard focus of ethnographic interpretation. Descriptions of how, where, and by whom pollution phenomena are situationally embodied are also critical (Crumbley 2008; Masquelier 2005). Many cases from African and African diaspora religions illustrate how the situational embodiment of religious phenomena is relational, meaning that dynamics of embodiment can involve intersubjective and collective experiences of affliction, healing, and, here, symbolic pollution.

Despite its cultural and phenomenological prevalence across many southern African communities, dark matter as symbolic pollution is differently embodied (or rather disembodied) depending on the socioecological and political context. This chapter shows how contemporary negative valences of sinyama in the region echo a history of racialization originating in modern European Christian colonialism. An ethnographic comparison across national and cultural boundaries also reveals how gender and race are key variables in symbolic pollution's diverse forms of (dis)embodiment. Recalling Yolanda Covington-Ward and Jeanette Jouili's introduction in this book, sinyama has become a racialized representation of Black religion in several societies sharing this stigmatizing colonial history and its hangovers.[2]

Using terms like *polluting* or *contagious* for the embodiment of religious phenomena is provocative because of their culturally negative connotations (Crumbley 2008, 94). These terms are historically and ethically fraught, having been used in colonialist discourses as means to symbolically "other" and denigrate Black people's bodies. Black African and African diaspora embodied religious experiences and rituals, like spirit "possession," have long been subject to spurious representations or political control. For example, anthropologist Deidre Crumbley's (2008) insights on women's bodies (including her own) and menstrual pollution in southern Nigerian Aladura churches speak to how the anthropology of religion in Africa and its diasporas is itself ethically charged in its political history and ethnographic methods.[3] She leads us to ask, What forces deem someone or something polluting? What lines of difference are drawn in this attribution of embodied experience, and how are relational dimensions of this experience excised, erased, or expanded? What meanings are foregrounded in particular representations of these experiences, and how?

My own consideration of these ethical dynamics in African studies of religion involves documenting "the ways people interact with and recognize each other across different social worlds" and the ways "such interactions are qualified through peoples' simultaneous engagement with global and material aspects of those worlds" (Golomski 2016, 461). Perceptual and material dynamics in religious performance are then also ethical, as is the fact that religious performances and their communities are politically differentiated and made historically unequal.[4] Globally, the long-term scaling of modern European colonialism scattered and segregated peoples into altogether new social worlds and also bound these worlds together in shared legacies of violence and radical cultural change through racialized and gendered tropes of modernity (Pierre 2013). The cultural and religious lives of contemporary peoples in Africa and its diasporas embody these dynamics of displacement and differentiation and shape how ethical recognition of and among religious phenomena and communities unfold. This also foregrounds the necessity for cross-cultural comparison and interpretation.

To wit, this chapter offers a comparison of funereal dark matter in southeastern Africa—including corpses, embodied experiences of bereavement, and mortuary ritual ephemera and spaces—to show how its materialities are diversely valued and (dis)embodied while deriving from a shared cultural domain. Specifically, it shows how dark matter emerges differently between South

Africa and Eswatini, and brief comparison of the two places helps situate my interpretive motive.

Regionally, Eswatini—which since 2018 is the new official name of the country formerly known as Swaziland—is a neotraditionalist bastion of African alterity. The small country of 1.3 million citizens is the continent's last absolute, divine diarchy, ruled by King Mswati III and his mother, Queen Mother Ntfombi Tfwala, along with a retinue of state-appointed princes and princesses who administer the country's 350 chiefdoms.[5] Prominent Swazi state representatives and businessmen often go shirtless and wear animal loinskins and customary textiles during international travel and at the United Nations. The national calendar is punctuated by ceremonies specific to the societal regimentation of gendered age sets, *emabutfo*. For example, each August at the Umhlanga rite, over forty thousand girls are summoned as "virgins" by the state for a weeklong rite to harvest reeds for presentation to the Queen Mother in celebration of their gendered identities and bodily-sexual purity. The kingship decrees seasonal tributary labor in communal projects of weeding, harvesting, and hunting, and its proclamations on what is authentic "Swazi culture" are taken as sagacious ultimatums by political elites and traditionalist citizens. These state-originated postcolonial cultural productions drive regional sensibilities about the veracity of African culture and identity, including those about "traditional" deathways.

With respect to sovereignty, geography, and population, Eswatini is radically different from its multicultural, multiracial, and democratic neighbor South Africa. Eswatini is dependent economically on South Africa, and the two have deeply intertwined histories of their Indigenous polities' territories and cultures being altogether transformed in European settler colonialism since at least the sixteenth century. The geographic lines where Eswatini ends and South Africa begins are a product of this history, and such modern borders complicate how everyday practices, whether those surrounding death or others, unfold. South Africa is far more urbanized; its 40.5 million citizens emerged from white-minority rule only in 1994, after the fall of apartheid, but today have one of the world's most liberal constitutions. Contrasting to this is Eswatini, which became independent from British colonial rule in 1968, with its autocratic leadership and small-scale societal dimensions in state-driven ethnocultural nationalism, shared language, and a religious synergy of (post)mission Christianity and traditionalism embodied in African independent churches (AICs), which predominate in the kingdom.

A comparative and historical perspective on formations of death pollution in these two places shows how some people and things come to be dark matter-out-of-place. In peri-urban Eswatini, dark matter condenses as a problem of women, where bereaved widows embody sinyama, signified in mourning rites and dress, with churches aiming to contain and dissipate its power. In urban South Africa, dark matter is a more diffuse, negating, diminishing force associated with immorality, criminality, and socioeconomic disintegration. It is a surfeit problem, portending communal affliction and religious ritual remedies. It is a more disembodied phenomenon. These differences reflect particular geographic and political configurations born out of colonialism in different places and at the same time reveal shared experiences of racialization.

To make this case, I draw from ethnographic research on death, dying, and funerals in Eswatini and document research on popular literary, cultural, and media texts in South Africa on the same matters. Much of the ethnographic material derives from my own participation in and observation of funerals in Eswatini (Golomski 2018a). Similarly, I observed many rituals in both Swazi and South African churches indicating measures to avoid or contain sinyama. Less of this material is explicitly phenomenological or experience-near, as fewer of my main consultants or interlocutors claimed to experience sinyama themselves, but they reported that others did. Using these sources along with popular literary and cultural accounts, my interpretation embodies a "methodological attitude that demands attention to bodiliness even in purely verbal data such as written text or oral interview" (Csordas 1999, 148) and critically combines phenomenological and textual evidence in making ethnographic knowledge about religion. I now trace how embodied knowledge and practices surrounding sinyama have been revalued over time in the broader region.

The Origins of Dark Matter

Several contemporary southeastern African communities have similar percepts of sinyama, sintima, or umnyama that denote blackness or darkness and are associated with night, shadows, malevolence and evil, illness, and death.[6] Death imbues sinyama as a dark penumbral emission that affects bodies, emotions, and relationships. The bereaved are said to feel it and have it. A related precept is *libhadi*, sometimes translated as "badness" or "bad luck," which may derive from sinyama and may sometimes be characterized as dark or black. Both are possessive and/or qualify the presence of this phenomenon: *kuyisinyama lapha*, "there is darkness here," or *unelibhadi*, "that person has bad luck." But what are the origins of these present connotations?

Tellingly, the ethnographic record shows that sinyama as an endogenous and precolonial percept has fewer negative and more empowering connotations. Domestic objects and leisure activities had positive connotations derived from their black colors.[7] For Zulu peoples, the ethnically "insider anthropologist" Harriet Ngubane (1977) located black color symbolism in cosmic orders of night and day and bodily processes of eating and defecating, noting that blackness had significant power. It was associated with the immensity of rain and thunderstorms, which produced both fertile rains and dangerous lightning. The South African–Swedish missionary ethnographer Axel-Ivar Berglund (1976) noted that Zulu ritual specialists produced blackened medicinal objects in the form of beads, brooms, and parts of animals to use as protection, invoke ancestral beneficence in sacrifices, and cure illness. "After completion of the period of treatment with black medicines, the evil of death and danger is believed to have been removed," Ngubane (1977, 126) wrote, and black can "stand for both goodness and badness" (113). Blackness was a constitutive, animating quality of bodies and materialities in the religious cosmologies in the region.

This endogenous ecological and religious ritual symbolism changed, however, in the historical confluence of colonial technologies, racial ideologies, and gendered Christian stipulations for death in the late nineteenth and early twentieth centuries especially.[8] Historians Rebekah Lee and Megan Vaughan (2008) comprehensively show how death and funerals were revalued and performed in this period, and their work is pivotal for understanding contemporary funerals. They do not, however, interrogate race and racialization (explicitly) as factors in the cultural production or valuation of ritually embodied practices surrounding death, despite the trenchant colonial racist sciences and policies that violently categorized peoples by skin color and other bodily qualities in the region (and globally). This Linnaean colorist system of classification rendered difference as rigid, requalifying persons and things as human and/or nonhuman and driving new associations among them along axes of unequal value.

Writing from the United States about colonialist and colorist racism there and in African countries in the early twentieth century, W. E. B. Du Bois argued that this contemporaneous "theory of human culture and its aims has worked itself through warp and woof of our daily thought with a thoroughness that few realize. Everything great, good, efficient, fair, and honorable is 'white' . . . a bad taste is 'brown'; and the devil is 'black.' These changes of this theme are continually rung in picture and story, in newspaper heading and moving-picture, in sermon and school book" ([1920] 2007, 22). Du Bois invoked "the sermon" to suggest that this diffusion and internalization of color-based racism is operable in religion too, opening up possibilities to see how religious forms of blackness, like sinyama, emerged and were embodied in different religious traditions.

More recently, Aisha Beliso-De Jesús (2015) traces this process in a dynamic she calls *blackening*. Beliso-De Jesús conceptualizes the religious ontologies of African and African diaspora societies as having been racialized, citing entangled histories and present realities of enslavement, tourism, migration, and wage labor that members of these societies experienced. In her account from Afro-Caribbean and diaspora contexts, Cuban Santeria religious practitioners' embodiment of religious phenomena happens both virtually and in cities, with the latter deemed perceptually dark places in the materialities of scents, religious media, sexual encounters, and funerary rites. Using Frantz Fanon's writings on racism, she posits that these dispersive virtual and urban dynamics of material assemblage are phenomenologically and racially "blackened" *as* African diaspora religions for both its practitioners and global audiences.

Drawing on these critical arguments that racialization is constitutive of African and African diaspora religions, I trace how this kind of blackening forms the "warp and woof" of present southeastern African deathways where contemporary experiences and terms of symbolic pollution are iconic of negative blackness. The diverse polities and religious practices in southeastern Africa give rise to diverse spiritualities associated with universal matters of death. And, finally, understanding why death is construed as a negative, polluting formation necessitates historicizing death itself in the face of a colonial racial gaze, which I comparatively explore in the following sections on Eswatini and South Africa.

Eswatini: Dark Matter and Gender

As the previous ethnographic examples show, blackness was not always determinatively negative as an element of local social worlds. Clothing was one such form of material culture where blackness was favored in Eswatini. Borrowing the style from Tsonga peoples, many esteemed and mature headmen wore grubwax head rings "as black as jet . . . [and] made to shine brightly" (Junod [1912] 1966, 129–130). Married women's attire formerly included long, pleated skirts made of blackened cowskin, a style that is made today from cotton or other fabrics and worn by brides at customary weddings.[9] The skins were derived from cattle sacrifices, the animals culled from family herds, or those exchanged as part of bridewealth ceremonies. These were and are valuable and beautiful pieces of customary clothing, *imvunulo*. This symbolism of ritual and clothing, along with the color symbolism of herbal medicines, represent a customary religious assemblage where blackness is a constitutive, enduring cultural value (Berglund 1976; Makhubu 1978; Ngubane 1977).

Contemporary perceptions of sinyama as a negative phenomenon in Eswa-tini surround both embodied experiences and materialities of death and can be traced through the civilizing missions of Christian churches and the racist poli-cies and ideologies of Afrikaner and British settler colonialism (ca. 1840–1968). The siSwati word *kugula* means "to be ill or sick" and is a synonym for *kuzila*, "to mourn," connoting difficult bodily experiences of bereavement, through which sinyama emerges in longing for tangible connections with the deceased. Clothing and other domestic or personal objects bind people together in Eswa-tini "as a materially embodied, intersubjective process wielded to enact pres-ence, absence and transition between self and other" (Golomski 2015, 325). The loss of an other is materially mediated through bodily ephemera to restore socioemotional well-being for widows especially, as the immediately bereaved, and then, by proxy, the community. Ngubane (1977) described this ritual and practical ordering of persons and objects in the socioecological environment as rendering cosmological "balance" (*ukuzilungisa*, or well-being among the living and between the living and the dead).

In precolonial and colonial mourning customs, Swazi widows formerly undertook elaborate clothing rites, turning their black cowskin skirts inside out and making and then later ritually destroying hats, ropes, and other at-tire made of grass (Kuper [1947] 1980). Beginning in the 1840s, Christian missions like the Wesleyans, Nazarenes, Methodists, and others (the prede-cessors of what are today called *mainline churches*) began unsettling indig-enous cultural stipulations of gender and clothing through overtly civilizing or modernizing missions related to existential, socioemotional, and material matters of death.[10] Through the colonial period, acculturative changes in clothing, including patterning, tailoring, and coloring of cotton fabrics, were spread through traveling merchants like Dups Bazaar. Today Dups is Eswa-tini's largest mortuary and funeral insurance retailer. European-style clothing mainly replaced clothing made of grasses and various animal skins and leath-ers. Today's formal mourning gowns are an outcome of this history, taking the form of completely black pinafore dresses, aprons, shawls, skirts, and tams. If not black, gowns are dark blue, sometimes indicative of the church groups that widows belong to.[11]

This negative clothing symbolism paralleled broader racially charged revalu-ations in colonial society. Hilda Kuper's ([1947] 1969) ethnography of race rela-tions in colonial Eswatini shows white settlers' veritable racialization of Swazis *as* "black" and stereotyping of them as hypersexual, barbaric, and stupid. The royal Dlamini Swazis she worked with understood skin-color variation as beau-tiful but came to self-deprecate themselves for their technological inferiority to whites. These stereotypes were further embedded in unequal economic policies and the dispossession of Swazis' land during the colonial era. These racist representations and policies endured into the postcolonial era (Dlamini 2007), laying the structural grounds for variable embodiment of a negating blackness.

Despite the history of black customary medicines' potency for healing and purification, Christian churches across the ecumenical spectrum today propound eschatologies that describe grief and mourning as symbolically dark or black. This is stronger in mainline churches and newer Pentecostal churches in Eswatini. Pentecostal churches are notable for their ideological assault on anything deemed traditional. Some Pentecostal churches are criticized for being racist against Black southern Africans (van Wyk 2014, 77–78) and are arguably the principal religious institutions driving these negative valuations today. At a Pentecostal church I attended in Matsapha in 2010, I documented a Bible-study session on the topic of "dark African customs" surrounding death, dying, and funerals. The pastor, a prominent public theologian, spoke at length about sinyama. The following quote is from a recording of the pastor's words (my translation, along with other passages in this chapter, from siSwati), with key vernacular terms in brackets:

> People talk about death's dark matter [kufa kwesinyama] and bad luck [libhadi lesikufa], but here in church we talk about death in God. Dark matter moves and affects all of your relatives as they move around too. At funerals we see people whispering to the corpse [sidumbu]. They think if they don't say or do something ritually, the spirit will be flying here and there, like "Ffft! Ffft!" These are not going out from the body to kill us. God is there, and these rituals do not protect us as we go around or our children go to school. We Africans think death is unnatural; we take it as bad luck happening all around us.

In his contrastive retelling, Africans (wrongly) associate death with darkness and evil. The soul or spiritual entity is set loose from the body, if not contained by some (non-Christian) rite. The circumstances surrounding death portend unnatural, ungodly forces that potentially undercut the bereaved and their families. The fleeting velocity of unleashed spirits is dangerous, almost ungraspable, and affects daily routines and travel; his sounds of "Ffft! Ffft!" were meant to indicate something flying around like an insect. At a later point in his lecture, he mimicked women crying in front of the body at the funeral, saying that they should think about the dead's godly resurrection rather than wallow in grief.

FIGURE 12.1. Women cover widows of the deceased in blankets at the graveside during the burial at an AIC funeral, southwestern Swaziland (now Eswatini), May 2011. Photograph by author.

Contemporary funeral rites condense sinyama and libhadi in bereaved persons' bodies, especially widows, which effectively contain symbolic pollution and can affect others. Men who are widowers in Eswatini face none of the sinyama-related rites and prophylaxes detailed here. As in the Pentecostal example, bereaved women and widows are the main subjects of ritual criticism and control. This is most evident in customary religious rites and those of AICs. Their rites operate on embodied processes of sequestration and purification. Most funerals have a night vigil, *umlindzelo*, where mourning wives, daughters, and other women are kept separate from other attendees in a room or small house on the homestead with the body. Their spatial containment is repeated at the burial site during interment, where they are shielded from attendees' view with blankets held up by other women. This can be seen in figure 12.1, in which women drape a dark, rose-ringed blanket across their shoulders, arms linked, to shield one of the deceased man's widows, who is crouching behind the blanket at their feet. After the burial, some widows have their heads shaved. When attendees return to the homestead for a morning feast after the burial, kettles are commonly used to pour water over people's hands to both purify and wash them before eating. That this water is sometimes mixed with ash, especially in AICs, hearkens to older forms of purification using black medicines (Makhubu 1978).

After the funeral is over, widows are effectively made into social pariahs according to traditionalist stipulations: their presence and the wearing of black mourning gowns make them iconic of sinyama, from which people elaborate a host of ideas about their ability to emit libhadi. Many in-laws confine widows to a patrilocal home and induce abstention from sex. Widows' physical activity and mobility are limited beyond the home, where they remain silent and deferential. When I was living in a rural community in 2011 next to the late chief's compound, his widow rarely left the homestead. When she did, it was in the company of one of her brothers-in-law. This man was also her prospective new husband, as widows are often entrusted to their deceased husband's brothers, a rite of levirate marriage that some claim is solely part of Swazi culture but that was also arguably revalued as Swazi after the introduction of Old Testament biblical lore in the colonial era (Nyawo 2015).

Widows are often headliners in Eswatini's two national newspapers in stories about stolen mourning gowns, in-law disputes over property and personal autonomy, and women's and their natal families' refusals to ritually mourn. I estimate I collected over fifty widow-specific stories between 2006 and 2009. Widows are later purified from their condition in a rite organized by their in-laws that takes place after one to three years or winters, called kugeza emanti, meaning "to wash [with] water." It involves the bodily application of water and a reintroduction of the purified widow to her relatives, church members, neighbors, and potential new husband (her brother-in-law). At some widows' reintegration rites I attended, the widow was again covered with blankets as gifts for her mourning work (figure 12.2), symbolically reaffirming the containment of the woman's body as part of her deceased husband's patriline. The thanksgiving, purification, and containment of sinyama associated with widows show how pollution surrounds mourning and is gendered in the confluence of (post)mission Christian and endogenous religious practices.

This negative valuation of widows and their bodies also moves from domestic domains to the public. Widows are sometimes avoided on public transport, in workplaces, and in queues and are joked about as apparently emitting libhadi. One interviewee I spoke to in 2011 was a women's rights and gender-based violence researcher at the Eswatini office of the Women and Law in Southern

FIGURE 12.2. Widow with gifts and wrapped in blankets at a purification and reintegration rite (*kugeza emanti*) at an AIC night vigil, southeastern Swaziland (now Eswatini), August 2008. Photograph by author.

Africa Trust. She explained how women faced undue gendered pressures as widows under the guise of tradition:

> Some women will leave the house wearing the gowns, but when they get to work, they take them off. Then when they leave the office for the day, they put them back on to go home. . . . People will not want to speak to her at the front desk. They may send her in the back then to do things like make tea, but then even the men at the office will not want to drink the tea that she makes. . . . You see, maybe the mourning thing was fine in the old times when women just stayed in the house all day, but now they are going out to work, and then it causes problems.

In her account, men especially perpetuate the idea that because widows embody blackness, they are bad luck and contagious in the exchange of food-stuffs and movement in public spaces. At the end of the interview, I made a reflexive cautionary note, saying that others I met could perceive my research as potentially dangerous, at least according to the etiology of libhadi we had discussed. "Oh no, they won't say that," she said. "Libhadi is just for us Swazis. For you [as a white person], you may talk to her or even brush up against her [a widow], but libhadi won't go to you." As Ngubane (1977, 24) suggested for the category of *ukufa kwabantu*, "African disease," the women's rights researcher explained that I would not be affected. Only other Black African Swazi could succumb to widows' darkness or bad luck, a discrete ontological configuration of death-related illness where no affliction is transmitted outside of a single racial category.

In Eswatini, dark matter condenses like a bruise or welt that slowly disappears over time but from which contagion emerges and moves surreptitiously. Pollution is strongly gendered as a problem of women as widows (rather than men as widowers). Modes of containment and prevention happen in women's mourning seclusion, traditionalist or AIC rites of purification, and their discursive obviation in Pentecostal settings. The local concentration of these rites is arguably due to ongoing cultural elaborations of death amid HIV/AIDS in the shadows of state-driven authentications of culture (Golomski 2018a). But as the next case shows, when moving across modern geopolitical borders to multicultural urban South Africa, sinyama becomes a phenomenologically diffusive ground for embodying tradition in more violent terms and places in which people live and die.

South Africa: Dark Matter and the Metropole

Again, modern geopolitical borders should not belie continuities of cultural formations like death-related symbolic pollution, although the settings people find themselves in also reconfigure these formations and their lived experiences. For example, as the Eswatini–South African border was created in the late nineteenth century, Swazis found themselves living in South Africa and outside of their sovereign then-protectorate kingship. These South African areas later became designated as segregated "native" territories or "homelands." Many men from Eswatini were conscripted into circuits of labor migration to the geographic area of South Africa known as the Rand to work in the infamously dangerous gold mines. The effects of capitalist industrialization and its concomitant racial segregation under apartheid thus inflect the religious pluralism and multiculturalism that predominate in South Africa.

Having lived and worked with many folks and families in urban and peri-urban areas in South Africa's Gauteng and Mpumalanga provinces in 2009, 2014–2015, 2017, and 2019, I documented several domestic rites of ancestral thanksgiving and attended worship services at Pentecostal charismatic and mainline Catholic and Protestant churches. Sinyama, or the isiZulu equivalent umnyama, did not feature as strongly in biblical exegeses or ritual concerns as it had in Eswatini religious ritual settings. What more systematic ethnographies of religion in South Africa, as well as contemporary fictional literature by South African authors, show is that dark matter is indeed present, but it casts much wider shadows.

Dark matter surrounding death is indeed a problem for women in South Africa, who may be made peripheral in accordance with "African tradition." An important difference, however, is that widows there also embody a powerful will to live and mobilize politically. Women whose (male) partners died in the fight against state racial oppression featured prominently at African National Congress (ANC) political rallies. Widows were foregrounded at massive funerals for their husbands—rather than hidden like in Swazi funerals—in the 1980s–1990s as the antiapartheid struggles reached their climax, publicly embodying survivorship of racialized violence. Widows also had central testimonial positions in the Truth and Reconciliation Commission in the aftermath of apartheid (Ramphele 1997). In 2014 the figure of the politicized widow returned to the televised spotlight as the primary bereaved family members of the forty-plus who were protesting male miners killed by state and private security forces at the Marikana platinum mine. Here the strife of widows and their bereavement were mobilized against the violence of enduring racialized political economies.

This is not to say that widows or the bereaved are not associated with sinyama. Rather, in South Africa, like in Afro-Caribbean contexts (Beliso-De Jesús 2015), this penumbral phenomenon is more pervasively disembodied. It constellates uneasily across multicultural persons, objects, and technologies in congested, underdeveloped urban spaces. Cities are where death is imminent because life is uncertain. Dark matter materializes as a problem of the postcolonial metropole and can afflict urban dwellers in their daily lives. Melekias Zulu and Matthew Wilhelm-Solomon (2015, 138–140), for example, describe how some Johannesburg migrant-residents are tainted by umnyama, a "flow that captures an environment" and morally and physically affects and transmits among bodies and objects. A site of death—like a bloodstained stairwell of a high-rise following a suicide or murder—can be perceived as dark matter, as are entire inauspicious "dark buildings" with precarious electricity connections and streetcorners rife with criminals.

The uncertainty, mobility, and dynamics of evictions and failing infrastructure constellate, for some migrants, as zones iconic of darkness, which are also effectively non-white because of their inhabitants' racial demographics.

Julia Hornberger (2008, 288) describes how state electrification in the Black-occupied segregated townships like Soweto came about only in the 1970s to quell increasing political protests. Instead of the brighter white-colored mercury-based lighting that was systematically erected in white-occupied areas, townships were provisioned with low-lit, orange-colored sodium-based lighting. "Because of [sodium-based lighting's] monochromatic nature, it does not allow for color rendering and dips everything within its reach into an abnormal atmosphere. . . . [T]o have a less distorted nightlight became the privilege of the city" rather than the township.

On weekends in Johannesburg and other major, often-violent South African cities, funerals are followed by huge parties called "after tears," sometimes held near the bereaved family's house or at urban megacemeteries like Avalon in Soweto. Francis Lukhele (2016, 36) describes this "mourning" practice as "gangsterly"; attendees are partiers whose "happy-go-lucky demeanour conceal[s] a frightening brutality," that of the death, injuries, and struggles that mark the lives of postapartheid urban youth. Men broadcast music videos on their laptops, drive expensive cars over grave mounds, rival each other's sound systems, and drink heavily with women in a "nonchalant, consumerist exhibitionism incongruously coexist[ing] with the parasitic appearance of hordes at funerals," writes Lukhele. Rather than being covered fully, as widows in Eswatini would be, women (and men) at after-tears parties dress stylishly or as if they were going to a club. The scene can be considered profane in what is seen as a transgression of customary or ethical ritual conduct.[12] Or, as a lecture class of University of Johannesburg undergraduate anthropology students collectively explained to me and the Swazi anthropologist Thandeka Dlamini-Simelane in 2019, "South Africans like partying too much."

Further evidence of darkness as a problem of deathly urbanity can easily be drawn from contemporary South African literature. In Niq Mhlongo's (2007) novel *After Tears*, for example, the protagonist Bafana's licentious uncle Nyawana describes the urban cemeteries of Johannesburg as sexually rife locations where sex drives death, subsequent funerals, and new risky sexual encounters *at* funerals: "'Some [women] wear revealing miniskirts just to challenge you, man. That's why Avalon cemetery is full, it's because these ladies are living advertisements for Aids. . . . I got this new chick at a funeral some months back. When I saw her by the graveside that day, I knew she was going to be mine,' he said, touching his left breast tenderly" (48–49). Later, Nyawana is shot on New Year's Eve and kept alive in a vegetative state but dies while being transported in an ambulance to another hospital during a township-wide electricity blackout. The family argues about the choice of undertaker, saying the one Nyawana's sister chooses is owned by racist Afrikaners, extending the settler colonial legacy of "killing abodarkie [a derogatory term for Black people]. The only difference is that these days they're making a huge profit out of it because they kill you today and bury you tomorrow" (196).

The historical process of blackening is articulated as funeral attendees and township residents understand their lived reality of home, work, and now burial places as one of racialized structural violence. Given the superdiverse, cosmopolitan space of the city, a multitude of Black African traditional religious rites and practitioners are mobilized to contain sinyama and related forces. In Mhlongo's novel *Way Back Home*, the protagonist is Kimathi Tito, a sly, aging nouveau riche war hero and hustler, his personality seemingly embodied in features like "black smudges around the edges of his neglected lower teeth" (2013, 64). He is haunted by the ghost of Senami, a young woman and his national comrade, whom he killed while they were fighting pro-apartheid forces in exile in Tanzania. Years after he kills Senami, she returns in the night in "dark, bloody dreams" (74). Darkness pervades Tito's bodily being, and to contain it and relieve his illness, he is forced to go to Senami's parents' home and hire the healer Makhanda. Because Senami died and was buried in exile, the family has to hold a "symbolic funeral"; it is a veritably disembodied rite without her corpse. Makhanda makes ritual incisions on Tito's joints and applies "black medicines" to the wounds (64) to contain the haunting presence of the dead young woman, but only for a short while.

This sinyama emerges from antitheses or failures to mourn and only condenses uneasily in funeral rites similar to those found in Eswatini. In *After Tears*, at Uncle Nyawana's funeral (which takes place at the same Avalon cemetery where he found sex and which he also derided), some funeral attendees keep his corpse covered at night and peripheral from the proceedings; Bafana deems this "strange" rather than customary (Mhlongo 2007, 190). Like in Eswatini, ritual attempts to contain sinyama and purify mourners from dark matter at funerals involve using "big steel baths of dirty water. Everyone who came from the cemetery was required to wash their hands and erase all thoughts of death and human decay as they did so" (200) before eating. The substance of purification or containment is here again black medicine, but the timbre of the novel's conclusion, which involves Bafana failing out of college owing to financial limitations, and his effective social death, suggests that purification has been less than efficacious.

In Mhlongo's novels, men are lecherous and women are made to be sexual or spiritual culprits, victims of the violent precarity of postcolonial life without moral means to mourn. Their urban environment is consistently painted as dark, and life runs aground in spates of misfortune. Dark matter is all-consuming of life in the metropole, not just embodied in women's bodies or rites. In fact, widows' bereavement may embody the symbolic potential to regenerate communities altogether in the wake of racist political violence. The religious practices they engage in here and in other literary (Mda 1995) and ethnographic examples (van Wyk 2014; Zulu and Wilhelm-Solomon 2015) of urban South African cultural life are similar to what is found in more traditionalist domains like Eswatini, yet their value is configured to accommodate a surfeit of dark matter not relegated to the embodied purview of a particular gender.

Conclusion

> What, then, is this dark world thinking? It is thinking that as wild and awful as this shameful war was, *it is nothing to compare with that fight for freedom which black and brown and yellow men must and will make unless their oppression and humiliation and insult at the hands of the White World cease. The Dark World is going to submit to its present treatment just as long as it must and not one moment longer.*
> —W. E. B. Du Bois, "The Souls of White Folk," 1920

> It is early Sunday evening under the trees outside the Matsapha Prison liquor store: we wring out a few dance moves, drink beer and whiskey over ice, and watch a wintering sunset beyond His Majesty's Correctional Services College. Black and white birds grace the sky. "Kumnandzi sintima," says my friend Mphile—"It is nice in the darkness."
> —Author's field notes, Eswatini, June 3, 2017

Documenting how experiential phenomena like embodied metaphors of darkness and pollution emerge in situ counts as important methodological grounds for comparative inter- and intracontinental African diaspora studies of religion. The geopolitical influence of settler colonialism and apartheid structured the material world for many southeastern African religious practitioners by driving the unequal development of more monocultural and multicultural spaces. Arguably, in the case of both Eswatini and South Africa, discourses and policies devaluing the lives of non-white peoples and women shored up negative prejudice about darkness as a quality of materiality in religious ritual deathways. This is a continental example of the dynamic of global historical blackening that Beliso-De Jesús (2015) describes and a formation of materially ethical life (Golomski 2016) that we must account for in understanding Black African and African diaspora embodied religious phenomena.

Historically, blackness has been structurally-symbolically and diametrically opposed to whiteness, the outcome of European- and American-driven extractive colonial projects and war, rendering a mirage of distinctive racialized social worlds. That this was affirmed in the imperatives and "*souls* of white folks" in the modern era (Du Bois [1920] 2007; emphasis added) suggests that violence is immanent in the sacred. Anthropologists of religion must historicize what are presumed to be universal perceptions and ethical values. Blackness has not always been negative in Black African and African diaspora religious cosmologies, as I documented here. It has been spiritually potent and medicinally restorative in the face of illness and death and, as my brief field notes in the epigraph hint at, leisurely and aesthetically pleasing. Blackness has also obviously been a symbolic and embodied resource for political liberation. Overall, the (in)auspicious penumbra of dark matter, as I take it, is a manifestation of ongoing ethical and embodied engagements with a changing world, indicative of the ways that the world has been materially shaped by modernity and life in the postcolony.

ACKNOWLEDGMENTS

This chapter is crafted from ethnographic material and theoretical ruminations from a variety of venues. Thus, I thank many people: my informants in Eswatini and South Africa, Mark Auslander, Thandeka Dlamini-Simelane, Jessica Hardin, Michael Jackson, Anna Jaysane-Darr, Laura John, Ieva Jusionyte, Sarah Lamb, Janet McIntosh, George Paul Meiu, Casey Miller, Danai Mupotsa, Sonene Nyawo, Gcobani Qambela, Ellen Schattschneider, Mrinalini Tankha, Allison Taylor, and Hylton White, and also, from the University of Pittsburgh workshop, Mari Webel, Yolanda Covington-Ward, Jeanette Jouili, Stephanie Mitchem, Rachel Cantave, Jaison Youssef Carter, Bertin Louis, and Jacob Olupona.

NOTES

1. In astrophysics, dark matter is hypothetically high-density, high-energy matter born from particles that cannot absorb light and is undetectable by visible-light telescopes. I draw rather on past metaphorical uses of the term in Black or African American and African diaspora studies to signal sociocultural and religious dynamics of racism, such as in W. E. B. Du Bois's ([1920] 2007) invocations in *Darkwater: Voices from within the Veil*.

2. When quoting from a source that uses lowercase *b* in *black*, I maintain the author's original usage. Of note, it is conventional in Southern Africa not to capitalize black when it is used in racial terms.

3. Crumbley (2008, 95) argues that gender-segregating menstruation-related rites in these churches are less about women members' polluting qualities and more about keeping separate elements valued as profane and sacred. In Yoruba cosmology, for example, menstruation has the power to make life and "may indicate cosmological subtleties of holy otherness," she writes. Ethnographically, Crumbley prohibited herself from entering the church during her period as part of her ethnographic methods, a situational act she ethically aligned with Aladura principles that women should not approach altars because of their bodily powers.

4. Michael Jackson (2009) and Michael Lambek (2010) write that religious communities organize themselves by culturally intellectualizing, performing, and materializing what are fundamentally human ethical practices.

5. By royal decree, and marking fifty years of independence from the British, King Mswati III changed the country's name to Eswatini from Swaziland in June 2018. Eswatini means "land of the Swazis" in siSwati, which, along with English, is one of the country's two official languages.

6. Specifically, I am referring to siSwati-, isiZulu-, isiXhosa-, xiTsonga-, (Southern) siNdebele-, and seTswana-speaking peoples.

7. Among Tsonga peoples, Henri-Alexandre Junod recorded a lullaby to soothe babies invoking blackness: "'Keep quiet *Makaneta*, of the black hut,'" meaning a "village where the huts have had time to become black; they have never been destroyed by enemies, as no enemy dares to attack your clan! So the roofs have blackened inside from the effects of the smoke and outside from those of rain!" ([1912] 1966, 361). Here blackness indicated natural environmental and domestic processes of lived accretion, rather than violent destruction. Blackness was also a valued quality in leisure activities like "saliva contests" in men's hemp-smoking games, where when spitting from their pipes "the saliva must be blackish . . . produced by hemp, and not the ordinary white saliva" (344–345).

8. See Comaroff (1993) and Junod ([1912] 1966). The latter wrote about Tsonga funerary practitioners, for example, that their "heathenism is so poor . . . even if we had no religious convictions at all, should we not earnestly desire that, for these people, the bright comforting Christian hope may dispel the darkness of their thoughts and the sufferings involved in their rites?" (168).

9. I use the term *customary* to reflect local terms used in Eswatini to describe these phenomena as "traditional" or part of "Swazi law and custom," which people there contrast to "modern" or "white people's" ways of doing things. *Traditionalists* is the term I use for Swazi citizens who overtly promote the kingship's political regime and their associated cultural productions.

10. The kingship and traditionalists have incorporated diverse forms and values of Christianity into their religious practices since the late nineteenth century. For example, the kingship supports the largest network of AICs, which combine forms of customary healing and symbolism with biblical lore. Newer Pentecostal charismatic "ministry" churches have also mushroomed there, as they have across the continent in the past twenty years; royalist elites maintain pastoral and prophetic positions in both these types of churches. Altogether, they make up a religiously plural field in which religious ritual phenomena, like sinyama, are ecumenically negotiated (Golomski 2018b).

11. For neighboring Tswana Apostolic churchwomen, "a blue dress . . . lets people know that your husband has passed away, but it doesn't make them think about death in the way a black dress does. . . . [A] black dress cuts your heart, intensifying your grief because anyone who sees you is reminded of death" (Klaits 2005, 55).

12. Karabo Ngoepe, "'After Tears' and Mourning in the 21st Century," *News24*, April 21, 2016, https://www.news24.com/SouthAfrica/News/after-tears-and-mourning-in-the-21st -century-20160412.

REFERENCES

Beliso-De Jesús, Aisha. 2015. *Electric Santeria: Racial and Sexual Assemblages of Transnational Religion*. New York: Columbia University Press.

Berglund, Axel-Ivar. 1976. *Zulu Thought Patterns and Symbolism*. Bloomington: Indiana University Press.

Comaroff, Jean. 1993. "The Diseased Heart of Africa." In *Knowledge, Power and Practice: The Anthropology of Medicine and Everyday Life*, edited by Shirley Lindenbaum and Margaret Lock, 305–329. Berkeley: University of California Press.

Crumbley, Deidre. 2008. *Spirit, Structure, and Flesh: Gender and Power in African Instituted Churches among the Yoruba of Nigeria*. Madison: University of Wisconsin Press.

Csordas, Thomas. 1999. "Embodiment and Cultural Phenomenology." In *Perspectives on Embodiment: The Intersections of Nature and Culture*, edited by Gail Weiss and Honi Hern Faber, 143–162. New York: Routledge.

Dlamini, Nhlanhla C. 2007. "The Legal Abolition of Racial Discrimination and Its Aftermath: The Case of Swaziland, 1945–1973." PhD diss., University of the Witwatersrand.

Du Bois, W. E. B. (1920) 2007. "The Souls of White Folk." In *Darkwater: Voices from within the Veil*, edited by Henry Louis Gates Jr., 15–25. New York: Oxford University Press.

Golomski, Casey. 2015. "Wearing Memories: Clothing and the Global Lives of Mourning in Swaziland." *Material Religion* 11 (3): 303–327.

Golomski, Casey. 2016. "Religion and Migration: Cases for a Global Material Ethics." *African Studies* 75 (5): 449–462.

Golomski, Casey. 2018a. *Funeral Culture: AIDS, Work and Cultural Change in an African Kingdom*. Bloomington: Indiana University Press.

Golomski, Casey. 2018b. "Work of a Nation: Christian Funerary Ecumenism and Institutional Disruption in Swaziland." *Journal of Southern African Studies* 44 (2): 299–314.

Hornberger, Julia. 2008. "Nocturnal Johannesburg." In *Johannesburg: The Elusive Metropolis*, edited by Achille Mbembe and Sarah Nuttall, 285–297. Durham, NC: Duke University Press.

Jackson, Michael. 2009. *The Palm at the End of the Mind: Relatedness, Religiosity, and the Real*. Durham, NC: Duke University Press.

Junod, Henri-Alexandre. (1912) 1966. *The Life of a South African Tribe*. Vol. 2. New York: University Books.

Klaits, Frederick. 2005. "The Widow in Blue." *Africa* 75 (1): 46–62.

Kuper, Hilda. (1947) 1969. *The Uniform of Colour: A Study of White-Black Relations in Swaziland*. New York: Negroes University Press.

Kuper, Hilda. (1947) 1980. *An African Aristocracy: Rank among the Swazi*. Oxford: Oxford University Press.

Lambek, Michael, ed. 2010. *Ordinary Ethics: Anthropology, Language, and Action*. New York: Fordham University Press.

Lee, Rebekah, and Megan Vaughan. 2008. "Death and Dying in the History of Africa since 1800." *Journal of African History* 49 (3): 341–359.

Lukhele, Francis. 2016. "Tears of the Rainbow: Mourning in South African Culture." *Critical Arts* 30 (1): 31–44.

Makhubu, Lydia. 1978. *The Traditional Healer*. Kwaluseni: University of Botswana and Eswatini.

Masquelier, Adeline, ed. 2005. *Dirt, Undress, and Difference: Critical Perspectives on the Body's Surface*. Bloomington: Indiana University Press.

Mda, Zakes. 1995. *Ways of Dying*. New York: Picador.

Mhlongo, Niq. 2007. *After Tears*. Johannesburg: Kwela Books.

Mhlongo, Niq. 2013. *Way Back Home*. Johannesburg: Kwela Books.

Ngubane, Harriet. 1977. *Body and Mind in Zulu Medicine*. New York: Academic Press.

Nyawo, Sonene. 2015. "'Sowungumuntfu ke nyalo—Now You Are a Real Person': A Feminist Analysis of How Women's Identities Are Constructed by Societal Perceptions on Fertility in the Swazi Patriarchal Family." PhD diss., University of KwaZulu-Natal.

Pierre, Jemima. 2013. *The Predicament of Blackness: Postcolonial Ghana and the Politics of Race*. Chicago: University of Chicago Press.

Ramphele, Mamphela. 1997. "Political Widowhood in South Africa: The Embodiment of Ambiguity." In *Social Suffering*, edited by Arthur Kleinman, Veena Das, and Margaret Lock, 99–118. Berkeley: University of California Press.

van Wyk, Ilana. 2014. *The Universal Church of the Kingdom of God in South Africa*. Cambridge: Cambridge University Press.

Zulu, Melekias, and Matthew Wilhelm-Solomon. 2015. "Tormented by Umnyama." In *Healing and Change in the City of Gold: Case Studies of Coping and Support in Johannesburg*, edited by Ingrid Palmary, Brandon Hamber, and Lorena Núñez, 135–148. New York: Springer.

Contributors

RACHEL CANTAVE is an anthropologist and an assistant professor of international affairs at Skidmore College. Her research interests include race, religion, identity politics, and social movements in Latin America and the Caribbean. She has published in the *Journal of Religious Studies, History and Society.* Dr. Cantave is also cofounder of TheEbonyTower .com and coproducer of the documentary *Chèche Lavi*, a film documenting the experiences of Haitian migrants at the border between Tijuana, Mexico, and the United States.

YOUSSEF CARTER is an assistant professor of religious studies and Kenan Rifai Fellow in Islamic studies at the University of North Carolina at Chapel Hill. His training brings together anthropology with the interdisciplinary fields of Islamic studies and Black studies. His research and publications focus on contemporary and historical interactions between West African and African American Muslims in South Carolina and Senegal. He is working on a book called "The Vast Oceans: Remembering God and Self on the Mustafawi Sufi Path," a multisite ethnography of a transatlantic spiritual network of African American and West African Sufis who deploy West African spiritual training to navigate historical-political contexts in the US South and Senegal.

N. FADEKE CASTOR is an assistant professor in religion and Africana studies at Northeastern University and an award-winning author of *Spiritual Citizenship: Transnational Pathways from Black Power to Ifá in Trinidad* (Duke University Press, 2017). A Yorùbá initiate, Black feminist ethnographer, and African diaspora studies scholar of Trinidadian heritage, she is inspired by, and aspires to create, Black liberation imaginaries. Her writing, prayers, and creative works emerge from the intersection of Spirit with the Black radical tradition, social justice, and decolonial praxis.

YOLANDA COVINGTON-WARD is department chair and associate professor in the Department of Africana Studies (with a secondary appointment in anthropology) at the University of Pittsburgh. Her first book, *Gesture and Power: Religion, Nationalism, and Everyday Performance in Congo* (Duke University Press, 2016), was awarded the 2016 Amaury Talbot Award for African Anthropology and the 2017 Elliott P. Skinner Book Award. She has new projects examining migration and identity for Liberian immigrants and religious embodiment in the nineteenth-century American South. She has received a number of fellowships and grants from the National Science Foundation and the Ford, Mellon, and Fulbright foundations, among others, and is currently the president of the Association for Africanist Anthropology.

CASEY GOLOMSKI is a cultural and medical anthropologist and Africanist with strong interests in the humanities. He is the author of articles in *Transforming Anthropology*, *Africa*, and *American Ethnologist* and of the book *Funeral Culture: AIDS, Work and Cultural Change in an African Kingdom* (2018). As accolades from the American Anthropological Association, he has received the 2010 Carrie Hunter-Tate Award and the Society for Humanistic Anthropology's 2019 Ethnographic Poetry Prize. He is a board member of the North Eastern Workshops on Southern Africa and of the Seacoast African American Cultural Center and, at the University of New Hampshire, an associate professor of anthropology, core faculty in women's and gender studies, and program coordinator of Africana and African American studies.

ELYAN JEANINE HILL is an assistant professor specializing in African and African diaspora arts, material culture, and performance in the Department of Art History at Southern Methodist University. Her research interests include narratives of slavery, visual culture, and Black women's history-making practices in Ghana, Togo, Liberia, and their diasporas. Her first book manuscript, "Spirited Choreographies: Ritual, Identity, and History-Making in Ewe Performance," engages with the body politics and multivocal histories of migration featured in rituals and festivals in Ghana and Togo. Her field-based research has been funded by the Fowler Museum at the University of California, Los Angeles; the West African Research Association; the Africana Research Center at Penn State University; and a Mellon postdoctoral fellowship in the Wolf Humanities Center at the University of Pennsylvania.

NATHANAEL J. HOMEWOOD is a postdoctoral fellow and assistant professor of religious studies at DePauw University. He is the general secretary of the African Association for the Study of Religion. His research on global Christianity focuses on African Pentecostalism and the entanglement of spirits, sexualities, and bodies.

JEANETTE S. JOUILI is associate professor of religion at Syracuse University. Her research and teaching interests include Islam in Europe, North Africa, secularism, pluralism, race, counterterrorism, popular culture, moral and aesthetic practices, and gender. She is the author of *Pious Practice and Secular Constraints: Women in the Islamic Revival in Europe* (2015) and has published articles in various peer-reviewed journals. Currently, she is working on her second book manuscript, "Islam on Stage: British Muslim Culture in the Age of Counterterrorism."

BERTIN M. LOUIS JR. is an associate professor of anthropology and African American and Africana studies (AAAS) at the University of Kentucky and the inaugural director of undergraduate studies for AAAS. He is the former editor of Conditionally Accepted, a career advice column for *Inside Higher Ed*, and serves as president-elect of the Association of Black

Anthropologists (2019–2021). Dr. Louis studies the growth of Protestant forms of Christianity among Haitians transnationally, human rights, anti-Haitianism in the Bahamas, and antiracist social movements in the US South.

CAMEE MADDOX-WINGFIELD is an assistant professor of anthropology at the University of Maryland, Baltimore County. Her ethnographic research interests center on cultural activism and identity formation in Caribbean and African diaspora dance communities, with a primary focus on the French Caribbean. As a dance ethnographer, Dr. Maddox-Wingfield analyzes the various ways that dance expression contributes to the emotional health and wellness of communities suffering from colonial and/or racial oppression. She is currently working on her book project on the cultural politics of the *bèlè* drum-dance revival in contemporary Martinique, with a particular focus on the intersections of spirituality, religion, and French secular nationalism.

AARON MONTOYA is an anthropologist whose work has taken him from southern Mozambique to southern Colorado. He currently directs a National Science Foundation Hispanic-Serving Institution grant to improve undergraduate STEM education by implementing culturally responsive and place-based education initiatives at Adams State University that more accurately reflect the people of the San Luis Valley. Building from his research on bicultural sensibilities (*mestiçagem*) in Mozambique, his current work asks how education in Southwest North America can better cultivate bicultural development that supports both students' scientific identifications and their cultural formations rooted in their heritages and social experiences.

JACOB K. OLUPONA is professor of African religious traditions at the Harvard University Divinity School, with a joint appointment as professor of African and African American studies in the Faculty of Arts and Sciences. His research ranges across African spirituality and ritual practices, spirit possession, Pentecostalism, Yoruba festivals, animal symbolism, icons, phenomenology, African immigrant religions, and religious pluralism in Africa and the Americas. He is the author of *Òrìsà Devotion as World Religion: The Globalization of Yorùbá Religious Culture* (2008), *City of 201 Gods: Ilé-Ifè in Time, Space, and the Imagination* (2011), and *African Immigrant Religions in America* (2007), among others. Professor Olupona has received grants from the Guggenheim Foundation, the American Philosophical Society, the Ford Foundation, the Davis Humanities Institute, the Rockefeller Foundation, the Wenner-Gren Foundation, and the Getty Foundation. He has also served as president of the African Association for the Study of Religion.

ELISHA P. RENNE is a professor emerita in the Department of Anthropology and Department of Afroamerican and African Studies at the University of Michigan–Ann Arbor. She has published articles and chapters on African ethnology and infectious disease, fertility and reproductive health, gender relations and Islam, and the anthropology of cloth. She also has authored several monographs and edited volumes, which include *Cloth That Does Not Die: The Meaning of Cloth in Bunu Social Life* (1995), *The Politics of Polio in Northern Nigeria* (2010), the edited volume *Veiling in Africa* (2013), *Veils, Turbans, and Islamic Reform in Northern Nigeria* (2018), and *Death and the Textile Industry in Nigeria* (2020).

Index

Page numbers in italics indicate figures

Alásùwadà conference, 70–87, 85, 86, 87, 89n2, 93n28

albinos, xiii

alchemy, as inward transformation, 54–55, 60, 63

Al-Jazeera, 206

Allah, remembrance of (dhikr), 49

Alleviating the Difficulties of the Hajj (Salman bin Fahad al-Oadah), 135, 136–137

Amatodos (AIDS dance performance piece): accusatory narrative, 233–237; AIDS-free subjectivity promoted, 14, 224, 231, 238–239; antecedents to and political background, 224–228; audience embrace of ecstatic energies, 224, 233–242; audience interpretations of, 223, 228–239, 242; ballet in, 233, 236, 246n9, 246n10; Changana language used in, 236, 246n12; colonial history reflected in, 236–237; condom character, 223, 224, 233; mother-to-child AIDS transmission scene, 236–237; musical choices in, 233–234; nyamusoro dancer scene, 239–241; restrained vs. villainous subjects in, 222, 230, 232–233; as sacred dance, 239–242; as secular dance, 231–239; secular sensorium promoted by, 231, 236, 239, 241, 243, 245n6; theoretical and methodological approach to, 228–231; and "think about life!" campaign, 232–234, 239, 243; "Too Late for Mama" scene, 235, 236

American Indian communities, 177

Ammerman, Nancy, 276

ancestors, 8, 40; and African-descended Muslims, 49–51; appeasing, 39, 77–80; collective (Egungun), 12, 70–73, 77–79, 81–84, 87, 87–89, 89n3, 90n10; dance as connection to, 238; Ilé-Ifè of Yorubaland, 78; Martinican, 186–187; stigmatized, incorporated into social fabric, 35; transatlantic connections with, 72–73. See also Mama Tchamba dance rituals

ancestral matrix, 79, 87, 90n8

Andersson, Efraim, 273

Anse Cafard slave memorial (Martinique), 186, 192n15

Anthony, Saint, 277

Antilleans. See bèlè drum-dance tradition; Martinique

Antonian movement (Kongo Kingdom), 276–277

Apostolic churches (Botswana), 7, 315n11

Appadurai, Arjun, 91n19

Asad, Talal, 10

àṣẹ (spiritual energy), 75, 82, 83, 84, 92n27

Assemblies of God (Assembleias de Deus), 118n4

assimilation, 238; French model, 176–177, 179, 191, 192n6

audience: and bèlè, 184; discomfort with racialized choreography, 233–239; embrace of ecstatic energies, 224, 233–242; of Ewe rituals, 24–26; interpretations of state campaigns, 223, 228–229; and Islamic hip-hop, 200–201, 203–205; unruly spectator, 242; Western, 45n12

authentication narratives, 198, 202–204, 242, 299, 308

Avalon cemetery (Soweto, South Africa), 310

"Awesome (My God Is)" (Jenkins), 163–164, 164

Baganda people (Uganda), xiii

Bahamas, 13, 152–172; African influence on, 157–158; anti-Haitian sentiment, 153, 155, 157, 161, 168–169; Bahamian church services in English, 161; centrality of religion to social life, 153, 158; Constitution, 170n5, 170–171n7; diverse identities in, 153, 157–158; Haitian as term in, 170n1; independence from Britain, 157; Protestantism in, 152–154, 156, 160–161, 169; religious plurality among Haitians, 152–153; and West Indian laborers, 158; xenophobia in, 13, 154, 157–158. See also Haitian-Bahamians

Bakhtin, Mikhail, 44n9

BaKongo ethnic group, xii, 273

Baluarte, David, 162–163

Bamalli, Alhaji Nuhu (Magajin Gari Zazzau), 129

bangunza (prophets, traditional healers), 274, 278, 282–283, 290, 292n2

Baptist women, Black, 5

Beidelman, T. O., 125

bèlè drum-dance tradition (Martinique), 1, 13–14, 175–196; artists, 184; Bele Djouba biennial festival, 186; bèlè légliz (church bèlè), 178, 183–184, 190; bèlè linò, 175–176; carré (square formation), 187, 192n16; circular procession, 185; Coordination Lawonn Bele, 180–181, 192n7; cultural associations, 180, 192n14; danm bèlè (female dancers), 188; ethical values, 180–181; as fecundity rite, 185; as laïque (secular) spirituality, 178; lespri bèlè (the spirit of bèlè), 184; monté o tanbou (greeting of drummer), 187, 192–193n16; rebirth of, 179–182; as revitalization movement, 176–177, 191; as secular, 176, 177, 181; as secular spirituality, 188–189; spiritual engagement with, 176, 177–178; swaré bèlè system, 180, 184, 188; tracing African and diasporic cosmological thought, 185–187; as way of life, 175–176. See also Martinique

Bèlè Légliz (documentary), 184

Belgian Congo. See Democratic Republic of the Congo

Beliso-De Jesús, Aisha, ix, 7, 302, 312

Bello, Ahmadu, 125, 135

Bello, Malam Muhammed, 130

belonging, 4, 13, 57, 80, 87, 91n17, 153, 180; French national, 178–179; and spiritual ethnicity, 71, 73, 75

Bennett, Michael, 216

Berglund, Axel-Ivar, 301

Berkeley County Museum and Heritage Center, 51, 65n4

Bight of Benin, 23, 76

bin Fahad al-Oadah, Salman, 135, 136–137

BisiKongo ethnic group, 273–274

Black Atlantic, 3, 7, 55–57, 214, 218n6

black color, as culturally valued, 302, 313, 314n7. *See also* dark matter (*sinyama*)

blackening, historical process of, 302, 311

"Black Leg-Irons" (Tukur), 141

Black Panther (film), 92n23

Black radical traditions, 14, 74

Black Skin, White Masks (Fanon), 177

Bochow, Astrid, 258

Boddy, Janice, 6

body: agency of, 264–266; being-in-the-world of, 267; Black, and West African Sufism, 60–63; of Black Muslim woman, writing, 206–213; body-mind dualism as racialized, 2; communication and sociality derived from, 229; consciousness changed by habitus, 103–104; corporeal pedagogy, 53; deceased, 304–305, 311; deliverance body, 254, 260–262; discipline of, 103–105, 107–108, 110, 261; distanced relationship with, 237; "double person" concept, 285, 293–294n15; and European hegemony, 2–5; faithful/faith-filled, 105; imitation of techniques from others, 31–32, 142, 144; indeterminacy of, 264; as intelligent somatic practice, 229, 241; intercorporeality, 10–11, 14, 216; and kinesthesia, 224, 228–230, 232, 238, 242–243, 254; of king, xiii–xiv; and knowledge production, 9–10, 53–55, 241; meaning created by movement, 266–267; mindful, 2, 49, 53, 55, 57–58, 63–64; ontological status of, 9; as pious entity, 54–55, 58, 63; and power relations, 33, 102, 267; and ritual process, xii–xiv; as site for producing relationality, 214–217; social, xii, 6–7, 44; somatic awareness of, 229–230, 265, 268, 271; subjectivity of, 229; techniques of, and embodied religion, 140–142; techniques of, for *hajj*, 135–140; transcorporeal perceptivity of, 215. *See also* embodiment

Boom Shaka, 234

Botswana, 7

Bourdieu, Pierre, 126, 154

Brazil, 7, 12, 100, 193n17; Candomblé, 7, 56, 104, 108–109, 118n1; capoeira Angola, 178

brekete drumming, 32, 45n14

British Empire, 75–76, 157

British Muslims of African descent, 14, 198, 218n4; spoken-poetry scene, 201; *umma* (community), 214; women Black Muslim hip-hop artists, 198–221. *See also* Islamic hip-hop; Poetic Pilgrimage (Muslim female hip-hop duo)

Brivio, Alessandra, 44n9

Brotherhood Movement of Nigeria, 143

Browning, Barbara, 31

Burdick, John, 193n17

Butler, Judith, 215, 216

Butler, Octavia, 45n16

Calabar, Nigeria, 281

Candomblé, 7, 56, 104, 118n1, 178; *terreiros* (temples), 108–109

capoeira Angola, 178

care of the self, 12, 61, 189

Caribbean: Cuba, 7, 76, 178; Trinidad, 12, 70, 75–76, 80. *See also* Bahamas; Haiti; Martinique

Caribbean and Atlantic Diaspora Dance: Igniting Citizenship (Daniel), 234–235

carnivalization, 29–30, 38, 44n9

Catholicism, 76; and *bèlè* drum-dance tradition, 14, 178, 183–184; in Brazil, 101, 118n3; Martinique's predominant religion, 182; Second Vatican Council and inculturation, 183–184; as target of UCKG, 101

Celestial Church of Christ, 282, 283

Centro de Estudos Culturais (Center for Cultural Studies, Mozambique), 225

Césaire, Aimé, 179

Chants D'Éspérance (Songs of hope, Baptist hymnal), 161

Cherubim and Seraphim Church (Nigeria), 293n11

children: absence from UCKG sessions, 109–110; *allo* and *ilmi* schools for, 127, 129; funeral for Haitian, 166; Haitian-Bahamian, 159, 160, 163, 165, 168; and Mama Tchamba dance rituals, 31–32; mother-to-child transmission of AIDS, 236–237; women's importance for raising, 127–128, 145n9

Chong, Kelly, 156, 165

choreographies, 23–26; *Amatodos* scenes, 223–230, 239–240, 243–244; of spirit possession, 25–26, 31–33. *See also* dance practices; Mama Tchamba dance rituals

Christianity, x, 4, 65n11; AICS (African independent churches), 274, 280–281; AIDS charities, 236–237; anthropological bias against, 190; Antonian movement, 276–277; compulsory, 236; death and funerals revalued by, 301; distanced relationship with body, 237; lgbtq Christians, 254, 259, 270. *See also* Catholicism; Dibundu dia Mpeve Nlongo mu Afelika (DMNA); God's Global Path Church (Ghana); Pentecostalism; Victory Chapel Church of the Nazarene

Church of the Holy Spirit in Africa. *See* Dibundu dia Mpeve Nlongo mu Afelika (DMNA)

Church of the Lord-Aladura, 282, 283, 298, 314n3

class differences, 80

clothing, 276; abaya (gowns), 138; *al-zayy al Islami* or *al-zayy al-Shari' i* attire, 143; *atamfa hajji* (printed hajj) cloths, 138–139; black, favored in Eswatini, 302; communal perspective, 206; European-style as replacement for traditional, 303; *gyale* (rectangular veil), 130–133, 135; *hijab*, 13, 122–144, *133, 139,* 146n15, 147n22, 203–217, 219n12; *hijab* forbidden in France, 126; *ihram* clothes for men, 123–124, 134–138, *138,* 140–144, 147n21, 147n26; *imvunulo,* 302; and Islamic hip-hop, 198, 205–206; *jellabiya* gowns, 136, 143; for Mama Tchamba rituals, 23–24, *30,* 42, 44n10; modesty as result of dress, 203–204; textile mills, 139; white, and DMNA church, 279, 283–285, 291, 292, 293n10

Code Noir (1685), 182–183

cognitive processes, 57, 102–103, 254

collective histories, 11, 24, 57; of violence, 210–211, 214–215

collectivity, 40–41; and dance, 234, 241; ritual, 12, 75, 79, 90–91n13

Collingwood, Dean, 158

Collins, Patricia Hill, 26

collusio (interactive field), 154

colonialism, 2–5; Americas, assault on ethnic identities in, 73–74; blackness as opposed to Whiteness, 313; and colorist racism, 301–304; countering through Islamic moral education, 125–126; French, 177–179, 183; persecuted religious movements, 276; Portuguese, in Mozambique, 223–225, 237–238; postcolonial state influence on culture, 225–227; psychological imbalances due to, 177; and racialization of *sinyama,* 297–298; racialized ideologies, 223–224; separate and unequal social formations, 231, 239; social worlds created by displacement and differentiation, 298, 301; and women's education, 127

colors: black as culturally valued, 302, 313, 314n7; colorist system of classification, 301–304; herbal medicine symbolism, 302, 304, 305–306, 311, 313; skin tone, 29, 44n8, 79; white cloth, symbolism of, 279, 283–285, 291, 292, 293n10, 293n11, 293n12. *See also* dark matter *(sinyama)*

Comaroff, Jean, 115–116, 117

"Common Mistakes Women Make during Hajj or Umrah" (Asma bint Shameem), 138

communitas, 72, 75, 77

community formation, 4, 8, 26, 213

Companhia Nacional de Canto e Dança (CNCD), 222–246; background, 224–228; members' interpretation of *Amatodos,* 223, 232; *Dances: Em Moçambique o sol nasceu,* 226; *A grande festa,* 226; *As mãos,* 226; *N'Tsay,* 226–227; *Ode à paz,* 228; *Pós-Amatodos* (Beyond *Amatodos*), 244, 245–246n8. *See also Amatodos* (AIDS dance performance piece)

compassion, 214–217, 244

Congo, Lower, 273–296; BaKongo ethnic group, xii, 273; bangunza (prophets), 274, 278, 282–283, 290, 292n2; BisiKongo ethnic group, 273–274; history of women as spiritual leaders, 276–277; KiKongo language, 273–274, 289–290; Swedish Protestant mission, 274, 278, 292n4. *See also* Democratic Republic of the Congo; Dibundu dia Mpeve Nlongo mu Afelika (DMNA)

Connerton, Paul, 57

consciousness, changed by habitus, 103–104

conversion, 13, 57, 66n15, 101, 106–107, 182

Convict and the Colonel, The (Price), 177

Coordination Lawonn Bele (Coordination around Bele), 180–181, 192n7

Copeland, M. Shawn, 4

copresence, 7

cosuffering, 215, 216

counternarratives, 73, 74, 90n12

Covington-Ward, Yolanda, 80–81, 82

Craton, Michael, 159

Creole languages: Haitian, 160, 161–162; Martinique, 180

creolization, 76

Crumbley, Deidre, 280, 282, 283, 298, 314n3

Csordas, Thomas J., 10–11, 300

Cuba, 7, 76, 178. *See also* Santería (Lucumí, Regla de Ocha)

cultural genocide, 179

cultural literacy, choreography as, 31

cultural transmission, 24

Curtis, Edward, 56

customary, as term, 314n9

Dagbamba people, 45n14

daily cultural practices, 223–224

dance: and colonial history, 236–237; "Indigenous," 237; popular nightlife, 234; sacred connotations in Africa and diaspora, 230–231; secular, 231–239; transcendent, 234–235; and transformational states, 224–225, 230–231

dance practices: capoeira Angola, 178; *danmyé* (Martinican martial art combat dance), 185–186, 191n5; as journey of transformational states, 224–225; nation-state regulation of, 225; neotraditional, Mozambique, 226; possession vs. concert, 31; regulation of, 73–74, 225, 237. *See also Amatodos* (AIDS dance performance piece); *bèlè* drum-dance tradition (Martinique); choreographies; Mama Tchamba dance rituals

dance studies, 25, 229–231, 241

"dance writings," 31

Daniel, Yvonne, 82, 178, 186, 234–235, 239

Dankwa, Serena Owusua, 258

danmyé (Martinican martial art combat dance), 185–186, 191n5

Dansso, Mamissi Sofivi, 24–25, 30, 44n4; descended from both purchasers and enslaved persons, 27–28, 36; October 2015 ritual held by, 31–33

dap greetings, 75, 81, 91n18

dark matter *(sinyama)*, 15–16, 297–316; "after tears" parties, 310; black color symbolism, 301–313; blackening, historical process of, 302, 311; cross-cultural comparison, 298–300, 312; dark buildings, 309–310; embodied in women, 300, 304–306, *305*; and gender, in Eswatini, 302–308; *libhadi* (badness, bad luck), 300, 304–308; measures to avoid or contain, 300, 304–308, *305, 307*, 311; origins of, 300–302; precolonial concepts of, 300–301; racialization of, 297–298, 300; South African views of, 308–312; *umnyama* (isiZulu equivalent), 309; widows, treatment of, 304–312, *305, 307*. *See also* death

death: bloodless, through servitude, 39; enslaved people as "bad dead," 39, 46n21; historicizing, 302; Pentecostal Christian views of African beliefs, 304; *umlindzelo* (night vigil) at funeral, 305

death pollution. *See* dark matter *(sinyama)*

debt to enslaved ancestors, 37–38, 43, 45n16; intergenerational effect of, 40–41

decolonial critiques, 187, 216

DeFrantz, Thomas F., 33

dehumanization, 73–74, 165

deliverance, 253–272; acceptance of church while rejecting deliverance, 263, 268; as act of surveillance, 261, 265; body controlled by pastorate, 260–261; as cosmic battle, 255–256, 261; defined by bodily movement, 254; docility as goal of, 254, 263, 265, 270; failed attempts, 263, 268–269; Foucauldian response to exorcism, 265–269; of lesbian women, 255–263; outing of lesbians, 258–259; as physical ritual, 255; services, 255; somatic refusal of script, 265; violence during, 255–256, 262–263, 269. *See also* God's Global Path Church (Ghana); healing

Democratic Republic of the Congo (DRC), 7, 273; as Belgian Congo, 273–274; healing, role in, 274; independence, 274, 276; Kongo Central province, 274; Kongo prophetic movements and churches, 8. *See also* Congo, Lower; Dibundu dia Mpeve Nlongo mu Afelika (DMNA)

détresse créole (creole distress), 177

dhikr (*zhikr*, remembrance of Allah), 65n5; as form of social memory, 51; and listening practices, 62–63; and mindful body, 2, 49, 53, 55, 57–58, 63–64; in Mustafawi circles, 52–53; performative nature of, 53; as spiritual technology of remembering, 63. *See also* Islam; Masjidul Muhajjirun wal Ansar (*zawiyah*-mosque)

Diago-Pinillos, Iya Regla, 79

Dibundu dia Mpeve Nlongo mu Afelika (DMNA), 15, 274–296, *281*; call-and-response singing, 280; founding of, 275, 277–279, 286; gender makeup of congregation, 280; Kongo lived religion, 276, 289; Kongo women in, and prophetic tradition, 286–291; lived religion in, 275–276, 287–288, 290–291; *lusakumunu* blessing, 289, 290; marginalization of women in, 274; menstrual blood as justification for gendered treatment, 275, 282–284, 314n3; sexual impropriety as justification for gendered treatment, 282–283; slippage, moments of, 286–287; threatened by women's authority, 291; white cloth, symbolism of, 279, 283–285, 291, 292, 293n10; women in, and rejection of as spiritual leaders, 279–286

Dickerson, Vanessa D., 216

"Dieu Tout Puissant" (Almighty god [praise song]), 161

dignity, 153–155, 169

disabilities and physical differences, xiii

discipline, 261, 263–264

(dis)embodiment, 297, 298

distance, ritual, xiii–xiv

divergent diaspora, 105, 114–117

divination, xi, 76–77

djouba (dance), 186

Dlamini-Simelane, Thandeka, 310

Dlamini Swazis, 303–304

dobale (ritual prostration), 81–82

"double person" concept, 285, 293–294n15

Douglas, Sukina, 199, 202, 205–213; "I Carry," 208, 212–213, 214–216

Drame, Fode (Imam), 49

drug narratives, 105–108

drumming, 70; Afro-Creole traditions, 175–176, 178; *bèlè* tradition, 1, 13–14, 175–196; *brekete*, 32, 45n14; drum as divine entity, 181; drum as tool of the devil, 184; materials used for drum, 191n2; *matinik* drum, 186

Du Bois, W. E. B., 301, 312, 313

Dups (mortuary and funeral insurance retailer), 303

Durkheim, Émile, xi–xii, 124, 126, 128

ecstatic practices, 12–13, 118n7; and DMNA church, 278; Ewe Vodun, 24; Neo-Pentecostal, 101, 114; and performance of *Amatodos*, 224, 230–231, 233–242; and *qasidas*, 59

education: *allo* and *ilmi* schools for children, 127, 129; Eurocentric (disembodied), 58, 66n16; Islamic, for married women, 124; and Islamic dress, 13, 123; for married women in Zaria City, 128–134; mode of transmission, 126–127; moral, 13, 123–128, 135, 141–142, 144, 145n6, 145n9; moral, and Islamic reform, 125–128; moral, France, 126; in secular subjects for Muslims, 128; Senegambian Qur'anic schooling, 10; as technique of body, 142; Western, opposition to, 58, 66n16, 145n6

egos (*tazkiyyat-ul-nafs*), 10, 54

Egungun (collective ancestors), 70–73, 77–79, 81–84, 87, 87–89, 89n3, 90n10

Egyptian cosmic knowledge, 187

Egyptian Islamic Revival, 103

elders, viii–ix, 32, 70, 72, 77, 84, 186; embodied humility shown to, 82–83, 85, 86, 87, 180

Elementary Forms of the Religious Life (Durkheim), xi–xii

embodied perception, 260, 267–268, 271; resistance through, 263–65, 269–270

embodied resistance, 14, 180–181, 242, 259–260, 270

embodiment, 170n3; adornments assembled on body instead of altar, 39; bodies trained to remember narratives, 43–44; cosuffering, 215, 216; and cultural transmission, 24; (dis)embodiment, 297, 298; of epistemology, 7, 215; ethical cultivation through, 50; of FRELIMO discourses, 228; in Haitian-Bahamian worship practices,

163–164; of hip-hop ethics, 202–204; of Holy Spirit in church members, 274, 286; of humility, 82–83; *kupupula* (physical action accompanying healing), 290; learning of, 81; learning through, 266–267; and lived religion, 276; memory of enslaved others, 27–31; muscle memory, 82–83; self-formation, epistemology, and intersubjectivity, 8–11; self-remaking through, 13; shared, 286. *See also* body; *dhikr* (*zhikr*, remembrance of Allah); habitus; habitus, religious; memory

Émile, or On Education (Rousseau), 127–128

Emanuel African Methodist Episcopal (AME) massacre (2015), 61

enslaved people, 1, 11, 23; as *amefleflewo*, 26; as "bad dead," 39; manifested in Tchamba practitioners, 28–29; *quilombos* (maroon communities), 108. *See also* Mama Tchamba dance rituals

enslavement: African-descended Muslim understandings of, 51; domestic, 26, 29, 44n6, 44n7; embodied memories of enslaved others, 27–31; memories of, 23; mnemonic geographies of, 23, 41; wealth, discourses of, 26, 27, 28, 36, 39. *See also* slavery

enslaving families, 27–30, 36, 45n15

ephemeral literature, 130

epistemology, 8–11; embodied, 7, 215

Erinfolami, Alagba Baba (Chief), 72, 84, 90n8

Esaie, Masamba, 277–279, 291

eschatological perspective, 211, 217, 304

Escola Nacional de Dança (END), 231–232, 245n8

essentialization, 190

Eswatini (former Swaziland), 15, 299–308; dark matter and gender in, 302–308; *emabutfo* ceremonies, 299; siSwati language, 303, 314n5; state-driven authentications of culture, 308; traditionalists, 314n9, 314n10

ethical attunement, 200

ethical relationships, 298; and Black Muslim hip-hop, 14, 202–204, 206–207; and Islam, 50, 200, 209, 216–217; and Mama Tchamba rituals, 11; mediated, 215–216; and *sinyama*, 16

ethics, neoliberal, 105, 107

ethnic group identity, 104

ethnicity. *See* spiritual ethnicity

ethnocide, 159

evangelical traditions, ix, 7, 115, 117, 156, 165. *See also* Pentecostalism

Evans, Curtis, 5

Ewe society, 23, 26, 29, 39, 44n1

Ewe Vodun: debt to enslaved ancestors, 37–38, 40–41, 43, 45n16; as site of social commentary,

Haydara, Mustafa Gueye (Shaykh), 50, 66n20

healing, 4, 118n3, 314n10; African American folk
healing practices, 7; in the DRC, 274; gender
politics of, 15, 273–296; *kupupula* (physical action), 290; *lusakumunu* blessing, 289, 290; and
moforibale, 83; and prophets, 273–274; *qasidas*
(odes) used to activate, 51–52, 57–60, 62–64;
from racial trauma, 12, 50, 54, 61–64; for social
body, xii, 6–7, 44; and United Church of the
Kingdom of God, 101, 118n3, 118n14. *See also*
deliverance; trembling, spirit–induced

herbal medicine color symbolism, 302, 304,
305–306, 311, 313

Higginbotham, Evelyn Brooks, 5

hijab, 13, 122–144, *133*, *139*, 146n15, 147n22, 203–
217, 219n12; and conduct on stage, 203–204; and
family conflict, 131–132; and fashion, 205–206;
forbidden in France, 126, 141; in hip-hop lyrics, 207; and modesty, 131–132, 134–135, 138,
142–144; opposition to in Zaria City, 130–131; as
"shackles of Gumi," 131; sports model, 147n22

Hindu prayer, 103

hip-hop, "original," 197, 198–199, 201, 218–219n8.
See also Islamic hip-hop

Hirschkind, Charles, 63, 66–67n21, 200, 214, 231,
243, 245n6, 245n7

Hispanic, as category, 71

historical imaginaries, 12, 29–30, *30*, 40–41;
imagined homelands, 49–51; North, in Mama
Tchamba rituals, 22–23, 27, 29, 37, 44n2; Yorùbá
spiritual ethnicity, 72, 80, 91n17

histories: attached to lived realities, 28, 41–42;
entanglements, and spiritual ethnicity, 75–77,
91n17; processual approach, 37–38; "what happened" vs. "what is said to have happened," 30

Holy Spirit, 15; embodiment of in church members, 274, 286; and UCKG, 111–113. *See also*
trembling, spirit–induced

homelands, imagined, 1, 49–51, 57; ancestral connections, 78–79; journeys taken to *shuyukh*, 54

Homewood, Nathanael J., 242

homosexuality: discretion as situation of, 258; as
enchanted battlefield, 255–256; within Ghanaian Pentecostalism, 15, 253–272; outing of in
Pentecostal churches, 258–259

Hornberger, Julia, 310

Houtman, Dick, 140

humility, 82–83, 203

"I Am Malcolm X" tour, 209

Ibn Taymiyah, 137

Ibrahim, Sa'idu Yunus, 130, 140

identities, 66n13; Afro-Brazilian, 104; colonial
assault on, 73–74; Ewe, 29–31, 38; group
politics, 114; Haitian-Bahamians, 153, 157–160;
influences on, 104; local and ethnic, 1–2, 30;
psychological imbalances due to colonialism,
177; religious, and race, 104–105; religious habitus as tool for building, 155; shared, 71; social,
construction of, 8, 54, 78, 104; transatlantic,
56–57

ideology, individualist, 105

Ifá religion, viii–xii; conference, Trinidad, 12;
Egungun (collective ancestors), 70–73, 77–79,
81–84, *87*, 87–89, 89n3, 90n10; Ilé-Ifè, in
Yorùbá cosmology, 80; Obatala, xi, xiii; Odu
Ọ̀sá Ogúndá, 82, 89n2, 92n24; twins, ix, xi,
xii; white cloth, use of, 293n12; Yorùbá-based
lineage of, 76–77. *See also* Orisha; spiritual
ethnicity; Yorùbá/Yoruba religion

Ifakolade, Awo, 84

ihram clothes, 123, 124, 135–138, *138*, 140–144,
147n21, 147n26

Ilé Aiyé (Spirit of the Earth), 79, 92n25

Ile Eko Sango/Osun Mil'osa; IESOM (Orisha
shrine), 70, 72

Ile Oluji, Nigeria, xii

incorporation, 29, 35, 53, 62, 65n7

indigenous hermeneutics, 103

indigenous religions, viii, ix, 80, 181–182

individualism: and affect, 12–13; challenged by
Ewe Vodun practitioners, 40; children's absence
reinforces, 110; and musical practices, 110–111;
and neoliberalism, 102, 104, 105–108, 114; and
Neo-Pentecostalism, 102, 104

individuality/dividuality, 7

influence, religious, 99–121

intercorporeality, 10–11, 14, 216

interdependence, 188, 216

intergenerational transmission, 38, 40–43

interiority, 2, 4, 9

internalization: of color-based racism, 301; of Izala
reforms, 131, 132, 142, 144; of neoliberal ideals,
107; of power, as relational, 10; of religious
embodiment, 6, 13, 41, 51; of religious experience, 153–155

International Monetary Fund, 227

intersubjectivity, 8–11; of collective care, 54;
defined, 40; and ecstatic practices, 12–13; and
intergenerational transmission, 38, 40–43; and
Islamic hip-hop, 198; ritual performances as a
type of, 23. *See also* subjectivity

Kongo prophetic movements and churches, 8, 288, 291–292; Belgian persecution of, 277, 292n5, 293n7. *See also* Dibundu dia Mpeve Nlongo mu Afelika (DMNA)

Kouzen Zaka (Vodou *lwa*, spirit), 186

Kumina tradition, 181

Kuper, Hilda, 303

laïcité (secularism), 141, 178–179, 182, 183; *bèlè* as form of, 188–189; nonmetropolitan context, 178, 190, 191n4

laïque spirituality, 188–189

Laman, Karl, 284

Latin America and Caribbean, 5; Protestant growth in, 156

Latinx devotees of Orisha, 79–85; Afro and Anglo devotees, 80

learning, through embodiment, 266–267

Lee, Rebekah, 301

Lemba (therapeutic healing and trade association), 290

Lemu, A. sha, 124, 125–126, 127, 142

lesbianism, hidden in Ghana, 258. *See also* deliverance; God's Global Path Church (Ghana)

Lesser Antilles, 175, 177

libations, 33–34, 38, 185

Liberia, 42, 46n22

Liberian Gola people, 42

libhadi (badness, bad luck), 300, 304–308

Liman, Usman, 137, 140, 142, 147n20, 147n24

lineages, 89n3; embodied reinforcement of, 82–83; types of, 78; Yorùbá-based lineage of Ifá, 76–77

listening practices, 62–63, 200

liturgical dance, 163–264, *164*; *bèlè légliz* (church *bèlè*), 178, 183–284, 190

lived religion, 275–276, 287–288, 290–291

Lived Religion: Faith and Practice in Everyday Life (McGuire), 275–276

Lomé, Togo, 24

Lopez, Donald, 36

Louis XIV, 182–183

Lucumí (Regla de Ocha, Santería), 7, 56, 81, 178, 302

Lukhele, Francis, 310

Luozi (Democratic Republic of the Congo), 15, 274. *See also* Democratic Republic of the Congo; Dibundu dia Mpeve Nlongo mu Afelika (DMNA)

Luso-America, 56

Luvuvamu (Democratic Republic of the Congo), 289

Macedo, Edir, 100, 115

Madarasatul Anwarul Islam school, 128

"magical" practices, ix–x

Mahi nation, 186

Mahmood, Saba, 103, 155

Mahmud, Alhaji Habib Umar, 138–139

Makonde people (Mozambique), 226

Mama Tchamba dance rituals, 1, 11; *brekete* drumming, 32, 45n14; children's learning of, 31–32; clothing represents enslaved Northerners, 23–24, 30, 42, 44n10; dancing, 31–33; dark-skinned people incorporated, 29; hierarchical tensions performed, 36–38; improvisational movements indicate spirit possession, 34–36, *36*, 40; initiates, 41–42; Muslim aesthetics in, 23–24, 29–30, *30*, 36, 42; North, imagined, 22–23, 27, 29, 37, 44n2; pantheon of dangerous spirits, 23, 38; potentiality of, 37–38; power reversals in, 33–38; priests and priestesses (*hounoun* and *mamissi*), 24–25, 35; *senterua* (attending initiates), 35, 45n17; spectators, behavior of, 24–26; stigmatized ancestors incorporated into, 35; *Tchambagan* (Tchamba rings), 28, 39; and unspeakable fears, 38–40; walking variations, 32–34, *33*, 39–40, *43*; wealth, debt, and illness addressed by women, 25, 26, 37, 39. *See also* choreographies; Ewe Vodun

Mandombe, Mikala, 277

Maputo, Mozambique, 14

Maranke and Marowe churches, 281–282

Maroon traditions, 181

Marshall, Dawn, 152–153

Martinique, 13–14, 175–196; Anse Cafard slave memorial, 186, 192n15; cultural autonomy, Creole, 183; danmyé (martial art combat dance), 185–186, 191n5; general strike, 192n8; Haitian folklore, overlap with, 186; mental health/neocolonial distress, 176, 177, 188; place of religion in, 182–183; *quimbois* (conjuring and folk healing), 183, 192n9; radical-left youth activists, 179–181, 191. *See also bèlè* drum-dance tradition (Martinique)

Marxist political ideology, 179

Masjidul Muhajjirun wal Ansar (*zawiyah*-mosque), 12, 49–53, 57–64, 65n4. *See also dhikr* (*zhikr*, remembrance of Allah)

Mason, Michael, 81, 83

Massé, Raymond, 177

mastery: of Ewe ritual dance, 25; inward spiritual, 12, 50, 58, 64

materiality, xi–xii, 4, 8, 16, 140–141, 293n11, 312; and exclusion of women from positions of authority, 274–276, 283, 291–292; food taboos, xi, 284, 307; loss and bereavement mediated by, 303; racialization of, 2. *See also* body; clothing; dark matter (*sinyama*); embodiment

Matsayin Hijabi a Musulunci (Ibrahim), 130

Mauss, Marcel, 2, 124–125, 142, 144

mayi (Mahi nation dance), 186

Mbonga, Telezi, 277

McGuire, Meredith B., 9, 103, 275–276

Mecca. *See hajj* (pilgrimage to Mecca)

Mecca II Medina (Islamic hip-hop group), 203

Mellor, Philip, 154–155, 170n3

memory, 4, 7–8, 66n14; collective, 9, 23, 187; commerce of memory making, 190; *dhikr* (remembrance of Allah), 49–64; embodied, 11, 24, 29, 51, 88; embodied, and diasporic time, 77–80; embodied, of enslaved others, 27–31, 43–44; embodied, of shared recognition, 82; of enslavement, 23, 26; European notions of challenged, 36; habitual, 8, 57; imagined landscapes of, 40; local frameworks, 26; mnemonic practices, 23, 41; reversion, 57, 66n14, 66n15; social, and transatlantic connections, 51, 55–57; victims, remembrance of, 212–213

menstrual blood: as justification for women's exclusion from authority, 275, 282–285, 314n3; power of, 284, 285–286, 314n3

mental health, Martinique, 176, 177, 188

Merino, Stephen, 105

Meyer, Birgit, 140

Mhlongo, Niq, 310–312

Middle Eastern Muslims, in Britain, 199

migration, 56, 117, 308–309; of Haitians to Bahamas, 156–158

Miles, William, 177

Miller, Ivor, 73, 74, 75, 85, 87, 89–90n4

mind-body dualisms, vii, 9; Vodun intersubjectivity as counter to, 40–41

mindful body, 2, 49, 53, 55, 57–58, 63–64

missionaries, Western, 5, 277–278, 303

Mitchell, Kerry, 189

Mitchem, Stephanie, 4–5

mnemonic practices, 23, 41

mobility, 4, 8

"modernity," 74

modesty, 103, 261; and *hijab*, 131–132, 134–135, 138, 142–144; and Islamic hip-hop performance, 203–205, 219n14; and male hip-hop artists, 203

moforibale (full-length prostration), 81–84, 85, 87

Moncks Corner, South Carolina, 49, 51, 53, 60–61, 64n2. *See also dhikr* (*zhikr*, remembrance of Allah); Masjidul Muhajjirun wal Ansar; Sufism

Monrovia (Liberia), 42

Montconthour, Father (Martinique), 184

moral education, 13, 123–128, 135, 141–142, 144, 145n6, 145n9; in France, 126, 141; and Islamic reform, 125–128

moral geography, 215

movement dialectics, 38

moyo (life essence), 285, 293–294n15

Mozambique, 14, 222–249; AIDS-free subjectivity promoted in, 14, 224, 231, 238–239; AIDS prevalence in, 245n2; civil war, 227, 245n5; cultural institutions, state-sponsored, 225–226; dance as journey of transformational states, 224–225, 230; Escola Nacional de Dança (END), 231–232, 245n8; FRELIMO, 225–226, 232, 243; independence (1975), 225; industry of information, education, and communication (IEC) campaigns, 223, 231, 232, 244; Marxist-Leninist state, 225–227; peace accords (1992), 226–227; "think about life!" campaign, 232–234, 239, 243. *See also Amatodos* (AIDS dance performance piece)

mpeve (vital principle), 286

Mswati III (King of Eswatini), 299, 314n5

Muhammad, Prophet, 59, 65n3, 67n22, 131, 144

Muneera. *See* Williams, Tanya Muneera

Murphy, Ann V., 216

Muslim Mothers' Association, 135

Muslims, African American, 12; and racial trauma, 50, 54. *See also* Islam; Masjidul Muhajjirun wal Ansar

Mustafa, Shaykh, 52, 54, 61; "Al-Bahrul Muhit" (The Vast Ocean), 58–59; "The Cloak of Protection and the Soldiers of Divine Care," 58–59, 66n20

Mustafawi Sufi Order, 49–52, 57–60, 62–64

Nana Asma'u, 127

National Hajj Commission of Nigeria, 124, 138

nationality, just sanguinis and jus soli, 159

Nationality Support Unit (NSU, Bahamas), 162–163

National STD/AIDS Control Programme (Mozambique), 232

Nazarene Christianity, 152–153, 156, 165. *See also* Victory Chapel Church of the Nazarene

neoliberalism, 3, 14, 87, 105–108; *Amatodos* and promotion of, 230; and Black disconnection from Africa, 116–117; and drug narratives, 105–108; and individualism, 102, 104, 105–108, 114; Mozambique, 14; neoliberal ethics, 104, 107; privatization, 105, 106–107; supported by religious sensuous habitus, 100

Neo-Pentecostalism, 100–102, 114–117; Afro-Brazilian religions, opposition to, 100, 108, 115; prosperity theology, 101, 107, 118n5; and race, 104–105. *See also* Pentecostalism

Ngubane, Harriet, 301, 303, 308

Niass, Ibrahim (Sheikh), 145n3

Nigeria, 13, 77; Buhari administration, 135; Pilgrim Welfare Board, 138; state pilgrimage boards, 123, 124, 135–136; techniques of the body in, 140–142; Yorùbá/Yoruba Aladura churches, 282, 283, 298, 314n3; Yorubaland, 77–78. *See also* Izala (Jama'atu Izalat al-Bid'a wa Iqamat al-Sunna); Zaria City (Nigeria)

nitu (outer person), 285

nkawa (stick used in healing), 287

nkisi (sacred medicine), 284n293n14, 285

Noland, Carrie, 265, 267–268, 270–271

Nonconformist missions, 5

nonhuman material bodies, 11

Novack, Cynthia Jean, 229

Ntfombi Tfwala (Queen Mother), 299

Obatala (Yorùbá/Yoruba deity), xi, xiii

obreiras (trained volunteers or workers), 109–110, 114, 116

O'Brien, Susan, 145n8

Okenwa, Saleh, 137–138

Olódùmare (Yorùbá/Yoruba deity), 89n1

Olomo, Oloyè Aina, 89n3

ontologies, racial, 216–217, 302

oral traditions and histories, viii, 29, 201–202

Orí (spiritual head), x–xi, 82, 92n27

Orifice as Sacrificial Site, The (Aho), xii

orifices, xii

Orisha (Orixá), ix–xi, 181; and Afro-Cuban rumba, 178; Cuban lineages, 76; definition, 89n1; gatherings, 90–91n13, 91n15; Latinx devotees, 79–85; Nigerian Yorubaland lineage, 77; sensed and felt on body, 7; Trinidad lineages, 76. *See also* Ifá religion; spiritual ethnicity

Orisha Shrine (Ile Eko Sango/Osun Mil'osa; IESOM), 70, 72

Orixás, caboclos e guias: Deuses ou demônios? (Orixás, caboclos, and guides: gods or demons?) (Macedo), 101

Oshun (Yorùbá/Yoruba deity), 83, 185

Other: northerners from Togo as, 29–30; as part of self, 34, 40; religion used to categorize, 4

othering, of embodied sacred practices, 231

Oyotunji Village (South Carolina), 72

Parish, Steven, 103

past: Africa as place of origin, 7–8; collective envisioning of, 57; counternarratives, 73; European notions of as fixed record, 36; healing of, 12; recreated in ways appropriate for present, 36, 41; transatlantic identities and contextualization of, 56–57

Pearls of Islam (Islamic rhythm and *nasheed* duo), 204

Pentecostalism, ix, 7, 12; charismatic Christianity, limits of, 255; in Eswatini, 314n10; first wave, 118n3; Ghanaian, 15, 255; Neo-Pentecostalism, 100–104, 114–117; racism toward Black southern Africans, 304; sins described in detail, 262. *See also* deliverance; God's Global Path Church (Ghana); United Church of the Kingdom of God ()

perception, 102–103, 114, 154; embodied, 260, 263–265, 267–271

performances, 13–14; accusatory narrative, 233–237; collective envisioning of past, 57; dap greetings, 75, 81, 91n18; ethical and moralizing, 62; of Islamic hip-hop, 202–206; of knowing, 55; protection in, 57–60; social relationships affirmed by, 82; of spiritual ethnicity, 71–74, 84. *See also specific dance and religious practices*

Perry, Imani, 218n6

piety: embodied practice of, 54–55, 58, 63; and Islamic hip-hop, 198, 200–202, 204; sensory experiences, pious, 12–13, 200; women's movement in Cairo, Egypt, 155

Pilgrim Welfare Board (Nigeria), 138–139

Pinho, Patricia de Santana, 115, 116

Pinn, Anthony, 4–5, 267

Piot, Charles, 37

Poetic Pilgrimage (Muslim female hip-hop duo), 198, 199, 205–217, 207; "I Carry," 208, 212–213, 214–216; "Star Women," 208; "White Lilies," 208, 209–212, 213–215; writing the body of the Black Muslim woman, 206–213. *See also* Islamic hip-hop

political apperception, 215

pollution, symbolic, 297. *See also* dark matter (*sinyama*)

Pópóọlá, Olóye Ṣọlágbadé, 77, 92n24

Portuguese colonialism, 223–225, 237–238. *See also* Mozambique

Pós-Amatodos (Beyond *Amatodos*), 244, 245–246n8

possession. *See* spirit possession

Possession at Loudun, The (Certeau), 265–66

power, 10; destabilized by rituals, 11; ecclesiastical, 261, 266–267; embodiment as a source of,

80–81; Foucauldian paradigm, 264–265; genius of, 266; incorporation of dark-skinned people indicates proximity to, 29; re-placement of with Allah, 62; reversals in Mama Tchamba rituals, 33–38; and spatial location of body, 257; and spirituality, 189; struggle for centered in body, 265; women's bodies as source of, 211

power relations, 11, 33, 102, 267

"Practical Steps in Performing the Hajj Rites" (Okenwa), 137–138

praise dancing, 163–164, *164*

prayer: Islamic *(ṣalāt),* 155; at Victory Chapel, 165–168, *166–167*

predestination, xi

Price, Richard, 177

Progressive Liberal Party (Bahamas), 158

prophetic movements and churches, 8, 15, 273; angels, visions of, 278, 283–284, 293n11; revelations, belief in, 275, 278, 287, 288, 291. *See also* God's Global Path Church (Ghana); kingunza (prophetic) movements; trembling, spirit–induced

Protestantism: in Bahamas, 13, 152–154, 156, 160–161, 169; growth of in Latin America, 156; Haitian, 156, 160–161; mainline churches in Eswatini, 303–304; transnational, 161, 164. *See also* Nazarene Christianity; Neo-Pentecostalism; Pentecostalism

Puar, Jasbir, 264

purity, xiii, 15, 279, 283–286, 293n10, 293n11, 293n13, 299, 305–306, 311

Qādiriyya Brotherhood, 145n10, 145n12, 146n13

qasidas (odes), 51–52, 57–60, 62–64, 65n5

quilombo (maroon community), 108

quimbois (conjuring and folk healing), 183, 192n9

Qur'an, 59, 61, 63, 64n2, 67n22; 20:114, 145n10; and *dhikr* sessions, 53; and Izala movement, 122–124, 127; memorization of, 53, 55; Sura 2 on education, 128; Sura 24:30, 134; Sura 74 (The Enfolded), 122, 144; women's groups for reading, 127

Qur'anic schooling, 10, 66n16

race: relational assemblage of Black bodies, 116; as technology of affect, 105; tensions with religious identities, 114–115

racialization: of affect, 100; as constitutive of African and African diaspora religions, 302; of dark matter *(sinyama),* 297–298, 300; of Haitians, 155; of illness, 307–308; of material practices, 2; of morality, 4; and Orisha, 80; of skin tone, 29

racism: colorist, 301–304; French colonial, 177–179; internalization of color-based, 301; religion counters impacts of, 62–63; structural, 213–215

radicalism, vii

Radical Middle Way organization, 209

Rai, Amit, 264

Rastafarian religion, 5–6

reason, 2

Reddie, Richard, 218n4

Regla de Ocha (Lucumí, Santería), 7, 56, 81, 178, 302

relationality, 4, 8; body as site for producing, 213–217; of Obatala and the disabled, xiii; as ontological process, xiii; of *ori,* x–xi; reciprocal, 84; of self, vii, 10–11; and senses, 102; sensuous, 100; and spiritual healing, 7; of subjectivity, 10–11

religion: colorist racism in, 301–302; influence, religious, 99–121; lived, 275–276, 287–288, 290–291; non-Western religions, downgrading of, 2–4; routinization of, 274, 280; secular-religious binaries, 224, 230, 238–239, 242, 245n7; spirituality, difference from, 189; world religions, viii. *See also* Catholicism; Ifá religion (Yorùbá/Yoruba religion); Islam; Vodou; Vodun; specific religions

RENAMO (Resistencia Nacional Moçambicana), 227–228, 245n5

Renne, Elisha P., 293n11

representation: politics of, 4, 6, 8, 225; state attempts to regulate, 225

resistance: rescripting of by power, 266; through embodied perception, 263–265, 269–270

resistance, embodied, 14, 180–181, 242, 270; and Ghanaian Pentecostal church, 253–254, 259–260

respectability, 5–6, 130, 204

reversion, 57, 66n14, 66n15

revitalization movements, 176–177, 191

Rey, Terry, 154, 156, 160

Roberts, A., 40

Roberts, M., 40

Romain, Charles-Poisset, 156

Rosenthal, Judy, 41

Rousseau, Jean-Jacques, 127–128

routinization, 274, 280, 314n4

Rush, Dana, 37, 39

Rushdy, Ashraf, 40

Sackey, Brigid, 281, 282

Sacred Heart Church (Balata, Martinique), 182

sacred/secular dichotomy, 178

Vaughan, Megan, 301

Venezuela, 75–76, 80

Victory Chapel Church of the Nazarene, 153–154, 160–171; liturgical dance, 163–164, *164*; popular culture, use of, 163; prayer at, 165–168, *166–167*; worship format, 161–162

violence: collective histories of, 209–211, 214–215; during deliverance ritual, 255–256, 262–263, 269; as immanent in the sacred, 313

Vita Kimpa, Dona Beatrice, 276–277

Vodou, 44n1, 76, 178, 185; hybrid Catholic, 13; *lwa* (spirit) Kouzen Zaka, 186; Rada rituals, 186

Vodun, 44n1. *See also* Ewe Vodun; Mama Tchamba dance rituals

vuvudi (outer body), 285

Wakanda *(Black Panther)*, 92n23

Wali, Hajiya Rabi, 135–136

Wallace, Anthony, 176–177, 7, 191

war, violence of, 213–214, 311

Ware, Rudolph, 10, 53, 55, 66n16

Warnier, Jean-Pierre, 204

Way Back Home (Mhlongo), 311

Weeks, John, 284

Weiss, Gail, 216

wellness communities, 92n26

Wendl, Tobias, 39

Wesleyan Missionary Society, 156

West African Islam, 50, 53, 55–56, 58, 65n12, 146n19, 201–202; and Black body, 60–63

Western interpretive models, vii, viii, 2–5

West Indians, 80

West Indies: 1848 emancipation, 183

"What We Believe" (Universal Church USA), 111

Where I Stand (Gumi), 125

white cloth, symbolism of, 279, 283–285, 291, 292, 293n10, 293n11, 293n12

widows: of ANC fighters, 309; in Eswatini, 304–308, *305*, *307*; in South Africa, 309–312

Wilhelm-Solomon, Matthew, 309

Williams, Tanya Muneera, 199, 205–213; "White Lilies," 208, 209–212, 213–215

Willis, John Thabiti, 89n3

witness, 62–63

women, 15; Afro-Brazilian, and UCKG churches, 101; *banganga* (traditional healers and ritual specialists), 277; Black Baptist, 5; Black Muslim hip-hop artists, 198–221; bodies of as sources of power, 211; cloth coverings in Islam, significance of, 123; dark matter *(sinyama)* embodied in, 300; "disorders" of, 282–283; education of counters Western intellectual hegemony, 125–126; education's importance for raising children, 127–128, 145n9; European Christian views of, 4; Ewe rituals, leadership positions in, 25; and gender politics of healing in DMNA church, 273–296; Hausa Muslim, 127–128; menstrual blood as justification for gendered treatment, 275, 282–284, 314n3; modesty, comportment, and gender, 134–135; piety movement in Cairo, Egypt, 155; as prophets, 274; seclusion *(kulle)* 127; self-defined standpoints of, 26; as spiritual leaders in Kongo Kingdom, 276–277; use of histories-in-process, 26; violence against bodies of, 209–211; widows, 304–312, *305*, *307*; writing the body of Black Muslim, 206–213

Women and Law in Southern Africa Trust, 306–307

worthiness, 154

"wretched of the earth," 212, 216

Wynter, Sylvia, 216–217

xenophobia: in Bahamas, 13, 154, 157–158; in France, 178–179

Yahya, Mohammed, 201–202, 203

Yorùbá/Yoruba Aladura churches, 282, 283, 298, 314n3

Yorubaland, 77–78. *See also* Nigeria

Yorùbá/Yoruba religion. *See* Afro-Cuban religion (Lucumí, Santería, Regla de Ocha); Afro-Brazilian religions; Ifá religion; Mama Tchamba dance rituals; Vodun; Vodou

Zaria City (Nigeria), 122–151, 144n2; Anguwar Kwarbai quarter, 128; *anguwoyi* (quarters or wards), 129; Friday mosques, 145n12; Izala and education for married women in, 128–134. *See also* Izala (Jama'atu Izalat al-Bid'a wa Iqamat al-Sunna); Nigeria

zawiyah-mosque. *See* Masjidul Muhajjirun wal Ansar (*zawiyah*-mosque)

zhikr. See dhikr (zhikr, remembrance of Allah)

zones of contact, ix

Zulu, Melekias, 309

Zulu people, 301